A PILGRIM

Camino

Lisbon –Porto – Santiago

Camino da Costa

Camino Central

Senda Litoral

Variante Espiritual

A Practical & Mystical Manual for the Modern-day Pilgrim

John Brierley

First published in 2005. This revised 14th edition published in 2024.

ISBN: 978-1-912216-32-1

An eBook edition is also available for this guide:

ISBN: 978-1-912216-75-8 (epub)
978-1-912216-74-1 (mobi)

British Library Cataloguing-in-Publication Data.
A catalogue record for this book is available from the British Library.

Printed and bound in Czechia

CAMINO GUIDES
An imprint of Kaminn Media Ltd
272 Bath Street,
Glasgow, G2 4JR

Tel: +44 (0)141 354 1758
Fax: +44 (0)141 354 1759

Email: info@caminoguides.com
www.caminoguides.com

Pontesampaio – The modern camino, part of the original Roman Road *Via Romana*

CONTENTS:

"We walk to God. Pause and reflect on this. Could any way be holier, or more deserving of our every effort, our love and of our full intent?...

A Course in Miracles.

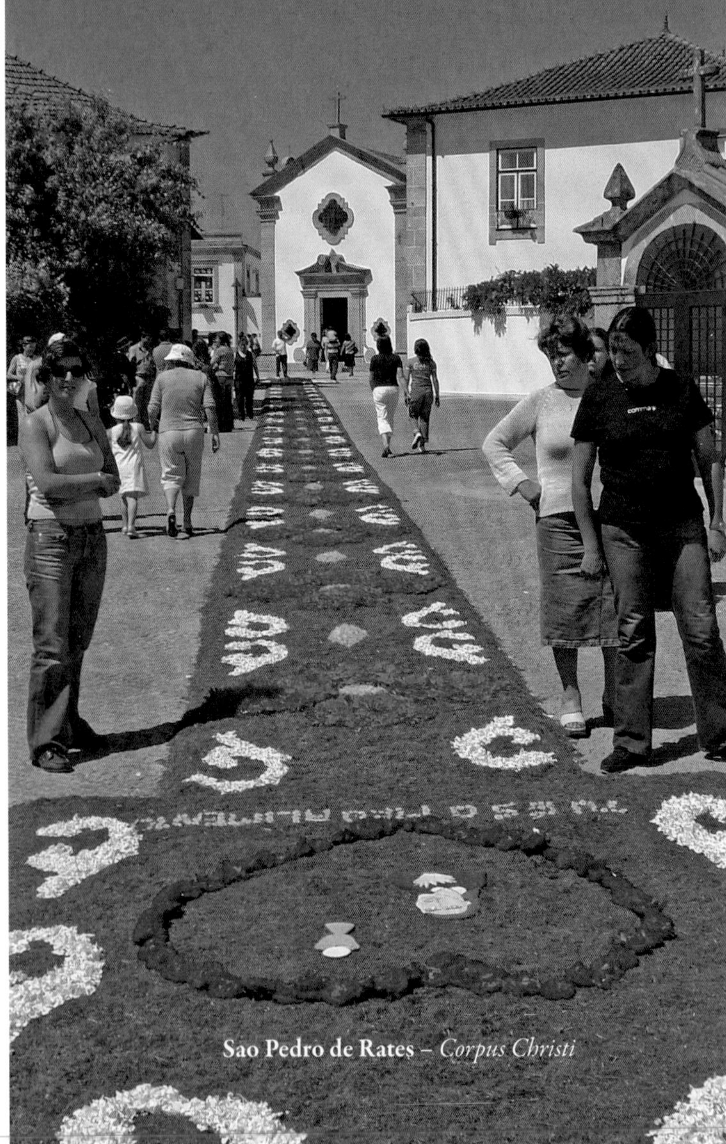

Sao Pedro de Rateṣ – *Corpus Christi*

•Portugal GMT +0 ✆+351 ---------------->

•España GMT +1 ✆ +34 ---------------->

About the author: *John Brierley 1948 - 2023*

John in Santaigo. Portrait by Patti Silva

For a quarter of a century the Caminos de Santiago inspired John Brierley. He fervently believed in their inherent power to foster positive change, in our individual lives and in the world through changing the way we view our place in it. These guides are the product of a calling he felt to encourage pilgrims to embark on both an *outer* journey, as well as to consider their steps along an *inner* journey. The following pages are filled with his enthusiasm and profound belief in the importance of both. They also contain clear and concise information on where to find a cup of coffee in the morning, a ritual as important to him as prayer.

In 2023 John took his final steps on this earthly pilgrimage, but his passion, wisdom and energy live on in the works he left behind. While the practical information in these guides continues to be updated by his daughter, the message is, and will always remain his. To make each step a prayer, to open our hearts with loving kindness and always to keep exploring both the *outer* world around us and our own *inner* landscape.

Acknowledgements: I would like to thank *Joana Castro, Antonio Martins, Pedro Macedo, Fernanda* & *Jacinto Gomes Rodrigues* and their families, all of whom have welcomed me into their hearts and homes and provided me with a sound basis for my love and deep appreciation for Portugal and her people. Gratitude is also due to all those pilgrims who have walked this path over the centuries. Each one has helped to shape and make this path what it is today. From St. James himself who risked life and limb to carry the message of love and forgiveness to the Iberian peninsular and now – some two thousand years later – the Friends of the Way in Portugal who voluntarily give of their time to waymark the route so that we might find our way safely to Santiago de Compostela.

I would like to acknowledge the help of the pilgrim association Via Lusitana including *José Luis Sanches, Natércia Sanches & Helena Bernardo* who provided invaluable help in the early stages. *Emídio Almeida & Vanda Silva of APAAS, Ilídio Silva, João Moreiro, Ana Castro, Kirsten Kleinfeldt, Alison Raju, Paul Crocker, Christopher Johnson, António Pires, Nuno Ribeiro, Manuel Miranda of Via Veteris Associação Jacobeia Esposende* and *Lúcio Lourenço Associação Albergue Cidade de Barcelos...* all offered valuable feedback. And let us not forget all those people who live along the *caminho* and offer welcome and shelter to us as we pass by...

muito obrigado. John Brierley

Notes to the 14th Edition: As we prepare this latest edition we are struck that once again the greatest change we see on the Camino Portugués is the dramatic increase in pilgrim numbers. In 2005, when the first edition of this guide was published, the total number of pilgrims recorded on the route was 5,507. In 2022 it was 123,802. Of these pilgrims only 87 had chosen to walk the coastal route in 2005 whereas in 2022 the number was 30,602, making the Camino da Costa the third most popular road to Santiago. Though the growing popularity of the alternative coastal routes among pilgrims is clear, some opposition remains from those who would seek to preserve the camino *as it was.* But the camino is constantly evolving, reminding us that we too must change and grow if we are to help shift human consciousness from fear and greed to generosity and love.

Another change that is afoot is the attention being given to the early stages of this route from Lisbon to Porto. Last year only 2,981 pilgrims were recorded as commencing their journey in Lisbon, but the sheer volume of pilgrims on the Camino Francés shows us that there is an appetite amongst us for longer pilgrimages. We know that pilgrim facilities and infrastructure grow as pilgrim numbers grow but also that pilgrim numbers increase when there are the facilities to support them. A growing international effort is working to address this in the hope that more pilgrims will consider Lisbon as their starting point in future. For now, however, this stretch remains a *road less travelled* and one suited to seasoned pilgrims with an adventurous and flexible approach. The pilgrim association based in Lisbon offers a 24 hour help line **Via Lusitana** (+351) 915 595 213.

Contrary to popular belief the Portuguese Way is one third by earthen tracks and woodland pathways. This is true for both the Lisbon (33.2%) and Porto (32.5%) sections. While over half the first stage out of Lisbon is on pathways (much of it along the rio Tejo estuary) the waymarked route out of Porto along the camino central has no natural pathways so options are provided as to how to avoid the busy road network around Porto city itself. Last year sections of newly waymarked pathways have been established to help minimise time spent on asphalt. This is welcome and the main reason why overall distances have changed slightly.

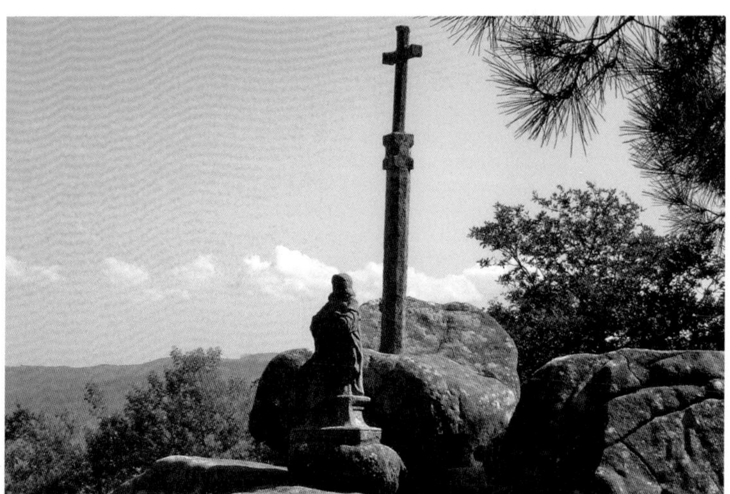

Foreword: *In the beginning was the Word...* John 1.1

We live in a dualistic world of past and future, left & right and right & wrong. This world of time and space, of judgment and condemnation often feels contradictory and threatening. How do we honour our worldly commitments and make time to go on pilgrimage? How do we balance work and play and still find time to pray? How do we resolve a world of seeming opposites and our prejudice and judgement of others?

Perhaps pilgrimage, the Path of Enquiry, will lead us to that point of understanding where there is no longer any separation between path and goal, where life itself is pilgrimage and every step a prayer. In the meantime, we stumble along in dark clouds of unknowing and that is, perhaps, the essential beginning place; to have the courage to admit we are lost and the humility to ask directions.

When I was stumbling around wondering how best to start this guide, a neighbour appeared with a newspaper cutting with the heading, *what is the best guide to the camino?* The instant I asked for help I was handed the answer. The words and timing were perfect: *The best guide to* **what** *camino?* There are many guides to the physical path but if we attend only to the practical we miss the mystical and perhaps we miss the whole point. We walk down a cul-de-sac called despair with only our own mortality waiting for us at the end. There is no way out of our conundrum but in — through the inner landscape of soul.

So suddenly I was prompted to write a foreword, a beginning. And it occurred to me that unless I put God first in everything I do, I will not find my way out. If I look on the world through my lower self with my physical eyes alone I see an image of divisiveness and chaos with the only certainty being death and decay. From the perspective of lower mind the world itself is already half way through its biological life — even the sun will die. I find these thoughts wonderfully liberating because it frees me from my bondage to the material and opens a way to knowledge of Higher Worlds.

Synchronicity was also working when, after walking for five days in perfect weather along the peaceful pathways that make up the Camino Portugués, I arrived in town and was confronted with a televised image of three Western kidnap victims in Iraq with their Islamic guards standing ominously in the background and the imminent threat of beheading. It was a dreadful image of intense pain and suffering that left me feeling shocked and nauseous. I wandered out into the sunlight in a vain effort to erase the terrifying image. An hour later, I found myself in a chapel before an image of St. James the Slayer of the Moors *Santiago Matamoros* occupying the central position over the altar. This was a place of modern Christian worship and the nausea returned as I realised that I was kneeling before an image of St. James with sword raised decapitating Islamic 'Infidels'. The way to forge peace can never be achieved through jihad and crusade.

Whether we believe in many Gods or One and whatever term we use to describe what cannot be described seems immaterial. God, Allah, Creator, Source... will do just fine, provided we direct our prayers towards an image of Love and Light. Words are powerful symbols and we need to be careful how we frame them. We may need to alter our images and think twice before we ask our questions and to whom we direct them. A loving deity may provide a very different answer to a vengeful one. We need to watch our terminology, mindful that those who look for separation and dissent will find it, but those who seek the truth and a unified purpose will find that also.

Along every Path of Enquiry there comes a point that requires a leap of faith. A point where we have to abandon the security of outdated dogma handed down to us over millennia. To let go of the familiar story taught to us by our tribe and develop the courage to dive instead into the mysteries – this is the story of the Grail Knights and the heart of modern-day pilgrimage too. When we meet that void no one else can cross it for us. We have to let go the safety of the familiar and dive into the unknown, with nothing but our faith in God to support us.

That is why I call these guides A Practical *and* Mystical Manual for the Modern-day Pilgrim. That we might find a place to eat and sleep at the end of a long days walking – but also, and crucially, that we might support each other to dive into the mysteries of our individual soul awakenings, without which all journeying is purposeless. We have a sacred contract, a divine function, and a reason why we came here. Perhaps your calling to go on pilgrimage will be the opportunity to find out what that purpose is and to provide the necessary space to re-orientate your life towards its fulfilment. Maybe this is the point in your life where all your neat and tightly held beliefs get shattered so that you can begin to piece together Who you really are and what your part in God's plan really is. We don't really have a choice, except to delay. Why wait for the inevitable?

So I end this foreword by giving the last word to the great mystic poet, Kabir.

Friend, hope for the truth while you are alive.
Jump into experience while you are alive!
Think... and think... while you are alive.
What you call 'salvation' belongs to the time before death.
If you don't break your ropes while you are alive,
Do you think ghosts will do it after?

The idea that the soul will join with the ecstatic
Just because the body is rotten —
That is all fantasy.
What is found now is found then.

If you find nothing now,
You will simply end up with an apartment in the city of death.
If you make love with the divine now, in the next life
You will have the face of satisfied desire.
So plunge into the truth, find out Who the Teacher is,
Believe in the Great Sound!

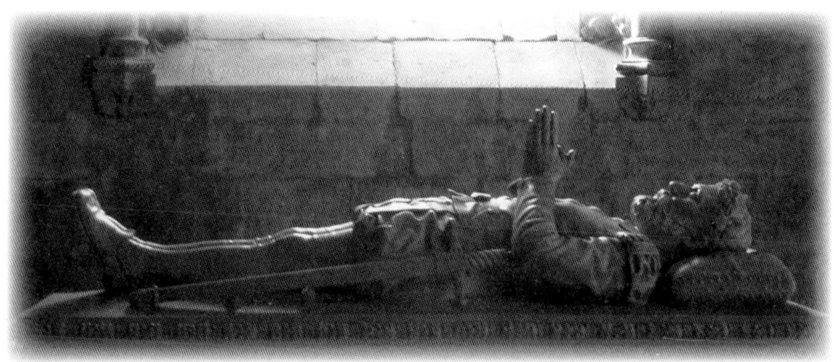

The Portuguese Way *Camino Portugués* *Caminho Português*

The Towers of the West *Torres del Oeste*

Along this route lies Monte Santiaguiño where St. James first preached Christ's lesson of unconditional love and forgiveness thus helping to write the first pages of Christian history. This pivotal event is represented on the front cover. St. James subsequently returns to Jerusalem to face martyrdom and his body is returned to this self-same spot – the boat carrying his mortal remains sailing up past the Towers of the West *Torres del Oeste* at Catoira to fetch land again at Padrón, his body finally being transported to Libredon – now renamed Santiago de Compostela. The Camino Portugués is thus both a starting point and an end point in the legendary Santiago story.

Much of the route follows the original Roman military road that connected Portugal with Spain and then France via the major 'crossroads' town of Astorga *Asturica Augusta*. You will pass by Roman milestones *miliários* to confirm that you are directly on the *Via XIX*. We will cross Roman bridges built 2,000 years ago, but this period, which marks St. James life and teaching, was to fade into obscurity for 800 years until the discovery of his tomb in the Roman town of *Liberum Donum*. The legend of the 'Field of Stars' *Compo-Stellae* was born just in time for the Christian re-conquest *reconquista* of the Iberian peninsular from the Islamic caliphate based in Córdoba. The renaming of Libredon to *Santiago de Compostela* was to follow. And here we also see the emergence of the terrible image of St. James the Slayer of the Moors *Santiago Matamoros*. This was an ideal image to spearhead the re-conquest but one far removed from the message of love of God, self, and stranger that is portrayed in the image of St. James the Pilgrim *Santiago Peregrino*. It is this latter figure that was to lead the revival of Christian pilgrimage as early as the 10th century and was to make Santiago de Compostela the third greatest pilgrim destination after Jerusalem and Rome. Most of the bridges that we walk over today were built during this medieval period, sometimes using the earlier Roman foundations. But it is at the dawn of the 21st century that we witness an extraordinary revival of pilgrimage that now places the Camino de Santiago at the forefront of this extraordinary modern phenomena and the most popular Christian pilgrimage route in the world today.

However, this brief overview is only part of the story, for there is not one camino, but many (see map back cover). In 2019 (pre-Covid) the Camino Francés accounted for 189,937 pilgrims (54% down from 85% 10 years ago) and the Camino Portugués central has become the second most popular route carrying 94,649 (27% up from 6% in the same period but still leaving the Portuguese Ways relatively uncrowded as they are split between 4 itineraries (Central, Costa, Litoral and Variante Espiritual). We follow in the footsteps of Pagan, Celtic, Roman, Islamic and Christian wayfarers going back over millennia. Today we seek the very same treasure they looked for – to find and embrace that loving Presence that offers us the gifts of joy and peace. In this fearful and war-torn world our mission has never been clearer or more urgent – every step now becomes a prayer for peace. The Way is open again for everyone, irrespective of gender or generation, colour, class or creed and from every religion, or none. This inclusivity marks it apart from virtually every other pilgrim itinerary around the world

Alternative routes: Before setting off you should at least hold an overview of the alternative routes that come under the general heading *O Caminhos Portugueses.* Not all of these are fully waymarked but enough have been painted with the familiar yellow arrows to cause possible confusion at certain points where they merge and branch off again. What follows is not an exhaustive list but it contains the major routes that have been used over the centuries and which *may* still be in existence today in some form or another. It is an indication of the popularity of the cult of St. James in Portugal during the Middle Ages that so many routes were available at that time. There are, perhaps, two contrasting reasons for its decline – the arrival of the industrial revolution in the 19th century and the apparition at Fátima in the early 20th century which changed the focus of attention. The early 21st century witnesses a marvellous awakening and renewal. Gratitude is due directly to you for being part of its re-emergence and I trust that it will feed and nourish you to the extent that you feed and nurture it.

❶ **Central Way *Caminho Central*** *Caminho Real* – the main historic route described in this guidebook from Lisbon to Porto and Porto to Tui which lies just over the border in Spain where more than half of all the pilgrims start the 'Portuguese' way ending in Santiago. Also referred to as the *Caminho Medieval*

❷ **Coastal Way *Caminho da Costa.*** This route is gaining in popularity with 22,292 (6% of total). It is well waymarked and includes the variant known as the senda litoral and is also included in this guidebook.

❸ **Seashore Path *Senda Litoral*** it is haphazardly waymarked but basically follows the seashore and beaches offering a distinctly tourist vibe. Both routes converge at Caminha to cross the Minho estuary into Spain at A Guarda and then via Baiona and Vigo to rejoin the main Central Camino at Redondela.

❹ **Sea Route *Ruta del Mar*** also known as **Spiritual Variant *Variante Espiritual*.** This follows the historical sea route up the Ria Arousa. Due to its increasing popularity it is now included in this guide. Commencing in Pontevedra it wends its way along delightful forest tracks around Armenteira to the coast at Vilanova de Arousa. Here you can take a dramatic boat trip up the río Ulla past Catoira and Towers of the West (photo previous page) to Pontecesures along the unique maritime *Via Crucis* with its stone crosses rising from the seabed... or continue by foot alongside the river estuary into Padrón.

❺ ***Caminho Nascente*** *(where the light is born)* was instigated in 2015 by the Associação de Amigos dos Caminhos de Fátima. The route between Tomar and Fátima is 29 km but difficulties have arisen due to competing paths that cross

it (Caminhos do Centenário) recently developed by Portuguese Tourism and another path with the same name commencing in Tavira in the south of Portugal. These paths have no connection with the historic Camino de Santiago. If you wish to visit Fátima consider taking a day return visit by bus from Tomar.

❻ **Braga Way *Caminho por Braga*** a little used variant from Porto to Braga thence joining with one of the several interior routes. It is mostly along busy main roads which deters many pilgrims. Braga is regarded as the ecclesiastical centre of Portugal and rich in religious monuments. The most widely visited 'tourist' site in Portugal is the intriguing church of Bom Jesus *Santuario do Bom Jesus do Monte* which lies on a hill overlooking Braga and the cathedral *Santa Maria de Braga*. The extent and wealth of its historical monuments is, perhaps, one of its biggest drawbacks for the modern-day pilgrim. Its popularity as a tourist destination means that roads into and out of Braga are busy and accommodation is relatively expensive. The city can be visited easily by bus from Barcelos with regular daily schedule (see under Barcelos for details).

❼ **Interior Way(s) *Caminho Interior*** a network of ancient and largely obsolete ways with limited facilities that are slowly being 'rediscovered' and waymarked. They include: ***Camino Portugués de San Rosendo*** (Lobios, Band, Verea, Celanova, A Merca, Barbadás, Ourense). ***Ruta da Raínha Santa Isabel / Saint Rudesind's Way / Geira Romana*** (first century CE – through the remote Peneda Geres National Park. Caldas da Rainha, Braga, Geres, Ribadavia, Codeseda, Pontevea / Celanova, Ourense, Santiago). Other variants via Viseu, Vila Real, Chaves connecting to the ***Camino Sanabrés*** in Verín. A variant crosses in Lamego to rejoin the central way in Ponte de Lima. ***Caminho Português de Lamego*** a variant from Coimbra to Lamego. The original route continued north via Chaves.

❽ **The Way of the Star *Caminho de Via de Estrela*** from Caceres to Braga. This route follows (in theory) the line of a Roman road that branched off from the Via de la Plata. While it has ancient roots it is only now re-emerging as a possible viable alternative pilgrim route. It crosses the remote and beautiful Monte Estrela through Belmonte. It will, in time, connect with Viseu and the Interior Way.

❾ **The Northern Way *Caminho do Norte*** via Lanheses. This route is poorly waymarked and the lack of lodging makes it difficult to negotiate. It combines the early stages of the Coastal route and then swings eastwards towards the Central route before branching off again near Barcelos (Abade de Neives). It then climbs steeply through the Serra de Padela *Parque de Valinhas* to descend sharply to cross the Rio Lima into Lanheses. From here it is another steep climb up through the Serra de Arga before dropping down to join the Coastal route at Vila Nova de Cerveira and thence to Valença or A Guarda. This route is arduous, taking in the steep mountains of the Serra de Arga.

❿ **Fátima: *Caminho de Tejo*** This route follows the camino de Santiago from Lisbon as far as Santarém where it branches off to the west. To pilgrimage in Portugal we need to understand that Fátima and Portugal are synonymous. Since the vision of the Blessed Virgin appeared to three young shepherd children (Lúcia, Francesco and Jacinta) in Fátima in 1917, it has become a major pilgrimage centre and place of veneration in its own right and one of the great Marian Shrines in the Catholic world. While the thousands who travel there every year do so mostly by bus, you may well come across happy bands of pilgrims walking to Fátima,

sometimes as many as 100 in a group! Lúcia survived the flu epidemic that ravaged Europe after the First World war and the one to whom the *Three Secrets* were revealed. The first was a horrifying vision of hell and a call for repentance. The second was similar and concerned the threat of world war and persecution. The third was the most prophetic but has never been fully revealed. The Vatican has suggested it concerns the attempted assassination and death of Pope John Paul II *(A bishop dressed in white who falls to the ground as if dead)* but others suggest it prophesies the fall of the Church itself *(due to scandals at the very heart of the hierarchy)*. The bullet extracted from the Pontiff has now been inserted into the crown of the statue of the Virgin at Fátima. (Photo of the Basilica above).

Lúcia died near Coimbra in 2005 and the Congregation of the Doctrine of the Faith will publish the full text of her message in due course and after suitable preparation. However we might individually interpret such prophecies, the fact remains that in order to breakthrough to a new reality we have to allow old thought-forms and dogma to die. The death of the old is generally experienced as painful, but the emergence of the new often brings elation. As we begin to shift from an imperfect outer authority to our innate inner wisdom we might experience an intensity of both anxiety and a sense of freedom. Fátima struggles with this self-same acceleration of both negative and positive forces. A headline in a Portuguese newspaper declared: *'Another Interfaith Outrage Blessed by Fátima Shrine Rector. Appearing on Portuguese television, Msgr. Guerra regurgitated the long-discredited ecumenical slogan that different religions should concentrate on what we have in common and not on what separates us.'* Pilgrimages of reparation still take place to atone for this outrage – and what, pray, is this defilement? A Hindu priest was permitted by Msgr. Guerra to offer a prayer for peace and reconciliation at the Catholic altar in the Little Chapel of the Apparitions!

Fátima clearly struggles with a traditional and more progressive faith. This snapshot of Fátima will hopefully provide a context to understand the general lack of interest, even suspicion within Portugal, towards Santiago. The town of Tomar on the historic Santiago route lies 35 km east of Fátima and represents the Gnostic perspective held by the Order of the Knights Templar. This is no less threatening today as it was in 1312 when the Order was outlawed by the Vatican for it proclaims the sanctity of the God that lies within every individual soul and is therefore less dependent on external authority. It is, perhaps, one of the reasons why no official pilgrim hostels were available on the Lisbon section until 2012, although they were everywhere in the medieval period. However, this lack of any single authority trying to take sole responsibility for the camino permits a more open and eclectic orientation. It might also help us understand why the familiar yellow arrow pointing to Santiago is often accompanied by a blue arrow pointing in the *opposite* direction – to Fátima.

If you intend to detour to Fátima contact the tourist office in the town ⓘ ***Turismo*** ✆ 249 531 139 or Armando Pereira at Hostel Pereira ✆ 960 330 636. The route can be walked in 2 days from Santarém (56 km). A route continues via Caxarias to rejoin the Caminho Central in Ansião or Alvaiázere (44 km or another 2 days). Regular bus service Tomar/ Fátima from €5 ± 1 hour. Taxi €30 ± 1 ½ hour. Information: *https://caminhosdefatima.org/pt/caminhos/caminho-do-tejo*

Pilgrimage is experienced on many different levels. At one end is the physical challenge of walking a long distance route with a group of friends in a limited time frame, always with an eye on the calendar. Perhaps now is an opportunity for you to experience pilgrimage at the other end, at a pace that allows for the inner alchemy of introspection. How deep you choose to make the experience is, of course, up to you. Nevertheless the basic counsel is to go on foot, alone. The extended periods of silence will open up space to reflect on your life and its direction. Go alone and you may find that you are never alone and that may prove a pivotal turning point.

The Camino Portugués is shaking off centuries of slumber and ready to play its part in the great flowering of human imagination, cooperation and consciousness. In the oft-repeated words of Christopher Frye from *A Sleep of Prisoners*, "...Affairs are now soul sized. The enterprise is exploration into God. Where are you making for? It takes so many thousand years to wake, but will you wake for pity's sake."

... And so, like a latter-day Rip Van Winkle we rise to dust off our boots and join the merry band of pilgrims making their way up through the welcoming beauty and peace of northern Portugal to the city of St. James in neighbouring Galicia. You will meet other fellow wayfarers and the native folk whose lands you pass over, but above all you may meet your Self, and that may make all the difference. Whatever you do, don't forget to begin. Journey well, *buen viaje, boa viagem!*

Historical Snapshot and Brief Chronology: What follows is not an authoritative discourse on the history of Portugal or its pilgrim routes. It appears on a yellow panel so you can skip this section if you have read it elsewhere or if it is of no interest. It merely seeks to draw together some of the innumerable strands that make the Portuguese Way central to an understanding of the Santiago story. From St. James first landing at Padrón to convert the pagan inhabitants in his guise as *Santiago Peregrino* to his re-invention to spearhead the crusades to vanquish Islam as *Santiago Matamoros* the memory of St. James is indelibly linked to these shores. The route has remained in obscurity for too long and deserves to be more widely discovered and acknowledged.

- **Palaeolithic period c. 20,000 B.C.**

1992 saw one of the great archaeological discoveries of the modern era in Vila Nova de Foz Côa, in the Douro valley 120 km due East of Porto. Here we find one of the oldest t displays of Palaeolithic art dating back some 22,000 years. It was declared a UNESCO World heritage site in 1998. The Douro river valley has been a cradle of civilisation long before the Age of Discoveries was launched from her harbours.

- **Megalithic period c. 4000 B.C.**

This period is best known for the building of great *mega* stone structures sometimes referred to as Dolmens or Mamoas. They generally had evidence of human remains and have been linked to prehistoric graves. They were also aligned to the winter solstice sun and so are connected to sun worship. An example lies on our route near Arcos (see stage 2 for details). Petroglyphs or rock carvings are another feature of this period. This megalithic culture was deeply religious in nature and left a powerful impact on the peoples who followed.

- **Early Celtic period c. 1,000 B.C.**

Central European Celts settled in north-western Portugal and Spain intermarrying with the Iberians and giving rise to the Celtiberian tribes. Remains of their Celtic villages *castros* or *citânias* can be seen dotted around the countryside especially in the Minho area. These fortified villages were built in a circular formation usually occupying some elevated ground or hillock. They are found today in place names on maps, but one of the most striking examples can be visited just off our route at Monte de Santa Tecla overlooking the mouth of the Minho (photo>). The extensive mineral deposits of this area gave rise to a rich artistic movement and bronze and gold artefacts of Celtic design and origin can be admired in museums all across Europe. The Phoenicians established a trading centre in Lisbon around 900 B.C.

- **Early Roman period c. 200 B.C.**

The Roman occupation of the Iberian peninsular began in the 2nd century BCE and they too were attracted by the rich mining potential of the Northern region.

Ponte de Lima *(Lethe)*

In 136 B.C. the proconsul Decimus Junius Brutus led his legions across the Lima and Minho rivers where he met resistance not only from the fierce inhabitants but also from his own soldiers wary of crossing the river that was thought to represent one of the rivers of Hades – the river of forgetfulness *Lethe*. Brutus became the first Roman general to make it across and on to the end of the known world at Finis Terrae. A Roman garrison was established there that would become city of Dugium – present day Duio. This early Roman settlement played host to pilgrims from many different traditions and it was to the king (governor) of Dugium that St. James' disciples were directed by queen Lupa for permission to bury his body (see *A Pilgrims Guide to the Camino Finisterre*).

While the Phoenicians are, perhaps, best known for their syllabic writing which influenced the Aramaic and Greek alphabets developed from their base at Byblos (from which comes our word Bible) they were the great merchant nation of antiquity. They also developed the sea routes to the British Isles to promote the tin trade in particular, helping to develop the Atlantic ports such as Cadiz, Lisbon and Finisterre on the way. In 61 B.C. Julius Caesar became governor of Hispania Ulterior establishing *Olisipo* (modern day Lisbon) as his base from where he conducted naval expeditions along these shores to finally win control of the Atlantic seaboard from the Phoenicians. The most significant Roman remains in Portugal are in Conímbriga which was a major military and trading post on the Via Roman XVI between Olisipo (Lisbon), Cale (Porto) and Bracara Augusta (Braga). The Roman road from Braga to Valença was known as the Via XIX also referred to as the Antonine Itinerary *Itinerario de Antonino*.

• Early Christian Period c. 40 A.D.

While there is little historical evidence to support the view that St. James (The Greater, Son of Zebedee to distinguish him for St. James the Just) came to the Iberian peninsular there is ample anecdotal testimony to that effect. It would appear that he sailed to Padrón and commenced his ministry there. By all accounts his mission was largely unsuccessful and after an apparition by the Virgin Mary in 40 A.D. he returned to Jerusalem where he was decapitated in the year 44 at Herod Agrippa's own hand (and sword). James thus became the first of the apostles to be martyred and his faithful disciples decided to return his body to the place of his earlier ministry at Padrón. On the instructions of the pagan queen Lupa the relics of St. James were taken to Finisterre where permission for burial was refused by the Roman legate. In the famous story of betrayal the disciples managed to escape with their sacred cargo and the body of St. James was finally laid to rest in Libredon (Liberum Donum). These remarkable events then faded from memory until...

• The Middle Ages c. 476 – 1453

The decline and fall of the Roman Empire was hastened in Portugal with the arrival of Visigoth and Suevi tribes from Germany. The Suevi settled further north around the Douro establishing headquarters at the roman port of Portucale (present day Porto and from which we get the name Portugal). The influence of the Visigoths extended further south around the Lisbon (Olisipo) area. It was from their base in Toledo that their incessant internal squabbles resulted in one group seeking support from the Muslim enclave in North Africa – the Moors duly obliged, arriving in 711. Within a decade Islam had effectively conquered the majority of the Iberian peninsular. While we are more familiar, perhaps, with the Arab influence in Spain, they occupied the entire of Portugal where their rule appears to have been much more favourable than life under the Visigoths who initiated the first expulsion of Jews from the peninsular while the Moors allowed freedom of religious expression. The last Islamic stronghold was the coastal area of southern Portugal, which they named al-Gharb (meaning the West) that today we know as the Algarve. Contrary to popular understanding, Mozarabes (Moçárabes) was the name given to freely practising Christians under Moorish rule. It was during this period, in the year 813, that a 'celestial light' led the hermit Pelayo to the Field of Stars *Compo Stellae* and the discovery of the tomb of St. James. This visionary event was immediately endorsed by the bishop of Iria Flavia in whose diocese Libredon was, and the following year King Alfonso II commenced the building of a basilica church.

The discovery of the tomb arrived just in time for St. James to become the figurehead for the Christian re-conquest of the Iberian peninsular from Islam. The night before the battle of Clavijo St. James appeared to the Christian troops as a knight dressed in armour astride a white charger, which was to rally the Christian army that the Arab forces were duly defeated. The re-conquest ebbed and flowed with Almanzor arriving at the door of Santiago cathedral in 997 but the relics of the saint had been removed so the Moors took the bells instead and had them carried by Christian slaves to his base in Córdoba. Al-Mansur provided a further setback in 1190 but Portugal's turning point came with Afonso Henriques and the battle of Ourique in 1139 and the taking of Lisbon in 1147. On the strength of these re-conquests he became Dom Afonso I, first King of Portugal. Dom Afonso III (1248-1249) finally providing the *coup de grâce* by winning back the al-Gharb in southern Portugal.

Santiago Matamoros

Pilgrimages to Santiago began around the middle of the 10th century, becoming increasingly popular and reaching something of a climax by the middle of the 15th century. While thousands of simple peasants, priests and paupers made the journey, we learn mostly of the exploits of nobility, kings and queens. By this time the main routes via Barcelos, Braga and Viana had become well established. In 915 Dom Ordonho II granted land in Correlhã, near Ponte de Lima, to the city fathers at Santiago de Compostela. This marks the first significant recognition of Santiago as a major pilgrimage destination through Portugal. By coincidence the only chapel dedicated to Santiago (in ruins) on the route in Portugal remains in the townland of Correlhã (see stage 16). D. Henrique and Dna. Teresa ratified the gifting of these lands on their royal pilgrimage to Santiago in 1097. Other monarchs followed with Afonso II in 1219, Dom Sancho II in 1244 and then Queen Isabel (the Saintly) made her first pilgrimage in 1325.

• The Age of Discoveries c. 1500

Portuguese Caravel *(replica)*

Under Manuel I, otherwise known as The Fortunate we see the navigation of the sea routes to India by Vasco da Gama in 1498 and the creation of the first viceroy to India some years later. In 1500 Pedro Alvares discovers Brazil, establishing a link that remains strong to this day. The ensuing foreign trade made Portugal one of the richest countries in the world and saw the flowering of Christianity, art and commerce with trade agreements as far flung as China, Persia, India and South America. King Manuel I became a great patron of the arts and this period and its beautiful architectural style is known as *Manueline*. Manuel, a deeply religious man, went on pilgrimage to Santiago in 1502. Amongst other dignitaries who made the pilgrimage through Portugal was Cosme III of the Medicis in 1669. It seems that the famous Italian pilgrim, Doménico Laffi, perhaps inspired by the Medici pilgrimage, made the journey in 1691. The first detailed account of the pilgrimage was by a German traveller, Jeronimo Münzer in 1495. This was followed by the better-known account of Juan Bautista Confalonieri an Italian priest who accompanied Monsignor Fabio Biondo on his pilgrimage in 1592.

• A snapshot of modern Portugal 1807 – 2019

In 1807 Napoleon reached Portugal and the royal family withdrew to Brazil and made their seat of government there. After Napoleon's forces were finally defeated in 1811 unrest within Portugal led to a Constitutional Monarchy in 1820 and an era of relative stability under D. Pedro V and D. Luís I. However civil strife at the turn of the century led to revolution and the establishment of a Republic in 1910 and Manuel José de Arriaga was elected as first president. Political unrest continued through the period of the first World War up to 1926 when an army coup installed General António de Fragoso Carmona to head a new government. He appointed António de Oliveira Salazar as minister of finance. Salazar was deeply religious and set about restoring the power of the church after becoming prime minister and effectively a dictator in 1932.

In 1936 Salazar supported General Francisco Franco during the Spanish civil war and both countries signed a non-aggression pact and declared neutrality during the Second World War. Salazar's rigid regime and economic policies led to low wages with poor labour rights and, inevitably, unrest. The regime resisted all opposition, crushing a revolt in 1947. The 1960's marked another difficult period for Portugal with rebellion in the overseas territories of Goa, Angola, Guinea and Mozambique. Portugal resisted these moves for independence in its African colonies receiving UN condemnation. In 1968 Marcello **Caetano** succeeded Salazar as prime minister. The repressive policies continued at home and in the colonies and Portugal's economic stability was again threatened and this led to a coup by the army in 1974, which installed Gen. António de **Spinola** as president. Spinola oversaw democratic reforms at home and in the African territories and during this period General Francisco da Costa Gomes was elected president. Nationalisation of industry, the banking system and the repossession of many large agricultural estates ensued.

Over the following decades political unrest between right-wing, communist and socialist factions led to a deepening of the economic and social problems of Portugal and the government has swung from left to right with alarming regularity. Soares (Socialist Party PS) played a prominent role during this period introducing an austerity program that led eventually to Portugal's entry into the European Community in 1986. In 2002 the centre-right coalition elected José Manuel **Barroso** as Prime Minister who resigned in 2004 to head up the European Commission and Santana **Lopes** was sworn in as Prime Minister.

The euro crisis saw the Socialist Party (PS) back in power under José **Socrates** but the austerity plans following the EU/IMF bailout agreement in May 2011 led to his resignation. Social Democratic Party (PSD) Prime Minister Pedro Passos Coelho's government took office in June 2011 to implement austerity. Portugal lurches from left to right with the shortest Constitutional Government in history lasting just twelve days in 2015! The gap is currently filled by a Socialist minority government sustained by an alliance of two far left parties all with an anti-austerity agenda. How long this will last is anyones guess.

• A snapshot of modern Galicia 1975 – 2019

After Franco's death in 1975, King Carlos nominally succeeded and appointed political reformist Adolfo Suárez to form a government. In 1982 the socialist party (PSOE) won a sweeping victory under Felipe **González** who successfully steered Spain into full membership of the EEC in 1986. In 1996 conservative José María **Aznar**, leader of the right wing *Partido Popular* (PP), won a narrow mandate but in November 2002 the oil tanker Prestige ran into a storm off Finisterre and the ensuing ecological catastrophe sank not only the livelihood of scores of Galician fisherman but, in due time, the right wing government as well. The disregard for the environment displayed by the President of Galicia and the Spanish environment minister of that time resulted in a popular cry up and down the country of 'never again' *nunca maís*. It only took the government's unpopular support of the invasion of Iraq coupled with the Madrid bombings in March 2004 to put the socialist's back in power under the youthful leadership of José Luis Rodríguez **Zapatero**. The new government set in motion an immediate change in foreign policy and, more controversially, a sudden but decisive shift from a conservative Catholic to a liberal secular society that led to one newspaper headline declaring, '*Church and State square up in struggle for the spirit of Spain.*' The economic crisis led to the election of Mariano **Rajoy** of the centre-right PP in December 2011.

Anger over corruption and immigration is changing the political landscape and seeing the rise of new parties such as *Podemos 'We Can'* led by radical academic **Pablo Iglesias.** In June 2018 **Pedro Sanchez** of the socialist party PSOE formed a new socialist alliance ousting the ruling PP. And seemingly immune to all these social and political upheavals the *Camino Portugués* goes quietly about her gentle spirit of transformation with the rising sun ushering in a fresh start to each new day...

Preparation – A Quick Guide:

❶ Practical Considerations:

• **When?** Spring is often wet and windy but the route is relatively quiet with early flowers appearing. Summer is busy and hot and hostels often full. Autumn usually provides the most stable weather with harvesting adding to the colour and celebrations of the countryside. Winter is solitary and cold with reduced daylight hours for walking and some hostels will be closed.

• **How long?** Clear the decks and allow some spaciousness into your life. This route is divided into 24 daily stages so it fits *(just)* into a 3 week break. Interim lodging allows each stage to be varied according to differing abilities and pace.

❷ Preparation – Outer: what do I need to take...

• Buy your boots in time to walk them in before you go.
• Pack a Poncho – Galicia in particular is notorious for its downpours.
• Bring a hat – sunstroke is painful and can be dangerous.
• Look again if your backpack weighs more than 10 kilos.

... *and* consider leaving behind.

• Books, except this one – all the maps and prompting you need are included.
• Extras, Portugal has shops if you need to replace something.
• Everything that is superfluous for pilgrimage. Take time to reflect carefully on this point as it can form the basis of our questioning of what is really important in our life and spiritual awakening. We have become reliant, even addicted, to so many extraneous 'things'. We need to de-clutter if we are to clear space for what truly matters to arise in our awareness.

❸ **Language:** learn at least some basic phrases now, *before* you go.

❹ Pilgrim Passport, Protocol & Prayer

• Get a *credencial* from your local confraternity – and join it (see p.265)
• Have consideration for your fellow pilgrims and gratitude for your hosts.
• 'May every step be a prayer for peace and an extension of loving kindness.'

❺ Preparation – Inner: why am I doing this?

Take time to prepare a purpose for this pilgrimage and to complete the self-assessment questionnaire (page 27). Start from the basis that you are essentially a spiritual being on a human journey, not a human being on a spiritual one. We came to learn some lesson and fulfil our sacred contract –this pilgrimage affords an opportunity to find out what that is. Ask for help and expect it – it's there, now, waiting for you.

Whatever you do – for heaven's sake don't forget to start.

● **Practical Considerations:** This guidebook provides essential information in a concise format, with information on where to eat, sleep and points of interest along the way. The maps have been designed to show relevant information only and accurate distances between points are printed on the map and correspond with the text – they are generally spaced at around 3.5 kilometre intervals which corresponds to around one hour of walking at an average pace. These maps directs you *to* Santiago; if you intend to walk 'in reverse' source different maps.

Each stage begins and ends at a town or village where some suitable accommodation can be found with details and alternatives provided in the text. Interim accommodation is also listed so that you make your own start and finish point. Your body will remind you when you need to eat or drink but my advice is never to pass a drinking font without using it – a minimum of 2 litres a day will help ward off injury and fatigue.

● **How long will it take?** Allow time to complete the journey gracefully. There's already too much pressure in our lives – so clear the decks and allow some spaciousness into your life. Walking pace naturally varies between individuals and when you add in variations in weather, detours (planned and otherwise) and various route choices this results in a heady mix of possibilities. The route has been divided into 24 stages (13 from Lisbon to Porto and 11 from Porto to Santiago). Fit walkers could accomplish the entire route in 3 weeks but this would allow for no rest days, no detours, no injuries and little time for reflection and integration of experiences along the way. A month is ideal and equates to an average of 26 km per day with 3 rest days, allowing time to explore along the way and 2 days to travel to Lisbon and home again from Santiago. (Allow 2 weeks Porto to Santiago).

Be mindful that most injuries occur in the early days while pushing the body beyond what it has been conditioned for. It takes the body a few days to adjust to the regular walking with full backpack. Give body, mind and soul time to acclimatise. Don't push yourself at the beginning. It is always advisable to put in some physical training before you go. Walking poles, if used properly, can also greatly reduce wear and tear on the body and minimise the likelihood of injury.

Distance and Time: This guide has a daily *average* of 26 km but can – *and should* – be adjusted to suit individual needs. Remember pace will slow, often considerably, towards the end of a long day's walking. Pace also varies depending on the gradient and contour maps are provided to alert you to strenuous *up*hill stretches. Familiarise yourself with the map symbols used in this guide (see p. 31) and note that in addition to the *actual* distance an *adjusted* time is provided based on the cumulative height climbed during each stage. This is based on the Naismith rule of an additional 10 minutes for each 100m of ascent. Average pace is taken as 1 km in 15 minutes or 4 kph.

Pilgrims often question the measurements given for the *last* section of each stage suggesting it was *double* the distance indicated (it took twice as long as expected). They were right about the time but not the distance! Take heed of the Chinese proverb, ***'On a journey of a hundred miles, ninety is but half way'***!

Decide where to stop according to your individual level of fitness. The maps in this guide are designed for an 'average' pace and based on what fits neatly on one page. Alternatives are limitless by using interim accommodation.

● **When to go?** The summer months can be very hot and accommodation, particularly in July and August, in short supply. This problem is aggravated during Holy or Jubilee Years, any year when the feast of St. James (25th July) falls on a Sunday. Temperatures as high as 40^{C} have been recorded in July although the average for the month is 25^{C} with rainfall of only 20mm. The coast has a moderating influence on temperature but the Atlantic can throw up storms and high winds. Autumn tends to be kinder than spring with an average temperature of 24^{C} and rainfall of 51mm in September compared to 15^{C} and 147mm in March.

The main season for pilgrim services runs from April through September. Outside these months some accommodation and services will close. However, costs are lower and the bulk of tourists have left so some of the most mystical and transformative trips can be in the quieter low season. I have never wanted for a bed to sleep at any time of year but if travelling during the winter bring warm waterproof clothes and remember that daylight hours are reduced to 8 hours maximum so the daily distance that can be covered must be adjusted.

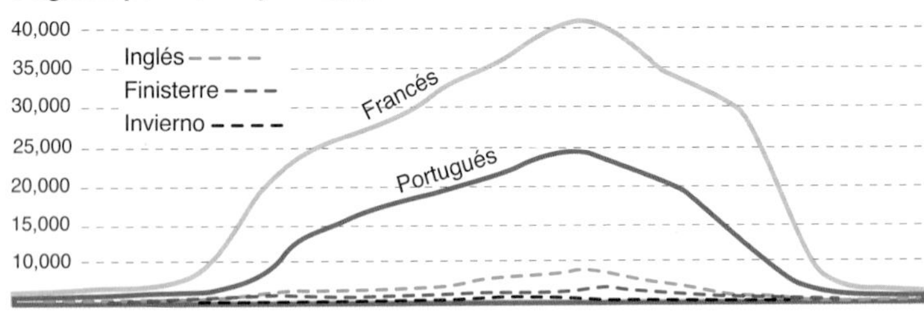

● **Travel:** Competition from airlines means there are good budget travel options from/to Porto, A Coruña, Vigo and Santiago by air. There are also regular bus and rail services to each airport which allows for easy onward travel. For example Autna and Alsa have regular services direct from Porto airport to Valença if commencing at Tui. Depending on point of departure the good bus and rail links also provide ample options for those who wish to avoid flaying.

◖ **How to get there:** The following international •**AIRLINES** fly into **Lisbon**: TAP/ BA / EasyJet / Thomsonfly / Aer Lingus / Air France / Ibéria / Vueling / KLM / Lufthansa / Vueling / Finnair / and SATA International: ***Departure airports*** in the UK include London, Bristol, Birmingham, Liverpool and Manchester. All major cities throughout Europe are covered in addition to direct flights from Canada and the USA. Recent expansion at **Vigo** has added flights from Dublin, London and Edinburgh. International •**RAIL** & •**BUS** services to Porto are more limited but there are daily services direct from Paris and Madrid – check with **Portuguese rail** *www.cp.pt* with an online booking service in English also **Rail Europe** *www.raileurope.com/en* **Eurolines** has daily services from London to Lisbon via Paris *www.eurolines.com* Bus and rail within Portugal are efficient and comprehensive. Check schedules with *www.rome2rio.com*

◖ **...and back:** If you are **returning from Porto** there are 2 daily rail services from Santiago to Porto (Campanha) with frequent onward connections to Lisbon with

Spanish Rail www.renfe.es This is a splendid trip along the Minho river valley and the Portuguese coast that gives a flavour of the Caminho da Costa. You can stop off in Viana do Castelo and wander the old quarter next to the train station. **Alsa** www.alsa.es have a regular service to Santiago from Porto. **Autna** www.autna.com operate daily direct from Vigo bus station to Porto airport via Valença.

▮ **AIR**: ***Ryanair*** fly direct to **Santiago** from London Stansted, Frankfurt, Rome, Madrid, Malaga, Barcelona, Alicante. ***Vueling*** fly from Paris direct. ***Aer Lingus*** fly Santiago direct from Dublin (summer schedule) and ***BA*** and ***Iberia*** and other major airlines offer regular services throughout the year via various connecting airports in Spain, mainly Madrid. ***Vueling*** fly direct A Coruña to London.
▮ **RAIL** – you can book online through **Spanish rail *Renfe*** www.renfe.es/horarios/english or Rail Europe at www.raileurope.co.uk **Bus** you can book online with **Alsa** www.alsa.es (English language option)
▮ **FERRY** The advantage of sailing home is that you get a chance to acclimatise slowly – check with Brittany Ferries / Santander - Plymouth 19 hours and Santander - Plymouth 23 hours (twice weekly).
▮ **CAR HIRE** If you can find other passengers to share the cost then this is often a relatively cheap and convenient way to travel on to such places as Santander or Bilbao and flying or sailing home from there.

● **Credentials *credenciales* & Certificate of Completion *compostela*:** In order to stay at official pilgrim hostels you need to have a pilgrim passport *credencial* impressed with a rubber stamp (in Spanish: *sello* Portuguese: *carimbo)* at hostels, churches, town halls etc. along the way (2 stamps per day within Galicia). On the Spanish section of the Camino Portugués this is generally done in the official pilgrim hostels *albergues* that are reserved exclusively for pilgrims to Santiago (or Fátima if you are doing the route in reverse). This *credencial* must be presented at the pilgrim office in Santiago in order to receive a Compostela as proof that you have walked at least the last 100 kilometres (200 if cycling). Those who do not accept a spiritual motivation as part of their reason for making the pilgrimage can obtain a ***certificado*** which is essentially a certificate of completion.

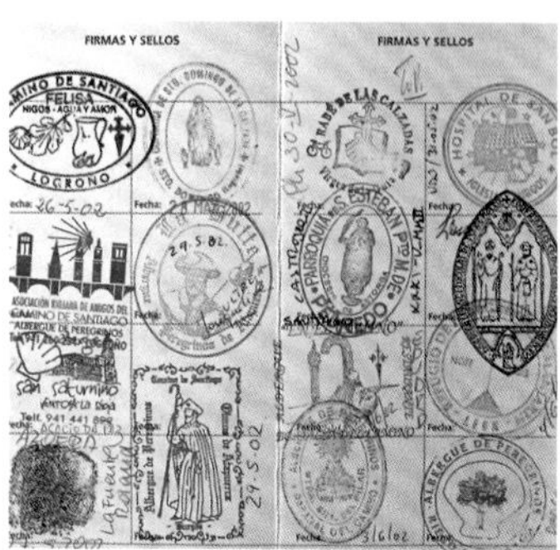

You can obtain a 'pilgrim passport' *credencial* before travelling from the Confraternity of St. James in London or possibly from a local confraternity in your country of origin (see *useful addresses)*. An official *credencial* can also be obtained from Lisbon, Tui or Porto cathedrals and at the Church of the Martyrs or St. James in Lisbon. Also in several albergues. (see Lisbon city plan p.32).

● **Pilgrim hostels** *albergues de peregrinos* ●*Alb.* vary in what they provide but lodging is usually in bunk beds with additional overflow space on mattresses *colchones*. Number of beds and dormitories are shown in brackets *[8÷2]* / *[40÷1]* (simple division will provide an idea of density!) + private rooms *+4*. The first dedicated pilgrim hostel in Portugal was opened in 2012 and facilities are improving fast. Youth hostels *Pousadas de Juventude* provide special pilgrim discounts from

€8 central booking +351 707 233 233. Opening times vary depending on time of year but are generally cleaned and open again from early afternoon to welcome pilgrims. Advance booking in official municipal and association albergues is not possible and phone numbers are provided for emergency calls or to check availability in winter.

While the section from Porto to Santiago has excellent facilities with most hostels offering kitchen /dining / sitting areas the early stages out of Lisbon have more limited choice. However there is a growing international effort aiming to address this with plans top open a new albergue on the first stage out of Lisbon.

● **Alternative accommodation** is generally available in *H* hoteles, *M* moteles, *Hs* hostales, *P* pensiones *pensãos*, fondas, residenciales or simply camas (literally beds). In addition Portugal has *Q quintas* or manor houses in the luxury bracket (€50 to €90). In Spain a similar standard of accommodation is provided in a type of up-market B&B known as a *CR casa rural* literally 'rural house'. Number of rooms (*x2* versus *x102*) indicates type (intimate -v- anonymous) and likely facilities on offer. Pilgrim discounts are often available – check before booking).

● **Bedbugs** ***Percevejos (Chinches** in Spanish)* are a source of concern in any accommodation where people sleep in close proximity. Bedbugs live in mattresses etc. feeding at night, so until the accommodation is treated the problem remains. Carrying a pre-treated pillowcase and bed sheet (e.g. LifeAventure 3X) can be a useful preventative measure. If affected (3 or more bites in a row is a good indication) you need to ❶ immediately advise the place you are staying and also the next hostel(s) so that they can take preventive measures. ❷ wash and/ or tumble dry all clothes at highest settings for 2+ hours and ❸ Seek medical attention in severe cases (Hydrocortisone). Vinegar is reported to reduce itchiness, but advice is often contradictory so seek help from those who have experience of the problem or a local chemist.

● **Other Costs:** Allow for a basic €25 a day to include €8 euros for overnight stay at a municipal hostel (av. €15+ private) and remainder for food and drink (3 course *menú del dia* €9. *Tapas* often served free with drinks!). Some hostels provide a communal supper on occasions (dependent on the warden *hospitalero*) and most have a basic kitchen *cocina* where a meal can be prepared. Alternatively most locations have one or more restaurants to choose from. If you want to indulge in the wonderful seafood *mariscos* available expect to double the basic cost.

● **Equipment:** Light walking boots or shoes are fine for this route. No pack need exceed 50 litres or 10 kilos (22 lbs). If you are not fluent in Portuguese or Spanish then buy a small phrase *and* pronunciation guide. Opposite is a pilgrim checklist with Spanish and Portuguese translations to help strengthen your vocabulary and assist you to buy or replace items along the way. This is not necessarily a recommended list; what you need will vary according to the season and individual need. But it may serve as a useful starting point when considering what to bring.

Packing Notes:

CHECK-LIST:	*Español*	*Português*
Clothes:	***Ropas:***	***Roupa:***
hat (sun)	*sombrero*	*chapéu*
sunglasses	*gafas de sol*	*óculos de sol*
shirts [ ]	*camisa*	*camisa*
travel gilet	*chaqueta de viaje*	*chaleco de viaje*
jacket -	*chaqueta -*	*casaco*
... waterproof	*... chubasquero*	*... capa de chuva*
... breathable	*... transpirable*	*... transpirável*
underpants [ ]	*calzoncillos*	*cuecas*
shorts	*pantalones cortos*	*calções / shorts*
trousers	*pantalones largos*	*calças*
handkerchief	*pañuelo*	*lenço*
socks [ ]	*calcetines*	*peúgas*
Shoes:	***Zapatos:***	***Sapatos:***
boots (mountain)	*botas (de montaña)*	*botas (de montanha)*
shoes (walking)	*zapatos (de andar)*	*sapatos (de caminhar)*
sandals (leather)	*sandalias (de piel)*	*sandálias (de couro)*
Size:	***Tamaño:***	***Tamanho:***
larger	*más grande*	*maior*
smaller	*más pequeño*	*menor*
more expensive/cheaper	*más caro / barato*	*mais caro / barato*
model / number	*modelo / número*	*modelo / número*
Essential documents	***Documentos esenciales:***	***Originais essenciais:***
passport	*pasaporte*	*passaporte*
pilgrim record	*credencial de peregrino*	*credencial do peregrino*
wallet/ purse	*monedero / cartera*	*porta-moedas*
cash	*dinero en efectivo*	*dinheiro em efetivo*
credit card	*tarjeta de crédito*	*cartão de crédito*
travel tickets	*pasaje de viaje*	*passagem de viagem*
diary	*diario*	*diário*
emergency addresses	*dirección de emergencia*	*endereço de emergência*
phone numbers	*números de teléfono*	*números de telefone*
Backpack	***Mochila***	***Mochila***
rain cover	*protección de mochila*	*capa para mochila*
sleeping bag	*saco de dormir*	*saco de dormir*
towel	*toalla*	*toalha*
water bottle	*botella de agua*	*garrafa de água*
penknife	*navaja*	*navalha*
Toiletries:	***Artículos de tocador:***	
soap	*jabón*	*sabão*
shampoo	*champú*	*champô*
tooth brush	*cepillo de dientes*	*escova de dentes*
toothpaste	*dentífrico*	*pasta de dentes*
hair brush	*cepillo de pelo*	*escova de cabelo*
sink stopper / plug	*tapón de fregadero*	*tampa de ralo*
shaving cream	*espuma de afeitar*	*espuma de barbear*

razor (blades)	*cuchilla de afeitar*	*lâminas de barbear*
face cloth	*guante de aseo*	*luva de asseio*
sun cream (lotion)	*crema solar (loción)*	*protector solar*
after sun cream	*leche solar (after sun)*	*loção pós-sol*
moisturiser	*crema hidratante*	*hidratante*
toilet paper	*papel higiénico*	*papel higiênico*
tissues	*pañuelos de papel*	*lenços de papel*
sanitary pads	*salva-slips*	*salva-slips*
tampons	*tampones*	*tampões*
First Aid Kit:	***Botiquín botiquín de primeros auxilios***	***Estojo de primeiro socorros***
painkiller	*analgésico*	*analgésico*
aspirin/ Paracetemol	*aspirina/paracetamol*	*aspirina/paracetamol*
plasters	*esparadrapo*	*penso rápido*
blister pads	*apósito para ampollas*	*penso para bolhas*
compeed-*second skin*	*compeed-segunda piel*	*compeed-band-aid*
antiseptic cream	*crema antiséptica*	*loção anti-séptica*
muscular ache (ointment)	*pomada para dolores musculares*	*pomada para dores musculares*
homeopathic remedies	*remedios homeopáticos*	*remédios homeopáticos*
Medicine (prescription):	***Medicina (prescripción):***	***Medicamentos (receita)***
asthma inhaler	*inhalador para el asma*	*inalador para a asma*
hay fever tablets	*medicina para las alergias*	*remédio para as alergias*
diarrhoea pills	*pastillas para la diarrea*	*pílulas para a diarréia*
other (doctor)	*otros (médico)*	*outros (médico)*
Accessories: (optional)	***Accesorios: (opcional)***	***Acessórios: (opcional)***
binocular	*prismáticos*	*binóculos*
torch	*linterna*	*lanterna*
wrist watch	*reloj de pulsera*	*relógio de pulso*
alarm clock	*despertador*	*despertador*
poncho	*poncho*	*poncho*
sleeping mat	*esterilla*	*esteira*
clothes pegs	*pinzas para la ropa*	*molas de roupa*
clothes line (cord)	*cuerda para tender ropa*	*corda para pendurar roupa*
knife	*cuchillo*	*faca*
fork	*tenedor*	*garfo*
spoon	*cuchara*	*colher*
Books: *(limited)*	***Libros: (cupo limitado)***	***Livros: (limitada)***
spiritual texts	*textos espirituales*	*textos espirituais*
inspirational quotations	*citas inspiradoras*	*citações inspiradoras*
phrase book -	*libro de frases*	*livro de frases*
... (Spanish)	*... (Español)*	*... (Espanhol)*
... (Portuguese)	*... (Portugués)*	*... (Português)*

Preparation for the inner journey: ***Why am I doing this?*** *These notes appear on a purple panel so you can easily skip over them if they are of no interest or use to you.*

Take time to prepare a purpose for this pilgrimage. Start from the basis that you are essentially a spiritual being on a human journey, not a human being on a spiritual one. We came here to learn some lesson and this may be your opportunity to find out what it is. While life may be the classroom, pilgrimage is one way to master the curriculum. It will never be mastered by walking the physical path on its own. You will need help, so ask for it – all the help you need is here, now, awaiting but your asking. We all have a different *Way* and what is right for one may be incomprehensible to another so don't feel pressurised to follow any particular path or opinion. You will know when something rings true for you – trust your resonance. A few suggestions are listed in the bibliography.

When we go on pilgrimage we bring along our individual personality and our physical, mental, emotional and etheric bodies. We may feel a need for healing in one or all of these areas. We do well to remember that the healing power of Love is a two-way flow. We both give and receive healing on the journey. Peter Dawkins of the Gatekeeper Trust, writing in *A Pilgrim's Handbook,* informs us:

> 'As the pilgrim moves through the landscape he or she follows certain paths. These paths become energised beyond the norm by the movement of the loving pilgrim. When Europe was given its name, taken from the myth of Europa and the Bull, it conveyed an important truth about the layout of Europe's inner landscape as a functioning pattern of energy and consciousness... There are many ancient pilgrimage routes which spread out across mainland Europe, leading to Santiago de Compostela in northern Spain, as if all the energy within Europe is drawn up to the crown and then focused in Santiago.'

This image is mirrored in the camino as the central star route in Europe. In *Paths of the Christian Mysteries, From Compostela to the New World* Virginia Sease and Manfred Schmidt-Brabant write:

> 'Those who travelled along the star route as far as Cape Finisterre had the experience: Here is the end of the sensory world, the abyss! And If I am able to comprehend it, the spiritual world approaches me from the other side. ... Compostela was a final, decisive juncture on an inner spiritual path that was simultaneously a path of nature initiation. ... Rudolf Steiner stated that people have a need to live not only with external history but also with the esoteric, hidden narrative which lies behind it: the history of "the Mysteries."'

These energy lines were well understood in earlier times and it is no coincidence that the Knights Templar set their Portuguese headquarters in Tomar. The power of the location was enhanced by the careful layout of the town and the orientation of its buildings in accordance with geomantic lore. This ancient knowledge would have been well known by St. James and his disciples and it will have been no accident of fate that they chose to enter Europe at its crown – sailing past the Towers of the West *Torres de Oeste* at Catoira to fetch land at Padrón. It is no wonder that the Camino Portugués remains such a powerful route today, its mystical allure still intact and aiding its rediscovery.

There is a growing sense of despair in the world as we bump up against the limits to growth. Belatedly it begins to dawn on us that we have lived beyond the means of the planet to sustain us and all of life that surrounds us. We have yet to care for all of humankind and the other sentient beings that occupy the earth in its wholeness. We have, collectively, ignored the plight of nature herself. But the existential crisis that we face is not limited to ecology but to a breakdown in the socioeconomic patterns of life and to a loss of common purpose.

However, we will not find what we are looking for by re-arranging the outer circumstances of our lives – but by recognising Who we are at the deepest level. 'Know Thyself' has been the great exhortation of spiritual teachings and mystics through the ages. And a primary purpose of pilgrimage is Self-discovery or re-discovery of a Self we had forgotten. Yet we are faced with a spiritual paradox for in trying to answer the perennial existential question, 'Who am I' we realise the question is not meant to be answered, *it is designed to dissolve the questioner*. When the ego identity dissolves we will know Who we are. But we have built a defence against this awareness because, like Narcissus, we have fallen in love with the reflection of our individual ego and body identities and we don't want to let them go. However, we can never know our true Self by clinging to the false self. We can never be fulfilled until we have emptied out the old. And here lies one of the great gifts of the camino because it allows time away from the familiar to contemplate a future quite unlike the past. Walking, with right intention, through the Landscape Temple that is the camino we can begin to allow our old identities and outworn belief systems to dissolve in the spaciousness of the very essence of Who we are. Greta Thunberg and her generation look at the world we are bequeathing them and ask, 'where are the adults?' We need to find the wisdom of the elders, and perhaps it lies closer than we think... in ourSelves! Rabbinic sage Hillel the Elder asks the rhetorical question, If not me, who? If not now, when?

Now, today, I can change the way I think and act. I can move from fear to love. I can choose to respect my fellow travellers and the natural world that is my home. I can... but will I? Each of us is part of the whole we call humankind and artificial borders can separate us no more. Indeed, they never have but only in our deluded and limited understanding of the nature of reality. Coronavirus taught us that we are all part of the same delicate balance of life on earth. Will we heed its warning or revert to business as usual ... until the next crisis strikes again?

The Camino is a global family that connects each of us to every nation on earth. The great insight of the First Nations has always been to remind us; *Man did not create the web of life, he is merely a strand in it. Whatever he does to the web, he does to himself... we may yet find we are brothers after all.*

SELF-ASSESSMENT *INNER WAYMARKS*

This self-assessment questionnaire is designed to encourage you to reflect on your life and its direction. View it as a snapshot of this moment in the ongoing journey of your life. In the busyness that surrounds us we often fail to take stock of where we are headed and our changing roles in the unfolding drama of our life story.

You might find it useful to initially answer these questions in quick succession as this may allow a more intuitive response. Afterwards, you can reflect more deeply and check if your intellectual answers confirm these, change them or bring in other insights. You can download copies of this questionnaire from the *Camino Guides* website – make some extra copies so you can repeat the exercise on your return and again in (say) 3 months time. This way you can compare results and ensure you continue to follow through on any insights that came to you while walking the camino.

☐ How do you differentiate pilgrimage from a long distance walk?
☐ How do you define spirituality – what does it mean to you?
☐ How is your spirituality expressed at home and at work?

☐ What do you see as the primary purpose of your life?
☐ Are you working consciously towards fulfilling that purpose?
☐ How clear are you on your goal and the right direction for you at this time?
☐ How will you recognise resistance to any changes that might be necessary?

☐ When did you first become aware of a desire to take time-out?
☐ What prompted you originally to go on the camino?
☐ Did the prompt come from something that you felt needed changing?
☐ Make a list of what appears to be blocking any change from happening.

☐ What help might you need on a practical, emotional and spiritual level?
☐ How will you recognise the right help or correct answer?
☐ What are the joys and challenges in working towards your unique potential?
☐ What are your next steps towards fulfilling that potential?

How aware are you of the following? Score yourself on a level of 1 – 10 and compare these scores again on your return from the camino.

☐ Awareness of your inner spiritual world.
☐ Clarity on what inspires you and the capacity to live your passion.
☐ Confidence to follow your intuitive sense of the right direction.
☐ Ability to recognise your resistance and patterns of defence.
☐ Ease with asking for and receiving support from others.

OUTER WAYMARKS: Thanks to the efforts of various pilgrim associations yellow arrow/shell waymarks clearly point the way to Santiago. In the event you lose your way it is likely you allowed your thoughts to wander and your feet followed! Re-trace your steps until you pick up the waymarks again. Where alternative routes are available your choice is aided by the colour coding in the guidebook (on the ground they will generally have the familiar yellow arrow). In this guidebook the quieter ***natural pathways*** are coloured green ●●● and might be considered by pilgrims seeking more solitude along *the way less travelled.* These 'scenic' routes are generally through woodland or alongside rivers *parque fluvial.* If you are a solo pilgrim and concerned about safety ask someone to walk with you or stick to the ***main camino*** shown with yellow markings ●●● and carrying around 80% of all pilgrims thus affording greater camaraderie and largely following public roads and laneways. The ***Coastal route*** is shown in blue ●●● and the ***Senda Litoral*** in sand ●●●. An additional category of remote 'purple' pathways ●●● is shown for experienced walkers seeking the silence of nature and a more solitary and reflective experience. Alternative routes are not always waymarked so always choose the options *you* are comfortable with.

SUN COMPASS: Finding your way as a pilgrim in Portugal is complicated by presence of the pilgrimage to Fátima. Meaning the route is generally waymarked in two directions – to Santiago always with a yellow arrow and to Fátima always with a blue arrow. A Sun Compass is provided on each map to aid to orientation. Even in poor weather we can generally tell the position of the sun. The route through Portugal is primarily in a northerly direction so the sun will rise to our right in the morning. At midday it will be behind us and by afternoon will appear over our left shoulder.

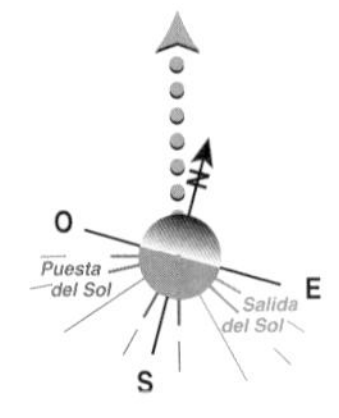

Mobile Phones: I have been walking the caminos for over 25 years. While the most obvious change over this period is the rise in pilgrim numbers a more recent impact is the rise in mobile phone use. This constant connectivity with our familiar *outer* world can keep us disconnected from the expansiveness of our *inner* world and diminish our relationship to each passing moment, the camaraderie of our 'camino family' and connection to our divine essence. Imagine Who we might meet in the space created by letting go these distractions? While many of us may feel the need to carry a mobile phone perhaps we can, collectively, be more conscious about how and when we use them so as to minimise disturbance to ourselves and other pilgrims. See *www.walkingtopresence.com*

Safety: The camino offers a remarkably safe environment in an inherently unsafe world. When viewed in this context few cases of crime or harassment are reported but they have been known to occur. If you are a solo pilgrim and ever feel nervous or unsafe consider avoiding the more remote alternative routes and keep other pilgrims in sight on the path, or ask to walk with someone until you feel comfortable again. In the event of an emergency or to report an incident the **EU wide emergency number is 112**. In Spain a new app Alertcops allows you to connect directly with the police via your smartphone.

MAP LEGEND: Symbols & Abbreviations

Total km	Total distance for stage
equiv.	Adjusted for cumulative climb (each 100m vertical +10 mins)
(850m) **Alto**	Contours / High point of each stage
< A H >	Intermediate accommodation (*often less busy / quieter*)
3.5	Precise distance between points (3.5 km = ± 1 hour)
50m > / ^ / <	Interim distances 50m right> / s/o=straight on^ / <left
	Natural path / forest track / gravel *senda*
	Quiet country lane (asphalt)
	Secondary road (*grey*: asphalt) / Roundabout *rotonda*
N-11	Main road [N-] *Nacional* (*red*: additional traffic and hazard)
A-1	Motorway *autopista* (*blue*: conventional motorway colour)
	Railway *ferrocarril* / Station *estación*
	Main Waymarked route (*yellow*: ± 80% of pilgrims)
	Alternative Scenic route (*green*: more remote / less pilgrims)
	Alternative road route (*grey*: more asphalt & traffic)
	Optional detour *desvío* (*turquoise:* to point of interest)
	Primary Path of pilgrimage (***purple***: inner path of Soul)
X ? !	Crossing *cruce* / Option *opción* / Extra care *¡cuidado!*
	Windmill *molino* / Viewpoint *punto de vista* / Radio mast
	National boundary / Provincial boundary *límite provincial*
	River *río* / Riverlet Stream *arroyo / rego*
	Sea or lake *Mar o lago* / Woodland *bosques*
	Church *iglesia* / Chapel *capilla* / Wayside cross *cruceiro*
F	Drinking font *fuente* / Café-Bar / Shop *(mini)mercado*
menú V.	Restaurant / *menú peregrino / V. Vegetariano(a)*
	Tourist office *turismo* / Manor house *pazo* / Rest area *picnic*
	Pharmacy *farmacia* / Hospital / Post office *correos*
	Airport / Bus station *estación de autobús / gasolinera*
XIIc.	Ancient monument / 12th century
H P C	Hotels •*H-H*** €30-90 / Pension •*P** €20-35 / •*CR (B&B)* €35-75
x12 €35-45	Number of private rooms *x12* €35(single)-45 (double) *approx*
H A A	*Off* route lodging / A Reported closed - check for updates
A 1 2 J	Pilgrim hostel(s) *Albergue* ●*Alb.* + Youth hostel ●*Juventude*
[32]	Number of bed spaces (usually bunk beds *literas*) €5-€17
[÷4] +12	÷ number of dormitories / *+12* number of private rooms €30+
Par.	Parish hostel *Parroquial* donation *donativo* / €5
Conv.	Convent or monastery hostel *donativo* / €5
Mun/ Xunta	Municipal hostel €5+ / Galician government *Xunta* €8
Asoc.	Association hostel €8+
Priv. (*)	Private hostel (network*) €10-17
	[all prices average (low season) for comparison purposes only]
p.55	Town plan *plan de la ciudad* with page number
(Pop.– Alt. m)	Town population – altitude in metres
	City suburbs / outskirts *afueras* (*grey*)
	Historical centre *centro histórico / barrio antiguo* (*brown*)

OVERVIEW: The Camino Portugués *Caminho Português Lisboa–Porto* is well waymarked from Lisbon. 2,651 pilgrims commencing their journey from here last year. The first 3 stages, as far as Santarém, coincide with the *Caminho da Fátima (caminho de Tejo)* so this section has more pilgrims. In Santarém the routes separate with the historic Camino de Santiago veering off to the northeast through the Templar town of Tomar whence pilgrims become few and far between –until we reach Porto. Facilities along this section have improved in recent years and it is now ready to be enjoyed by seasoned pilgrims; an ability to speak basic Portuguese being an asset. The section from Porto to Santiago continues to welcome pilgrims of all abilities. Within Portugal some Fire Brigades *Bomberios Volunatários* may provide basic lodging to pilgrims (bed or floor) and Youth Hostels *Juventude* accept pilgrims with a *credencial*. Telephone prefix for Portugal is +351 and numbers starting with 9 are mobiles. Museums etc generally closed on Monday.

Lisbon is a wonderful city with an interesting mix of old and new. One of the smallest capital cities in the European Union it is relatively easy to navigate and full of vitality and a sense of pride in its long and fascinating history. Originally known as Olisipo it was a major administrative centre and trading post for the Romans before the Visigoths took over; followed by 4 centuries of Arab rule when Afonso Henriques ousted them in 1147. In the 15th century it became the main base for the 'Discoveries' and many of the greatest explorers in history such as Columbus, Cabral, Magellan and Vasco da Gama set sail from here and established Lisbon as one of the great trading capitals of the world. Inevitably, an economy based on colonial spoils (rather than production) began to wane and the financial plight of Portugal took a lurch for the worse at precisely 9:40 a.m on November 1st 1755 when one of the most destructive earthquakes ever recorded hit the city. The Great Lisbon Earthquake and ensuing tsunami destroyed 90% of its finest buildings and killed a quarter of its population. The Marquis of Pombal emerged as the hero of the day and set about reconstruction in the form of the wide boulevards and squares that we see today. The tower of Belém and the adjoining Manueline-style Jerónimos monastery are 2 of the outstanding historic buildings that remain.

Tourist Offices: ⓘ **Airport Arrivals** ✆ 218 450 660 (07:00–24:00). The airport is close to the city centre (20 minutes or 10 minutes to Oriente). Buses leave every 15 minutes. ⓘ **Santa Apolónia rail station** ✆ 218 821 606 (08.00-13.00) it's a short walk or taxi ride to the 'lower' area along the river Tagus *rio Tejo* known simply as ***Baixa*** and forming the heart of the modernized city. On the main square adjoining the river ⓘ **Centro Turismo de Lisboa / *Welcome Center*** ✆ 210 312 810 (09.00-18.00) on Praça do Comércio with its distinctive ***Arco da Rua Augusta*** also ⓘ **Tourist Kiosk** in Rua Augusta (10:00–18:00 summer).

Rossio with its numerous cafés and restaurants spilling out onto the pavements is the main chic shopping district. Spread out along the grid of streets between *Praça do Comércio* and *Praça Dom Pedro IV*. This is also where you will find many of the city's smaller *pensões* (rooms are often located on the top floor!). At the far end is the national theatre *Teatro Nacional de Dona Maria*, formerly the site of the Court of the Inquisition in front of which the hanging of heretics and ritual burning of many of Portugal's wise women took place. Just around the corner is the striking neo-Manueline (1886) façade of the old Rossio station and at the bottom end of Avenida da Liberdade is Palacío Foz now the Portuguese ⓘ **Tourist Board** ✆ 213 463 314. And overlooking all this history and activity (to the south) is the ***Bairro Alto*** which you can access via various antiquated elevators *Elevador San Justa, da*

Bica and *da Glória*. This area includes the chic ***Chiado*** district with its elegant shops and cafés including the famous *A Brasileira*, haunt of many of Lisbon's literary figures (past and present) and the *Basilica dos Mártires* (issues credenciales).

To the north of the city we find the atmospheric ***Alfama*** quarter that rises to the ***Castelo de São Jorge*** (top photo) passing Lisbon's old cathedral and the church of Santiago ***Igreja de S. Tiago*** occupying an elevated position above the cathedral on rua Santiago that leads to the castle. The church has a fine statue of Santiago Peregrino (but your only likely sighting will be the photo> here as the church is often closed).

The cathedral ***Sé Patriarcal de Lisboa*** an austere castellated structure restored after the earthquake (although this Alfama quarter was the least affected part of the city). The original foundations of the cathedral were laid in 1147 just after the town was captured from the Moors and was built on the site of the former mosque. Ongoing archeological excavations in the cloister area ***claustro*** have unearthed structures dating from 4th century B.C.E. The cathedral is open from 09:00 to 19:00 (17:00 Sunday, Monday and holidays). Entrance to the Cathedral is free / €2.50 for the claustro. Pilgrim credencial and stamp available at reception kiosk.

Tram # 28 rattles past the main historic sites including the cathedral and Miradouro S. Luzia directly opposite the Church of Santiago and adjoining a café and public viewing terrace with unrivalled views across the rio Tejo estuary. (see photo). The Alfama area also claims one of the best-known fado houses in Lisbon *Parreirinha d'Alfama* adjacent to Largo do Chafariz de Dentro. This mournful music quivers to the Portuguese guitar and the soloist *fadista* sings of the pining for *things that are no more, or will never be* – this is the core of fado with a secondary theme being the pathos of the emigrant and nostalgia for life in general *saudade*. Avoid the tackier tourist venues that are generally overrated and overcharge. The museum ***Museu do Fado*** in Largo do Chafariz is worth a visit. Open Tues-Sun 10.00-18.00 €5. The camino passes through this area with the first waymark starting at the cathedral entrance.

● **Pousadas de Juventude** ***Hi Lisboa*** ✆ 925 665 072 r/ Andrade Corvo, 46 *(Sé + **3.1** km).* ● ***Moscavide YHA*** – see stage 1 *(Sé + **9.5** km).* ■ **Hostels** *book online* @ www.booking.com or www.hostelworld.com (€10-20 in bunk beds): ❶ **Yes** ✆ 213 427 171 r/S. Julião,148. ❷ **Goodnight** ✆ 215 989 153 r/Correiros, 113. ❸ **Home Lisbon** ✆ 218 885 312 r/S. Nicolau, 13. ❹ **Amazing Hostels** *Sé /Alfama* ✆ 964 453 972 Beco Arco Escuro, 6. ❺ **This is Lisbon** ✆ 218 014 549 r/Costa do Castelo, 63. ❻ **Alfama Pátio** ✆ 218 883 127 r/Escolas Gerais, 3. ▌***Alfama district:*** (adj. Sé) •*P* **São João de Praça** €25-45 incl. ✆ 218 862 591 r/São João de Praça, 97. •*Hs*** **Petit Lusa** *8x* €75+ ✆ 218 872 773 opp. museu do Fado on Largo do Chafariz de Dentro, 24. ▌***Rossio and Baixa districts*** (lower city centre) wide selection of hotels and 'rooms' *quartos/dormidas.*▌***Chiado*** good value •*H*** **Borges** *40x* €38+ ✆ 213 461 951 r/Garrett 108 opp. *Basilica dos Mártires (credencial)* adj. popular ☕ *A Brasileira.* Patron saint S.Antonio *Festas de Lisboa* mid June.

Pilgrim passports *credenciales*: ***Via Luistana*** ✆ 915 595 213. ***APAAS*** Amigos de Apóstolo Santiago ✆ 966 426 851. ***Basílica dos Mártires*** r/Serpa Pinto ✆ 213 462 465 (10:00-17:00). ***Cathedral*** *Sé* (09:30-18:30).

○ **Historic Buildings and Monuments:** Much of the historic fabric of the city was lost in the 1755 earthquake. Saved were 2 outstanding examples of Manueline architecture: ❶ ***Mosteiro dos Jerónimos*** *XVI* Praça do Império (10:00-17:30). Work started in 1502 capturing this illustrious period in Portuguese history. At the entrance is a statue to Henry the Navigator and the interior houses the tombs of Vasco da Gama (below) and the 'Discoveries' poet Luís de Camões. Nearby is the ***Torre de Belém*** *XVI* built as part of Lisbon's port defences. Also In this area is the Monument to the Discoveries *Monumento dos Descobrimentos* built to celebrate the 500th anniversary of Henry the Navigator (trams # E15/ E18). ❷ ***Basilica dos Mártires*** with chapel dedicated to St. James. ❸ **Cathedral** ***Sé*** *XII* (# 28E) (09:30-18:30) work commencing in 1150 on Roman foundations to replace the former mosque. 400m above the cathedral ❹ ***Igreja de Santiago*** rua de Santiago ❺ ***Castelo São Jorge*** *XI* (9:00-21:00) Rua de Santa Cruz do Castelo

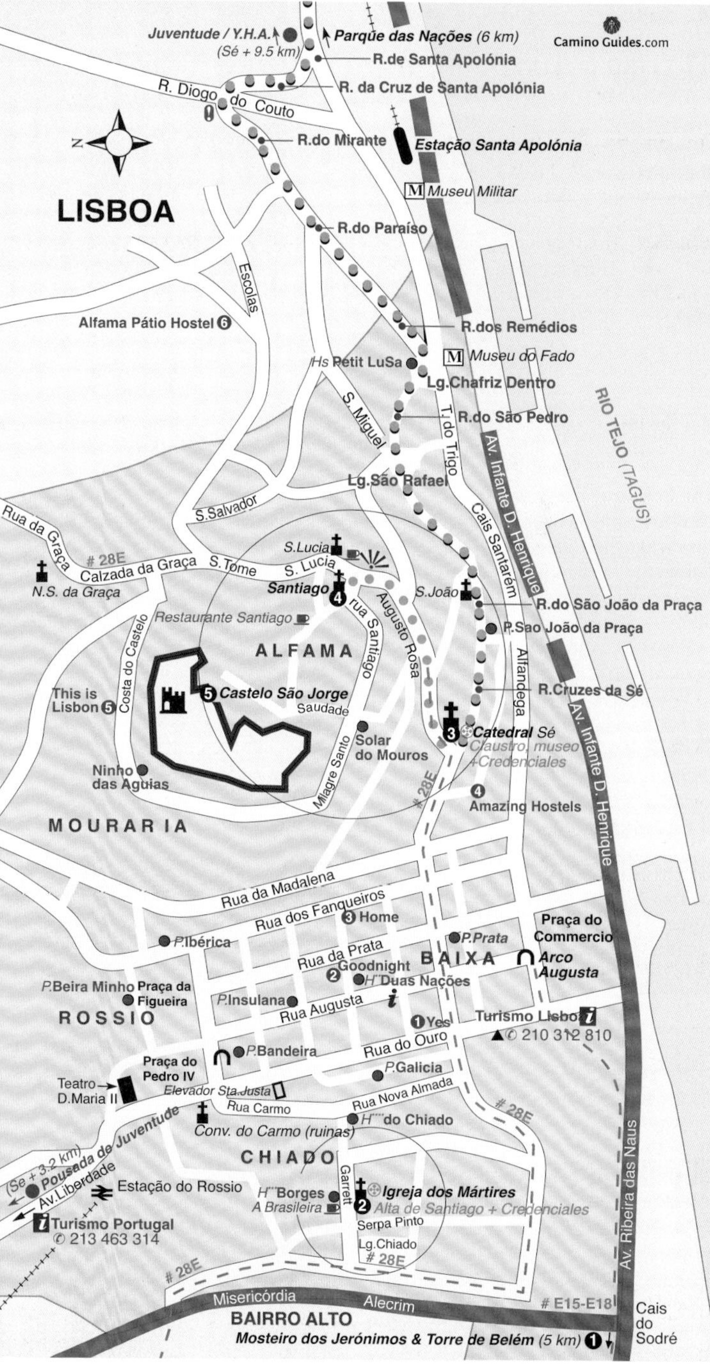

LISBOA
Camino Guides.com
Juventude / Y.H.A.
(Sé + 9.5 km)
Parque das Nações (6 km)
R.de Santa Apolónia
R. da Cruz de Santa Apolónia
R. Diogo do Couto
R.do Mirante
Estação Santa Apolónia
Museu Militar
R.do Paraíso
Escolas
Alfama Pátio Hostel 6
R.dos Remédios
Hs Petit LuSa
Museu do Fado
Lg.Chafriz Dentro
R.do São Pedro
S. Miguel
T.do Trigo
Lg.São Rafael
RIO TEJO (TAGUS)
Av. Infante D. Henrique
Cais Santarém
S.Salvador
Rua da Graça
28E
Calzada da Graça
S.Tome
S. Lucia
S.Lucia
N.S. da Graça
Santiago 4
S.João
R.do São João da Praça
P.Sao João da Praça
Restaurante Santiago
rua Santiago
Augusto Rosa
ALFAMA
Costa do Castelo
Alfandega
This is Lisbon 5
5 Castelo São Jorge
Saudade
R.Cruzes da Sé
3 Catedral Sé
Claustro, museo +Credenciales
Solar do Mouros
Milagre Santo
Ninho das Aguias
4 Amazing Hostels
MOURARIA
Rua da Madalena
Rua dos Fanqueiros
3 Home
P.Ibérica
P.Prata
Praça do Commercio
Rua da Prata
BAIXA
Arco Augusta
2 Goodnight
H'' Duas Nações
P.Beira Minho
Praça da Figueira
P.Insulana
Rua Augusta
ROSSIO
1 Yes
Turismo Lisboa
© 210 312 810
Rua do Ouro
P.Bandeira
Praça do Pedro IV
P.Galicia
Teatro D.Maria II
Elevador Sta.Justa
Rua Nova Almada
Rua Carmo
H'''' do Chiado
Conv. do Carmo (ruinas)
Pousada de Juventude
(Se + 3.2 km)
CHIADO
Av.Liberdade
Estação do Rossio
H''' Borges
A Brasileira
Garrett
2 Igreja dos Mártires
Alta de Santiago + Credenciales
Turismo Portugal
© 213 463 314
Serpa Pinto
Lg.Chiado
28E
Av. Ribeira das Naus
Misericórdia
Alecrim
E15-E18
Cais do Sodré
BAIRRO ALTO
Mosteiro dos Jerónimos & Torre de Belém (5 km) 1

01 LISBOA – ALVERCA *Verdelha*

	--- ---	7.7	--- ---	*51%*
	--- ---	4.2	--- ---	*14%*
	--- ---	10.3	--- ---	*35%*
Total km		**32.2** km *(20.0 ml)*		

Total ascent **550**m **+55** *minutes**

Alto ▲ Alpriarte **60**m *(197 ft)*

< A H > ➲Moscavide **9.4** km ➲Alpriate **22.5**

•S.Apolónia •Oriente •Sacavém •S.Iria •Póvoa •Alverca.

The Practical Path: Traversing any city presents a challenge. However, navigating your way out of Lisbon is relatively easy as we head down to the estuary of the river Tagus *Rio Tejo* at the Expo '98 Maritime Park *Parque das Nações.* We then follow the river to its confluence with the modest *río Trancão* finally leaving it to take a path up a tranquil green valley to the high point of today's stage at a mere 60m around Alpriate. It's then a gentle descent before entering the busy environs of Póvoa de Santa Iria. Here we cross the rail line to join with the alternative 'green' route alongside the Tejo before reaching Alverca do Ribatejo with a short detour to Verdelha de Baixo with lodging. Surprisingly for a city route we find over half is on pathways with the waymarked route now avoiding most of the dangerous N-10. ● ● ● ● A new boardwalk along the Tejo, opened summer 2023, reduces this stage by 7.8 km allowing for a delightful traffic-free walk.

Injustice anywhere, is a threat to justice everywhere. *Martin Luther King*

The Mystical Path: The wealth of Portugal was carved out of its colonial past and its seaports were a gateway for the lucrative slave trade from Africa to the Americas. Our affluent Western lifestyle has created enormous injustices in wealth distribution. Chesterton wrote *There are two ways to get enough; one is to continue to accumulate. The other is to desire less.*

Personal Reflections: I nearly upset the begging bowl as I stepped over her outstretched legs. Irritated at her pleading voice I avoided her eyes... inside the church was like a refuge but also a reminder of my privilege and responsibilities. As I sat I vowed to give a tithe of my daily expenses to those in need. As I left the church she was nowhere to be seen, but other opportunities will arise...

0.0 km Lisboa Catedral *Sé* The first waymark is right of the cathedral steps down into rua São João da Praça, Largo de São Rafael, rua de São Pedro into Largo de Chafariz (Museu do Fado) ***Option: Estação de Santa Ápolónia*** option to take commuter trains to intermediate stations. ***Oriente, Sacavém, Santa Iria, Póvoa, Alverca*** all offer possibilities but miss the delightful paths along the ríos Tejo and Trancão. The albergue in Alpriate is now closed but the new boardwalk (green route) now reduces this stage to a more manageable 23.8 km to off route lodging around Verdelha de Baixo.

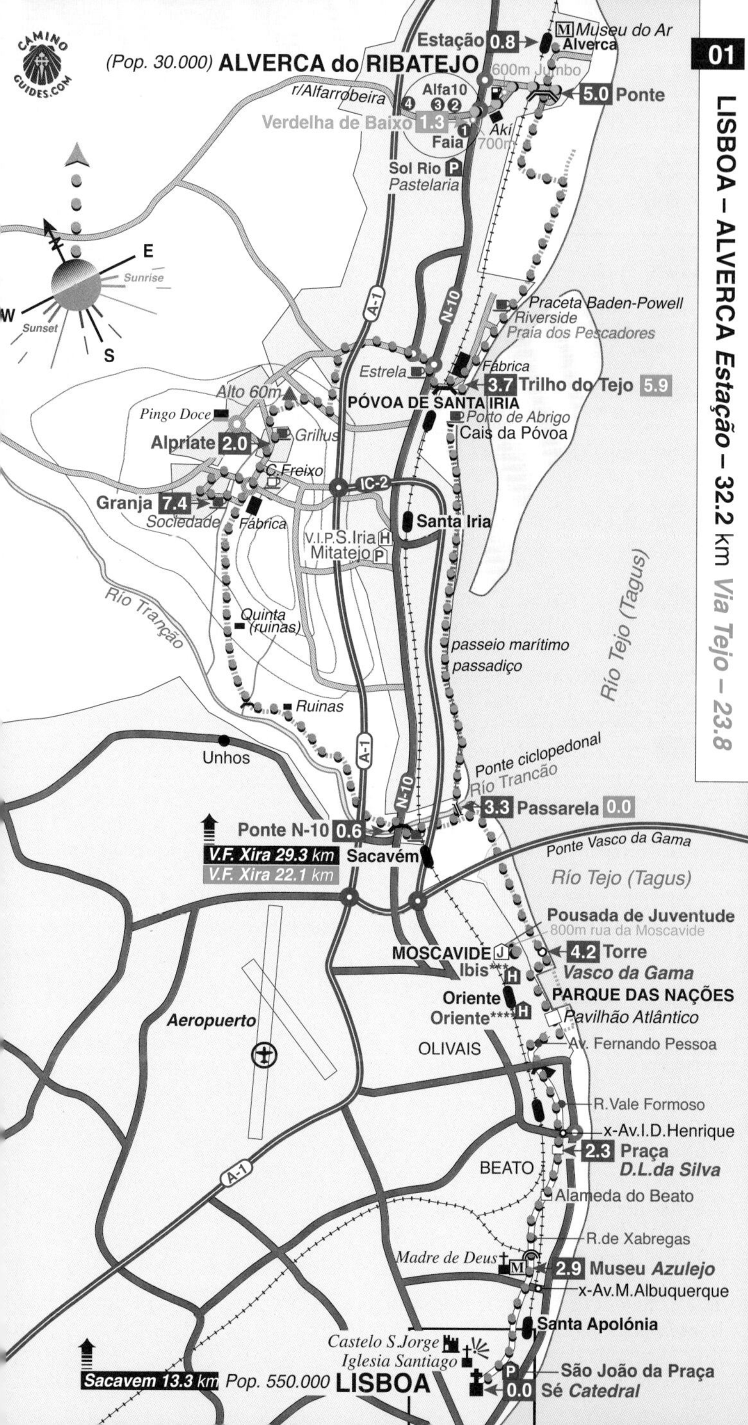
01
LISBOA – ALVERCA Estação – 32.2 km Via Tejo – 23.8
CAMINO GUIDES.COM
(Pop. 30.000) ALVERCA do RIBATEJO
Estação 0.8
Museu do Ar
Alverca
600m Jumbo
5.0 Ponte
r/Alfarrobeira
Alfa10
Verdelha de Baixo 1.3
Aki
Faia
700m
Sol Rio
Pastelaria
E
Sunrise
W
Sunset
S
A-1
N-10
Praceta Baden-Powell
Riverside
Praia dos Pescadores
Fábrica
Estrela
3.7 Trilho do Tejo 5.9
Alto 60m
PÓVOA DE SANTA IRIA
Porto de Abrigo
Cais da Póvoa
Pingo Doce
Grillus
Alpriate 2.0
C.Freixo
IC-2
Granja 7.4
Sociedade
Fábrica
Santa Iria
V.I.P.S.Iria
Mitatejo
Río Trancão
Quinta (ruinas)
passeio marítimo
passadiço
Río Tejo (Tagus)
Ruinas
Unhos
Ponte ciclopedonal
Río Trancão
3.3 Passarela 0.0
Ponte N-10 0.6
V.F. Xira 29.3 km
V.F. Xira 22.1 km
Sacavém
Ponte Vasco da Gama
Río Tejo (Tagus)
Pousada de Juventude
800m rua da Moscavide
MOSCAVIDE
4.2 Torre
Vasco da Gama
Ibis***
PARQUE DAS NAÇÕES
Oriente
Oriente****
Pavilhão Atlântico
Aeropuerto
OLIVAIS
Av. Fernando Pessoa
R.Vale Formoso
x-Av.I.D.Henrique
2.3 Praça
D.L.da Silva
BEATO
Alameda do Beato
R.de Xabregas
Madre de Deus
2.9 Museu Azulejo
x-Av.M.Albuquerque
Santa Apolónia
Castelo S.Jorge
Iglesia Santiago
São João da Praça
Sacavem 13.3 km
Pop. 550.000 LISBOA
0.0 Sé Catedral

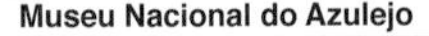

Museu Nacional do Azulejo

View over the Rio Tejo

For those with the intention to walk the entire route we continue up into rua dos Remédios and s/o via ruas Paraíso, Mirante and cross s/o *over* [!] rua Diogo Couto veering sharp right into rua da Cruz Santa Apolónia *(waymarks obscure)* over Av. Mouzinho de Albuquerque into Calçada da Cruz da Pedra and down into rua da Madre de Deus to:

2.9 km **Museu Nacional do Azulejo** here we find the splendid museum of Portuguese tiles with delightful courtyard and baroque church all housed within a former Manueline convent *Convento da Madre Deus.* Keep s/o under rail line into ruas de Xabregas, Grilo and Beato passing the Beato fire station *Bombeiros* and Convento and Alameda do Beato into:

2.3 km **Praça David Leandro da Silva** with public w.c.'s, taxi rank, and striking Art Deco façade of Fonseca & Poço. We now cross the wide ring road Av. Infante Dom Henrique into the narrow rua Vale Formoso de Baixo (antigo teatro left) through the underpass (rail line left) and turn right to crossroads and left into Av. Fernando Pessoa down to the roundabout and Expo site and ***Parque das Nações***. Our destination is the tower (see photo) reached via Alameda dos Oceanos and Pavilhão de Portugal ***or*** make your way directly to the Tejo estuary via Jardins da Água (blue waterfall) and Passeio de Ulisses (the start of our own Odyssey). This leads to the seafront past the Oceanário (one of the largest aquariums in the world) and cable car *Teleférico* and along boardwalks over the estuary to Lisbon's emblematic tower:

4.2 km **Torre Vasco da Gama** A variety of bars, restaurants & hotels spill out onto the pavements all developed as part of Expo '98. Including •*H**** **IBIS** *110x* €60 ✆ 210 730 470 *www.ibis.com r/do Mar Vermelho* and on *Av. Dom João II* •*H***** **TRYP Lisboa Oriente** *206x* €92-105 ✆ 218 930 000 *www.melia.com* and •*H***** **Tivoli Oriente** *280x* €96+ ✆ 218 915 100 *www.minorhotels.com* ***Moscavide: [+0.8km]:*** ●**Pousada de Juventude** *Asoc. [92÷6]* €14 *+20x* €30 ✆ 218 920 890 *www.pousadasjuventude.pt/en* r/Moscavide Lt 47-101. *Via* Av. da Boa Esperança and Alameda dos Oceanos into rua de Moscavide.

Ponte Vasco Gama — Statue of Catherine of Braganza *Queen of England (Charles II)*

We now join pedestrian walkways through a linear park along the banks of the Tejo. We pass a handsome bronze statue of *Catarina de Bragança* who left Lisboa in 1662 to marry Charles II. Her dowry included Bombay and tea! *(She and her court introduced tea to England).* Continue under the 17 km-long *Ponte Vasco da Gama* following the Tejo until it meets a small tributary **Foz del rio Trancão [2.5 km]**. This is a good place to rest and view the route north up along the Tejo. There are bench seats and shade and the first concrete bollard marking the *Caminho de Fátima* (blue arrows to Fátima, yellow to Santiago (see photo p. 36).

3.3 km **Passarela Option:** ●●●●
Here we have the option to take a new boardwalk *passeio marítimo* alongside the Tejo estuary. Opened in 2023 in time for Pope Francisco's visit to the city. This meanders over the marshland between the estuary and the IC-2. The boardwalk joins the original Trilho Riberinho at Póvoa de Santa Iria at ☕ *Porto de Abrigo* which also houses a small fisherman's museum. Both routes continue through the derelict industrial area to the Praia dos Pescadores.

The main route follows the modest Trancão inland passing under the ring road (IC-2) and rail line at Sacavém. Shortly afterwards we meet up with the old **N-10 [1.4 km]**. ☕ *café Kebab (bars off route left)*.

0.6 km **N-10 Ponte Sacavém** turn right over bridge and imm. left over the N-10 [!] (Toyota sign) onto remote path under the A-1 viaduct and along a raised bank by the river (often muddy / mosquitos) passing ruins (right) before leaving the *río Trancão* over a small stream to take the wide farm track up a tranquil green valley where time seems to have stopped (except for air traffic from Lisbon airport!). Various *Quintas* lie abandoned in ruins and lead us to the high point of today at 60m. The camino has now been rerouted through Granja village.

7.4 km **Granja** ☕ *Sociedade*. Continue through the village turning right opp. 🍴*Sabores* to main road and back down to roundabout. Turn left past *Casal do Freixo* ☕*Cultural* (right) & into tranquil village of:

2.0 km **Alpriate** Note the former albergue here is closed permanently. *[🚰]* ☕🍴

Grillus (Zézinha) rua Vasco da Gama where Maria José *Zézinha* cooks (except Thurs). Continue out the village over fields & road to path below A-1 and cross back *under* motorway and down Estrada dos Caniços past *Olival Parque* to the 2nd roundabout on the N-10:

3.7 km **N-10 Póvoa de Santa Iria** busy industrial town. [!] We now turn *back* towards Lisbon along the N-10 for 200m ☕ *Estrela* (right).

*[**Detour** s/o **+3.7 km*** along N-10 adj. Galp •*H**** **VIP Santa Iria** *124x* €63+ ✆ 210 032 300 *www.viphotels.com* adj. •*Hs* **Miratejo** *36x* €40 ✆ 219 591 216*]*.

Cross over the railway line by industrial park to connect with the boardwalk ● ● ● ● *Parque Linear Ribeirinho)* where both routes continue via a lane between derelict industrial buildings into Pracata Robert Baden-Powell at Praia dos Pescadores ☕ *Riverside bar. (The adj. sheds are used by the local scouts).* The path continues via the boardwalks to a wide gravel track alongside the railway up to road bridge and option point.

5.0 km **Ponte *Option*** ● ● ● ● Road bridge ◆ on the outskirts of Alverca with option for possible lodging in Verdelha. If you are continuing to Alverca or V.F. da Xira continue s/o to the railway station and next stage.

0.8 km **Alverca do Ribatejo *estação*** Rail station and air museum *museo do Ar*. **Alverca:** despite plans for a hostel in this ideal location the lodging previously available at **Fundação CEBI** and at **Vivenda Lurdes** are no longer taking pilgrims.

Detour *off* route: ● ● ● ● To stay the night in **Verdelha** leave the waymarked route at the bridge ◆ and make your way towards the **N-10** turn <left at the petrol station **Jumbo [600**m] and continue past the major **AKÍ** store to the 2nd roundabout and cross over [!] to the start of **Estrada de Alfarrobeira** [700m].

1.3 km Verdelha de Baixo *(distance from Lisbon cathedral – 32.7 km / from Moscavide 23.3 km)*. Here at a major intersection of roads we find a variety of rooms *quartos / Dormidas* and restaurants mostly serving the workers from the adjacent industrial parks (busy during weekdays). *On* **Estrada *de Alfarrobeira:*** @**Nº1** ❶ *P* 🍴 **Faia** *8x* €20-30 ✆ 219 596 197 m: 931 612 110. @ **Nº10** ❷ *P* **Alfa10** *15x* €15-30 ✆ 219 580 475 *www.alfa10.pt* see photo>(adj. Leal now closed). @**Nº17** ❸*P* **A Lanterna** *6x* €15-30 ✆ 219 576 488. @**Nº23** + 550m ❹*P* **Silvina Ferreira** *20x* €20-30 ✆ 219 583 911 adj. rotunda and autopista. On N-10 above *pastelaria* **Sol Rio** *x5* €55 ✆ 939 250 251 N-10.

Personal Reflections:

The paths we traverse today are called Paths of Faith *Caminhos da Fé.* How strong is our faith?... and faith in what?

***Santiago Peregrino** – rose window Lisbon cathedral.*

02 ALVERCA *estação* – AZAMBUJA

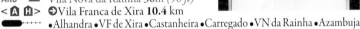

--- --- 10.0 --- --- *33%*
--- --- 12.6 --- --- *42%*
--- --- 7.7 --- --- *25%*
Total km **30.3** km *(18.8 ml)*

Total ascent **450**m +¾ *hr*
Alto ▲ Vila Nova da Rainha **30**m *(98 ft)*
<A H> ➔Vila Franca de Xira **10.4** km
•Alhandra •VF de Xira •Castanheira •Carregado •VN da Rainha •Azambuja

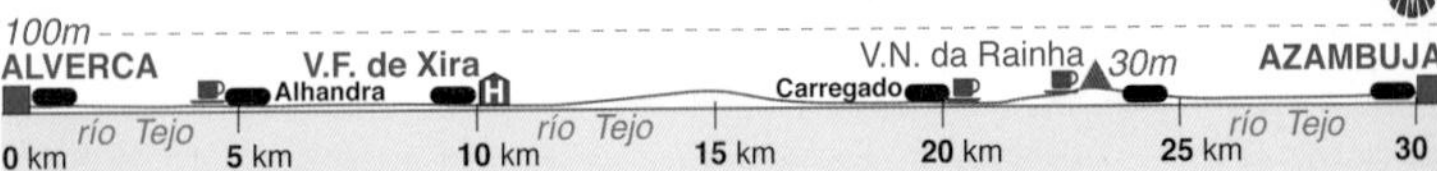

The Practical Path: A level day's walk much of it parallel to or *on* the busy N-10 which we have to join through built-up industrial areas, requiring extra vigilance. But, a delightful interim 8 km stretch has recently been opened allowing safe passage between Alhandra and Castanheira and a new route has been waymarked alongside the rail line between V.N. Rainha and Azambuja. Vila Franca de Xira makes a lovely interim stopover with selection of accommodation and good restaurants and the town occupies an unrivalled riverside location. The Caminho de Fátima coincides with our route until we reach Santarém.

It is more blessed to give than to receive. *Acts 20:35*

The Mystical Path: Giving and receiving are two sides of the same coin Accumulating for oneself alone is Self defeating. *It will be given you to see your brother's worth when all you seek for him is peace. And what you want for him you will receive.* ACIM

Personal Reflections: My roommate was French with penetrating eyes and dark beard. He told me he was anxious to get back to Toulouse but his bank had failed to transfer funds – he was short €20 for his fare. I judged him dishonest and chose not to help. It was only after we parted I realised my tithing commitment from yesterday was... €20 – its distribution proving oddly difficult – my mistrust and prejudice were deeper than I realised. Christ appears in many guises.

0.0 km *Verdelha de Baixo If you stayed in Verdelha return to the waymarked camino by the Bridge [1.3 km] and continue to Alverca rail station [0.8 km].*

0.0 km **Alverca** ***estação*** Cross the railway and veer right into rua Infante D. Pedro to skirt the town out past the playing fields onto pathway up through an industrial estate to the N-10.

3.4 km **N-10** ***Rotunda*** [!] This is a busy junction on the N-10 *Pingo Doce (left)* and we have to continue alongside it through *Sobralinha* for 2 kilometres [!] passing under 2 grain chutes. •Dormidas *Carborodrigues* €40 (left) ✆ 219 500 564 directly on the N-10 (serves workers from local factories and daytime trade!). We finally leave the main road to cross over rail bridge at **Alhanda** *estação* down to a

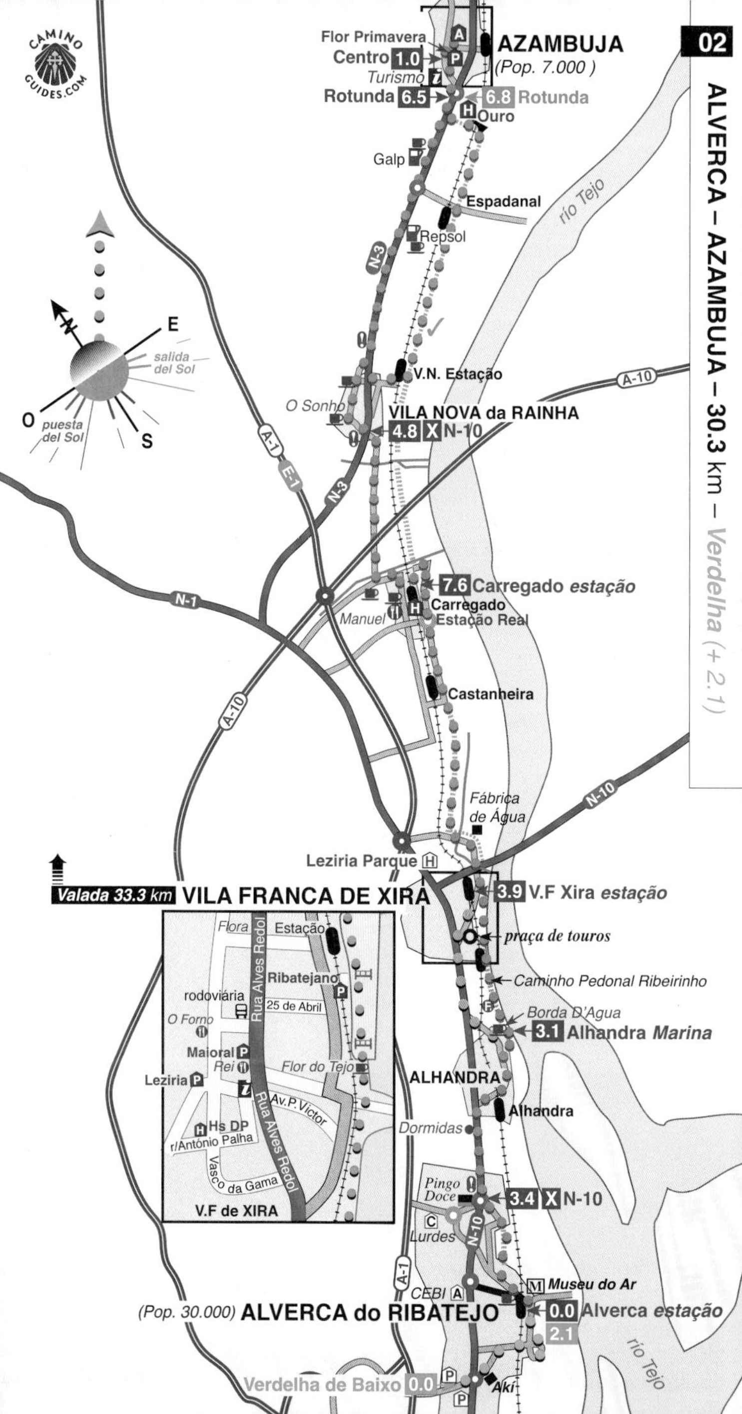
CAMINO GUIDES.COM
AZAMBUJA
(Pop. 7.000)
Flor Primavera
Centro 1.0
Turismo
Rotunda 6.5
6.8 Rotunda
Ouro
Galp
Espadanal
Repsol
río Tejo
N-3
E
salida del Sol
O
puesta del Sol
S
V.N. Estação
O Sonho
VILA NOVA da RAINHA
4.8 X N-10
A-10
A-1
E-1
N-3
N-1
7.6 Carregado estação
Carregado Estação Real
Manuel
Castanheira
A-10
N-10
Fábrica de Água
Leziria Parque
Valada 33.3 km
VILA FRANCA DE XIRA
3.9 V.F Xira estação
praça de touros
Flora
Estação
Rua Alves Redol
Ribatejano
rodoviária
25 de Abril
O Forno
Maioral
Rei
Flor do Tejo
Leziria
Av.P.Victor
Hs DP
r/António Palha
Vasco da Gama
V.F de XIRA
Caminho Pedonal Ribeirinho
Borda D'Agua
3.1 Alhandra Marina
ALHANDRA
Alhandra
Dormidas
Pingo Doce
3.4 X N-10
Lurdes
N-10
A-1
CEBI
Museu do Ar
(Pop. 30.000) ALVERCA do RIBATEJO
0.0 Alverca estação
2.1
río Tejo
Verdelha de Baixo 0.0
Aki

lorry park towards the river bypassing the town (left) where, like Alverca, there is no lodging in this sizable town but there are a variety of bars and shops. We pass Bombeiros Voluntários (no longer receiving pilgrims) and turn left at the end of Rua Vasco da Gama *Voltar ao Cais* by the river:

3.1 km **Alhandra *Marina*** *Borda DAgua* lovely riverside setting adj. small museum. Continue past the marina, sailing club *Vela* (with pilgrim stamp!*)* and municipal swimming pool onto delightful new riverside path *passeio ribeirinho pedonal (photo>)* with water fonts, murals and a coin operated w.c. The waymarked route now takes us all the way into Vila Franca de Xira past the impressive bullring *Plaza de Toros (other side of railtrack)* past the modern library *biblioteca* with to the intimate harbour area *Largo Cais* *Flor do Tejo* to the shaded municipal gardens by railway station.

3.9 km **Vila Franca-de-Xira *Estação*** This busy town stands at the edge of Portugal's main wetland reserve *Reserva Natural do Estuario do Tejo* home to large numbers of migrating and domestic wildfowl. Today it is better known for the breeding of fighting bulls and its popular 'running the bulls' that takes place during the 'Red Waistcoat Festival' *Festa do Colete Encarnado* first 2 weeks in July and again in October *Feira de Outubro* when accommodation is all but impossible to find. The town is linked with the English crusaders who landed here en route to the Holy Land naming it Cornogoa after Cornwall!

Lodging central: •*P* **Ribatejana** Vilatejo *10x* €20 ✆ 263 272 991 m: 925 912 679 (Mariano) r/da Praia, 2a. ●*Hs* **DP** *Priv.[16÷4]* €20 incl. +*14* €55 ✆ 263 288 012 m: 926 070 650 *www.hosteldp.com* (Fernando e Carolina) r/António Palha 2. •*HR* **Flora** *20x* €30-40 ✆ 263 271 272 r/Noel Perdigão 6 (closed). •*Estalagem* **Leziria** €8-25 ✆ 964 774 863 r/da Barroca De Baixo 17 •*Hs* **Maioral** €28-€38 ✆ 263 274 370 Trv.do Terreirinho 2.

Outskirts: EN-1 (+ 2 km) •*H* **Lezíria Parque** *102x* €65+ ✆ 263 276 670 *www.continentalhotels.eu* .Take time to explore this colourful town that prides itself in its bullfighting history *(the Portuguese version where the bull is not killed but deftly outmanoeuvred).* The *azulejos* clad market *mercado* is located next the bright terracotta *DP hostel* (see photo>). The town abounds in low budget eateries. For local *haute cuisine* try *O Forno* rua Dr. Miguel Bombarda 143. For a sundowner try *Flor do Tejo* by anchor on the harbour front *Largo Cais* (see photo>) which gets the last of the setting sun. ***Posto de Turismo*** *(summer) Câmara Municipal* ✆ 263 285 600 Praça Afonso de Albuquerque.

To proceed to Azambuja take the municipal park s/o past the rail station (left) out the park exit onto a straight stretch of road and under the N-10 (which goes over the Tejo at this point). A rough path runs parallel to the road and turns right after the **Fábrica de Água / Simtejo** [**2.7** km]. *[Note the original route went s/o over the bridge ahead and old arrows still point in that direction. The former route is dangerous and not advisable].* Veer right along delightful gravel track that meanders alongside a small stream past the modern **Estação Castanheira [1.8 km]. *Note:*** arrows right just *before* the station take a wide service track along the railway. A canal just before V.N.Rainha necessitates walkers to take a narrow path by the rail line which is dangerous. Plans are afoot to build a pasarela so in the meantime take the *pasarela* over rail line at **Carregado *Alenquer*** [**3.1** km].

7.6 km **Carregado** •*Hs* **ER Estação Real** *6x* €40-45 ✆ 911 808 461 (first rail station in Portugal opened by royalty) opp. *OManuel.* We now turn inland along a dyke and turn right> over bridge *[s/o 50m]* past EDP *termoeléctica*. The route continues under the A-10 and s/o over the N-3 [**!**] (underpass 50m right) into:

4.8 km **Vila Nova da Rainha.** *[For alt. route ❷ turn right along main road to rail station]*. For original road route ❶ and cafés continue s/o over N-3 *[!]* past [ ] (picnic area right) over río Ota into village past / *O Sonho* past *Dois M's* and *Retiro* to rejoin the N-3. *[to access alt. route ❷ at this point continue s/o over main road down to rail station]*. For road route proceed along main road for a 6.0 km 'slog' into Azambuja. Pass Repsol services s/o to roundabout at Galp on the outskirts of Azambuja: & (left).

6.5 km **Azambuja *rotunda*** Hotel •*H*** **Ouro** *40x* €35-45 ✆ 263 406 530 N-3 / Km 10 roundabout at entrance to the town.

For alt. 'green' route ❷ alongside railway go to **V.N. Rainha station** and take the ***pasarela*** [**0.8** km] *over* rail and out through gate to join wide farm track (take gap in fence). This avoids the busy main road but there are are no facilities or shade along this 6 km section. Pass *Espadanal* and at the far end take the new tunnel *under* rail (see photo>) and cross waste ground to join the road route at roundabout in Azambuja [**6.0** km].

6.8 km **Azambuja *rotunda*** road route joins at Aldi *supermercado*.

Continue s/o over roundabout ***Aldi*** past bullring and *Páteo Valverde* ❶ ***Turismo*** to the rear of the courtyard (left). Continue past the Bombeiros Voluntários on rua José Ramos Vides up to the town centre.

1.0 km **Azambuja *Centro Praça do Município*** Igreja Matriz & Pelourinho. Pleasant town (population 7,000) with variety of *cafés / bars / restaurants* and popular fiesta during the last week in May *Feira do Maio* with its own 'running of the bulls.' The area is also known for its robust red wines coaxed from the Periquita grapes. Rural Portugal is relatively poor but rich in heritage buildings. **Páteo Valverde** is a cultural centre with popular café, small museum and tourist office (summer). Here we find portraits of local bullfighters and one of the most fêted female matadors in Portugal, Ana Maria. The *Centro Comercial Atrium* on rua Eng. Moniz da Maia has free internet access.

AZAMBUJA: ●*Alb.* **Azambuja** *Asoc. [16÷1]* €10 ✆ 914 103 807 managed by Asoc. Via Lusitana has moved to the former museum in this central location at 69 rua Vitor Cordon (the main street see photo>) imm. (80m) beyond *O Diamante*. ▮ **Other Lodging:** •*Hs* **Flor da Primavera** *20x* €25-45 ✆ 263 402 545 *www.flordaprimavera.pt* rua Conselheiro Francisco Arouca, 19 (directly on camino). •*P* **Jacinto** *4x* €20 ✆ 965 535 677 [m] 263 402 504 on Rua dos Campinos, 3C... and •*P* **Casa da Rainha** *6x* €45 ✆ 969 512 143 *www.casadarainha.pt* on Travessa da Rainha, 6. For chic outdoor dining try *Tasco de Ilda* on adj. rua Jaime da Mota.

Personal Reflections:

03 AZAMBUJA – SANTARÉM

------ 19.2 ------ *58%*
------ 14.0 ------ *42%*
------ 0.0 ------ *0%*
Total km ------ **33.2** km *(20.6 ml)*

Total ascent **300**m +½ *hr*
Alto ▲ Santarém **135**m *(443 ft)*
< A H > ➲Valada **13.4** km ➲Porto Muge **17.0**
•Reguengo •Cataxo •Vale de Santarém •Santarém

100m AZAMBUJA · Valada · Port de Muge · Cardaso · Quinta da Burra · Alto 135m SANTARÉM
río Tejo · 0 · 5 km · 10 km · 15 km · 20 km · 25 km · 30 km

The Practical Path: Today we traverse the flood plains *lezíria* – ½ the route is via delightful farm tracks through this agricultural area with fruit and vegetable production (primarily tomatoes) and vineyards. This is the market garden of Portugal covered with the rich alluvial soil of the Tejo which has now narrowed to a more intimate river as distinct from its estuarine form but all the more hazardous for that as it can (and does) rise and flood this totally flat terrain – a rise of 8 meters has been recorded! The only climb today is up to Santarém at 110m. ***Note*** there are no facilities between Porto de Muge and Santarém (16.2 km!) so carry energy snacks and water. Some shade is provided by lines of poplar along the path.

The Mystical Path: *Do one thing in this life – eradicate prejudice.* Peter Ustinov. Everyone is an extension of the One Mind or Source of all that is – within reality. Illusion descends and appears to fragment that unified wholeness. To look on another with the vision of Christ is to recognise one's true Self in reflection. *The eye with which I see God, is the same eye with which God sees me.* Meister Eckhart.

Personal Reflections: I was dreamily contemplating the journey ahead when I realised my camera was being lifted from my pocket. I lashed out in anger and recognised the young boy from an earlier confrontation. The strength of my reaction alarmed me. I write now in the calm of the evening and re-dedicate this journey to eliminating prejudice from my heart and to making every step a prayer for peace and understanding... *He who angers you, conquers you.* Elizabeth Kenny.

0.0 km **Azambuja** Break-fast before you leave? Café Reguengo 11 km! From ***Praça do Município*** follow waymarks that down *rua Conselheiro Federico Arouca* to the railway station up the metal staircase and over the N-3 and rail line to follow a quiet tree-lined road on the far side past shaded picnic area to a bridge.

2.0 km **Ponte** Turn down sharp <left to riverside path over canal by quinta and pick up wide farm tracks to asphalt road by ***Aerodromo*** [**3.1** km]. Turn <left along quiet country road past ***Quinta Alqueidao*** [**2.8** km] back to the river with the Tejo lying 'hidden' behind the high flood barrier that follows the river at this point passing a welcome sign as we enter ***Reguengo*** [**3.1** km].

9.0 km **Reguengo** village with welcoming *Campino*: Continue by road to:

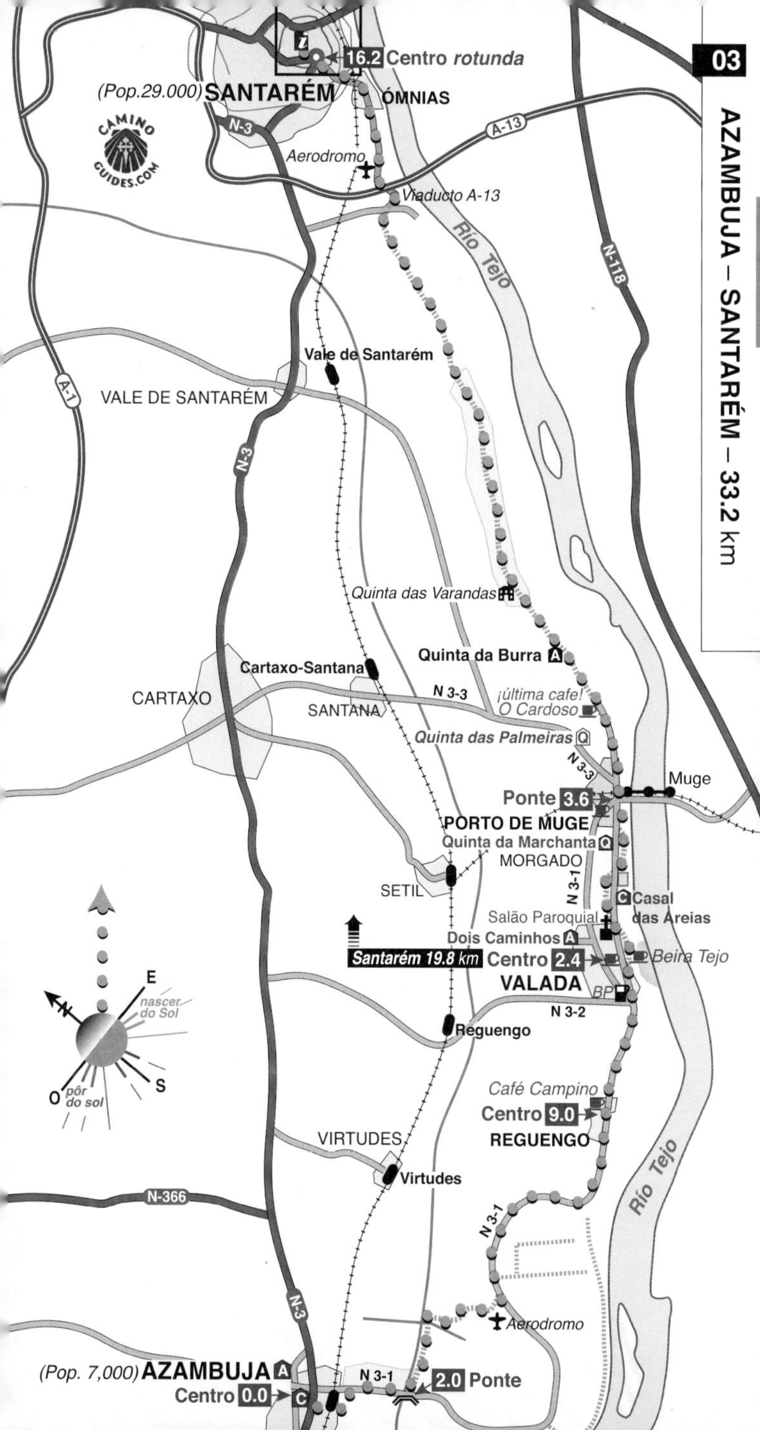

03
AZAMBUJA – SANTARÉM – 33.2 km
16.2 Centro rotunda
(Pop.29.000) SANTARÉM
ÓMNIAS
CAMINO GUIDES.COM
N-3
A-13
Aerodromo
Viaducto A-13
Río Tejo
N-118
Vale de Santarém
A-1
VALE DE SANTARÉM
N-3
Quinta das Varandas
Quinta da Burra
Cartaxo-Santana
CARTAXO
N 3-3
SANTANA
¡última cafe! O Cardoso
Quinta das Palmeiras
N 3-3
Muge
Ponte 3.6
PORTO DE MUGE
Quinta da Marchanta
MORGADO
SETIL
N 3-1
Casal das Areias
Salão Paroquial
Dois Caminhos
Santarém 19.8 km
Centro 2.4
Beira Tejo
VALADA
BP
N 3-2
E
nascer do Sol
Reguengo
S
O
pôr do sol
Café Campino
Centro 9.0
REGUENGO
Río Tejo
VIRTUDES
Virtudes
N-366
N 3-1
N-3
Aerodromo
(Pop. 7,000) AZAMBUJA
N 3-1
2.0 Ponte
Centro 0.0

2.4 km Valada *Centro* Quaint riverside village *Maioral Zé* to main square *Casa Tradição Helena Almeida [**Note: Casa Velha** & **Casa Rio** in Porto de Muge are closed].* *Mano Velho* + *Porfírio* welcomes at peaceful beachfront *Beira Tejo*. Pilgrims can sleep on the floor at ●**Salão Paroquial** Largo da Igreja basic lodging. & *Oliserve* on bypass road to rear of town & ●*Alb.* **Dois Caminhos** *Priv.[6÷3]* €15 Enrico ✆ 915 657 651 r/D. Diniz, 4. A flood bank separates the village from the sandy beach and a stone marks the flood level *-nivel-* where in 1979 it rose to the top! Igreja de N.Sª do Ó *XII* dates from 12thc.

Continue s/o past road to •*CR* **Casal das Areias** (+300m) €28-42 special pilgrim price for basic lodging from €10 Nuno (speaks English) ✆ 932 384 524 www.casaldasareias.com Morada. Keep s/o past water plant *(note an overgrown path runs along part of the flood wall)* into the outskirts of the next village **Porto de Muga.** Pass •*CR* **Quinta da Marchanta** €30 / €40 double ✆ 913 553 187.

3.6 km **Porto de Muge** ***Ponte*** *Morgado Quiosque* opp bridge. *[Detour +400m (left)* •*Quinta das* **Palmeiras** *x7 €85-95 ✆ 243 749 272].* Keep s/o along riverbank *rua do sabugueiro* past *O Cardaso* [**0.7** km].*(last café before Santarém).* Next we come to •**Quinta da Burra** [**0.5** km] *Currently closed following the death of popular hospitalera Paula. Awaiting update.* Continue along remote sandy tracks that meander for 10 km through this rich agricultural area *Lezíria* with variety of crops (tomato) past *Quinta das Varandas* where the first views of Santarém open up on the horizon. Join asphalt road under **A-13 Viaduct** [**10.9** km] past aero club and under the railway in **Ómnias** [**1.6** km] for the final steep ascent up into Santarém [**2.5** km]:

16.2 km **Santarém Centro** ***rotunda*** roundabout ***Largo Cândido dos Reis*** with *Hospital de Jesus Cristo* church adj. ***Santa Casa da Misericórdia*** offering pilgrim lodging to the rear (see next page). This also marks the point at which the Camino de Fátima branches off (left) and the Camino de Santiago continues s/o.

Santarém is a charming, historic city straddling a fortified hilltop well out of reach of the floodwaters of the Tejo. Its commanding position affords wonderful views of the river especially from the viewpoint *miradouro* also called Gates of the Sun *Portas do Sol* where extensive gardens form a viewing platform on what was formerly the Moorish citadel. The town provided a major stronghold for the Romans and Julius Caesar chose it as the administrative centre *conventus* for the region. When the Moors arrived it became a stronghold for Islam and was considered to be unassailable until the first king of Portugal *Dom Afonso Henriques* recaptured it in 1149 and returned the town to the Portuguese who have occupied it happily ever since.

Praça Sá da Bandeira

Personal Reflections:

Rio Tejo from Santarém

Historic Buildings and Monuments: At the entrance to the town ❶ ***Igreja do Hospital de Jesus Cristo*** *XV*[th]c (adjoining the Santa Casa da Misericórdia). ❷ ***Praça Sá da Bandeira*** this exquisite square includes a flight of steps up to ***Igreja N.Sra. da Conceiçáo e Seminário*** *XVII*[th]*c* which dovetails as the cathedral and on the opposite side is ***Igreja N.Sra da Piedade.*** Next on the circuit is the Manueline gem ❸ ***Igreja de Marvila*** with its wonderful display of ceramic tiles *azulejos* dating from *XVII*[th]c although the original site was donated by D. Afonso Henriques to the Knights Templars in the *XII*[th]*c.* ❹ ***Igreja da Graça*** *XV*[th]c with its fine rose window and which houses the tombs of Pedro Alvares Cabral (after whom the square is named) the 'discoverer' of Brazil whose simple stone slab is outdone by the ornate sarcophagus of Pedro de Menezes the first governor of Ceuta (Morocco). ❺ ***Portas do Sol*** 'Gate of the Sun' is a wonderful viewpoint *miradouro* occupying the site of the original Roman forum and the Moorish citadel. ❻ ***Porta de Santiago*** medieval pilgrims gateway. There is an alternative waymarked route around town (grey on plan). *Photo of the old Mercado below.*

Mercado & Azulejo

🅘 **Turismo** © 243 304 437 rua Capelo e Ivens, 63. ***Centro:*** ●*Alb.***Santa Casa da Misericórdia** *Conv.[24÷12!]* €5 © 243 305 260 Largo Cândido dos Reis (check-in front office or go to Antonio at *rear* reception after 17:00). *[Note: Alb.Santarém now closed].* ● **N1 Hostel Apartments** *Priv.[30÷4]* + €12–€40/60 © 243 350 140 *ww.n1hostelapartments.com* Av. dos Combatentes, 80. ●**Seminário** *Conv.[96÷24] (grupos 10+)* €10+ © *913 023 728 (Sra. Aida)* Praça Sá da Bandeira *(museo €4).* •*CH* **Casa Flores** Rua Pedro Canavarro, 9 © 965 612 001 (duplex sleeps 4 €50+). •*Hr* **A Casa Brava** *x16* €75-95 © 912 852 261 R. Guilherme Azevedo 31. •*P* **Coimbra** *x4* €15 pp © 243 322 816 Rua 31 de Janeiro, 42. •*Hr* **Beirante** *x40* €35+ © 243 322 547 rua Alexandre Herculano (near Mercado). •*H*** **Vitória** *x60* €35-55 © 243 309 130 rua Visconde de Santarém, 21. •*Hs* **Tagus Host** *12x* €30-37 © 913 476 949 *www.tagushost.pt* Av. Dom Afonso Henriques, 79A.

+ ***1.3*** *km* •*H**** **Santarém** *x105* €60-70 © 243 330 800 on Avenida Madre Andaluz. + ***1.5*** *km down in modern suburbs adj. Hospital.* •*H**** **Umu** *x67* €47-57 © 243 377 240 *www.enfis.pt/umu* Av. Bernardo Santareno 38. *Nearby* ● **BV** *Mun.[4÷1]* €10 © 243 377 900 Rua Brigadeiro Lino Dias Valente. *On way out* in Portas do Sol is the luxurious •**Casa da Alcáçova** *x7* €100+ © 243 304 030 Largo do Alcáçova,3.

❑ **Fátima** Bus 3x daily from Santarém. Journey time 45 mins €10 RedeExpressos *www.rede-expressos.pt/en* first bus 10:45–Fátima 11:30 / Fátima 17.45–Santarém 18:30. Taxi 35 mins €35 (see also under Tomar). ***Info:*** *Hostel Pereira Fátima © 960 330 636 (Armando Pereira) www.hostelpereira.com*

rio Tejo
(Tagus)
Ponte Alcôrce
Fonte Palhais
RIBEIRA DE SANTAREM
N-114
Casa da Alcáçova
Miradouro
5 Porta do Sol
Santa María de Alcáçova
6 Porta de Santiago
Calcada Atamarma
VALE DA ATAMARMA
Av. 5 de Outubro
waymarked routes...
Main Camino Santiago
Pedestrian alternative
Caminho Fátima
São João de Alporão (Museu)
4 Igreja N.S. Graça XV
N.M. Pedro Álvares Cabral
Lg.Pedro Álvares Cabral
3 Igreja Marvila (Manuelino)
Lg.de Miravila
Braamcamp Friere
Tv. Capuchas
S.Estevão
Lg.do Milagre
Igreja Milagre
Serpa Pinto
Misericórdia
1 Dezembro
Miguel Bombarda
Guilherme Azevedo
Ribatejo
Casa Brava
Capelo e Ivens
S.Nicolau
João Afonso
São Francisco
Coimbra
Piedade
O Saloio
Turismo
Av. António dos Santos
Fátima
2 Praça Sá Bandeira
N.S.Conceição (Sé)
Seminário (Grupos)
Pedro Canavarro
Flores
Terra P.
Santarém
Texeira Guedes
Camara
N-3
Beirante
Mercado
Ümu Bombeiros
Av. Sá da Bandeira
Lg.Cândido dos Reis
Calçada Fonte da Junqueira
Taberna do Quinzena
Casa de Misercordia
Igreja de Jesus Cristo 1
Vitória
Av.dos Combatentes
SANTARÉM
N1
Tagus Host
Santarém

04 SANTARÉM – GOLEGÃ

--- --- 16.0 --- --- *47%*
--- --- 11.3 --- --- *32%*
--- --- 7.1 --- --- 21%
Total km **34.4** km *(21.4 ml)*

Total ascent **305**m +½ *hr*
Alto Santarém **135** m *(443 ft)*
<A H> Azinhaga **26.9** km.
•*Santarém* •*Vale de Figueira* •*Mato de Miranda* •*Riachos-Golega.*

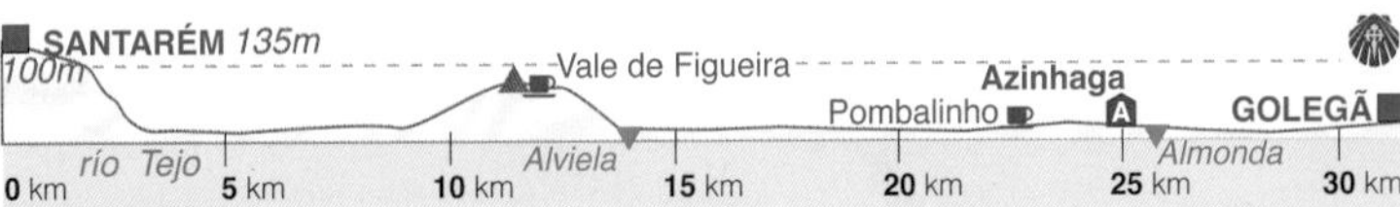

Practical Path: Pleasant stage 47% on remote farm tracks parallel to the river Tejo (66% on alternative path). ***Note:*** over-zealous friends of Fátima have waymarked the route from Santarém with yellow (not blue) arrows which can cause confusion – take extra care leaving town and head *down* onto the flat alluvial plane of the Tejo. Flooding in recent years has necessitated re-routing of the path into Golegã. Waymarks now direct us via Pombalinho with several cafés and Azinhaga which provides a good interim stopover with accommodation. The original route is shown as a lovely alt. 'green' option in dry conditions.

Mystical Path: *The possibility of the impossible is the subject of my novels.* *José Saramago.* Let me live in my house by the side of the road, where the race of men go by; they are good, they are bad; they are weak, they are strong, wise, foolish – so am I; then why should I sit in the scorner's seat, Or hurl the cynic's ban? Let me live in my house by the side of the road, and be a friend to man.

Sam Walter Foss

Personal Reflections: I was cold and wet and the batteries in my GPS suddenly went flat. I wearily retraced my steps and met her locking up the office by the side of the road. She knew of a place to sleep and, perchance, it was her birthday so she would be delighted to celebrate and share a meal with me. As I luxuriated in a hot bath it was not only the batteries that were being recharged – my heart was being filled with gratitude for unexpected friendship and trust offered to a total stranger by a lady at the side of the road... in Azinhaga.

0.0 km **Centro** *Rotonda* Waymarks now via rua João Afonso *(alt. via Serpa Pinto)* to **Porta do Sol** [**1.0** km] out through St. James Gate *Puerta de São Tiago* to head down steeply [!] on woodland paths and s/o <left across the N-114 [!] to rail line at **Ribeira de Santarém** [**1.1** km]. Pass *fonte de Palhais* and medieval bridge turn right> over *rio Alcorce* onto country road to farmhouse and path [**1.0** km]:

3.1 km **Camino** turn <left by *Casa Grande* onto path that now veers right> through crop fields running parallel to the road which we cross at [**3.5** km] and continue s/o along path to rejoin road by Quinta Cruz da Légua (ruins) past Quinta Boavista into **Vale da Figueira** [**5.1** km] a village typical of the *lezíria*:

8.6 km **Vale da Figueira** *Petiscos* & parish church. S/o past *Val Doce* and at

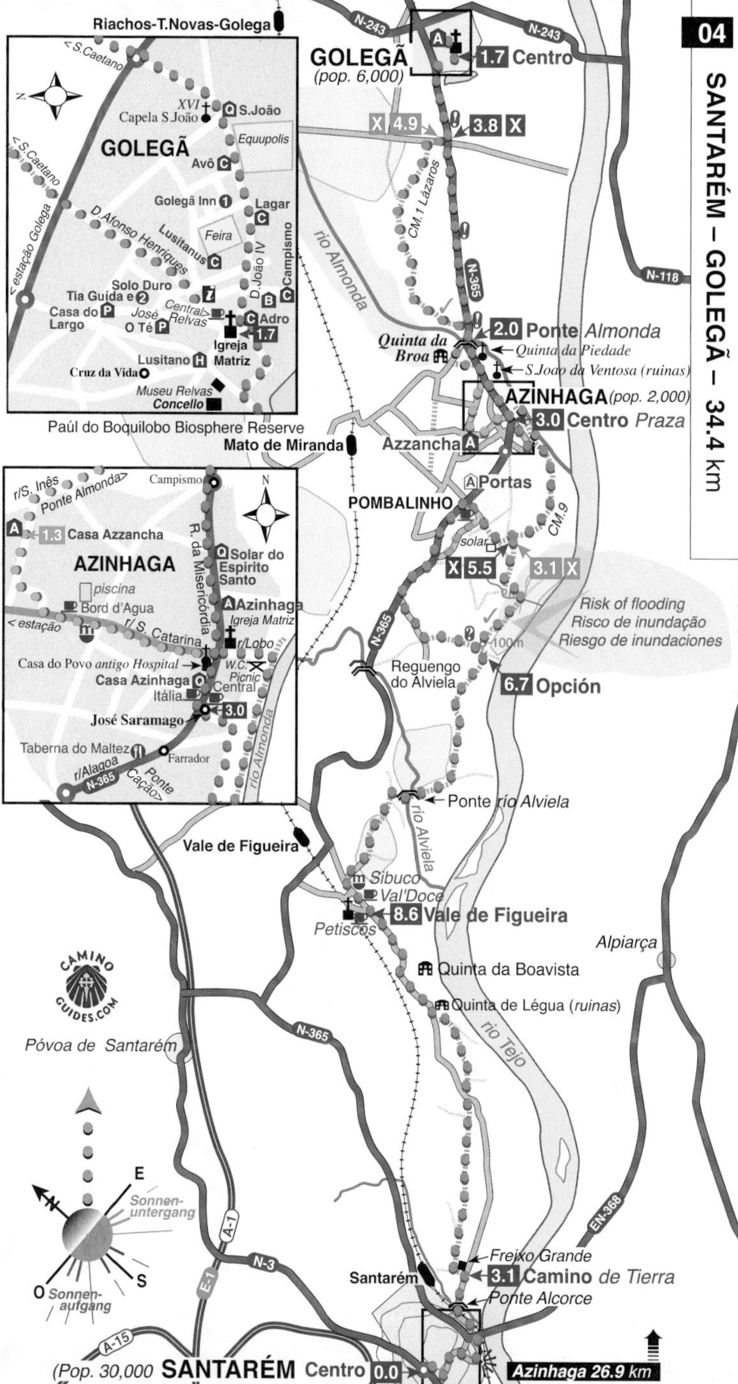
GOLEGÃ
(pop. 6,000)
1.7 Centro
Riachos-T.Novas-Golega
N-243
4.9
3.8
CM.1 Lázaros
rio Almonda
N-365
N-118
2.0 Ponte Almonda
Quinta da Broa
Quinta da Piedade
S.Joao da Ventosa (ruinas)
AZINHAGA (pop. 2,000)
3.0 Centro Praza
Azzancha
Portas
Mato de Miranda
POMBALINHO
Paúl do Boquilobo Biosphere Reserve
CM.9
solar
5.5
3.1
Risk of flooding
Risco de inundação
Riesgo de inundaciones
100m
Reguengo do Alviela
6.7 Opción
Ponte río Alviela
río Alviela
Vale de Figueira
Sibuco
Val'Doce
8.6 Vale de Figueira
Petiscos
Alpiarça
Quinta da Boavista
Quinta de Légua (ruinas)
rio Tejo
N-365
Póvoa de Santarém
CAMINO GUIDES.COM
E
Sonnen-untergang
O
Sonnen-aufgang
S
A-1
N-3
E-1
EN-368
Freixo Grande
Santarém
3.1 Camino de Tierra
Ponte Alcorce
A-15
(Pop. 30,000 SANTARÉM Centro 0.0
Azinhaga 26.9 km
GOLEGÃ
<S.Caetano
<S.Caetano
XVI
Capela S.João
S.João
Equupolis
Avô
Golegã Inn
Lagar
D.Afonso Henriques
Lusitanus
Feira
Campismo
D.João IV
<estação Golega
Solo Duro
Tia Guída e
Casa do Largo
José O Té
Central Relvas
Adro
1.7
Igreja Matriz
Lusitano
Cruz da Vida
Museu Relvas
Concello
AZINHAGA
r/S. Inês
Ponte Almonda>
Campismo
1.3 Casa Azzancha
R. da Misericórdia
Solar do Espirito Santo
piscina
Bord d'Agua
< estação
r/ S. Catarina
Azinhaga
Igreja Matriz
r/Lobo
Casa do Povo antigo Hospital
W.C. Picnic
Casa Azinhaga
Itália
Central
José Saramago
3.0
río Almonda
Taberna do Maltez
Farrador
r/Alagoa
N-365
Ponte Cação>

mercado O Sibuca [**0.2** km] turn down right> veering <left at fork (cork trees) and right> at next junction down to ruins (up right). Cross **bridge** [**2.8** km] rio Alviela (tributary of the Tejo) and turn <left through **gate *posts*** [**1.0** km]. The route now alternates between lanes and farm tracks through crop fields, mostly corn *maizales* past farmyard and Quinta (left) to T-Junction and option point [**2.7** km]:

6.7 km [X] **Opción** ▲ Following floods in 2012 the Município de Golegã waymarked a route via Pombalinho into Azinhaga. The original route ❷ is good in dry weather and is 2.4 km shorter (5.5 – 3.1) all by path and recently waymarked.

▲ **Option ❷** Turn <left on gravel track and ***imm.*** right> [**0.1** km] [**!**] onto path past **hut** [**0.2** km]. Several tracks branch off so stay vigilant for new waymarks. rejoin the other route on gravel track by solar panels [**2.7** km].
3.1 km X-Crosstracks Continue past gravel pits into Azinhaga.

▲ To continue on main track ❶ turn <left at option point & keep s/o and turn right> at **crossroads** [**1.2** km] (**Reguengo do Alviela** *left – no facilities).* Turn right> onto **N-365** [**1.0** km] [**!**] to wetland area and signboard [**0.8** km]. Keep s/o past road (right) and turn right> into **Pombalhino** [**1.1** km] with ☕ & 🛒. Keep s/o where N-365 veers left *[Note +* ***900m*** *•CR.* **Portas** *Alb.[8÷1]* €20 *4x* €58+ ✆ 243 459 044 *www.casadasportas.pt N-365.]* Continue past park [🚰] to end of the town where 5 farm tracks meet. Keep s/o to solar panels (right) to junction where alt. 'green' route joins from the right [**1.4** km].

5.5 km **X-Crosstracks.** S/o along delightful shaded farmtracks past ponds and water treatment plant to **Ponte do Cação** [**2.4** km]. Option here to continue on new riverside walkway to picnic area and toilets with access to Casa da Azzancha (see map). For main route follows waymarks into town centre [**0.6** km].

3.0 km **Azinhaga** ***Centro*** Largo da Praça & Foundation dedicated to Nobel Laureate ***José Saramago*** (photo below) who was born here in 1922 (died in 2010) becoming the first Portuguese writer to win the Nobel Prize for literature in 1998. He wrote, *"As citizens, we all have an obligation to intervene and become involved – it's the citizen who changes things."* Azinhaga is an attractive town with connections to the original medieval pilgrim route and a resident population of 2,000. **Lodging:** ●*Alb.* **Azinhaga** *[4÷1]* € *donativo* ✆ 919 209 621 •**Casa da Azinhaga** €70+ ✆ 249 957 146 (ivy-clad Quinta) and •**Solar do Espirito Santo** ✆ 249 957 252 equestrian centre with rooms from €65 both on main street, rua da Misericordia. To the rear of town (+1.3 km) is the popular •*CR* **Casa de Azzancha** *x4* €30pp +€65 dbl. incl. ✆249 957 253 m: 919 187 773 where Helena Santos welcomes pilgrims on Rua dos Altos Montijos, 68 (see photo>) *(adj. rua S. Inês continues to Golega direct).* Pilgrim menú at 🍴 *Taberna do Maltez* adj. blacksmith statue *Tributo ao Ferrador.*

Continue from town centre on rua da Misericordia (N-365) past ancient pilgrim hospital adj. Capilla Espíritu Santo to rotunda *Estátua do Campino* s/o past Capela S. João Ventosa (*XV* ruins–right) alt. track (left) to río Almonda bridge.

2.0 km **Ponte *río Almonda* Quinta de Brôa** *(left)*. From here the waymarked route is along the N-365 main road (with no margin [!]) all the way into Golegã. *[**Detour:** +4.5 km Mato Miranda (rail) Quinta de Miranda €55 ✆ 249 957 115].*

Option: Alt. un-waymarked route parallel to the dangerous N-365 [!]. It is 1.1 km longer (4.9–v–3.8) but avoids 3.7 km of busy main road: Turn <left over bridge onto CM.1 Estrada Lázaros [**0.2** km] veer right> onto farm track [**3.1** km] and right at T-junction [**1.4** km] to crossroads [**0.2** km] total 4.9 km.

4.9 km Cruce N-365 waymarked route joins from the right.

From Ponte Almonda continue along N-365 [!] past alt. route (left) straight to:

3.8 km **Cruce Crossroads** (alt. route joins from left). Continue s/o [!] past lake (right) and at end of tree-lined park turn right and up into the main square:

1.7 km **Golegã *Centro*** ■ ***Largo da Imac. Conceição*** *Igreja Matriz XIV fine Manueline porch (photo page 54).* ❶ *Turismo* ✆ 249 979 002 (Mon-Fri 10:00-6:00). ☕ *Central* & ☕ *Praça* + 🍴 *Páteo Gallega*. ■***Largo Dom Manuel I*** *Concello* & *Sporthotel equuspolis* ✆ 249 979 000 (groups). *Casa Museu Carlos Relvas* (10:30-18:00) early photographic material. ***Cruz da Vida*** sculpture by José Augusto Coimbra exploring boundaries between birth/death, human/animal adj. ☕ *Flôr*. ■ ***Largo Marquês de Pombal*** equestrian centre & home of the Lusitano.

Golegã is a lively town of 6,000 whose roots go back to the 12thc when a Galician woman (from "Galego" *Golegã*) set up an inn for travellers and pilgrims on the Royal Way *Estrada Real* from Lisboa to Porto. Known as the 'horse capital of Portugal' and famous for its international horse fair *Feira Nacional do Cavalo* held during the first 2 weeks in November (St. Martin's Day) when lodging is all but impossible to find.

Lodging: ***Centro:*** *(waymarked camino)* (adj. Igreja) •**Casa do Adro** €65+ ✆ 966 798 330 (Filipe) Largo da Imaculada Conceição, 58. ***Rua D. João IV*** **Bombeiros Voluntários** ✆ 249 979 070 possibility of floor in hall *salão* (shower in adj. campsite). •**Cavalo Branco** ✆ 249 979 003 bungalows from €40+ (3 beds) part of adj. •**Parque Campismo** ✆ 249 979 003. **Nº136** •*P* **Quartos do Lagar** *x5* €25 ✆ 917 591 833 (Josefino). **Nº141** •**Pátio da Avó Faustina** €65 ✆ 935 640 545. Nearby in ***r/da Cunha Franco Bloco 17*** *Alb.*❶ **Inn Golegã** *x12* €15-€35 Elsa ✆ 933 493 397. •**Quinta S. João** pilgrims from €25 incl. ✆ 961 015 131 (adj. Equuspolis). •*P* **Lusitanus** *x6* €40-50 Largo Marquês de Pombal ✆ 249 976 933. ***Rua José Relvas***: **Nº84** ★*Alb.*❷ **Solo Duro** *Priv.[14÷2]* €15 ✆ 249 976 802 *www.casadatiaguida.com* adj. •*CR* **Casa da Tia Guida** *6x* €45-60 (same owner). **Nº119** 🍴 *&*•*Hs* **O Té** €15-35 ✆ 249 976 404. •*H* **Casa do Largo** *10x* €55+ ✆ 249 04 850 Largo 5 de Outubro (roundabout). •*H**** **Lusitano** *x24* €75+ ✆ 249 979 170 *www.hotellusitano.com* r/Gil Vicente.

05 GOLEGÃ – TOMAR

(dotted)	13.4	42%
(grey)	13.5	42%
(solid)	5.2	16%
Total km	**32.1** km *(19.9 ml)*	

Total ascent **1,100**m *+1¾ hr*

▲ Alto *m* Grou **165**m *(540 ft)*

<A H> S. Caetano **6.1** km *V.N. da Barquinha **9.1 km** (+**1.1** km)* Atalaia **11.6** km Asseiceira **20.1** km.

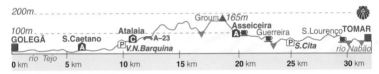

Practical Path: We set out today towards one of Portugal's most notable manor houses *Quinta da Cardiga*. The first half is along quiet country lanes relieved with the occasional farm track as we head back towards the Tejo where it takes a pronounced bend away from our path at Vila Nova da Barquinha and we leave it for the last time. This is the point where we leave the flat alluvial plains and head into more demanding countryside with gentle rolling hills covered in woodland offering shade. We also encounter villages at regular intervals with the possibility of refreshments and we end this stage in the historic Templar town of Tomar, the quintessential pilgrim halt, where the welcome offered to the medieval pilgrim is extended to those of us who follow in their footsteps.

Practise random acts of loving kindness and senseless acts of beauty. ***Anon.***

Mystical Path: Love simply *is* and needs no defence. It is the desire for love that makes it manifest and dissolves the barriers erected in a vain attempt to keep it hidden. Luís Vaz de Camões says it thus:

The lover becomes the thing he loves
By virtue of much imagining;
Since what I long for is already in me,
The act of longing should be enough.

Personal Reflections: I arrived in the heat of the afternoon and rested by the gate – I didn't have long to wait and was treated like an old friend with love and kindness. I merely mentioned an interest in visiting the castle at Almourol and was driven there without a moments hesitation along with a visit to Constância beautifully located at the confluence of the Tejo and Zezere. It was here, in the 16thc, that Portuguese poet Luís Vaz de Camões was forced into exile and wrote some of his masterful verse, oft compared to that of Shakespeare.

0.0 km **Golegã** ***Centro*** despite its compact size it is easy to get lost in the maze of streets; use the sun for orientation (if you stayed here last night head east towards the rising sun). *[For an alt. route (fading waymarks) head up the main shopping street Afonso Henriques and s/o over the bypass* ***N-243 [0.9 km]*** *onto track to intersection with road and* ***main route*** *[2.0 km]: Total 2.9 km.]*

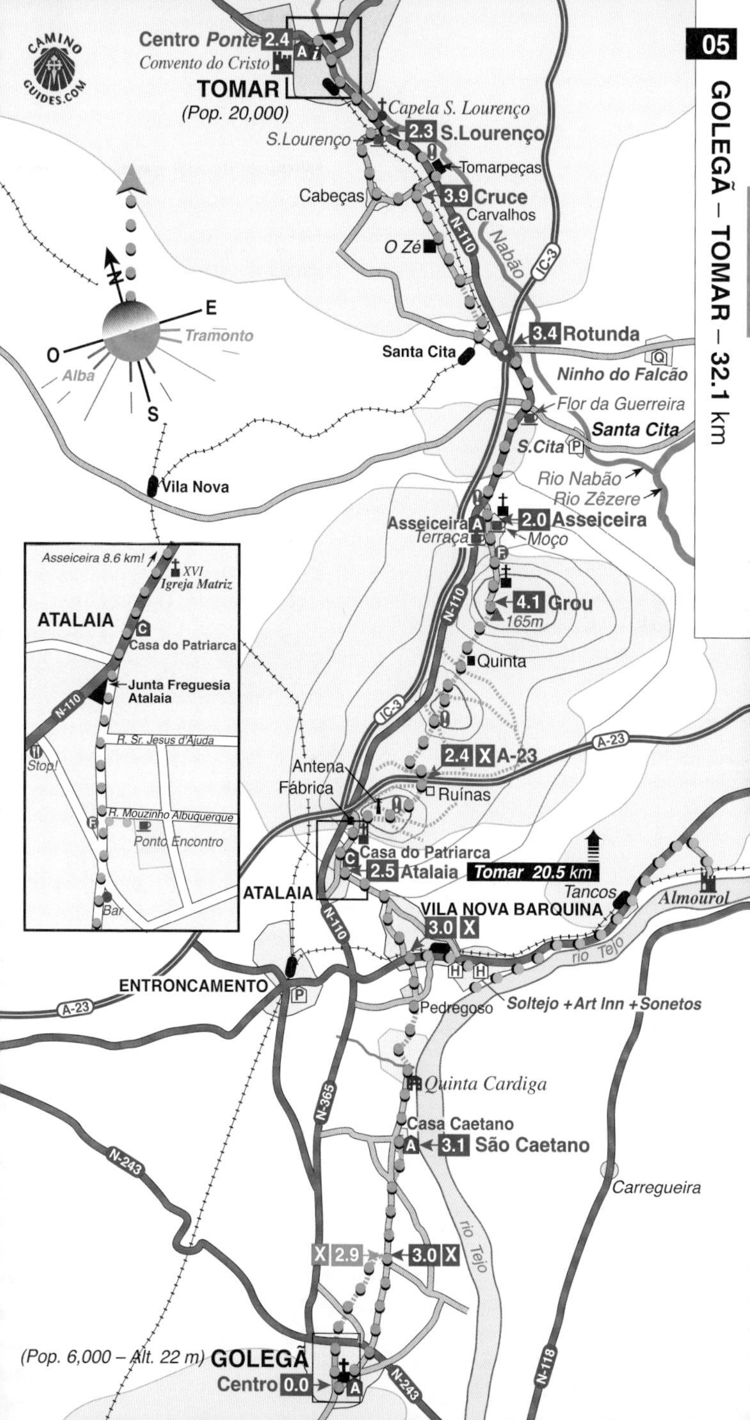
CAMINO GUIDES.COM
Centro Ponte 2.4
Convento do Cristo
TOMAR
(Pop. 20,000)
Capela S. Lourenço
S.Lourenço
2.3 S.Lourenço
Tomarpeças
Cabeças
3.9 Cruce
Carvalhos
O Zé
N-110
Nabão
IC-3
E
Tramonto
O
Alba
S
Santa Cita
3.4 Rotunda
Ninho do Falcão
Flor da Guerreira
Santa Cita
S.Cita
Vila Nova
Rio Nabão
Rio Zêzere
Asseiceira
Terraça
2.0 Asseiceira
Moço
4.1 Grou
165m
Quinta
Asseiceira 8.6 km!
XVI Igreja Matriz
ATALAIA
Casa do Patriarca
Junta Freguesia Atalaia
R. Sr. Jesus d'Ajuda
Stop!
R. Mouzinho Albuquerque
Ponto Encontro
Bar
2.4 X A-23
A-23
Antena
Fábrica
Ruínas
Casa do Patriarca
2.5 Atalaia
Tomar 20.5 km
ATALAIA
Tancos
Almourol
VILA NOVA BARQUINA
3.0 X
rio Tejo
ENTRONCAMENTO
Pedregoso
Soltejo + Art Inn + Sonetos
Quinta Cardiga
N-365
Casa Caetano
3.1 São Caetano
N-243
Carregueira
X 2.9
3.0 X
N-118
(Pop. 6,000 – Alt. 22 m) GOLEGÃ
Centro 0.0

Main route via rua D. João IV past Quartos do Lagar (right) Capela S. João (left) and s/o at roundabout on the N-243 [**1.6** km] to junction [**1.4** km].

3.0 km **Cruce** Here the alternative route joins from the left and we continue s/o by road passing Quinta do Matinho into the Land of the Templars *Terra de Templários* with Templar cross in the peaceful hamlet of:

3.1 km **São Caetano** ●*Alb.* **Casa São Caetano** *Priv.[10÷5]* €15 ✆ 914 951 076 village green *núcleo museológico* with ☕ (summer). S/o to **Quinta Cardiga** [**0**.7 km] *Stroll down the peaceful, tree-lined avenue where old retainers try to maintain some order out of the fading opulence. It started life as a castle in the 12th century before D.Afonso Henriques placed it into the care of the Templars. Along with Almourol (see below) it formed part of the defensive system against Spanish and Arab invasion. From castle it became royal palace (Philip II rested here in 1580 after his coronation), house to religious orders, hospital for pilgrims, home to nobility passing into... history?* Continue over stone bridge *Ribeira da Ponte da Pedra* the stream enters the Tejo imm. to our right (the gardens of the quinta front the river). The route now wends its way into Pedregoso passing sign for V. N. Barquina (right) pass Escola S.Maria (left) to main road (EN-3) and **railway** [**2.3** km].

3.0 km **Vila Nova da Barquinha** ***Option 0.0*** [?] We have several options.
Detour ❶ ***+0.5*** *km along N-3* ● ● ● ●
V.N. da Barquinha. Riverside town. •*H* **Soltejo** *x14* €40 ✆ 249 720 150. Mod. •*H* **River House** *Art Inn x15* €40-60 ✆ 918 735 242 *www.riverhouse.pt* Largo 1° Dezembro, 9 & •**Nature House.** •*CR* **Sonetos Do Tejo** *x6* €60-75 ✆ 919 280 663 *www.sonetosdotejo.com* restored quinta r/Tejo, 18. ❷ ***+5.5*** *km* ***Almourol*** medieval castle occupied by the Knights Templar and dramatically set on a rocky island in the Tejo (see photo). A visit would require an overnight stay. A boat (summer only) runs from Tancos which can be accessed either by riverside walk, rail or taxi. ❸ ***Constância + 10*** *km + hoteles* ❹ *+ **3** km* ***Entroncamento*** *hoteles*

S/o over rail in V. N. Barquinha up through suburbs merging into Atalaia via ruas D. Afonso Henriques & Paulino José Correia to [🚰] and rest area (see wall art by ***Last drinking font & cafés until Asseiceira 8.6 km!*** *[**Detour** right 50m onto r/ Mouzinho Albuquerque for ☕ Ponto Encontro or 🍴 Stop on Patriarca Dom José 90.]*

2.5 km **Atalaia** •*CR* **Casa do Patriarca** *x6* €40-60 ✆ 249 710 581 *Dª Luisa Oliveira* *www.casadopatriarca.com* rua Patriarca Dom José 134. Welcoming manor house (see photo>) directly on the camino. Continue up to the 16thc Parish church ***Igreja Matriz*** [**0.2** km] (National monument) with fine Manueline porch. We now head down towards the N-110 and turn right> onto track [**0.6** km] imm. *after* the sign for leaving Atalaia opp. industrial building.

[!] *Vigilance is needed through this section (to Grou) as clear-felling of trees in the area has removed some waymarks so look carefully for signs on pylons and rocks.* Keep to the main track through woodland up to a central clearing and intersection of forest tracks [**1.0** km] *(pylon right).* Keep s/o to open ground under pylons and veer right to track that takes a wide curve to pass derelict buildings *ruinas* (left) just before the bridge *ponte* [**0.6** km] over the A-23 motorway 'hidden' in a cutting in the landscape at this point (see photo below).

2.4 km **Ponte A-23** cross the bridge and turn <left back above the A-23 before turning up sharp right> [**0.3** km] [!] (narrow path through woodland, easily missed) onto a steep path up through the woodland to a clearing where overhead cables cross and several indistinct paths branch off. Take the main central path s/o to next intersection and turn <left [**1.3** km] and imm. right> down into the valley ahead (see 2nd photo opp) and at the bottom turn <left and imm. right> by *Resitejo* (waste management) over river-bed [**1.2** km] and up past quinta where the forest track yields finally to asphalt in Grou [**1.3** km]

4.1 km **Grou** views towards Tomar [ ]. Keep s/o along asphalt road past modern church (right) down the valley with [ ] and albergue up past *Terraça* with terrace overlooking church ruins – monument to the last battle of the civil war fought in the town in 1834. top of town and centre of **Asseiceira.**

2.0 km **Asseiceira** *Moço* & . ●*Alb.* **D.Dinis** *Mun.[5÷1]* €10 Junta ✆ 249 381 426 former schoolhouse (on way into town.) Continue s/o down to **N-110** [**0.9** km] turn right> along N-110 into **Guerreira** [**1.1** km] *Flor da Guerreira* ❖***Detour: Santa Cita*** *(+ 0.9 km)* ●●●● •*P*** ***Santa Cita*** ✆ 964 682 805 Largo Igreja. Continue by main road over *Ribeira da Bezelga* to **roundabout** [**1.4** km]:

3.4 km **Rotunda A-23 / IC-3 / N-110** [!] [❖ *Detour + 1.1 km right to* ***Quinta do Falcão*** ●●● •*P*** ***Ninho do Falcão*** €35+ ✆ 249 380 070 Estrada do Castelo Bode, 24. ***Focus*** [!] We now head *under* the flyover (new bypass around Tomar) following signs to Zona Industrial / Leiria *around* the next roundabout and *over* rail bridge [**0.4** km] and imm. turn down right> [!] onto path alongside railway keeping s/o at level crossing and up onto asphalt road [**2.0** km] (rua Casal Marmelo) to top of rise passing opp. [ ] *S.João* to T-Junction and option [**1.5** km].

3.9 km **Cruce/Opción** *[For the original road route turn down right> over railway to the main road at Tomarpeças. Turn <left along N-110 into São Lourenço to rejoin route below].* A new route <left now avoids some of the busy N-110. Turn <left

at T-junction & right> in **Cabeças** [**0.7** km] up into **Alto do Piolhino** [**0.9** km] down *under* rail into rua S. Lourenço and **N-110** [**0.7** km].

2.3 km **S. Lourenço** 🍴 *S. Lourenço. The chapel XVI*[th] *opp. was built in the manueline style to commemorate the spot where, in 1385, the troops of D. João I joined with those of D. Nuno Álvares Pereira prior to the battle of Aljubarrota resulting in the defeat of the Spanish and establishing the independence of Portugal under Dom João I. This decisive victory led to the construction of the monastery of Santa Maria da Vitória na Batalha (battle) now a UNESCO World Heritage Site where the king along with his English born wife, Philippa of Lancaster lie buried. The blue and while tiles depict this famous meeting. Behind the chapel is a memorial column O Padrao de D. João II.*

We now follow the busy **N-110** [**!**] alongside the river Nabão into Tomar suburbs to rail station. Inexplicably the route is now 'officially' and poorly waymarked (left) *under* the rail tunnel to take a circuitous route around the town past the rail and bus stations (right) and s/o past Museo Fósforos and adj. Igreja Francisco de Assis. Pass ☕ *Pica Pau* into narrow streets s/o over main road with 🍴 *Infanta* (right) into pedestrian rua Infanta all the way into the beautiful and lively main square **Praça da República** [**0.5** km] with statue of the founder of Tomar and Grand Master of the Knights Templar Dom Pais who takes centre stage and overlooks the beautiful Manueline church of S. João Baptista. The camino continues down the pedestrian street rua Serpa Pinto (Corredoura) to the 'old bridge' over the río Nabão ***Ponte Velha*** [**0.4** km].

2.4 km **Tomar** ***Ponte Velha*** *Praceta de Olivença.* Next stage s/o over bridge.

The original route is still waymarked and offers a more direct access. Continue up the commercial rua António Joaquim de Araújo past access to bus station and *Hs. Trovador* (left) to **roundabout** [**1.5** km] [🚰]. *[Keep s/o to go direct to Ponte Velha]* or turn <left into Av. Dr. Cândido Madureira by Taxi rank and turn right> by 106, Tomar, Portugal into Tv. do Arco. Continue s/o to the old bridge *Ponte Velha* or: Turn <left into Av. Dr. Candido Madureira and right> by 🍴 *Infanta* into rua Infanta to access the old town *cidade velha* and *Praça da República.*

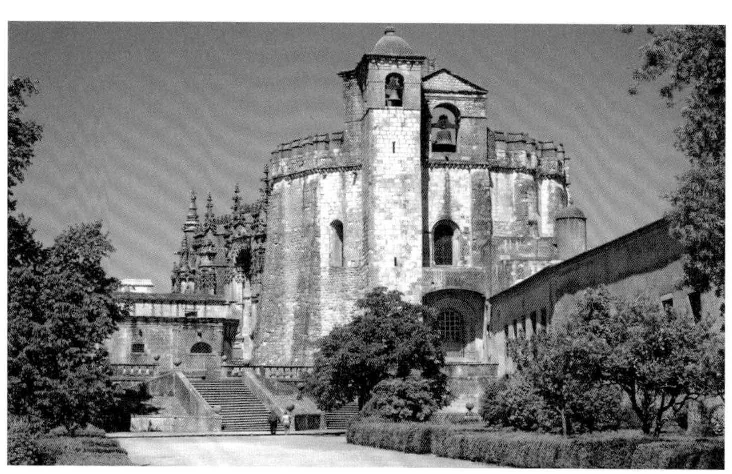

***Convento do Cristo** (above) **Quinta da Cardiga** (below)*

Personal Reflections:

Tomar is *the* quintessential medieval pilgrim town and the most perfect example of Templar layout and architecture to survive to this day. The main sites of historic interest are shown on the town plan opposite numbered ❶ – ❻. The Templar castle (picture previous page), Convent of Christ and the incomparable *Charola* occupy a commanding location overlooking the town and have been declared a World Heritage Site. Successive Grand Masters including King Henry 'The Navigator' helped to plan the Great Discoveries from here. Gualdim Pais, founder of Tomar is buried in the Templar Mother church on the far side of the river. This historic town has a population of 21,000 and excellent facilities with a good range of accommodation in all price brackets. ❶ An information board is located opp. the old bridge *Ponte Velha* at the start of the main pedestrian street – rua Serpa Pinto (locally referred to as Corredoura) and is a good place to start a tour of the town. Consider spending a rest day here to explore its Templar past and to soak up the peaceful atmosphere that pervades the old town. ❶ ***Turismo Regional*** 09:30-18:00 ✆ 249 329 800 Av. Dr. Cândido Madureira 531.

● **Lodging** *(sequentially from entrance)* ❶ *Hs* **Avenida** *x7* €15-€35 ✆ 960 077 991 Av. Dom Nuno Álvares Pereira, 41 (adj. Galp). ❷ *H*** **Trovador** *x30* €35-40 ✆ 249 322 567 r/10 de Agosto, 22 (adj. bus station). ❸ *P* **Thomar Story** *x12* €45-55 ✆ 925 936 273 r/João Carlos Everard 53 (by river). ***Central:*** ❹ *H***** **Republica** *x19* €125+ ✆ 249 193 400 *www.hotelrepublica.pt* Praça da República 41. ❺ *H**** **Casa dos Ofícios** *x16* €80+ ✆124 9247 360 *www.casadosoficioshotel.pt* r/Silva Magalhães N.º 71. ***Rua Serpa Pinto @Nº144*** ❻ *P** **Luz** *x10* €18-25 ✆ 249 312 317 *www.residencialluz.com* ***@Nº94*** ❼ *P** **União** *x26* €30-40 ✆ 249 323 161.***@Nº43*** albergue run by Sónia Pais ★❽*Alb.***Thomar 2300** *Priv.[32÷5]* €22 incl. *+4* €25-€35 ✆ 249 324 256 *www.hostel2300thomar.com* ***@Nº144*** ❾ *H*** **Cavaleiros de Cristo** *x16* €25-40 ✆ 249 321 067 rua Alexandre Herculano,7. ❿ *Hs* **Sinagoga** €30 ✆ 249 323 083 rua Gil Avo,31. ⓫ *P* **Luanda** *x14* €30-40 ✆ 249 323 200 *www.residencialuanda.com* Av. Marques de Tomar, 15, above *Rst.* on river. – opp. ***Far side of rio Nabão:*** ⓬ **Estalagem de Santa Iria** *x14* €35-40 ✆ 249 313 326 Parque do Mouchão (rio Nabão). Also on the river (further out of town) ⓭*H**** **dos Templarios** *x177* €103+ ✆ 249 310 100 *www.hoteldostemplarios.com* Largo Cândido dos Reis. **Over river:** ⓮ *H**** **Thomar Boutique** €55-65 ✆ 249 323 210 *www.thomarboutiquehotel.com* r/Santa Iria 14. ⓯ *H*** **Kamanga** *x15* €35-€45 ✆ 249 311 555 *www.hotelkamanga.com* r/Major Ferreira Amaral, 16 near **Bombeiros.**
● **Restaurantes:** Popular 🍴 Taverna Antiqua adj. Praça da República. 🍴 Beira Rio adj. río Nabão. 🍴 Brasinha r/dos Arcos 5 adj. Splash *lavanderia automatica.*

Town Centre & Templar castle *above*

Convento de Cristo *Chapter window*

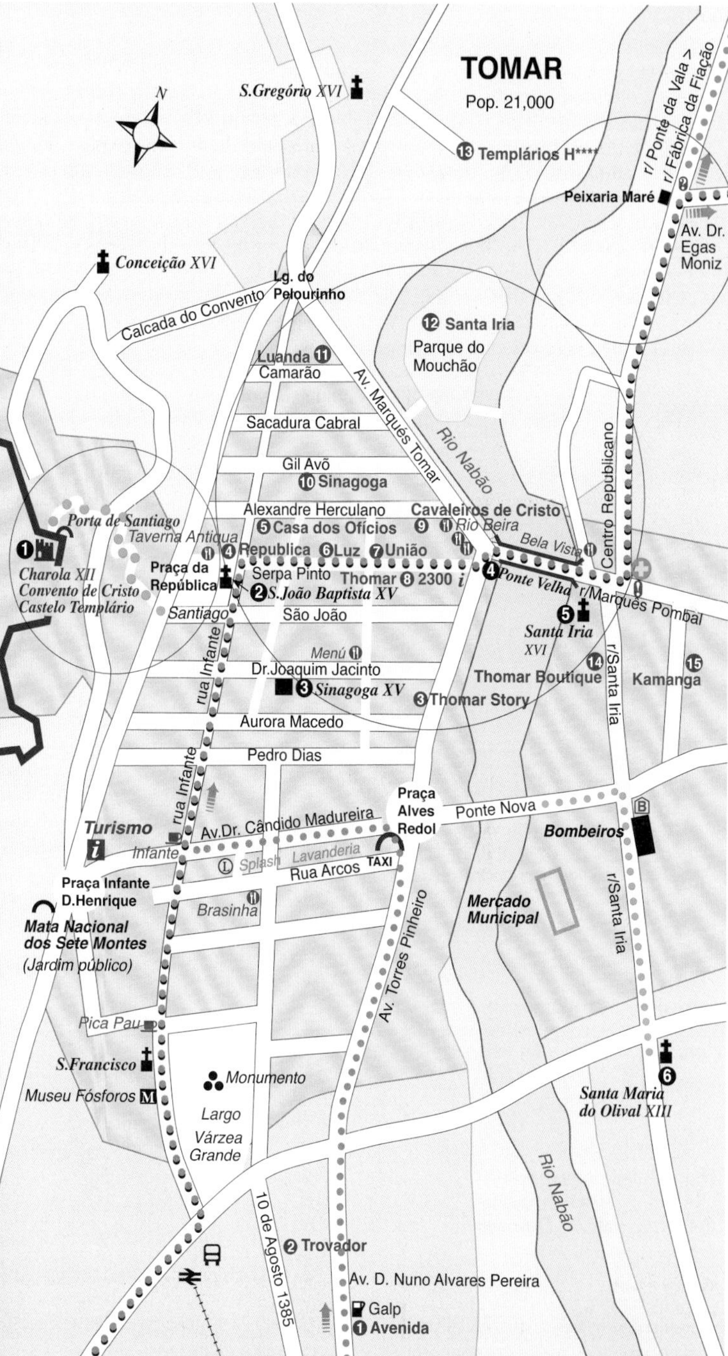

TOMAR
Pop. 21,000
N
S.Gregório XVI
13 Templários H****
r/ Ponte da Vala >
r/ Fábrica da Fiação
Peixaria Maré
Av. Dr. Egas Moniz
Conceição XVI
Lg. do Pelourinho
Calcada do Convento
12 Santa Iria
Parque do Mouchão
Luanda 11
Camarão
Av. Marquês Tomar
Rio Nabão
Sacadura Cabral
Gil Avô
10 Sinagoga
Centro Republicano
Alexandre Herculano
Cavaleiros de Cristo
Porta de Santiago
Taverna Antiqua
5 Casa dos Ofícios
9
Rio Beira
Bela Vista
1
Charola XII
Convento de Cristo
Castelo Templário
Praça da República
4 Republica
6 Luz
7 União
Serpa Pinto
Thomar 8 2300
4 Ponte Velha
r/Marquês Pombal
2 S.João Baptista XV
Santiago
São João
5
Santa Iria XVI
r/Santa Iria
Menú
14
15
Dr.Joaquim Jacinto
Thomar Boutique
Kamanga
rua Infante
3 Sinagoga XV
3 Thomar Story
Aurora Macedo
Pedro Dias
rua Infante
Praça Alves Redol
Ponte Nova
Turismo
Av.Dr. Cândido Madureira
Bombeiros
Infante
Splash
Lavanderia
TAXI
Rua Arcos
Praça Infante D.Henrique
Brasinha
Av. Torres Pinheiro
Mercado Municipal
r/Santa Iria
Mata Nacional dos Sete Montes
(Jardim público)
Pica Pau
S.Francisco
6
Monumento
Santa Maria do Olival XIII
Museu Fósforos
Largo Várzea Grande
Rio Nabão
10 de Agosto 1385
2 Trovador
Av. D. Nuno Alvares Pereira
Galp
1 Avenida

Tomar was founded in the 12th c by Gualdim Pais, first Grand Master of the Knights Templar, who established Tomar as the headquarters of the Order in Portugal. A statue of Pais takes centre stage in the beautiful *Praça do República* at the top end of the main pedestrian street where we also find the impressive ❷ ***São João Baptista*** built in the Manueline style with octagonal bell tower, opposite is the graceful 17th c town hall and rising above it all is the incomparable beauty and mystery of the Convent of the Knights Templar (transferred to the Knights of the Order of Christ in 1344) ❶ ***Convento de Cristo*** which forms the backdrop of the whole town. It is a pleasant 15-minute walk but allow a few hours to explore its dramatic buildings and beautifully maintained gardens. The entire complex forms the cradle of the Templar Order in Portugal and was inscribed by UNESCO as a World Heritage site *Patrimônio Mundial* in 1983.

Convento do Cristo – Charola

Gualdim Pais was a crusader knight who returned from the Holy Land to supervise the building of the fortress and the *Convento de Cristo* with its fascinating chapel *Charola* based on the octagonal shape of the Temple Mount in Jerusalem (alluding to the wisdom within Solomon's Temple). This became a hallmark of the Order whose roots were directly connected to the Temple where the original knights were based and from which grew its phenomenal power base and esoteric traditions. The chapel's double octagonal form gives the impression of a round building – indeed it was known as the Rotunda. Its richly embellished interior is full of mystery and occult symbols and the layout was reputedly designed to allow the knights to attend mass on horseback. The high altar and surrounding alcoves were subsequently decorated with monumental paintings and murals (a major restoration program of the Charola area commenced in 2008 and is ongoing).

When the Templar Order was outlawed by king Philip of France and suppressed by the papacy in 1312 the surviving knights fled to Portugal where Dom Dinis gave them sanctuary. In a stroke of genius he re-branded the knights under the title *the Order of Christ* redesigning the famous insignia by placing the red cross on a white band, symbolizing that the old order was now 'purified' which satisfied the Vatican and the vast Templar property including the Tomar headquarters now passed to the new order under the patronage of the Portuguese throne. Prince Henry 'the Navigator' became Grand Master between 1417 and 1460 and established his court here. Dom Manuel succeeded as Grand Master in 1492 before becoming King. Columbus, Vasco da Gama and other 'discoverers' were almost certainly received in these buildings as Dom Manuel and the Order became intricately involved in the financing and planning of the expeditions to the 'New World'. João III succeeded to the throne in 1521 and under his stewardship the Order became more religiously orientated and its hitherto political power base began to wane as it became more identified with monastic discipline. The Great Cloister adjoining the chapter house was commenced at this time marking the arrival of the Renaissance classical style in Portugal. The 7 interconnecting courtyards and extensive halls and dormitories which welcomed pilgrims en route to Santiago give some impression of the grand scale of the complex and the beauty and diversity of its architectural forms with examples of Romanesque, Mozarabic, Manueline and Portuguese Renaissance periods. Of particular note is the exquisite Chapter Window (see photo p.64) with its intricate sculptured maritime elements and topped by the cross of the Order.

The complex was allegedly connected by secret tunnels to the town below and to the Templar mother church St. Mary of the Groves ❻ ***Santa Maria dos Olivais.*** A drinking well to the right of the church was reputedly disguised as an aerating shaft as the tunnel itself was kept sealed. The church was the resting place of over 20 Templar knights and several Grand Masters including that of the town's founding father Gualdim Pais. In one of the many atrocities perpetrated against the Order the bodies were disinterred but fear of a political backlash convinced the Establishment to re-inter the body of Pais. In a further act of cultural sacrilege a new bypass was recently constructed through this ancient historical site – the modern power base may have shifted to the motoring lobby but the custodianship of the church and its mysteries still resides in the care of António who may provide a rich source of information. The simple layout of the church contains many hidden symbols of the Order.

Tomar has other sites to enthral the visitor and these include the 16thc chapel to the patron saint of Tomar ❺ ***Capela de Santa Iria*** which adjoins the lovely stone bridge over the river Nabão ❹ ***Ponte Velha.*** Near Praça República is the well-preserved ❸ ***Sinagoga e Museo Luso-Hebraico Abraham Zacuto*** in rua Joaquim Jacinto, 73. 15thc synagogue named after the astronomer who reputedly made the navigational equipment for Vasco da Gama's explorations. The town also hosts the famous Festival of the Trays ***Festa dos Tabuleiros*** with obscure origins dating back to the 16thc and generally considered to be related to the cult of the Holy Spirit. It is held in July every 4 years in 2023/2027 (the last one attracted over 600,000 visitors). The procession of the trays consists of around four hundred young women each carrying on her head a tray with loaves of bread and crowned with a white dove – the symbol of the Holy Spirit. The headdress weighs in the region of 15 kg so young men assist in the procession by escorting each maiden *(see right hand side of tile photo for headdress>)*

● **Fátima** is easily accessible from Tomar at only 35 km. Several buses operate daily from €5 ± 1 hour see schedule at *www.rome2rio.com* Taxi €30 ± ½ hour. (brief description p. 12).

06 TOMAR – ALVAIÁZERE

▥	--- --- 15.8 --- ---	*48%*
▬	--- --- 17.4 --- ---	*52%*
■	--- --- 0.0 --- ---	*0%*
Total km	**33.2** km *(20.6 ml)*	

Total ascent **1,340**m *+2¼ hr [!]*

▲ Alto *m* Alvaiázere **330**m *(1,080 ft)*

<A H> ➲Vila Verde **19.6** km ➲Tojal **23.1** km ➲Cortiça **26.4** km.

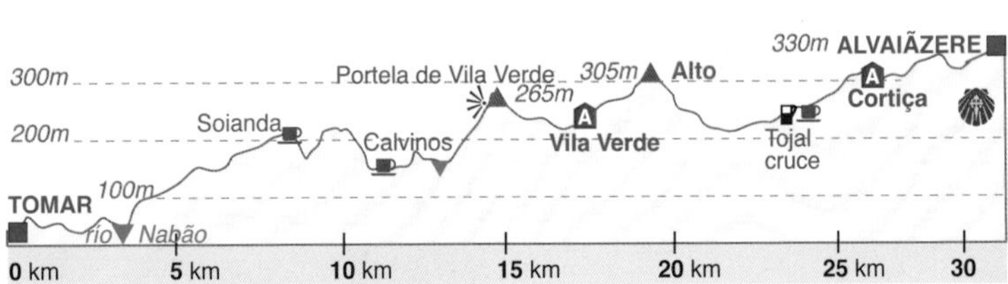

Practical Path: A day of varied terrain as we climb out of the flat plains of the Ribatejo into the central province of Beira Litoral over several hills *serras* to the high point today which is Alvaiázere itself at 305m. Several new interim hostels relieve this long stage which alternates between town pavements, earth tracks, roman roads, woodland paths and quiet country lanes. Few of the hamlets have facilities so stock up on water and some food before leaving Tomar.

Non nobis, Domine, sed nomini tuo da gloriam! *Psalm 113*

Mystical Path: *Not unto us, o Lord, but unto your name grant glory!* The words of this psalm were chosen by the Templar Knights as their Motto and serve us well today; self-glorification is a condition of our ego-orientated world and has made us blind to the Source of our true Self identity.

Personal Reflections: He was a mine of information but responded only to what was asked – humbleness exemplified. He indicated the general direction of the secret symbol but invited me to feel its power rather than observe its form. The Holy Grail is an inward understanding not a physical object. We have been looking in the wrong direction and found only emptiness in our blindness.

0.0 km **Tomar *Ponte Velha*** We leave town over río Nabão and turn <left at ***Farmácia Central*** [**0.1** km] *[original route s/o via rua Marqués de Pombal]* into rua Centro Republicano to small praça (Peixaria Maré left) and **option** [**0.4** km] ❖ ***[for recommended river route (in dry weather) keep s/o – see next page].*** For the main route turn up right into Av. Dr. Egas Moniz and veer <left at **bullring** [**0.4** km] diagonally into rua Antonio Duarte Faustino into Rua Principal da Choromela s/o at crossroads ☕ *Choromela* up steeply into rua Vincennes past military barracks (right) to high point of this stage 105m **alto** [**1.0** km] at new city heights ☕ *Cidade Nova* before finally dropping down to turn <left into rua Ponte Peniche onto wide track through olive orchards. River route joins (left) to the medieval stone bridge [**1.1** km].

3.0 km **Ponte de Peniche** Here alt. river route joins (left) to pass under the IC-9.

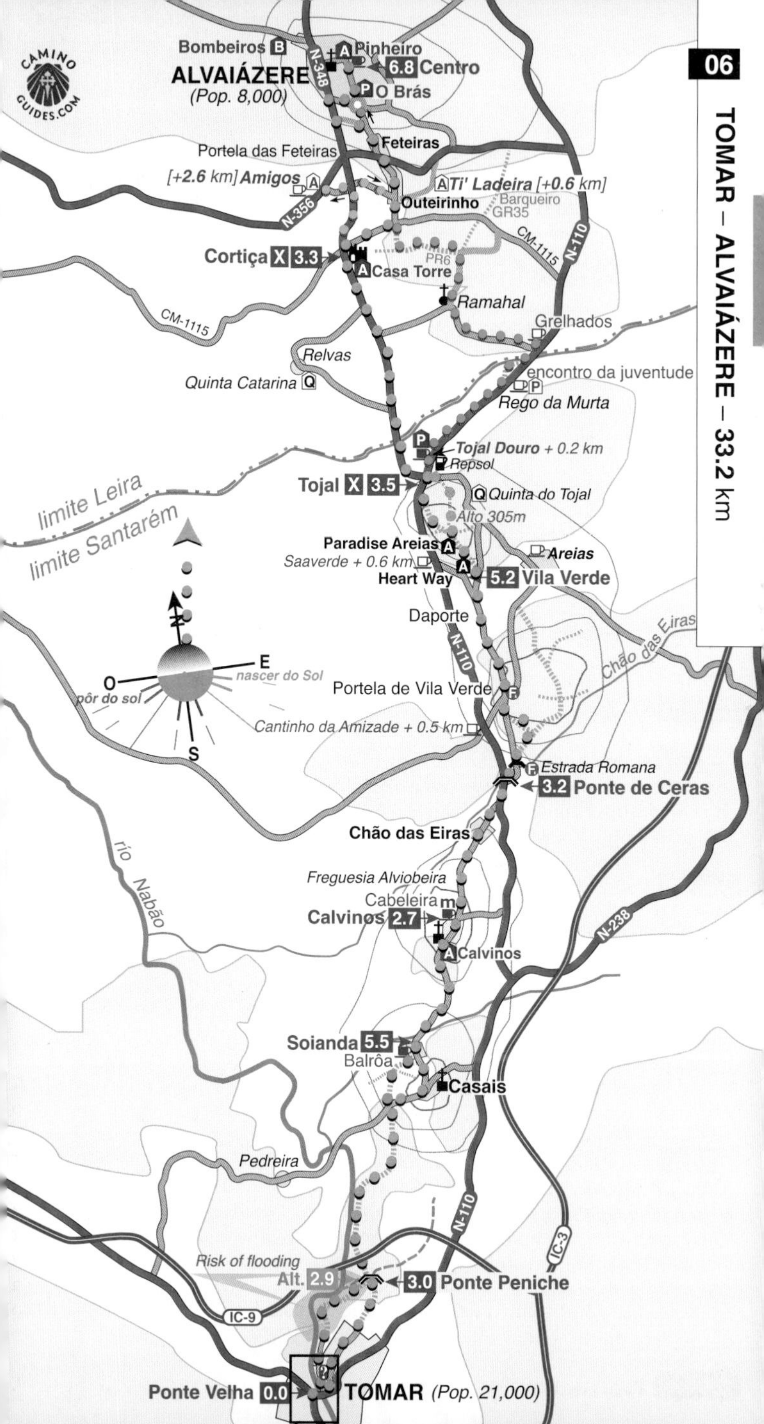
CAMINO GUIDES.COM
Bombeiros B
ALVAIÁZERE
(Pop. 8,000)
N-348
A Pinheiro
6.8 Centro
P O Brás
Feteiras
Portela das Feteiras
[+2.6 km] Amigos A
A Ti' Ladeira [+0.6 km]
N-356
Outeirinho
Barqueiro
GR35
CM-1115
N-110
Cortiça X 3.3
PR6
A Casa Torre
Ramahal
CM-1115
Grelhados
Relvas
Quinta Catarina Q
encontro da juventude
Rego da Murta
P
Tojal Douro + 0.2 km
Repsol
Tojal X 3.5
Q Quinta do Tojal
Alto 305m
limite Leira
limite Santarém
Paradise Areias A
Areias
Saaverde + 0.6 km
A
Heart Way
5.2 Vila Verde
Daporte
N-110
Chão das Eiras
N
E
O
nascer do Sol
pôr do sol
S
Portela de Vila Verde
F
Cantinho da Amizade + 0.5 km
F Estrada Romana
3.2 Ponte de Ceras
Chão das Eiras
río Nabão
Freguesia Alviobeira
Cabeleira
Calvinos 2.7
A Calvinos
N-238
Soianda 5.5
Balrôa
Casais
Pedreira
N-110
IC-3
Risk of flooding
Alt. 2.9
3.0 Ponte Peniche
IC-9
Ponte Velha 0.0
TOMAR (Pop. 21,000)

Alternative route 2.9 km -v- **3.0** km. offers a delightful riverside path in dry weather (low-lying and floods in wet weather). Keep s/o into Rua Ponte da Vala alongside disused canal and factory (left). The asphalt gives way onto a path up past *Tágusgás* depot and down to the majestic **rio Nabão** [**1.9** km] (from ponte velha). Continue alongside river passing weir and canal entrance (disused) past series of water wells to join the main route on wide earth track [**0.8** km]. Turn <left to bridge [**0.2** km] :

2.9 km **Ponte de Peniche.** Medieval bridge over tributary of río Nabão.

The route now continues on delightful earth track through pine and eucalyptus forest under the motorway **IC-9** [**0.3** km] to pick up the path again down to the rio Nabão where we turn right> along the river bank past a weir before turning up right> onto a steep path that cuts its way through the rock under power lines to take a track to the asphalt **road** [**3.1** km]. The route has been re-waymarked right> via **Casais** [currently no facilities] all by road to **Soianda** [**2.1** km]..

The original 'green' route continues s/o over road onto earth track through scrubland following old red / white GR signs. The track continues down s/o right ½ km and imm. s/o left up into woodland that winds its way back to the road in **Soianda** [**2.0** km] with popular café!

5.5 km **Soianda** *Balrôa* Continue s/o over stream into village of **Calvinos**.

2.7 km **Calvinos** ●*Alb.* **Calvinos** *Asoc.[10÷2]* €6 ✆ 927 627 647 r/Capela. *Cabeleira & (the last opportunity to buy refreshments before reaching Alvaiázere).* Turn <left (direction Chão das Eiras) to join the N-110 for a short stretch to the bridge in Ponte de Ceras.

3.2 km **Ponte de Ceras.** Do not cross the main bridge but take the side road *rua lagar do Boucha* (s/o right) to cross Ribeira do Chão das Eiras on the *Estrada Romana*. The road now turns right> uphill along rua das Azenhas before turning up [!] **sharp <left** [**0.6** km]. *[Note: the track continues s/o and winds it way into **Areias** with (albergue planned) to rejoin the main route at Tojal crossroads].* The steep track winds its way up a delightful forest path to country lane in **Portela** [**1.0** km] *de Vila Verde* [ ] with fine views of the surrounding countryside. The route maintains the high ridge and is well waymarked as it crisscrosses a maze of small country lanes through **Casal do Sobreiro** and **Daporta** to ***sign*** **Vila Verde** [**3.6** km] and short detour +300m to new albergue. *[Saavedra (on N-110)].*

5.2 km **Portela de Vila Verde** ***Areias sign***. ●*Alb.* **Heart Way** Liede ✆ 938 744 535 rua N.S da luz, 342 Areias / ●*Alb.* **Casa Paradise** Estrada das Galegas 305 - ***check if open following temporary closures***. Continue on Estrada da Porta left into rua do Casal dos Grilos and onto forest path through mixed woodland where waymarks maintain the contour to option [**1.7** km]. *[For original direct route avoiding N-110 keep s/o up past water tower (left – high point 305m) and down past specimen cork trees to Tojal crossroads [1.8 km].* For new waymarked route veer left down through grove of cork trees to chapel and join the N-110 [!] to Tojal crossroads [**1.8** km].

3.5 km **Tojal** ***cruce***. •*P.* **Tojal Douro** +200m €30 ✆ 925 374 578.

Alt. route via **Ramalhal 5.3** km -v- **4.1** km**:** Continue along busy N-110 [!] to •*CR.* ***Encontro*** [1.6 km]. Batista ✆ 913 234 298 rooms €20-35. Turn left off N-110 to *Grelhados* [0.4 km]. This route continues for [1.5 km] onto GR-35 and right at crossing [0.7 km] onto PR-6 into woodland and right over stream [0.6 km] to rejoin waymarked route at sign for Outeirinho [0.5 km].

[Note: At Tojal Carlos Pinheiro can arrange pick-up direct to Albergue Pinheiro (contact details below]. Waymarked route s/o via N-348 signposted Alvaiãzere Sul. We now have a dull stretch of road to Casa Torre at **Cortiça.**

*[**Detour Carrasqueiras 2.6** km + **1.2** km to rejoin route in Outerinho. ●Alb.* **Amigos** *Priv.[12÷1] €10 in dorm +tipi. free pick-up ✆ Paul 236 656 374 N-356 + menú & swimpool. S/o in Cortiça take second left 1.7 km onto track and left on N-356 1.0].*

3.3 km **Cruce** ***Cortiça*** ●*Alb.* **Quinta Cortiça** *Priv.[14÷2]* €20 incl. ✆ María 926 923 994 *www.quintadacortica.pt* (see photo>). Turn right at crossroads and left signposted **Outeirinho**. *[Detour 600m (right)* •*CR* **Ti' Ladeira** *x3* €25 incl. ✆ 927 493 141 *www.tiladeira.com family dinner available. Rua da Ladeira.].* S/o through **Feteiras** up into suburbs of Alvaiãzere along rua do Almagre. A new bypass has cut off the original access road into town. *[you can scramble down the bank onto the roundabout and save a long loop down to the N-348 and up again to this point!].* Official waymarks now direct down to N-348 and up again to the roundabout! Continue via the wide Rua 15 de Maio past •*P* **O Brás** *x12* €15-30 ✆ 236 655 405 [m] 966 495 337 *www.restauranteobras.pt menú* €10 into the centre:

6.8 km **Alvaiázere** ***Centro*** ★●*Alb.* **Pinheiro** *Priv.[20÷2]* €12 ✆ 236 098 343 *(free pick-up from Tojal)* [m] 915 440 196 Carlos and his family welcome pilgrims to their home on the main square and apply a pilgrim stamp with great aplomb and may issue a nip of port on arrival and Dª Irene has a useful launderette below! Several cafés and shops in the centre *Loja dos Frangos* (chicken shop! & takeaway) 200m. *Quintinha (Tita)* rua D. Sancho gets the evening sun. •**Bombeiros Voluntários** ✆ 236 650 510 may lodge pilgrims ½ km further out of town in Rua dos Bombeiros Voluntários just below the municipal gardens *jardim municipal.* The town has a population of 8,000 and the name Alvaiázere *(pron: Al-Vy-**Ah**-za)* comes from the Arabic *Al-Baiaz* 'land of the Falconer' and is linked with the Knights Templar.

07 ALVAIÁZERE – RABAÇAL

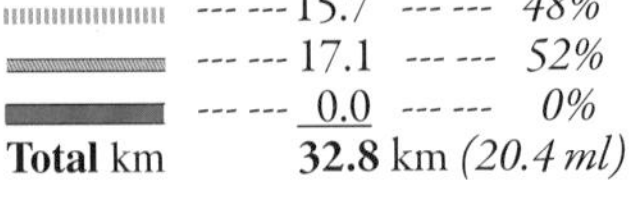

----	15.7	48%
----	17.1	52%
----	0.0	0%
Total km	**32.8** km *(20.4 ml)*	

Total ascent **1,050**m +*1¾ hr*

▲ Alto *m* Vendas **485** m *(1,590 ft)*

<Ⓐ Ⓗ> ➔Ansião **13.2** km ➔Alvorge **23.5**

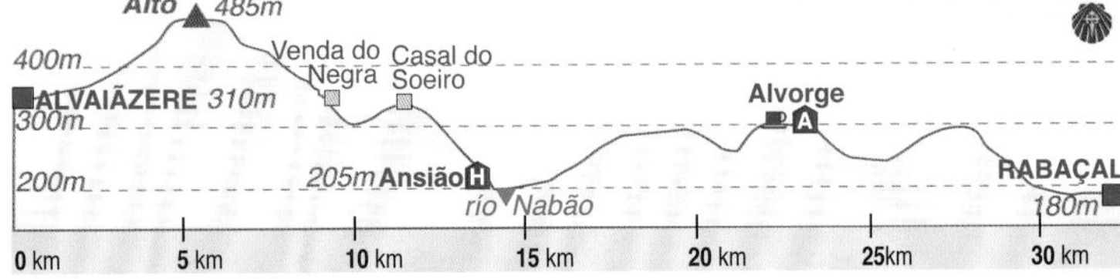

Practical Path: Another delightful day of undulating terrain through forested valleys interspersed with olive groves and small crop fields that brings us into Ansião, conveniently located around ½ way – a good place to take a midday break or possible stopover for the night. Note an alternative route to and from Fátima connects at Ansião so be careful not to follow any blue arrows.

Theirs is an endless road, a hopeless maze, who seek for goods before they seek for God. *Bernard of Clairvaux*

Mystical Path: There are many paths back to our divine origins but many that lead us in the opposite direction. We do well to remember that... *money will buy a bed but not sleep, books but not brains, food but not appetite, finery but not beauty, medicine but not health, luxury but not culture, amusement but not happiness, a crucifix but not a Saviour, a temple of religion but not heaven.*

Personal Reflections: She gave me a smile of such penetrating love that I was momentarily stilled, like one of her flock of peacefully grazing sheep and goats... And now I sit in this welcoming hostelry and eat the famous Rabaçal cheese, a mixture of local sheep and goat milk with the unique flavour of the pasture of this peaceful landscape... and the love of the shepherdess. I feel blessed and satiated.

0.0 km **Alvaiázere** From the town centre head down to the main street turning right> to main crossroads and municipal gardens where we veer up right and then <left (signposted Laranjeiras) and follow the road up into **Laranjeiras [2.5** km] shop and café (often closed) s/o up steeply into the *Serra dos Ariques* attentive for the waymarks as we twist and turn into **Vendas [1.3** km].

3.8 km **Vendas** small hamlet [✝] *S.João.* The steep climb continues to our high point of this stage at 485m. We now start the descent onto forest track (coincides with GR-26) to rejoin quiet country lane into:

3.2 km **Venda do Negra** *cruce* tranquil hamlet with small chapel (1673) and [✝] *sign Gramatinha (left).* Continue s/o over crossroads in *Venda do Negra* onto delightful path through scrubland crossing back over country lane and up

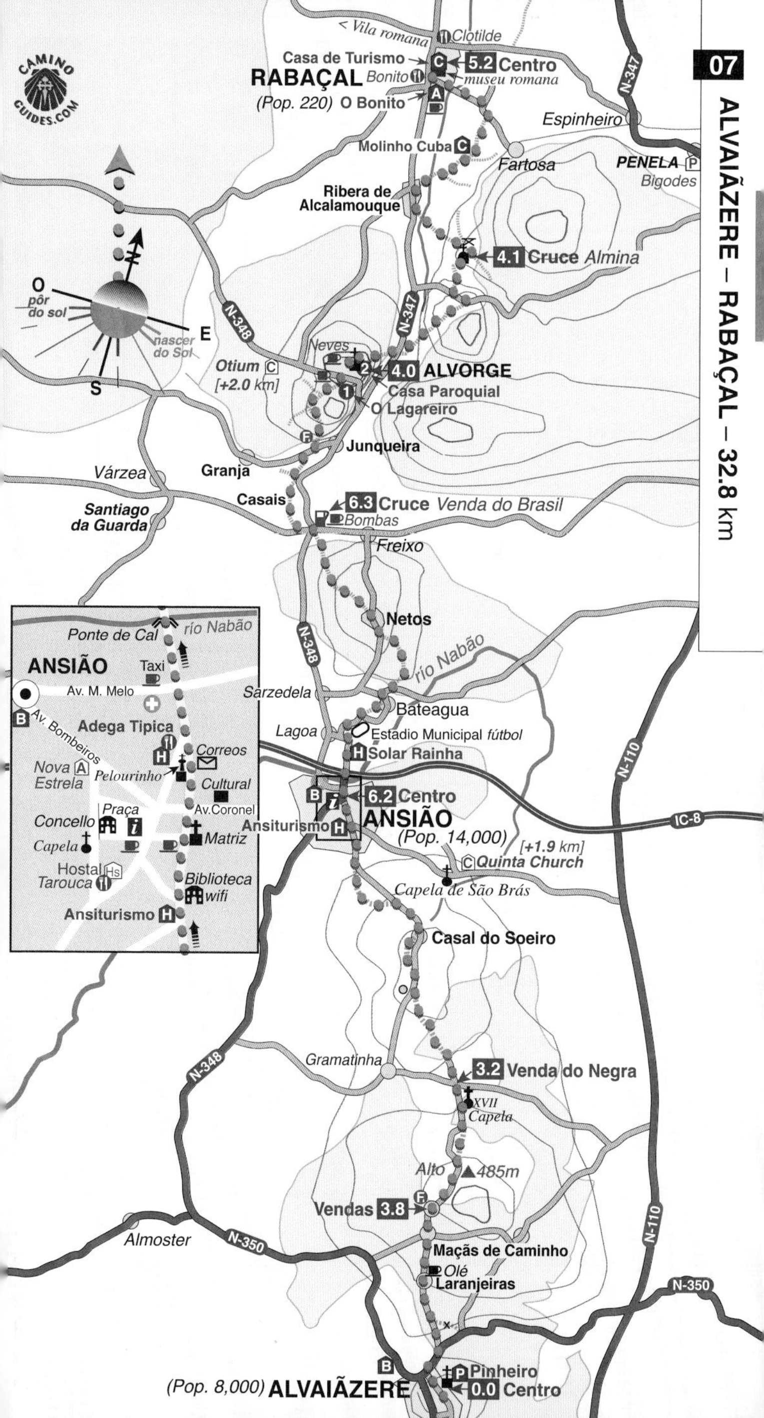
CAMINO GUIDES.COM
RABAÇAL
(Pop. 220)
Casa de Turismo
Bonito
O Bonito
< Vila romana
Clotilde
5.2 Centro
museu romana
Espinheiro
N-347
Molinho Cuba
Fartosa
PENELA
Bigodes
Ribera de Alcalamouque
4.1 Cruce Almina
O
pôr do sol
E
nascer do Sol
S
N-348
N-347
Neves
Otium
[+2.0 km]
4.0 ALVORGE
Casa Paroquial
O Lagareiro
Junqueira
Várzea
Granja
Casais
Santiago da Guarda
6.3 Cruce Venda do Brasil
Bombas
Freixo
Netos
N-348
rio Nabão
Sarzedela
Bateagua
Lagoa
Estadio Municipal fútbol
Solar Rainha
6.2 Centro
ANSIÃO
(Pop. 14,000)
Ansiturismo
[+1.9 km]
Quinta Church
IC-8
N-110
Capela de São Brás
Casal do Soeiro
Ponte de Cal
rio Nabão
ANSIÃO
Taxi
Av. M. Melo
Av. Bombeiros
Adega Tipica
Correos
Nova Estrela
Pelourinho
Cultural
Av.Coronel
Praça
Concello
Matriz
Capela
Hostal Tarouca
Biblioteca wifi
Ansiturismo
Gramatinha
3.2 Venda do Negra
XVII Capela
N-348
Alto
485m
Vendas 3.8
Almoster
N-350
Maças de Caminho
Olé
Laranjeiras
N-350
N-110
Pinheiro
0.0 Centro
(Pop. 8,000) ALVAIÃZERE

gently into **Casal do Soeiro** [**2.8** km] ***Chao de Couce / Cantinho doze*** *(no facilities)*. Continue down onto woodland track (local walks *Empeados de Cima* & wayside shrines *alminhas*) to main road [ ] (left) s/o over roundabout into the bustling market town of **Ansião** past •*H*** *spa* **Ansiturismo** *x10* €40-55 © 236 673 337 rua Jerónimo Soares Barbosa 34 pass library *biblioteca* & *Igreja matriz* (right) tourist office in main square *Praça municipal* (left) to the town centre and ***Pelourinho*** [**3.4** km] adjacent to Adega Típica.

6.2 km **Ansião** ***Centro*** population of 13,000 and source *nascente* of river Nabão. *[Ansião offers a detour route to Fátima indicated with blue arrows].* ***Lodging:*** •*P* **Adega Típica** *x8* €25-40 © 236 677 364 Carlos (speaks English) & brother João www.adegatipicadeansiao.com r/ dos Combatentes da Grande Guerra trad. Portuguese cooking opp. Concello & jurisdictional pillar *Pelourinho* (see photo>). Private •**Hostal** above tapas *Tarouca (Pedro)* top corner ***Av. Dr. Vítor Faveiro*** & at lower end •*H* **A Nova Estrela** *Sol* €20-30 © 236 677 415 [m] 918 838 605 recently renovated. Further down by main roundabout: •**Bombeiros Voluntários** © 236 670 600. On far side of river and IC-8 overpass (on way out) . •*P.* **Solar da Rainha** €25-35 © 236 676 204 r/Alto dos Pinheiras 339. *[**Detour +1.9** km off route •Cr **Quinta dos Church** €20 menú €10 © Olga (Church) 914 420 587 mod. house opp. Capela de São Brás – free pick-up]. Turismo: Praça municipal ©* 236 670 206 (summer) 10-13 & 14-18.

Leave Ansião over the 17thc bridge *Ponte da Cal* under the IC-8 up past Solar da Rainha and new sports ground *Estadio Municipal* onto short path around BateÁgua/ Além da Ponte and up steeply through woodland onto asphalt road into **Netos** [**4.2** km] *(no facilities)* turn right at the end of the village and <left onto a forest track that undulates sharply through pine forest where sap is still collected in funnel shaped receptors (see photo). The woodland is interspersed with olive groves to emerge at a crossroads in **Venda da Brasil** [**2.1** km]:

6.3 km **Venda da Brasil** ***Cruce*** major cross of 5 roads and service station with welcoming *das Bombas [**Detour 2½** km to A Santiago da Guarda with medieval Tower, fortified Palace and nearby accommodation at **Casa Vázea** © 236 679 057].* To continue to Rabaçal proceed in the direction of A Santiago and turn right> (100m) off the main road and right> again onto a short stretch of path by *Casais da Granja* to emerge on a dangerous corner of the **N-348** [!]. Proceed with caution back onto path to secondary road just before entering Junqueira on N-348. Turn left by functioning water wheel and ascend steeply through scrub to emerge by cemetery high point 310m. Continue to Alvorge crossroads main street and [ ]:

4.0 km **Alvorge** ***centro*** tranquil hilltop village ❶*Alb.***O Lagareiro** (mill) *Priv. [10÷2]* €12-17 *+1* €25-45 © 913 132 477 r/Boiças, 52 where Vítor has done a wonderful renovation. *Tira Peles* & ATM *Cruceiro menú.* *O Terreiro.* Rear of church for ❷*Alb.***Alvorge** *Par.[10÷1]* €5. also r/Padaria *& panderia Neves [**Detour +2.0** km s/o past Neves on N-348 •CR **Otium** €50+ © 914 784 547 www.otiumcountryhouse.com]. [**Note:** no facilities until Rabaçal 9.3 km].* The route continues steeply downhill on woodland path past fine rest area with picnic tables by old washing area *lavadero* in quiet olive grove. Cross the N-347 [!] onto delightful stretch of pathway that winds through open countryside to left of the conical hill on the horizon before turning down sharply left onto a secondary road for 300m to turn off right back onto path that winds it way up to T-junction with small wayside shrine *alminha*.

4.1 km **Cruce** ***Alminha*** high point 260m. Turn down left past remote picnic table back onto N-347 [!] **Ribeira de Alcalamouque** [**1.1** km] *(no facilities). [Off route + 1.5 km •CR **Vale Florido** €30+ © 236 981 716 Rua Santo Antonio].* Turn right and **turn off right** [**0.6** km] [!] **into** Rua de São Pedro *[Note: tired at the end of a long day don't miss this turn unless you want to go direct to Rabaçal by the busy N-347].* Pass windmills *CR.***Moinho do Cubo** *x1* €60 © 969 831 678 along quiet farm tracks that wind their way along the river valley to join country lane to crossroads across river to T-junction in Rabaçal [**3.5** km].

5.2 km **Rabaçal** ***Cruce*** ●*Alb.* **O Bonito** *priv.[16÷2]* €10 *x2* €25 +plunge-pool! Claudia © 916 890 599 adj. . Turn right down main street past *O Bonito* also run by the albergue and opp.•**Pousada do Rabaçal** *x10* €15 © 918 752 990 not well maintained. Part of the cultural centre & ***museo romano*** © 239 561 856 entrance €1.50 (10:00-13-00 & 14:00-18:00) *(The museum arranges tours of the Roman Villa at the far end* out *of town).* The population of 200 supports a (opp. museo) and *Cantinho de Clotilde* at lower end of town.

Residencial *(left)* **Museo** *(right)*

Grande Rota Terras de Sicó: There are 200 km of local walks in the area centred around the limestone massif *Sicó*. The limestone soil combined with the Mediterranean climate imparts a unique flavour to local agricultural products incl. honey and the renowned Rabaçal cheese. The area is also rich in Roman remains and artefacts.

*[**Detour 8** km ● ● ● ● to Penela, one of the oldest municipalities in Portugal founded by D. Afonso Henriques in 1142. A fine castle sits atop the hill* pena *and is a listed monument. Several hostals incl. • Hs Sicó In & Out* €15 Zona Industrial. •*H**** **Duecitânia** €50+ © 239 700 740].*

08 RABAÇAL – COIMBRA

	10.2	*35%*
	15.4	*53%*
	3.6	*12%*
Total km	**29.2** km *(18.1 ml)*	

Total ascent **920**m *+1½ hr*
Alto *m* Alto Santo Clara **215**m *(705 ft)*
<A H> Conímbriga **12.3** km.
*Condeixa a Nova **12.3** +1.0 km]*
Cernache **17.6** km . *Palheira **22.3** + 0.5 km]* S.Clara **28.2** km.

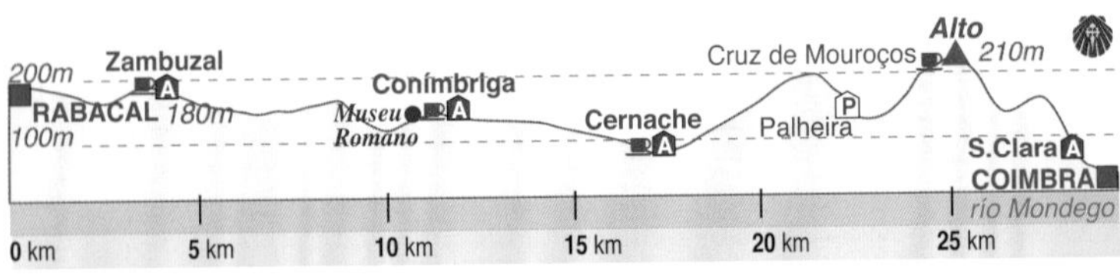

Practical Path: The terrain is gentler as we leave the *serras* behind, our highest point of the day is Alto Cruz Dos Morouços 225m overlooking Coimbra and the Mondego river valley. We follow part of the original Roman road that linked Olisipo (Lisboa) with Bracara Augusta (Braga) and pass the famous Roman ruins of Conímbriga. This first part of the day is through quiet countryside alongside the rio dos Mouros with a mixture of pine and eucalyptus woodland interspersed with vineyards and olive groves. However, the latter half of this stage ends less romantically as we navigate through the maze of roads and motorways that weave around the outskirts of Coimbra. Note *two* steep climbs at the end of this stage!

Live out of your imagination, not your history. *Steven Covey*

Mystical Path: "Healing does not mean going back to the way things were before, but rather allowing what is now to move us closer to God" *Ram Dass*. Come back to the present – arrive into now – embrace the joy of this moment – come alive.

Personal Reflections: I let my mind wander and my feet followed aimlessly, oblivious to the glorious Landscape Temple surrounding me; I might as well have been walking in my own back garden for all the benefit I was receiving or giving. As I retraced my steps I began to examine my choice – to stay dwelling on the past or focused on the wonder-filled present – the switch is simple awareness.

0.0 km **Rabaçal** From the centre proceed down the main street and turn right> [**0.3** km] (direction Panela) and <**left** [**1.2** km] onto track over stream by small bridge and merging onto asphalt into **Zambujal** [**2.3** km].

3.8 km **Zambujal** parish church & •*Alb.* **Casa das Raposas** *priv.[18÷2]* €15-20 © Sérgio Elias 965 006 277. Continue through the village and down over the river and over **road** [**0.9** km] s/o passing •*Refugio Peregrino Nicolau* who offers refreshment 'enter in peace' and tents (donativo) into **Fonte Coberta** [**1.4** km].

2.3 km **Fonte Coberta** Chapel and image of Santiago (photo above). S/o out of

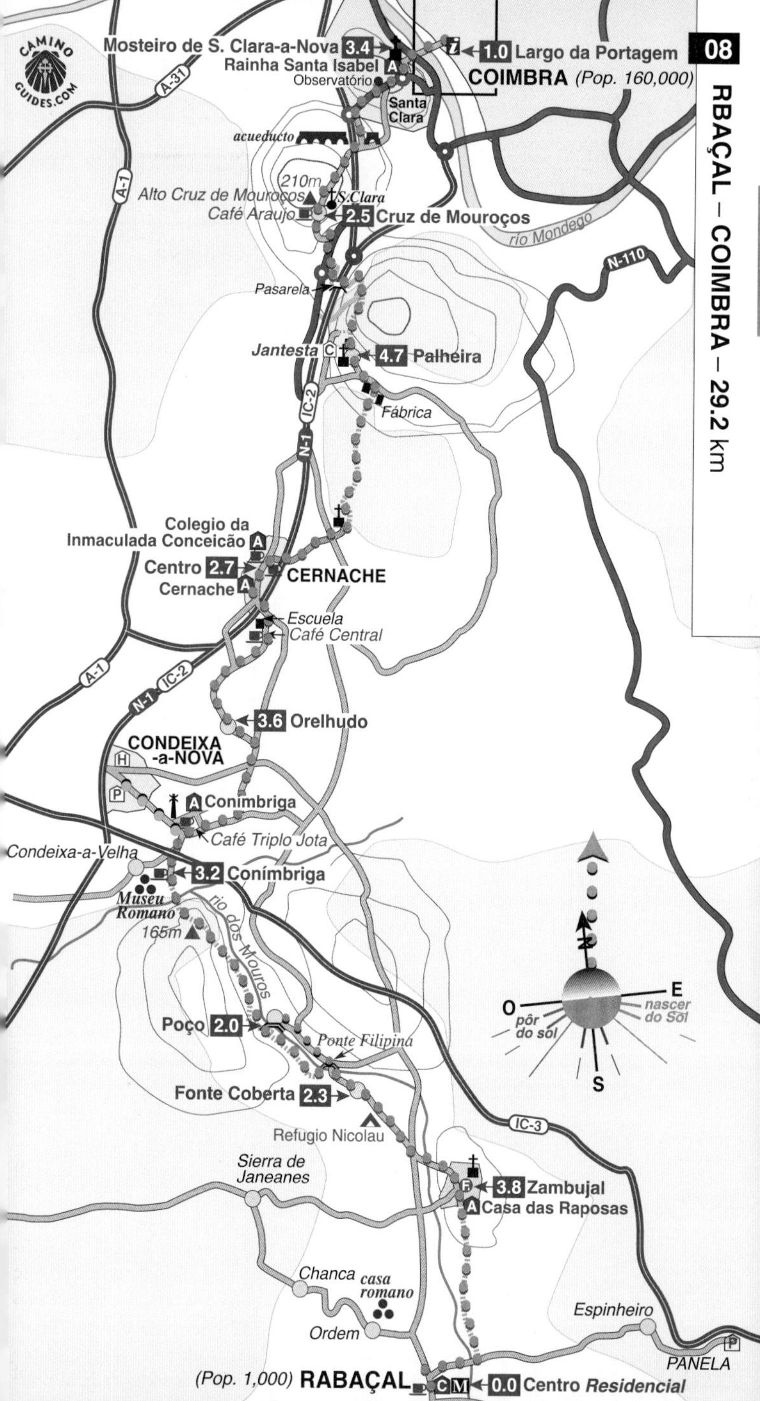

CAMINO GUIDES.COM
08
RBAÇAL – COIMBRA – 29.2 km
Mosteiro de S. Clara-a-Nova 3.4
Rainha Santa Isabel
Observatório
1.0 Largo da Portagem
COIMBRA (Pop. 160,000)
Santa Clara
acueducto
A-31
A-1
210m
Alto Cruz de Mouroços
S.Clara
Café Araujo
2.5 Cruz de Mouroços
río Mondego
N-110
Pasarela
Jantesta
4.7 Palheira
Fábrica
IC-2
N-1
Colegio da Inmaculada Conceicão
Centro 2.7
Cernache
CERNACHE
Escuela
Café Central
3.6 Orelhudo
CONDEIXA -a-NOVA
Conimbriga
Café Triplo Jota
Condeixa-a-Velha
3.2 Conímbriga
Museu Romano
165m
rio dos Mouros
Poço 2.0
Ponte Filipina
Fonte Coberta 2.3
Refugio Nicolau
IC-3
Sierra de Janeanes
3.8 Zambujal
Casa das Raposas
Chanca
casa romano
Ordem
Espinheiro
PANELA
(Pop. 1,000) RABAÇAL
0.0 Centro Residencial
N
E
O
S
nascer do Sol
pôr do sol

this historic pilgrim hamlet onto path and <left onto a delightful track just *before* the 17thc Ponte Filipina (see photo above with sign pointing to the road route). The track runs parallel to the rio dos Mouros into another tiny hamlet of Poço:

2.0 km **Poço.** We continue on a remote track alongside the river climbing gently up into woodland before dropping down more steeply to cross a tributary of the rio dos Mouros up to the historic Roman site at:

3.2 km **Conímbriga** *(Condeixa-A-Velha)* The largest and best preserved Roman settlement in Portugal and classified a National Monument. The Romans arrived here in 139 BCE under the command of general Decimus Junius Brutus who established a base on what was a Celtic settlement (*Briga* is Gaelic for 'fortified place'). Excavations have unearthed Iron Age remains going back to the 9thc BCE. The extensive ruins occupy an attractive wooded site and include a museum with ☕. We exit the ancient site via a tunnel under the modern motorway IC-3 and make our way towards the radio mast adj. ☕ *Triplo Jota*. ●*Alb.* **de Conímbriga** *priv.[8÷1]*. €12 ✆ 962 870 633 Rua da Lagoa, 15. *Directions*: Continue for 100m and turn left to next junction. Albergue in rear garden of house ahead.

Detour: ● ● ● ● ***Condeixa-A-Nova*** *1 km off route. Regional centre for hand-painted tiles.* •*H***** **do Paço** *x43* €65-79 ✆ 239 944 025 *www.conimbrigahoteldopaco.pt*. •*P* **Borges** €25 ✆ 932 824 949 Rua Dona Maria Elsa Franco Sotto Mayor Nº 65 + @ Nº 53 •**Casa de Hóspedes Ruínas** ✆ 239 941 772.

The waymarked route continues s/o along a series of intersecting secondary roads. Stay focussed so as not to miss any of the frequent turnings into and through:

3.6 km **Orelhudo.** Continue up passing ☕ [**1.5** km] and turn <left after school over the IC-2 into Cernache past Correio to the town **centre** [**1.2** km].

2.7 km **Cernache** ***Centro*** ☕ & ●*Alb.* **Cernache** *priv.[14÷3]* €8 ✆ 917 619 080 (Pedro) / 968 034 708 Rua Álvaro Anes, 37 in the centre of Cernache. At exit of town lodging available in Jesuit college •**Colégio da Imaculada Conceição** ✆ 239 940 630 (closed). Turn right> roundabout and exit under the IC-2 and s/o at crossroads up to church and start of forest track [**1.6** km] which continues for a tranquil [**2.5** km] emerging by modern factories. Turn <left on main road and cross over into **Palheira** [**0.6** km]:

4.7 km **Palheira** ***Igreja*** the route now undulates sharply up onto a woodland track to alto (210m). *[**Detour +0.5** km •CR **Jantesta** x15 €25+ ✆ 239 437 587 www.bemestar-coimbra.com Rua Da Jantesta, 35. It can be accessed directly by path off the waymarked route].* We now drop down steeply to take the pedestrian bridge *pasarela* over the IC-2 motorway up to new roundabout at Antanhol then sharp <left up again to the high point Miradouro da Cruz Dos Morouços (225m):

2.5 km **Cruz dos Mouroços** ☕ *Araujo* and •**Casa Tia Lena** *€20* ✆ *965 863 055.* From the *miradouro* on *Plaza de la Igreja* we get the first view over the Mondego river valley as we descend steeply down to the maze of roads and flyovers that bypass Coimbra 'old town'. Recent roadworks have obliterated some waymarks but the Roman **aqueduct** is our destination and clearly visible ahead. Cross bridge over the new city bypass **IC-2** [**0.8** km] which ploughs through the middle of the ancient aqueduct. Continue down to the valley floor and turn up right> at **roundabout** [**1.0** km] into rua Central da Mesura (signpost Santa Clara) and up again steeply into rua do Observatório passing observatory (left) before the second highpoint Alto de Santa Clara (210m) and modern suburb of Coimbra **roundabout** [**1.1** km] *cafés.* Continue past school and ⊕ *farmacia Duarte* as begin our sharp descent with panoramic views over Coimbra. Continue down to convent [**0.5** km].

3.4 km **Mosteiro de Santa Clara-a-Nova** ❶ An austere convent built in 1648 to replace the mediaeval Monastery of Santa Clara-a-Velha located on the nearby Mondego river which became liable to flooding. The fine altarpiece houses the tomb of the much loved Queen Isabel who was canonised in 17th century and re-interred from the old convent. Open daily church + cloisters €2. An incongruous military barracks adjoins as does the popular ☕ and ●*Alb.* **Rainha Santa Isabel** *Conv.[30÷3]* €10 ✆ 239 441 674 / Vitor [m] 911 736 610 with patio cafe ☕.

Continue down to roundabout and lower 'old' *Convento de Santa Clara-a-Velha* (right) along the river. *[Original resting place of Santa Isabel, wife of King Dom Dinis and subsequently patron saint of Coimbra. Known as 'The Peacemaker' she was daughter of King Pedro III of Aragon and was married to Dom Dinis at the age of 12 and suffered greatly under his austere rule and bouts of jealousy. She infuriated her husband by giving constantly to the needy. One of the early miracles associated with her (that would lead to her beatification) was how she hid gold coins to bring to the poor disguised in a basket and when stopped and searched by her husband the gold turned to roses thus escaping (or perhaps inflaming) his wrath. When Dom Dinis died in 1325 she distributed her remaining wealth to the poor and became a Poor Clare in the original convent. This also housed the remains of the tragic Dona Inês de Castro...*

...The life and gruesome death of Dona Inês de Castro is the subject of many an epic story and formed the subject (and title) of Victor Hugo's first play. Beautiful daughter of a Galician nobleman she caught the eye of Dom Pedro who vowed to marry her.

Pedro's father King Afonso IV fearing Spanish influence on account of the Galician connection forbade the marriage. However they married in secret but Afonso hearing of the union had her murdered in the grounds of the mournful park close by (to the right of our route) known as 'The Fountain of Tears' Fonte das Lágrimas. When Dom Pedro succeeded to the throne in 1357 he exhumed her body from the convent here and had her corpse crowned and seated on a throne in Santa Cruz de Coimbra where courtiers were forced to pay homage and obliged to kiss her decaying hand!]

We now make our way down and over the mighty river Mondego whose source is the Serra da Estrela. Cross the Ponte de Santa Clara into the welcoming square *Largo da Portagem* that marks the entrance to the city:

1.0 km **Coimbra *Largo da Portagem*** with cafés and helpful *Turismo* (right). Coimbra was capital of Portugal from 1145 until 1255 but is better known for its famous university founded in 1290 which crowns the hill and whose students bring a lively atmosphere to this ancient and historic city, formerly the Roman town of Aeminium. A population of 100,000 provides one of its main charms; its compact size which makes it easy to visit the main sites, some directly linked to the medieval camino de Santiago. Coimbra 'old town' was declared a World Heritage site in 2013. Spend a day in this enchanting city if you can for, like Tomar, there is much to do and see. The main historic and tourist sites are all grouped around the city centre and lie either directly on or within a few hundred metres of the waymarked camino. *Note: At Igreja Santiago ❷ the original route (yellow) turns left into R.Adelino Veiga. An alternative route s/o via R.Eduardo Coelho and R. Sofia is now waymarked.*

❶ ***Turismo: Largo da Portagem*** www.centerofportugal.com/destination/coimbra © 239 488 120. ▌**Hoteles & Pensões:** *(€12pp-€60)* on/adj. to the waymarked camino •*Hs* **Portagem** *x8* €15pp © 917 569 143 r/Couraça Estrela 11. •*P.* **Larbelo** © 239 829 092. adj. •*P.* **Atlantico** © 239 826 496. •*H******Astória** © 239 853 020. •*P.***Internacional** © 239 825 503. adj. •*P.***Avenida** © 239 822 156. Near cathedral *Sé* •*Hs* **Serenata** Largo Sé Velha © 239 853 130 & •*Hs* **Sé Velha** © 239 151 647 r/Norte, 11. •**Casa Pombal** © 239 835 175 r/ Flores 18. Between Igreja Santiago and the rail station •*P.* **Moderna** © 239 825 413, r/Adelino Veiga @ N°49 & •*P.* **Dómus** © 239 828 584 @N°62. There are several other hotels and Pensões in the busy streets in the area of the railway station itself. *Note* there are 3 railway stations in Coimbra, the central station 'A' Estação Nova is the one referred to here. On the far side of the university in rua Henrique Seco is a modern youth hostel ●**Juventud** *x70* €12 © 239 829 228 r/ Dr. Henriques Seco, 14 a 20 minute walk or take bus N° 46 from central station 'A'. **Bombeiros Voluntários** Av. Fernão Magalhães.

Wide variety of restaurants catering to all tastes and pockets down virtually every street which includes the popular but tiny 🍴 *Zé Manel Dos Ossos* © 239 823 790 Beco do Forno 12 (behind the Astoria). Sounding a different note but adj. to the cathedral is *fado* 🍴 *O Trovador* with its atmospheric interior of ceramic tiles and

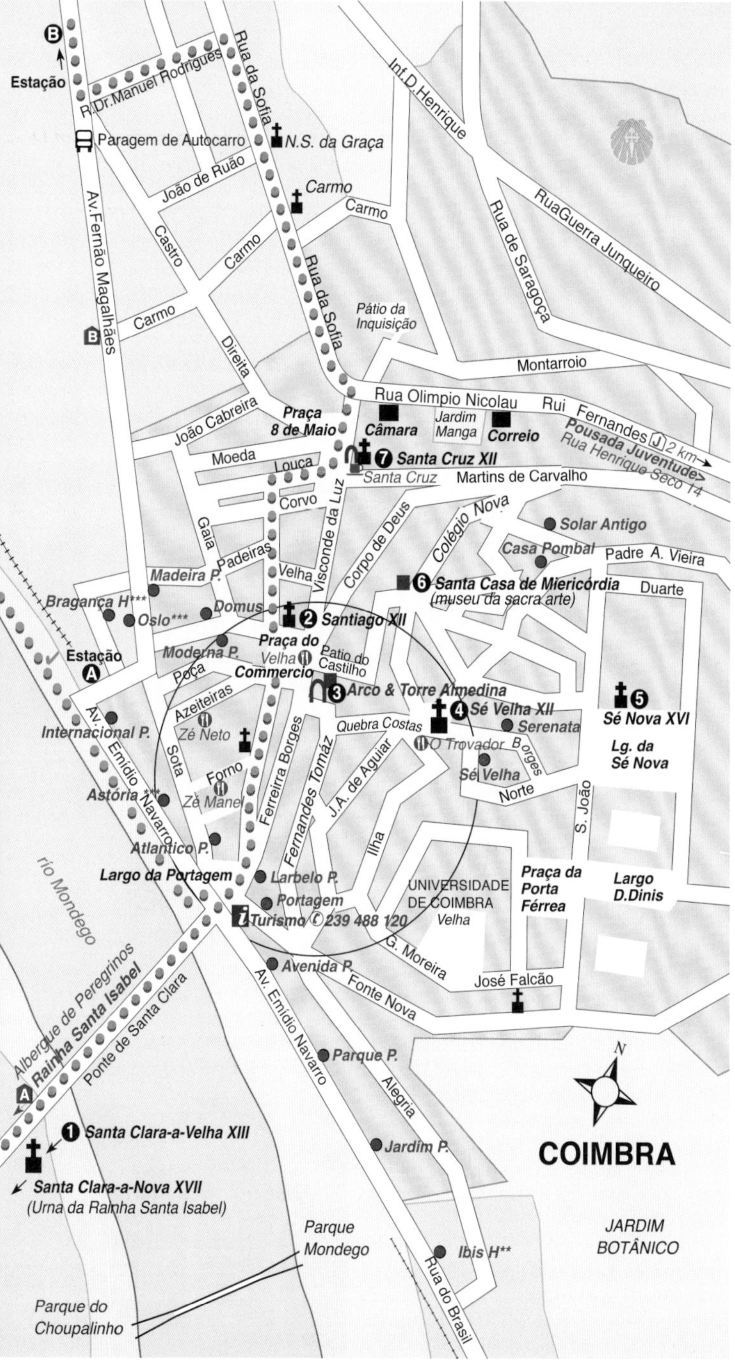

Estação
R.Dr.Manuel Rodrigues
Rua da Sofia
Paragem de Autocarro
N.S. da Graça
Inf.D.Henrique
João de Ruão
Carmo
Carmo
Av.Fernão Magalhães
Castro
Carmo
RuaGuerra Junqueiro
Rua de Saragoça
Rua da Sofia
Carmo
Pátio da Inquisição
Direita
Montarroio
Rua Olimpio Nicolau
Rui
Fernandes
2 km
Pousada Juventude
Rua Henrique Seco 14
João Cabreira
Praça 8 de Maio
Câmara
Jardim Manga
Correio
Moeda
Louça
7 Santa Cruz XII
Santa Cruz
Martins de Carvalho
Corvo
Visconde da Luz
Corpo de Deus
Colégio Nova
Solar Antigo
Gaia
Padeiras
Casa Pombal
Padre A. Vieira
Madeira P.
Velha
6 Santa Casa de Miericórdia
(museu da sacra arte)
Duarte
Bragança H***
Oslo***
Domus
2 Santiago XII
Estação
Moderna P.
Praça do Commercio
Velha
Patio do Castilho
Poça
3 Arco & Torre Almedina
Azeiteiras
4 Sé Velha XII
5 Sé Nova XVI
Av. Emídio Navarro
Internacional P.
Zé Neto
Quebra Costas
Serenata
O Trovador
Borges
Lg. da Sé Nova
Sota
Forno
Ferreirra Borges
Fernandes Tomáz
J.A. de Aguiar
Sé Velha
Norte
Astória***
Zé Manel
S. João
Atlantico P.
Ilha
rio Mondego
Largo da Portagem
Larbelo P.
UNIVERSIDADE DE COIMBRA
Velha
Praça da Porta Férrea
Largo D.Dinis
Portagem
Turismo © 239 488 120
Albergue de Peregrinos
Rainha Santa Isabel
Ponte de Santa Clara
Avenida P.
G. Moreira
Fonte Nova
José Falcão
Av. Emídio Navarro
Parque P.
Alegria
N
1 Santa Clara-a-Velha XIII
Jardim P.
COIMBRA
Santa Clara-a-Nova XVII
(Urna da Rainha Santa Isabel)
Parque Mondego
JARDIM BOTÂNICO
Ibis H**
Rua do Brasil
Parque do Choupalinho

wood panelling. Coimbra fado shares the same sombre melodies heard in the fado houses of Lisboa and Porto but supposedly with more scholarly lyrics! Just above the cathedral is the Museu Machado de Castro on Largo Dr. José Rodrigues and just above it we come to Largo da **Sé Nova** ❺ with the New Cathedral, which was founded by the Jesuits. The historic university ***universidade*** occupies the crown of the hill where the various faculties are located. The chapel and library are well worth a visit. The end of the academic year is marked with rowdy celebrations *Queima das Fitas* the 'burning of the ribbons' held in April. From here you can find your way down (or get deliciously lost) amongst the maze of narrow winding streets. Providing you head north (sun to your left if its afternoon) you will arrive back in the main shopping street.

○ **Historic Monuments:** *(see city plan)* ❶ ***Conventos Santa Clara*** on West side of the river (on the way in). From Largo da Portagem the waymarked route goes down rua dos Gatos into Adro de Cima past 18th c Igreja de São Bartolomeu and the ancient *Hospital Real* into Praça do Comercio lined with bars and restaurants and open air market to ❷ **Igreja de Santiago** (see photo>) 12th c church evoking the medieval pilgrimage. The flight of steps (right) brings us (off route) up to the main pedestrian shopping street rua Visconde da Luz. Turn left to the heart of the city in *Praça 8 de Maio* and ❼ **Igreja de Santa Cruz** (bottom photo far right). The monastery was founded in 1131 making it one of the oldest buildings still extant and housing the tombs of King Afonso Henriques and Sancho I. The Manueline 'Cloister of Silence' was added in 1517 and the triumphal arch in the 18th c. Adjoining it (right) and built on the original monastery buildings is the popular neo-Manueline café Santa Cruz with its vaulted stone interior. Also on the square is the Câmara Municipal behind which is the Jardim da Manga.

This minimal 'tour' would not be complete without a visit to the historic cathedral. Return via the pedestrian shopping street, past Santiago church and turn left up steps under ❸ **Arco de Almedina** the original main gate in the medieval defensive wall that ran for 2 km around the base of the hill. This is still the main entrance to the Old City or *High Quarter*. Continue up steeply into largo da Sé Velha where we find ❹ **Sé Velha** the old (original) cathedral before that function was transferred to the soulless Sé Nova situated further on up. One of the most important Romanesque monuments in Portugal built in 1162 on a former ecclesiastical site dating from the 9th c. Amongst the many ancient tombs is that of a former archbishop of Santiago de Compostela, D. Egas Fafes with a scallop shell emblem set in azulejos tiles. A side door provides access to a lovely Gothic cloister (see photo) the oldest extant cloisters in Portugal and well worth the minimal entry fee with proceeds going to community services. Back down towards the centre on r/Sobre Ribas: ❼ **Museu da Santa Casa da Misericórdia** XVI.

Some pilgrims choose to take the train or bus from Coimbra to Porto from here as most is by road and some along the busy N-110. However, facilities along the next stages are improving. A strenuous route from here to the *Camino Portugués Interior* via Penacova, Viseu, Vila Real and Verín is opening up to join with the Camino Sanabrés to Santiago – 500 km ±20 days. (see map back cover)

Personal Reflections

Igreja y Café de Santa Cruz

09 COIMBRA – MEALHADA

--- --- 6.6 --- --- *29%*
--- --- 13.4 --- --- *58%*
--- --- 3.1 --- --- *13%*
Total km **23.1** km *(14.4 ml)*

Total ascent **480**m+¾ *hr*
Alto *m* Santa Luzia **145**m *(475 ft)*
< > Fornos **8.5** km.

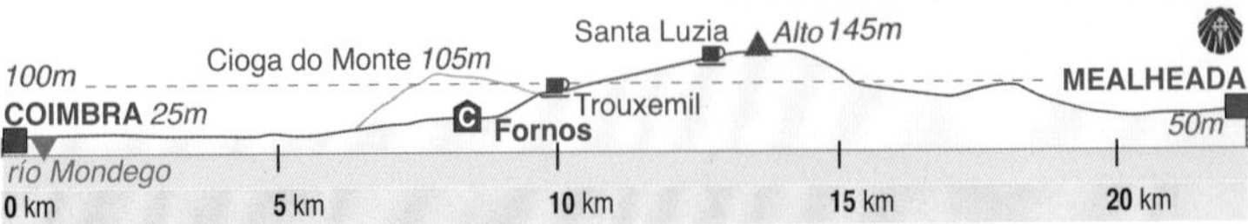

Practical Path: The terrain is now markedly different from the previous stages being virtually flat along various river valleys crisscrossed with flood and irrigation channels *acequia* (reminiscent of the Ribatejo plains). Our high point Santa Luzia at 145m. While we have short stretches of the roman road *calzada romana* much of today is spent on asphalt and there are several stretches of main roads where extra vigilance is required. A forest track has also been waymarked from Santa Luzia. Do *not* follow old waymarks along the busy N-1. A lovely 'green' route out of the city centre avoids the confusing and noisy 'official' waymarks (next page).

Bacchus hath drowned more men than Neptune. *Thomas Fuller*

Mystical Path: Between inebriety and sobriety lies a state of equilibrium; a middle path. Robbie Burns reflected thus: *"I love drinking now and then. It defecates the standing pool of thought. A man perpetually in the paroxysm and fears of inebriety is like a half-drowned wretch condemned to labour unceasingly in water; but a now-and-then tribute to Bacchus is like the cold bath – bracing and invigorating."*

Personal Reflections: It was like a battlefield, the bodies of the vanquished strewn all over the square. Some students were still comatose, others lay moaning in the cold light of dawn trying to awaken from the festivities. I picked my way out of the city and recalled my own youthful period of excess. Perhaps I am now more interested in quality rather than quantity, waking rather than sleeping. Despite the chaotic scenes around me, the light of this new day filled me with a sense of hopefulness, we will arise from our stupor.

0.0 km **Coimbra** ***Largo da Portagem*** Waymarked route via the main city sites down steps into Rua dos Gatos to Praça do Commercio *Igreja de Santiago* and Praça de Maio *Mosteiro de Santa Cruz.* Consider retracing your steps at this point to take the alternative 'green' route out along the river. Or continue out onto the busy Rua do Sofia turn <left at the Courts of Justice down Rua Dr. Manuel Rodrigues (opp. Igreja S. Pedro) to the main commercial Av. Fernão de Magalhães. Turn right> and continue out past bus station and imm. <left under the IC-2 and N-1 flyover (imm. past McDonald's 24 hour restaurant) down under rail bridge to join the alt. river route on new gravel canal to major roundabout *Rotunda.*

3.1 km **Rotunda** *(For alternative river route see next page).*

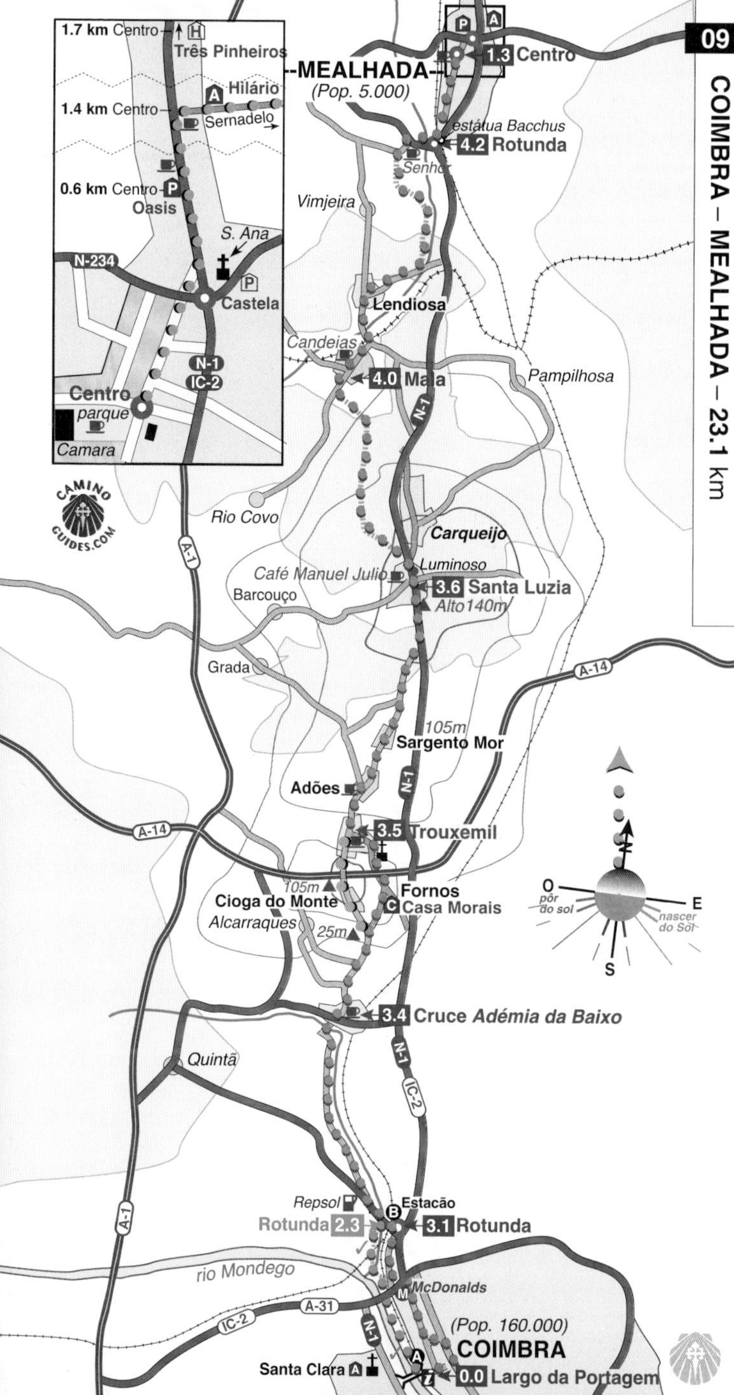
1.7 km Centro
Três Pinheiros
Hilário
1.4 km Centro
Sernadelo
0.6 km Centro
Oasis
S. Ana
N-234
Castela
N-1
IC-2
Centro
parque
Camara
MEALHADA
(Pop. 5.000)
1.3 Centro
estátua Bacchus
4.2 Rotunda
Senhor
Vimjeira
Lendiosa
Candeias
4.0 Mala
Pampilhosa
Rio Covo
Carqueijo
Café Manuel Julio
Luminoso
3.6 Santa Luzia
Alto 140m
Barcouço
Grada
A-14
105m
Sargento Mor
Adões
A-1
3.5 Trouxemil
105m
Cioga do Monte
Fornos
Casa Morais
Alcarraques
25m
3.4 Cruce Adémia da Baixo
Quintã
Repsol
Estacão
Rotunda 2.3
3.1 Rotunda
rio Mondego
McDonalds
A-31
(Pop. 160.000)
COIMBRA
Santa Clara
0.0 Largo da Portagem
O
pôr do sol
E
nascer do Sol
S
CAMINO GUIDES.COM

The 'green' route is not waymarked but follows the new (2022) pedestrian paseo along the river out under the A-31. Turn <left over pasarela to take a wide earth track along the rio Velho under rail bridge in the peaceful woodland park *Mata do Choupal (see photo next page under reflections).* We then follow the canal to the 'red & white' car park barrier visible ahead and take the road back to the join main route at roundabout.

S/o over roundabout and veer **right>** [**0.3** km] (*before* Repsol service station) onto asphalt road with the environs of Coimbra now firmly behind. Continue alongside canal parallel to rail line and turn right> **over bridge** [**2.9** km] up to main road **crossing** [**0.2** km]. Green route is not waymarked but follows the new pedestrian paseo along the river out under the A-31 and then turn <left over pasarela into the

3.4 km **Cruce** ***Adémia da Baixo*** s/o at **Trouxemil water works** [**1.4** km].

*[**Option**: for the original route turn left to Cioga do Monte (opp. Water dept.). continue up to **Cioga [0.9 km]** and on up steeply to cross over A-1 motorway and down gently to **Trouxemil [1.2 km]**: Same distance as new route].*

The new route is waymarked via **Fornos** [**0.6** km] •*CR* **Casa Morais** *x10* €50-60 ✆ 967 636 029 Rua Da Capela (formerly a medieval pilgrim inn). Up steeply by main road under the A-1 passing Manueline church (right) visited by Santa Isabel into **Trouxemil** [**1.5** km] where the original route joins from the left.

3.5 km **Trouxemil** ***Plaza*** turn up right> into **Adões** [**0.7** km] through **Sargento Mor** [**1.1** km] *café/mercado* and up gently to join the busy N-1 to traffic lights in **Santa Lúzia** [**1.8** km]:

3.6 km **Santa Lúzia** ***Luminoso*** ***Note***: a new route woodland track is now waymarked to the left of the N-1 *behind* *Manuel Julio*. Do *not* follow old waymarks along the N-1 but veer s/o left and join the **track** [**0.4** km]. The rough woodland path emerges onto a secondary **road** [**2.2** km] and we turn right> into **Mala** [**1.4** km].

4.0 km **Mala** *Candeias.* We continue over disused rail line into **Lendiosa** with chapel but no facilities. Pass sign for Vimjeira and veer right past [ ] and onto path by river through woodland to rest area with *Senhor* turn right to main road at roundabout at the entrance to Mealhada.

4.2 km **Rotunda** with god Bacchus astride a wine barrel (see photo below). Cross and turn <left over rail veering right> at Instituto da Vinho, past Correios to the town centre.

1.3 km **Mealhada** ***Centro*** town park with and shops.

Accommodation: •*P.* **José Ferreira Castela** *x5* €30 ✆ ✆ 231 202 275 basic but centrally located r/Doutor Paulo Falcão, 10 adj. church. Further out but directly on route (N-1) •*P.* **Oasis** *x16* €25-40 ✆ 231 202 081.

Mealhada: a busy town just off the A-1 and straddling the N-1 and rail line with a population of 5,000. The name derives appropriately from Meada 'meeting of the ways' and it was also a major crossroads town in Roman times being mile-post *miliário* XII on the Coimbra *Aeminium* – Porto *Cale* highway. A famous wine growing area where the municipal pamphlet takes a quote from Victor Hugo "God created water but man made wine." and urges us to "... render homage on our knees our hands in prayer, this is Bairrada wine, the divine liquid awaiting us." Praise indeed! And so that the culinary highlights of the district are not left out it leaves us with another popular saying, "God created the suckling pig, the devil the hedgehog!" Mealhada is famous for its spit roasted month-old piglet dish *Leitões*. However, our focus is, perhaps, more on accommodation possibilities and the pilgrimage ahead as we leave the centre of town.

Sernadelo *[Detour+0.6* km •*H*** **Quinta dos Três Pinheiros** x53 €40-52* © 231 202 391 www.trespinheiros.com +1.5 km but directly on route the popular ●*Alb.* **Hilário** *Priv.[20÷1] +15* €15-30 © 231 202 117 [m] 916 191 721 (Isabela) Av. da Restauração, 30 N-1 Sernadelo [1.5 km from town centre]. *Note Bombeiros Voluntários no longer receiving pilgrims.*

Personal Reflections:

10 MEALHADA – ÁGUEDA

(path)	3.1	*12%*
(road)	20.9	*82%*
(main road)	1.4	*6%*
Total km	**25.4** km *(15.8 ml)*	

Total ascent **160**m +¼ *hr*

▲ Alto *m* Anadia **85**m *(279 ft)*

<A H> ➲Sernadelo **1.5** km. ➲Anadia 7.7 ➲*Famalicão* ***9.1 km + 1.1***

100m MEALHEADA – Aguim – Anadia ▲85m – Avelãs – Aguada de Baixo – ÁGUEDA – rio Águeda
0 – 5 km – 10 km – 15 km – 20 km – 25

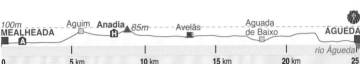

Practical Path: Another fairly level stage as the gently undulating terrain follows the path of the Cértima river valley, a tributary of the Vouga which we will pass on the next stage. It's also another relatively short stage but with much asphalt to contend with as we skirt several industrial areas. Vineyards and a stretch of woodland relieve the monotony of the road network and we have the attractive town of Águeda, built around the banks of the river, to explore on our arrival.

If we are not fully in the present moment, we miss everything.
Peace Is Every Step: *The Path of Mindfulness in Everyday Life* Thich Nhat Hanh

Mystical Path: Between alertness and stupor lies a liminal space of mindlessness. Day-dreaming can be a restful if the dreams are peaceful but it is not a place from which to navigate the paths of life with authority and power. To come fully alive we need to come fully present and act from mindfulness.

Personal Reflections: I had feasted on the local speciality and fallen under the spell of Bacchus and was feeling somewhat the worse for wear. So much for my judgement and condemnation of the youthful citizens of Coimbra. Here I am the following day lost because my mind is foggy from an excess of wine the previous night and I missed a key waymark. Mindfulness is the way of the pilgrim.

0.0 km **Mealheada** ***Centro*** from the town centre we make our way back to the N-1 passing *Residencial Oasis* and turn right> by *Espelho d'Agua* in the *direction* of **Sernadelo** and ●***Alb. Hilário*** [**1.5** km] veer off right> by house with modern concrete slatted windows onto path through **woodland** [**0.8** km] take left hand fork s/o into **Alpalhão** [**1.1** km].

3.4 km **Alpalhão** ***Igreja*** turn right> to **Aguim** [**1.5** km] with tiny *Capela de São Jose [**Detour 2.5 km Curia** with several hotels (thermal spa) incl. •Hs **Pharmacy** x7* €30+ ✆ 231 525 712*]*. Continue onto woodland **track** [**1.0** km] and s/o main road and roundabout *towards* Anadia past modern sports grounds *zona desporto* and continue up to next roundabout at top of the hill above **Anadia** [**1.8** km].

4.3 km **Rotunda** ***Anadia*** here we have an option to detour into the town for refreshments or stay the night: **ANADIA** •*H**** **Cabecinho** *x52* €50 ✆ 231 510 940 *www.hotel-cabecinho.com* on the roundabout (see photo top next page>).

MEALHADA – ÁGUEDA – 25.4 km

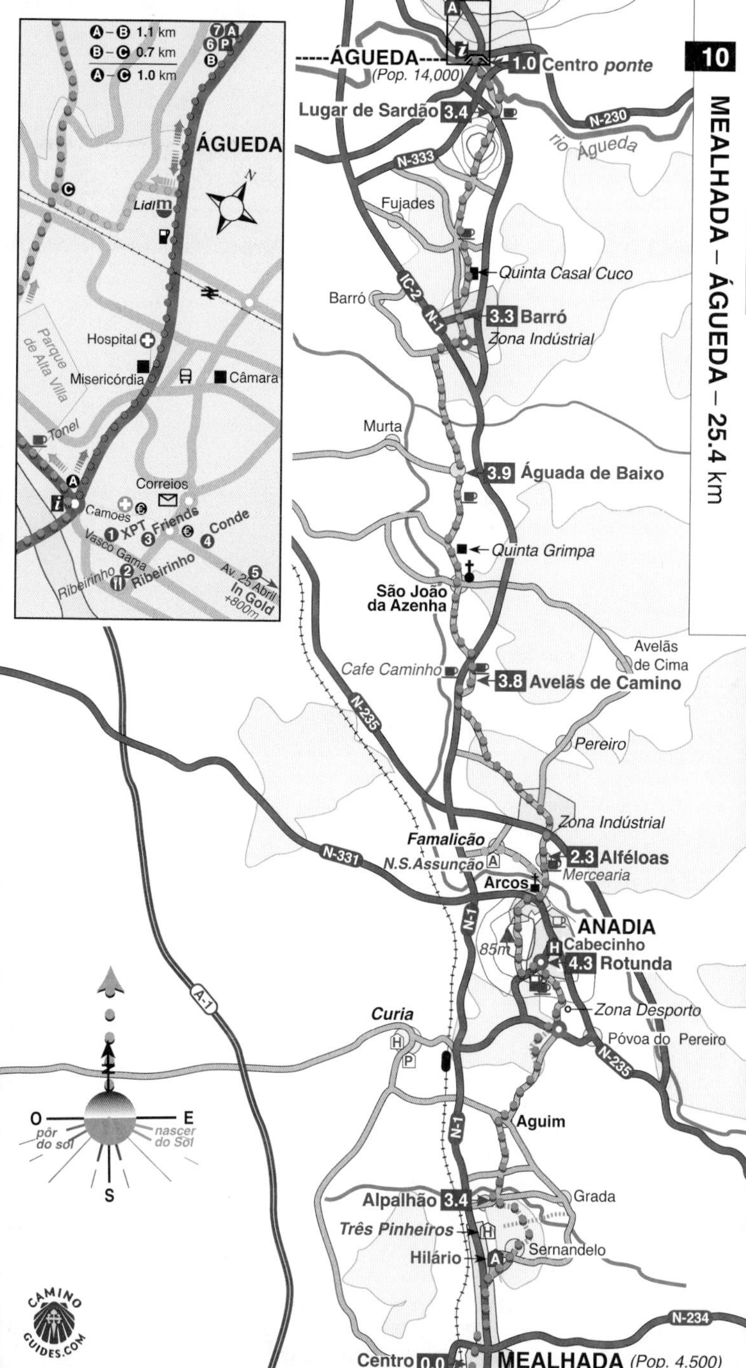

A – B 1.1 km
B – C 0.7 km
A – C 1.0 km
ÁGUEDA
Lidl
Hospital
Misericórdia
Câmara
Parque de Alta Villa
Tonel
Correios
Camoes
1 XPT
3 Friends
4 Conde
Vasco Gama
2 Ribeirinho
Ribeirinho
5 Av. 25 Abril In Gold +800m
ÁGUEDA
(Pop. 14,000)
1.0 Centro ponte
Lugar de Sardão 3.4
N-230
rio Águeda
N-333
Fujades
Quinta Casal Cuco
Barró
IC-2
N-1
3.3 Barró
Zona Indústrial
Murta
3.9 Águada de Baixo
Quinta Grimpa
São João da Azenha
Avelãs de Cima
Cafe Caminho
3.8 Avelãs de Camino
N-235
Pereiro
Zona Indústrial
Famalicão
N-331
N.S.Assunção
2.3 Alféloas
Arcos
Mercearia
ANADIA
85m
Cabecinho
4.3 Rotunda
Zona Desporto
Curia
Póvoa do Pereiro
A-1
O
E
pôr do sol
nascer do Sol
S
Aguim
Alpalhão 3.4
Grada
Três Pinheiros
Sernandelo
Hilário
N-234
Centro 0.0
MEALHADA (Pop. 4.500)
CAMINO GUIDES.COM

The waymarked route bypasses this lively market town with range of facilities. Turn <left at the roundabout past the petrol station and shops and turn up right> past the cemetery s/o up to our high point of this stage (75m) to drop steeply down passing [ ] into **Arcos** [**1.4** km] *Igreja São Paio Option* ▲▼:

*[**Detour Famalicão** ▼ **1.1** km to ●Alb. **Colegio N.S. da Assunção de Cluny** Conv. [50÷2] suelo €-donativo © 231 504 167 - **check if open before detouring**].*

▲ Main route s/o and imm. <left over river into **Alféloas** [**0.9** km]. *Mercearia*

2.3 km **Alféloas** s/o over the busy N-235 past various factories back down to the main road (traffic lights) into **Avelãs de Caminho**.

3.8 km **Avelãs de Caminho** variety of adjacent to the main road including the popular *Queiróz*. The suffix *caminho* denotes associations with the medieval camino. At the far end of the town we veer off <left by chapel into **São João da Azenha** past Bodega offices and **capela St. João** [**1.9** km] continue along the quiet country lane passing **Quinta da Grimpa** [**0.4** km] connected with the Bodega in São João and the famous Bairrada grape. The quinta's fine Manueline features were restored with stone from another site. We now head into the Município passing *Rossio* [**1.0** km] and up into the village of **Aguada de Baixo** [**0.6** km].

3.9 km **Aguada de Baixo** ***Centro*** *-pastelaría* s/o over river **bridge** [**0.6** km] turn right under the IC-2 / N-1 [**2.2** km] into the industrial area of **Barró** [**0.5** km]:

3.4 km **Barró** ***Zona Industrial*** leaving industrial area veer right> off, but parallel to the main road on the original Royal Way *Estrada Real* passing Quinta Casa dos Cucos turning up <left by and drop down steeply to cross the busy [!] N-1 at:

3.4 km **Lugar de Sardão** s/o through this ancient quarter with murals onto open ground (flood area) and through a tunnel under the by-pass and up over the old bridge *Ponte Velha* across the rio Águeda to:

1.0 km **Águeda** ***Ponte Turismo*** © 234 601 412 (summer) in the ***lower town*** on a tree-lined square. *The waymarked camino continues left along the river in the direction of A Parades.* Águeda is a lively town with a population of 14,000. The main activity is centred around the river area and main shopping street rua *Luis de Camões* with interconnecting mosaic-lined pedestrian streets off.

● **Lodging** ***Lower town:*** ❶ *P.* **XPT** *x9* €35-44 © 969 523 545 www.xpt.pt Rua Vasco da Gama, 37 and at Nº88. ❷ *P.* **O Ribeirinho** *x7* €35 © 234 623 825 + riverside ❸★*P.* **Friends** *Priv.[12÷2]* €18 incl. *x5* €40+ © 234 136 620 on Rua

José Maria Veloso, 8 and on Praça Conde de Águeda ❹ *H***** **Conde** *x30* €60-90 ✆ 236 610 390 *www.hotelcondedagueda.com* 900m further out on Rua Manuel de Sousa Carneiro ❺ *H***** **In Gold** *x60* €75+✆ 234 690 170 *www.ingoldhotel.pt* A seedy looking 'hotel' downtown may masquerade as a brothel...try the ***Bombeiros Voluntários*** de Águeda Av. 25 de Abril ✆ 234 610 100.

● **Lodging *Upper town:*** Access s/o up rua da Misericórdia veer <left at **park** [**0.3** km] *Jardim Conde Sucena* (bus station right) past Casa da Misericórdia & Hospital out past **Lidl** [**0.4** km] to **albergue** [**0.4** km]: ❻ *P.* **Celeste** *x12* €40+ ✆ 234 602 871 Rua da Misericórdia, 713 (N-1) also adjoining ★❼ *Alb.* **Sto. António** *Priv.[19÷4]* €12 (€17 incl.) pilgrim haven with kitchen, lounge and peaceful gardens (see photo).

To return to waymarked camino turn right at Lidl [**0.4** km] and left along disused railway to join waymarks [**0.3** km].

Personal Reflections:

11 ÁGUEDA – ALBERGARIA *A-VELHA*

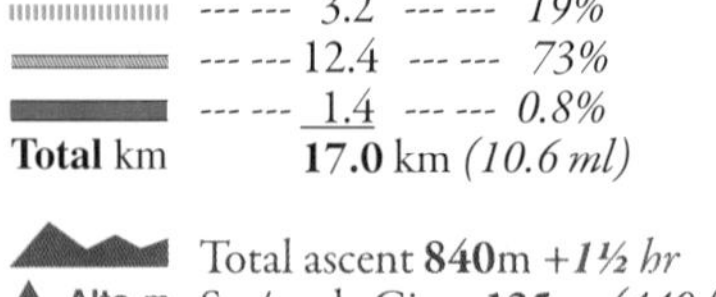

--- --- 3.2 --- --- *19%*
--- --- 12.4 --- --- *73%*
--- --- 1.4 --- --- *0.8%*
Total km **17.0** km *(10.6 ml)*

Total ascent **840**m *+1½ hr*
▲ Alto *m* Serém de Cima **135** m *(440 ft)*
<A H> *Zona Industrial* ***3.3** km* + ***0.4** km*

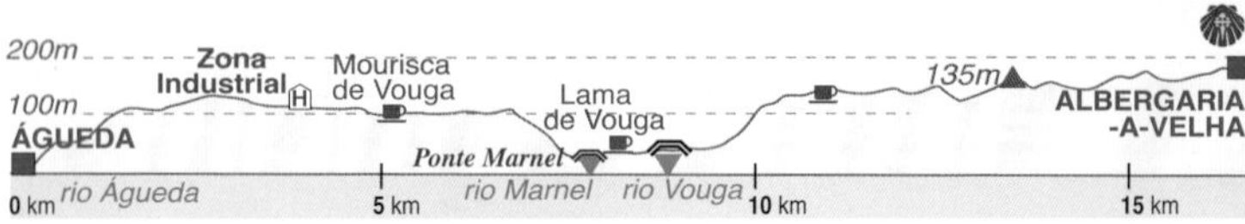

Practical Path: A short stage along reasonably flat terrain. A new albergue in Albergaria-a-Nova (23.1 km) offers a good alternative stage (see map). Again the majority is on asphalt roads relieved by a short but magical path through pine and eucalyptus woods along the original Via Romana XVI over a beautiful stone bridge across the rio Marnel – the ancient ambience and tranquillity marred only by the main road. Albergaria-A-Velha is a pleasant town with good facilities and provides an opportunity to just hang out and soak up its peaceful atmosphere.

We are all prostitutes... no matter how moral one takes oneself to be.
R. D. Laing

Mystical Path: The rape and pillage we see all around us, of our earth, our children and each other is calling for urgent change. The masculine principle is out of balance and requires the restoration of the Sacred Feminine as a crucial phase in the evolution of human consciousness. It is time for healing as we begin to embody the qualities of Love, Wisdom and Compassion – the Divine Mother, Mary, Sophia... known by different names but One and the same Source.

Personal Reflections: The goddess of love appears to have joined Bacchus god of harvest along this ancient stretch of calzada romana; Venus tempting the modern traveller with her charms. The fishnet tights looked out of place on the Roman bridge but blended easily in the modern motel. I, too, sell myself every time I try and manipulate the universe around me to meet my own needs. The liberal Coimbra students have taught me not to be too hasty in judging others.

0.0 km **Águeda** ***Ponte*** we continue out along the river via *rua 5 de Outubro* in the direction of *A Parades* and veer off right> [**0.5** km] up steeply and cross over railway [**0.6** km] *(Alt. route from Alb. S. António joins here)* s/o down steeply and up right again *rua do Portinho* through industrial estate and s/o over the **N-1** [**2.2** km] [!] ***[Detour +500****m right* *McDonalds adj.* •*P.* ***O Trindade*** *x16 €25-40 ✆ 234 645 830 adj.* •*P.* ***Castro*** *x22 €20-30 ✆ 234 644 356]*. [**3.1** km] *-Lince.* We now take the straight and narrow rua Liberdade (parallel with the N-1) into **Mourisca do Vouga** [**2.0** km] with its large mansions *Casas de Brasileiros* built by returning Portuguese who made their fortune in Brasil. Continue past ethnographic museum and shops to crossroads.

5.3 km **Mourisca do Vouga** *Bugatti.* S/o past *Mouripan* over the **N-1** traffic

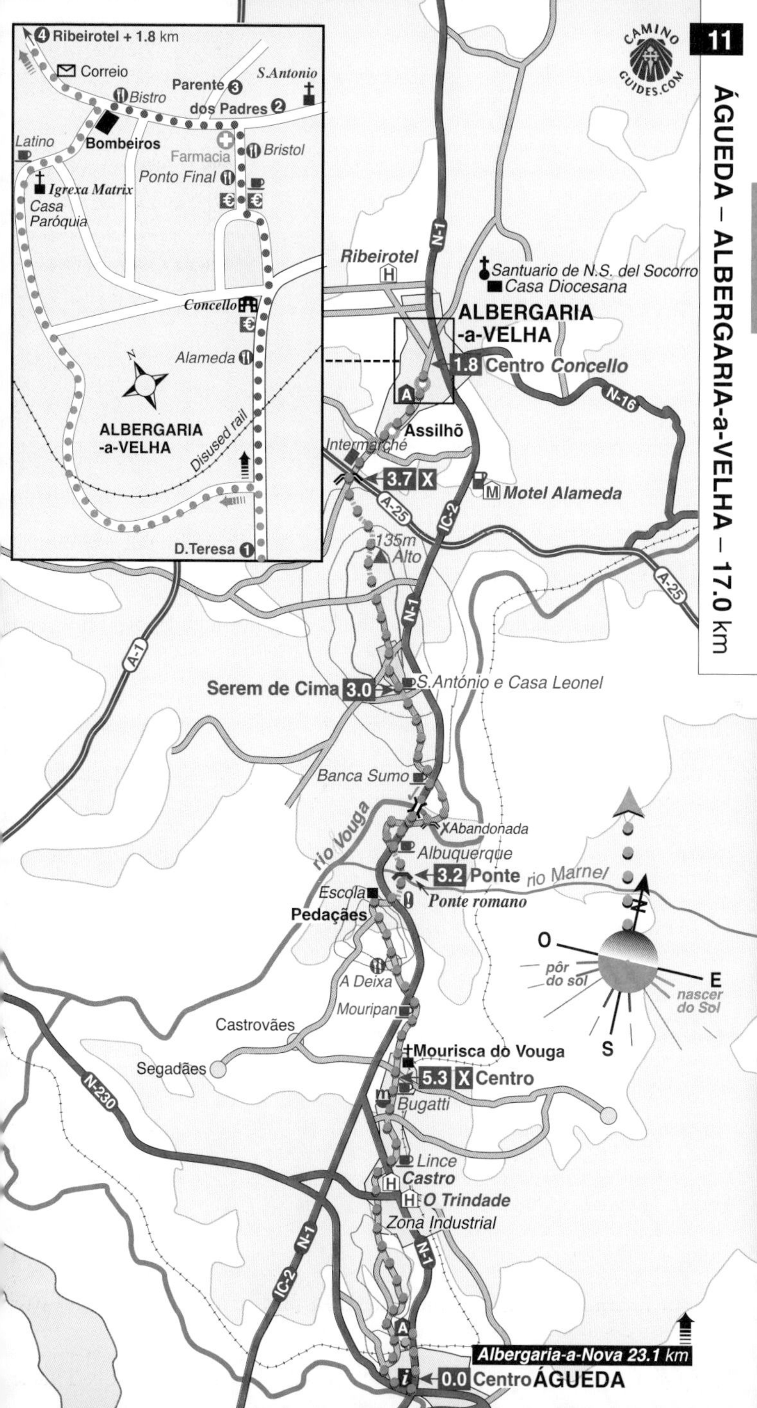
11
ÁGUEDA – ALBERGARIA-a-VELHA – 17.0 km
CAMINO GUIDES.COM
4 Ribeirotel + 1.8 km
Correio
S.Antonio
Parente 3
Bistro
dos Padres 2
Latino
Bombeiros
Farmacia
Bristol
Ponto Final
Igrexa Matrix
Casa Paróquia
Concello
Alameda
ALBERGARIA -a-VELHA
Disused rail
D.Teresa 1
Ribeirotel
Santuario de N.S. del Socorro
Casa Diocesana
ALBERGARIA -a-VELHA
1.8 Centro Concello
N-16
Assilhõ
Intermarché
3.7
Motel Alameda
A-25
IC-2
N-1
135m Alto
A-1
Serem de Cima 3.0
S.António e Casa Leonel
Banca Sumo
rio Vouga
Abandonada
Albuquerque
3.2 Ponte
rio Marnel
Escola
Ponte romano
Pedaçães
A Deixa
O
pôr do sol
E
nascer do Sol
S
Mouripan
Castrovães
Mourisca do Vouga
Segadães
N-230
5.3 Centro
Bugatti
Lince
Castro
O Trindade
Zona Industrial
Albergaria-a-Nova 23.1 km
0.0 Centro ÁGUEDA

lights into **Pedacães [1.7 km]** *A Deixa* (50m left). s/o into *rua de Espanha* and head down steeply, passing the Concelho Lamas do Vouga (school) to a dangerous bend on the **N-1** crossover [**!**] onto a delightful stretch of Roman road *rua da Ponte Romana* passing over the río Marnel on the restored medieval bridge (with Roman foundations – see photo next page) [**1.5** km]:

3.2 km **Ponte de Marnel** ***Vouga*** 2nd century and part of the original Via XVI. On the far side we enter the hamlet of **Lamas do Vouga** *Albuquerque* & [ ]. The secondary bridge over the río Vouga was badly damaged by floods so until repairs are effected we have no option but to take the curbside of the busy **N-1 / IC2**. (the original route via rua da Ponte Velha adds 400m). Keep s/o over new **bridge** [**1.1** km] (pedestrian walkway) turn off **left** [**0.5** km] by *Banca Sumo* up steeply to crossroads at **Serém de Cima** [**1.4** km].

3.0 km **Serém de Cima** *S. António* *Casa Leonel* continue along rua Central and cross over T-Junction and s/o ahead into eucalyptus forest [**1.3** km] the welcome respite from the asphalt road brings us to our high point of this stage (135m). The woodland track leads us to a bridge over the motorway [**2.4** km] and *Intermaché*.

3.7 km **Ponte A-25** *Os Mosqueteiros* down past *Sal e Pimento* and s/o at roundabout up into Largo da Misericórdia. Keep s/o along wide tree-lined avenue past and *Tianioa* (near hostel) pass *escola primaria* imm. adj. pilgrim hostel ❶ *Alb.* **Rainha D. Teresa** ✪*Asoc.[21÷3]* €8 (with bicicletas €12) ✆ 234 529 754 r/Bernardino Máximo de Albuquerque 14 managed by Via Lusitana (see photo). Continue to the roundabout with fountain.

1.8 km **Albergaria-a-Velha** ***Note:*** to access main square keep s/o at roundabout into *Plaza principal* **Concello** & *Casa da Alameda (see photo)*. The waymarked route bypasses the town centre on a path to the left of the roundabout over rail and up into town past the parish church *Igreja Matriz* adj. Casa Paroquia (floor *may* be available in high season). **Lodging:** ❷*Estalagem* **dos Padres** €45-€55 incl. Marta Duarte ✆ 930 610 380 *www.estalagemdospadres.pt* on r/Santo António, 34 well restored house in centre of town. ❸*P.* **Parente** €15 ✆ 234 521 271 r/Doutor Brito Guimarães, 11.

Outskirts ***Afueras*****:** ❹*H* **Ribeirotel** *x30* €30+ ✆ 234 524 246 *www.ribeirotel.com* Areiros, Zona industrial (½ off route). ·*Motel* **Alameda** *x20* €25-35 ✆ 234 523 402 *www.alameda-hotel.com* N-1 +***1.9*** km adj. *gasolinera* Total).

There is an appealing harmony to Albergaria-a-Velha, founded in the 12th century on the royal command of Dna. Teresa in 1120 to provide hospitality and refuge to pilgrims, a command that the townsfolk seem happy to fulfil 9 centuries later. Here is a place where old and new blend seamlessly – the façade of the historic Capelo Santo António sitting easily with the art-deco of the Cine Teatro. Whether writing your inner reflections in the shade of the alameda or availing of the free internet in the municipal library, enjoy the welcoming atmosphere. Popular restaurants incl. 🍴 *Casa Alameda* adj Concello – part of hardware store!) and 🍴 *Ponto Final* Av. Napoleão Luís Ferreira where João & Dorinda Geraldo serve meals through the day.

The popular albergue in Albegaria-a-Nova (see photo>) 6.1 km futher along the way on the N-1 offers a good alternative to those planning to stopover in São João da Madeira the following day (see next page for details). Note Albegaria-a-Nova town has limited facilities.

Personal Reflections:

Ponte de Marnel, rua da Ponte Romana

12 ALBERGARIA-*A-VELHA* – SÃO JOÃO *de MADEIRA*

▒▒▒	--- ---	5.7 --- ---	*19%*
▬▬▬	--- ---	20.9 --- ---	*69%*
███	--- ---	3.6 --- ---	*12%*
Total km		**30.2** km *(18.7 ml)*	

Total ascent **460**m +*¾ hr*

▲ Alto *m* São João da Madeira **240**m

<Ⓐ Ⓗ> ➲Albergaria-a-Nova **6.1** km ➲Outeirinho **9.4** km ➲Bemposta **12.6** ➲Oliveira de Azeméis **20.2** km

Practical Path: We start today along a lovely forest road through eucalyptus and pine but the route becomes progressively more urbanized as we approach São João da Madeira and have to cross the main road and railway several times. The terrain is now more irregular as we pass through several river valleys separated by gentle hills. Facilities along this stretch are good with several opportunities to eat and sleep along the way.

***Life is like riding a bicycle. To keep your balance you must keep moving.* Einstein**

Mystical Path: When we are out of balance we begin to wobble and fall further from our centre. We become irritable, tired, confused with the apparently limitless choices around us and distracted from our true purpose. As we move forward with awareness we regain our balance and find a new sense of peace and poise amid the mayhem. We become free to choose the right direction.

Personal Reflections: The bundle on her head was almost as big as her body yet she carried it with such poise. This theme of balance continues to flirt with me along the way. Between the sacred and the profane, between love and fear lies a place of acceptance and equilibrium. If I judge another as inferior or superior I make a distinction that drives the wedge of separation ever deeper into my human drama and psyche. I will keep moving forward and restore my equanimity.

0.0 km Albergaria-a-Velha We leave town via the fire-station *Bombeiros* and post office *Correio* (see town plan) along rua 1° Dezembro to **roundabout [1.0** km] *Casa Turco* tapas bar (*menú peregrino*). Cross the N-1 onto forest **track** turning <left at junction up to **crossroads** [**2.2** km] ***N. Sra. do Socorro*** statue of Our Lady *[retreat house •Casa Diocesana* © 234 522 422 *½ km* off *route up road right]*. Keep s/o along quiet asphalt road before turning off <left [**0.8** km] onto woodland path emerging onto asphalt road to cross over railway and turn right on **N-1** [**2.1** km] to **Albergaria-a-Nova.**

6.1 km Albergaria-a-Nova ●*Alb.* **Albergaria** *Priv.[12÷2]* €10 +6 €30 © 234 547 068 [m] 919 006 001 *www.albergaria.eu* where *Isabel Valente (Belinha)* and

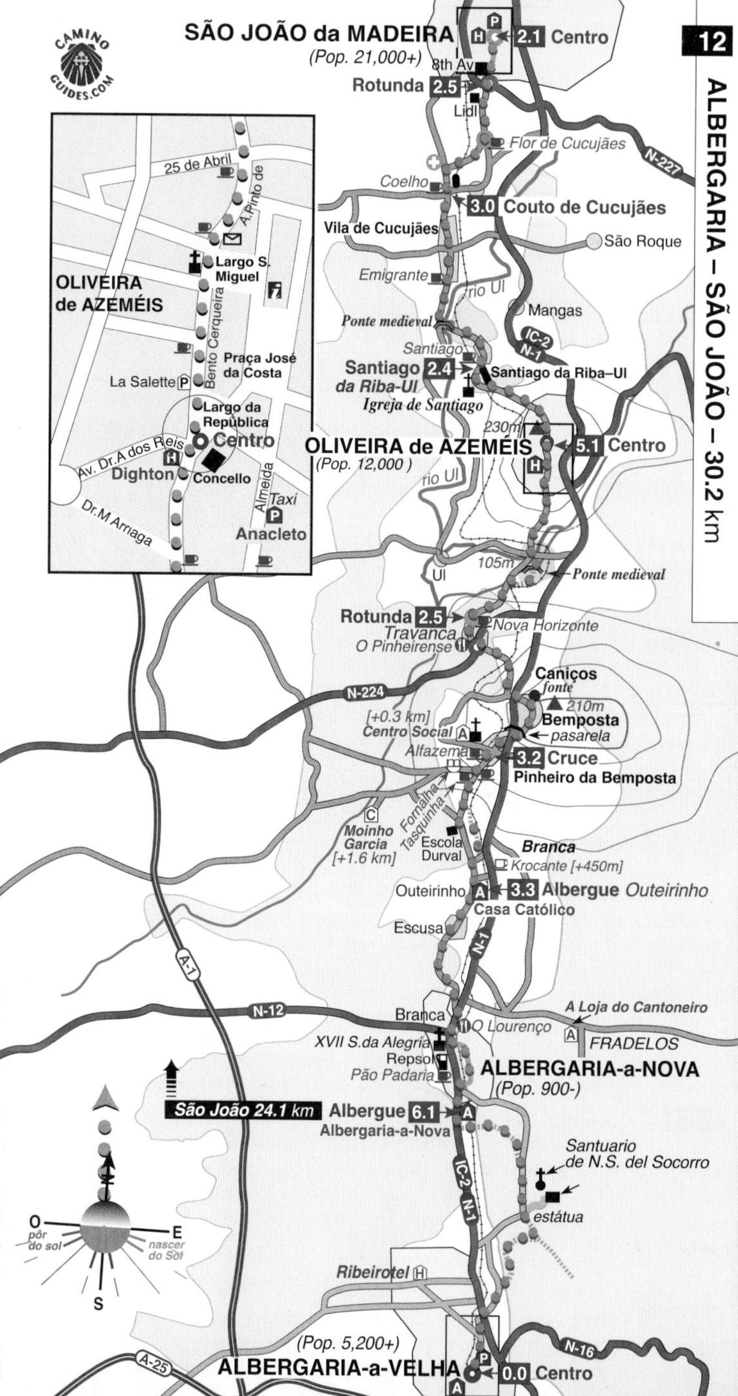
CAMINO GUIDES.COM
SÃO JOÃO da MADEIRA
(Pop. 21,000+)
2.1 Centro
8th Av.
Rotunda 2.5
Lidl
Flor de Cucujães
N-227
Coelho
3.0 Couto de Cucujães
Vila de Cucujães
São Roque
Emigrante
rio Ul
Mangas
Ponte medieval
IC-2 N-1
Santiago
Santiago 2.4
da Riba-Ul
Santiago da Riba–Ul
Igreja de Santiago
230m
OLIVEIRA de AZEMÉIS
(Pop. 12,000)
5.1 Centro
rio Ul
Ul
105m
Ponte medieval
Rotunda 2.5
Travanca
Nova Horizonte
O Pinheirense
Caniços
fonte
N-224
210m
Bemposta
[+0.3 km]
Centro Social
pasarela
Alfazema
3.2 Cruce
Pinheiro da Bemposta
Fornalha
Tasquinha
Moinho Garcia [+1.6 km]
Escola Durval
Branca
Krocante [+450m]
Outeirinho
3.3 Albergue Outeirinho
Casa Católico
Escusa
N-1
A-1
N-12
A Loja do Cantoneiro
Branca
O Lourenço
FRADELOS
XVII S.da Alegría
Repsol
Pão Padaria
ALBERGARIA-a-NOVA
(Pop. 900-)
São João 24.1 km
Albergue 6.1
Albergaria-a-Nova
Santuario de N.S. del Socorro
IC-2 N-1
estátua
O
E
pôr do sol
nascer do Sol
S
Ribeirotel
N-16
(Pop. 5,200+)
A-25
ALBERGARIA-a-VELHA
0.0 Centro
25 de Abril
A.Pinto de
Largo S. Miguel
OLIVEIRA de AZEMÉIS
Bento Cerqueira
Praça José da Costa
La Salette
Largo da República
Centro
Av. Dr.A dos Reis
Dighton
Concello
Almeida
Taxi
Dr.M Arriaga
Anacleto

the Valente family welcome pilgrims all year and endeavour to help pilgrims find alternative lodging if they are full. Garden to the rear now has a swimpool and bar. The route continues along the N-1 to traffic lights and option ▲▼:

▼ Continue on N-1 turning <left along r/da Portela for ●*Alb/Hs* **Currais** *Priv. [4÷1]* €25 *+2* €70 © 965 643 252, r/ Vale do lobo, 11 *www.curraisminihostelsuites.com* (650m). ▲ For main route turn right to pass through **Albergaria-A-Nova** *(limited facilities incl. pastelaria, café & mini-mercado)* re-emerging back ***on*** **N-1 [0.8** km]. Repsol garage/☕ (left 50m). Turn right along N-1 past ***Igreja N. S. da Alegria*** consecrated 1695 (with modern extension) past 🍴 *Lourenço* and veer left ***off*** **N-1 [0.5** km]. **Fradelos** *(off route+ 1.5 km just beyond Frutera [left]turn right sign Fradelos)* ●*Alb.Hs* **A Loja do Cantoneiro** *Priv.[18÷3]* €15 *+4* €30+ © 234 133 707 Filipe Marques. r/do Caima, 2 (pick-up maybe available).

[Note: from here to São João da Madeira we crisscross the N-1, the disused railway and a series of secondary roads that makes it impossible (and unnecessary) to detail all the twists and turns. It is sufficient to know that waymarking is adequate and with attention to signs no undue problems in navigating should arise). We now crisscross our way through **Branca** and **Escusa** *[**Detour + 1.1** km •**Quinta Relvas** Priv.[40÷3]* €15 *+10* €35 © *912 551 073 www.quintadasrelvas.pt eco community. Calçada das Relvas, Branca].* Keep s/o into **Outeirinho [2.0** km].

3.3 km **Outeirinho** ●*Alb.*Casa Católica *Priv.[18÷4]* €-donativo © 916 571 106 (Paulo) all facilities incl. terrace, fruit orchard & pilgrim dinner at r/das Silveiras, 22 (March–Nov incl. phone for winter opening). Continue along quiet country lanes and just before N-1 turn left onto path alongside disused **rail track [1.1** km]. Veer left into r/Escola past modern school in **Curval** and turn right leading to r/Gandara and right again on N-224 over rail *Pinheiro da Bemposta* past ☕ *A Tasquinha* up to **crossroads [2.0** km]:

3.1 km **Pinheiro da Bemposta** ☕ *Alfazema* [⛽]. *[2 options to sleep in the area* ❶ ***+0.3** km •**Centro Social Paroquial** senior citizens adj. the parish church offer a floor and basic facilities.* ❷ ***+1.6** km •**Moinho Garcia** Priv.[12÷2]* €16 *+5* €44 Nik Blum © *935 500 595 www.watermillmoinhogarcia.com Rua do Garcia 322. Beautiful old mill by waterfall. Simple menú €5 also kitchen. Directions: Turn left by A Tasquinha pass mini-mercado, Fornalha and gas station bearing left into rua do futbolclub Pinheirense].* Continue up through Caniços 🍴 *Pago Cheio* over the N-1 via *pasarela* up again steeply past ☕ *Areosa* to high point (alto 210m) over looking the valley (left) and ancient fonte (right). Continue down over N-1 past industrial estate 🍴 *O Pinheirense* and urbanised area in Travanca on Av. do Espírito Santo:

2.8 km **Rotunda** ***Travanca*** ☕ *Novo Horizonte* down over stream and turn up sharp right to pass *under* the **N-1** onto path alongside railway [**!**]. We now have a delightful one kilometre stretch of original pilgrim pathway as we descend down into the river valley along the *rua do Senhor da Ponte no Caminho de Santiago* over the rio Anceira via the **Ponte Romano** over railway back onto the asphalt road turning left into rua Cruceiro up rua da Portela through the suburbs into the (part) pedestrianised street *rua António Alegria* to the central square.

5.1 km **Oliveira de Azeméis** ***Centro*** Largo República overlooked by historic town hall *Câmara Municipal.* Oliveira presents a confident air with a growing population in excess of 12,000. It has all the facilities associated with a modern

town but also a fine historical centre (*see town hall pictured>*). The waymarked route brings us past the parish church of Saint Michael *Igreja Matriz de São Miguel* mentioned in documents as far back as 922 and an adj. Roman milestone *Miliário* evidence of the town's earlier foundations as part of the Via Romana XVI. We also find links with the camino de Santiago and the first 'official' camino bollard from the Xunta de Galicia. The town also has an important Marian shrine *La Salette.* The feast day of N. Sra. de La Salette takes place on 2nd Sunday in August and attracts huge crowds when beds are virtually impossible to find. The fine houses built at the end of the 19th century are known as *casas de brasileiro* built by former emigrants returning with their new found wealth. The story of their lives is captured by Portuguese writer Ferreira de Castro whose own house has been turned into a museum *casa-museu* in the village of Ossela 5 km to the East.

❶ ***Turismo*** (Summer only) ✆ 256 674 463 Praca José da Costa (see map). ● **Lodging:** •*H***** **Dighton** *x90* €55-65 ✆ 256 682 191 rua Dr. Albino dos Reis (opp. *Câmara*). •*P* **Anacleto** ±30 ✆ 256 682 541 Av. D. António José de Almeida, 310 (adj. taxi). *[+1.3 km South)* •**Bombeiros Voluntários** ✆ 256 682 122 *Rua dos Bombeiros Voluntários /Av. Dona Maria I].* **La Salette** rua Bento Carqueja (currently closed). Wide choice of **restaurants** around the central pedestrian main street.

We continue our way up along rua Bento Cerqueira past the Correios crossing rua 25 de Abril and then heading steeply down over the river turning <left at roundabout and up through the northern suburbs and industrial area, crisscrossing the railway with several short stretches of cobblestone as we make our way out to T-Junction in ***Santiago de Riba-Ul.***

2.4 km **Santiago de Riba-Ul** Igreja de Santiago and ☕ *Cha* (left). Turn right past ☕ *Santiago* and imm. left over rail bridge down narrow walled lane *corredoira* down to the medieval stone bridge over the river Ul ***Ponte do Salgueiro*** with miniature *alminhas* carved into the granite columns. We now make our way up past ☕ *O Emigrante* with the former Benedictine monastery *Mosteiro de Cucujães* on the hill ahead into:

3.0 km **Couto de Cucujães** ☕ *Coelho* (left) rail station down (right) up past Galp service station. We descend over river and up again over railway ***estação Faia*** (right) to emerge at roundabout ☕ *Flor de Cucujães*. S/o up past industrial area and Lidl (right) up to major roundabout at the start of the modern suburbs of São João da Madeira at 8th Avenue modern shopping centre.

2.5 km **Rotunda *8th Avenue*** ☕. Continue s/o past 🍴 *Planet Azul (Parque da Senhora dos Milagres right)* as we head up Av. Dr. Renato Araújo signposted *Centro* veering right at the 2nd roundabout (with fountain) and 🍴 *Grab & Go!* into rua Padre António Maria Pinho past the parish church of St. John the Baptist *Igreja Matriz (the original roman military thoroughfare Via XVI passed to the rear).* We now turn left into rua Visconde de São João da Madeira up into the central square:

2.1 km **São João da Madeira *Centro*** *Praça Luis Ribeiro* pedestrian roundabout with *cafés, bares, restaurantes* y *Hoteles.* An historic town of Roman origin – not obvious from the modernity that surrounds us. An industrial town built on the back of its worldwide reputation for the manufacture of hats and shoes with the ***Museo da Chapelaria*** on rua Oliveira Júnior, 501. The area around the central square *rotunda* is pedestrianised and has the 2 best hotel options and several café-bars including ☕ *Concha Doce* with its prominent pilgrim shell, the only evidence that we are actually directly on 'the way'. ℹ ***Turismo*** © 256 200 285 kiosko (summer) Praça Luís Ribeiro / Av. Liberdade.

● **Lodging:** Central rotunda Praça Luís Ribeiro @Nº165 •*P* **Solar São João** *x8* €25-30 © 256 202 540 www.solarsaojoao.pai.pt (see photo) & @Nº7 •*H*** **A.S. São João** *x36* €35+ © 256 836 100. •*S* **Central Suites 1** €35+ © 936 206 777 www.centralsuites.pt r/António José de Oliveira Júnior 54 +**Suites 2** Rua 5 de Outubro, 394 +**Suites 3** Av. Dr. Renato Araújo, 105. ● **Santa Casa da Misericórdia** *Priv. [12÷1] suelo* €-Donativo © 256 837 240 Rua Manuel Luis Leite Júnior 777. •*H**** **Golden Tulip** *x120* €60-64 © 256 106 700 Av. Adelino Amaro da Costa 573 +**0.8** km (off Av.Liberdade). *[•***Bombeiros Voluntários** © 256 837 120 r/ Oliveira Figueiredo, Z. Ind. +**2.2** km*]*.

ÃO JOÃO DA MADEIRA: Amongst the more notable buildings are: ● Chapel and Park of Our lady of the Miracles ***Capela e Parque de Na Sra dos Milagros*** built in the 1930's in the Neo-Romanesque style located near the roundabout on the way into town. ● Parish church of St John the Baptist ***Igreja Matriz de S. João Baptista*** reconstructed in 1884 with an altarpiece dating from the previous century, Off rua Visconde de São João da Madeira. ● Chapel of St. Anthony ***Capela de Santo António*** built in 1937 in the Neo-Romanesque style and located behind the central square in Largo de S. Antonio. ● House of Culture ***Casa da Cultura*** one of the best examples of a *Casa de Brasileiros* housing the town's Art Centre, exhibition rooms and auditorium, located off Alão de Morais beyond the Bombeiros. ● ***Museo da Chapelaria*** on rua Oliveira Júnior, 501 (on camino on way out of town).

Personal Reflections:

Stop. Look. Listen.

13 SÃO JOÃO da MADEIRA – PORTO

	3.1		*9%*
	21.8		*61%*
	10.9		*30%*
Total km	**35.8** km *(22.2 ml)*		

Total ascent **340**m +½ *hr*

▲ Alto *m* Malaposta **335** m *(1,033 ft)*

<A H> Malaposta **7.5** km Grijó **20.5**

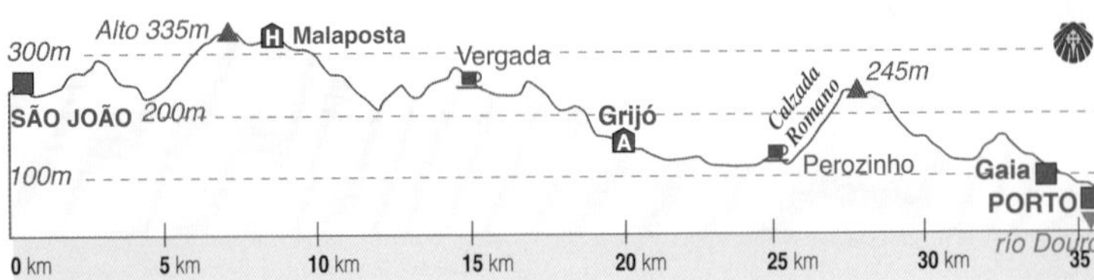

Practical Path: As we approach Porto the road network becomes ever busier so prepare for the long slog into the centre along hard city pavements This is a *very* long stage, much of it on main roads across undulating terrain. If you plan to make it to Porto in one stage leave São João at first light. The noise and danger of the roads is relieved by a short but delightful stretch of the old Roman road through woodland beyond Grijó at Perosinho. The albergue at Grijó offers a good midway halt (20.6 km) with a shorter stage the following day into Porto with extra time to explore this wonderful city (17.9 km to the *albergue*).

Greater is He that is in you, Than he who is in the world. *1 John 4:4*

Mystical Path: Physical sight shows us the superficial world of the ego fashioned by humanity with its incessant demands. Below the surface lies our true Identity. This higher Self is recognised by seeing it in others. The confusion between outer and inner between the ego and the divine forms the crux of our problem – one problem, one solution. It is time to awaken our spiritual vision.

Personal Reflections: How many more crossroads will I meet today – each one requiring a choice of direction... but I need to remind myself that I journey on two different levels. If I heed only the signs to Santiago I head towards an empty casket. The signs to the Source are not so obvious... but I miss them at my peril. I need to stay alert amongst the labyrinth of highways and byways of the inner camino if I am to reach my true Destination.

0.0 km **São João da Madeira** ***Centro*** from the Praça Luís Ribeiro we head out along rua Oliveira Júnior (to the left side of the Banco Espirito Santo) passing ***Museo da Chapelaria*** (left) [**0.5** km] veering <left opp. Repsol garage past industrial buildings s/o over crossroads by *supermercado* and over crossroads in **Arrifana** [**1.1** km] *Igreja Matriz* with fine façade of blue and white tiles *azulejos.* Continue up into Aldeia Nova and turn sharp right> at **Tareco** [**2.2** km] into rua S. António [ ].

3.8 km **Cruce** *Tareco*. S/o up rua S.Antonio past school and over the N-227

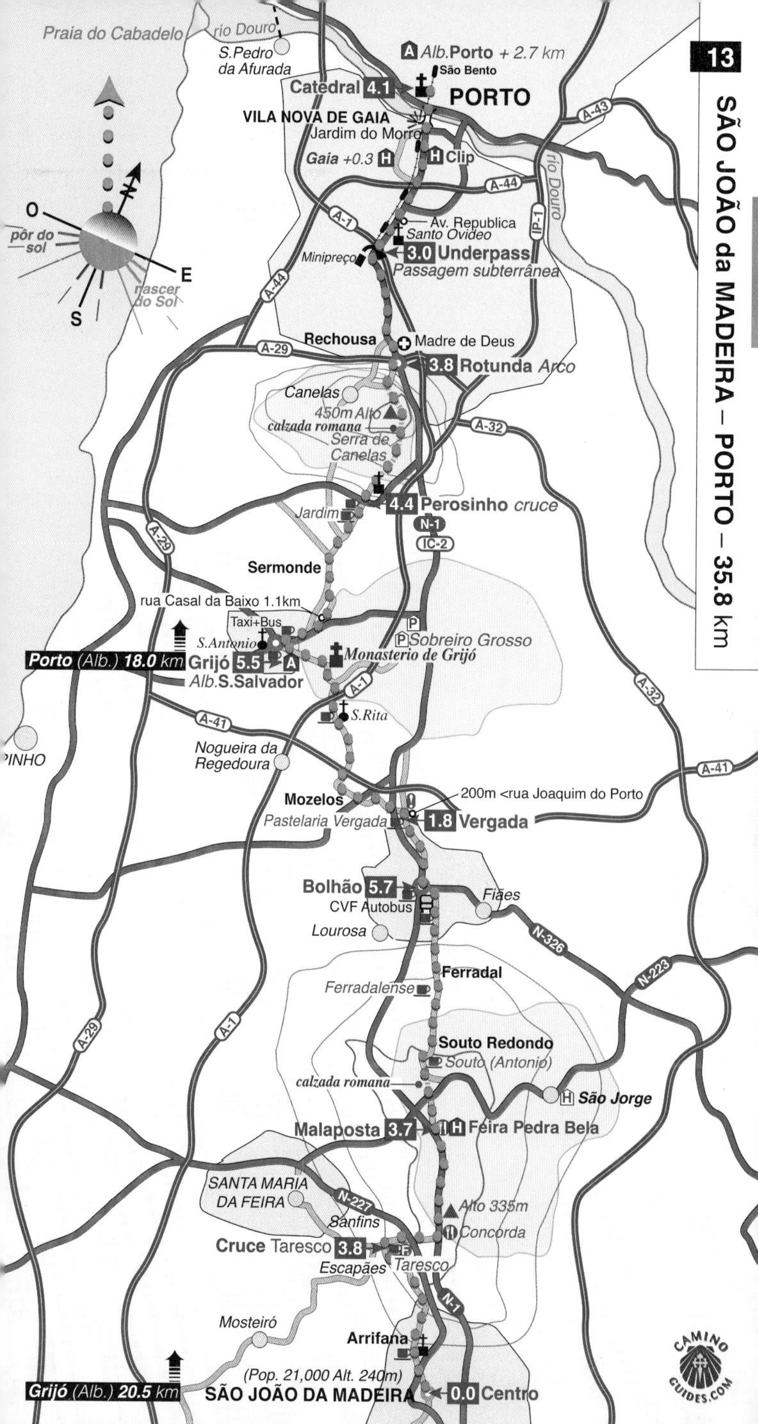
13
SÃO JOÃO da MADEIRA – PORTO – 35.8 km
Praia do Cabadelo
rio Douro
S.Pedro da Afurada
Alb.Porto + 2.7 km
São Bento
Catedral 4.1
PORTO
VILA NOVA DE GAIA
Jardim do Morro
Gaia +0.3
Clip
A-43
A-44
A-1
IP-1
rio Douro
O
pôr do sol
E
S
rascer do Sol
Av. Republica
Santo Ovideo
Minipreço
3.0 Underpass
Passagem subterrânea
A-44
Rechousa
Madre de Deus
A-29
3.8 Rotunda Arco
Canelas
450m Alto
calzada romana
Serra de Canelas
A-32
Jardim
4.4 Perosinho cruce
N-1
IC-2
A-29
Sermonde
rua Casal da Baixo 1.1km
Taxi+Bus
S.Antonio
Sobreiro Grosso
Monasterio de Grijó
Porto (Alb.) 18.0 km
Grijó 5.5
Alb.S.Salvador
A-1
S.Rita
A-41
A-32
Nogueira da Regedoura
PINHO
A-41
200m <rua Joaquim do Porto
Mozelos
Pastelaria Vergada
1.8 Vergada
Bolhão 5.7
Fiães
CVF Autobus
Lourosa
N-326
N-223
Ferradal
Ferradalense
A-29
A-1
Souto Redondo
Souto (Antonio)
calzada romana
São Jorge
Malaposta 3.7
Feira Pedra Bela
SANTA MARIA DA FEIRA
N-227
Sanfins
Alto 335m
Concorda
Cruce Taresco 3.8
Escapães
Taresco
N-1
Mosteiró
Arrifana
(Pop. 21,000 Alt. 240m)
Grijó (Alb.) 20.5 km
SÃO JOÃO DA MADEIRA
0.0 Centro
CAMINO GUIDES.COM

to the **N-1** [**1.2** km] to our uninspiring high point of this stage at 335m opp. *Concorde* turn left along the soulless N-1 (wide pavement) past Galp services through Sanfins into **Malaposta** [**2.5** km].

3.7 km **Malaposta** Modern •*H**** **Feira Pedra Bela** *x60* €35-50 ✆ 256 910 350 *www.hotelpedrabela.com* r/Malaposta / N-1 adj. We now leave N-1 onto short stretch of the original *Calzada Romana* *(left)* cross N-223 [!] *[**Detour right N-223 – São Jorge + 2.2** km* to variety of hotels €20 -50 in incl. •*P* **São Jorge** *x12* €28-33 ✆ *256 911 303]*. S/o into **Souto Redondo** [**1.7** km] / *Souto* where the amiable António delights in stamping credenciales. A short stretch of woodland path brings us into **Ferradal** [**1.6** km] *Ferradalense. [**Detour** Lourosa + 0.8 km B.V. Av. Principal* ✆ *227 443 189]*. Keep s/o to roundabout with CVF bus depot and cafés in **Bolhão** [**2.4** km].

5.7 km **Bolhão** Veer right> on Av. Principal past **Lidl** & *Diamante* s/o (right) into rua Central de Vergada to the town 'centre' and *A Flôr da Vergada*.

1.8 km **Vergada** ***centro*** Continue for turn-off left [**0.2** km] [!] into rua Joaquim do Porto (easily missed [!]) into *Mozelos* crossing the N-1 [!] *[distant view of the sea opens up on the horizon. Waymarking is good but keep focused on the web of roads ahead and the fast moving traffic]*. Continue down through **Vila de Nogueira da Regedoura** and down under the **A-41 flyover** [**2.0** km] onto short woodland path past **Capela S.Rita** [**1.5** km] (right) and *Ermo* (left) under **A-1** into the lush and relatively tranquil Grijó valley turning <left at mini-roundabout in **Padrão** [**0.5** km] with wall of Grijó monastery ahead. *[The pilgrim hostel in Grijó is nearby. For alt. lodging **(uphill)**. Turn right under A-1 into ruas do Sr. do Padrão, Quinta Fabrica and Americo Oliveira to •P. **Sobreiro Grosso*** ✆ *227 644 896 & **+1.6** km. Continue **+0.5** km to •P. **Catavento*** ✆ *227 640 054 on N-1]*. At the roundabout continue <left along walls of Grijó monastery up to the monastery entrance (right) and continue on Av. do Mosteiro to albergue [**1.3** km].

5.5 km **Grijó** ●*Alb.* **S. Salvador** *Par.[14÷2]* €7 António Pires ✆ 968 702 769 rua Cardoso Pinto, 274. Welcoming hostel good facilities and patio, popular with pilgrims arriving from São João da Madeira [20.6 km].

Mosterio S. Salvador de Grijó *XIII* where the medieval Italian pilgrim Confalonieri stayed during his pilgrimage from Rome to Santiago. The original buildings were consecrated in 1235 and were an important stop for both physical and spiritual nourishment to pilgrims. A sense of peace continues to pervade the parkland and offers the modern pilgrim respite from the traffic. Adjoining the monastery are the council offices *Freguesia de Vila Grijó* and public toilets.

Note: Despite the proximity to Porto there are still a few stretches of the original medieval pilgrim route ahead over the Serra dos Negrelos to relieve the noise and monotony of the roads. Waymarks now have to compete with other signs and you also need to stay alert to the fast moving traffic. Note the position of the sun and as you head due north keep it in the same general position which should be behind you over the left shoulder in the early afternoon to guide you into and through Vila Nova de Gaia which offers a range of intermediate accommodation. If you are not familiar with Porto it is probably best to go direct to the cathedral (along the *top* of the bridge – see alternative route later). This is the logical 'end point' of the Lisbon section where you can give thanks for your safe arrival, pick up a pilgrim passport *credencial* and / or stamp your existing one. Adjacent to the cathedral is a tourist office with map of the town and list of hotels. Just below the cathedral is a range of budget hotels and other accommodation (see under Porto). Note the new pilgrim hostel in Porto is a futher 2.7 km from the cathedral directly on the camino just beyond the pedestrian street rua de Cedofeita.

From the pilgrim hostel continue to the roundabout in Grijó ☕ *Central. [Taxi rank and bus stop Transportes Carvalhos every 30 minutes direction Porto Batalha via Jardin do Morro / Dom Luis I bridge for the cathedral – €2.45].* Continue right on main road (capela S.Antonio left) past modern shopping mall and turn off <left into rua Casal da Baixo. This marks the low point of this stage (95m) and we now climb steadily along a maze of country roads (well waymarked) up through Sermonde past school adj. ☕ *Jardim* to crossroads in:

4.4 km **Perosinho** several *cafés.* Continue s/o up past council office and parish church (right) and suddenly we find ourselves amongst the peaceful pines and eucalyptus of the Serra de Negrelos on the ancient Roman road *calzada romana* (see photo next page). The path continues for a delightful 2.5 km. It is sparsely waymarked but follow the main track straight ahead up to the high point (245m) and down to join an asphalt road by athletic club ACR. The route continues down steeply on rua do Mirante to Rechousa and the N-1:

3.8 km **Rotunda** ***Arco*** junction with the N-1 which we now follow over the A-29 past hospital Madre de Deus (right) and s/o at Galp services down past 🍴 *Terras dAlém* (right) and Minipreco (left) and under the A-1 motorway.

3.0 km **Underpass A-1** continue around modern apartment blocks and up steps to rejoin the N-1 at rotunda and Igreja Santo Ovídio and metro station. We head through **Vila nova da Gaia** along The N-1 which now becomes Av. de

República which we follow all the way to the cathedral over city bypass *Avenida dos Descobrimentos* past the *Belle Époque Casa de Cultura* following signs to *Centro Historico* past the grass platform (metro station *Estação de General Torres*). •*H*** **Clip** *x89* €49 © 223 745 910 *www.cliphotel.pt* Av. República, 1559 (opp bp). •*Hs* **Cruz Vermelha** *x9* €20-25 © 913 800 888 r/General Torres, 572 +300m. •*Hs* **Gaia** *x14* €18pp r/Cândido dos Reis, 374 +400m. Continue to dramatic viewpoint over the río Douro at *Jardim do Moro* and the city's iconic bridge ***Ponte D. Luís I***. A double-deck metal arch that spans the río Douro between Vila Nova de Gaia and Porto. Built in 1886 it became the longest span in the world at 172 m. Note [1]: Jardim do Moro is a good place to pause for breath – this has been a long stage and we are near the end point. [2] Take a moment to get your bearings – the viewpoint here gives a panoramic view of Vila Nova de Gaia spilling down *this* side to the Southern banks of the river with its Port wine lodges. •*H**** **Sandeman** *Priv.[28÷3]* €16 *+14* €120+ © 213 461 381 *www.thehouseofsandeman.pt* Largo Miguel Bombarda, 3 with the funkiest 'barrel-vault' bunk-beds in town!

On the *far* side is the city of Porto with the cathedral up to our right and the Ribeira harbour area down to the left and the main shopping area and hotels spread out behind. [3] If you haven't reserved accommodation decide now where to head for. There is a tourist office adj. the cathedral and note the new and welcoming pilgrim hostel is a further 2.7 km *beyond* the cathedral. [4] at this point a former waymarked route goes sharply down via Calçada da Serra to cross over the lower tier of the bridge to the harbour front and then proceeds either back up (steeply) to the cathedral or into the city centre. If you have no fixed plans it may be better not to lose the high ground but continue over the upper level of the bridge directly ahead directly to the cathedral.

4.1 km **Porto Catedral *Sé*** end point from Lisbon and start point for the various routes to Santiago where 27,924 pilgrims commenced their journey last year. Adjoining the cathedral entrance (by the statue of Vimara Peres atop his steed) is a *Turismo* and the offices of *Porto Tours* in the tower just below. See city map and details of accommodation in the next section.

Personal Reflections:

Serra de Negrelos – calzada romana.

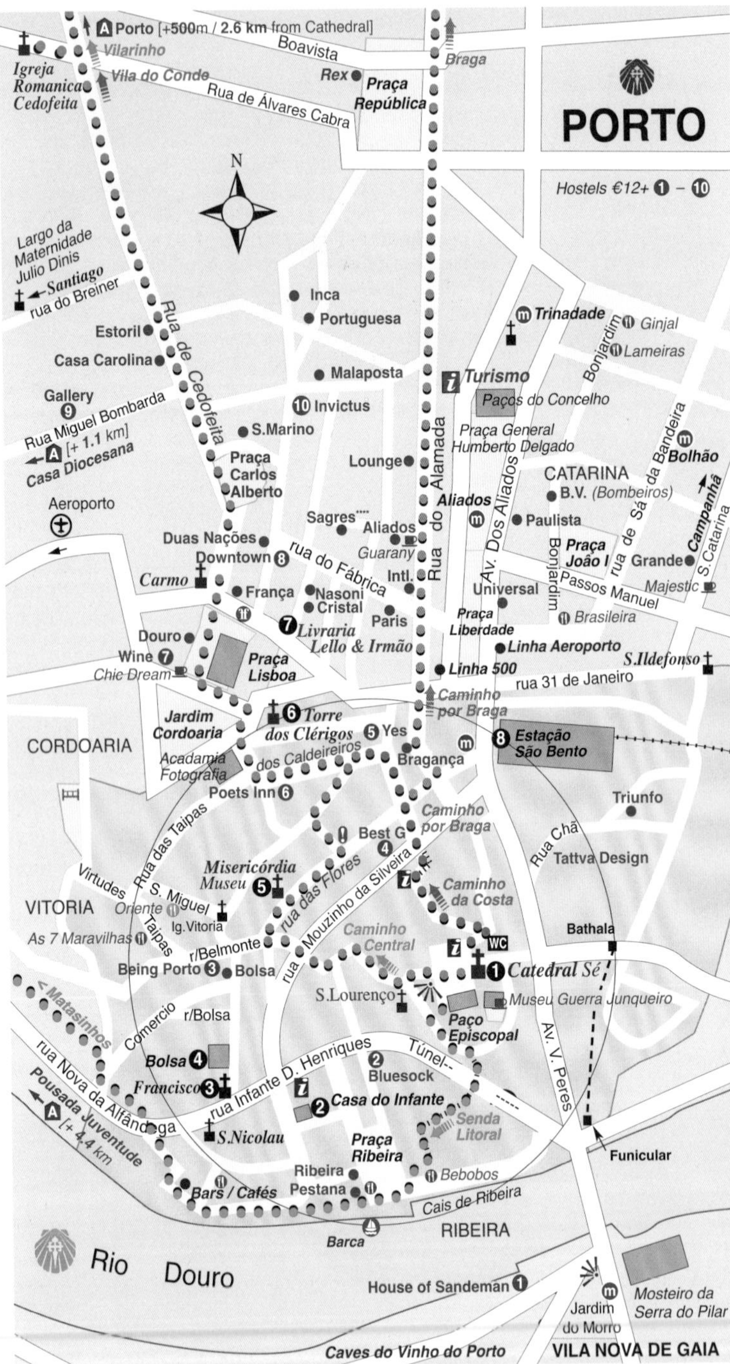

PORTO
Hostels €12+ 1 – 10
Porto [+500m / 2.6 km from Cathedral]
Vilarinho
Vila do Conde
Boavista
Braga
Igreja Romanica Cedofeita
Rex
Praça República
Rua de Álvares Cabra
N
Largo da Maternidade Julio Dinis
Santiago
rua do Breiner
Inca
Portuguesa
Estoril
Casa Carolina
Rua de Cedofeita
Trinadade
Ginjal
Lameiras
Bonjardim
Malaposta
Turismo
Paços do Concelho
Gallery 9
Rua Miguel Bombarda
10 Invictus
S.Marino
Praça General Humberto Delgado
[+ 1.1 km]
Casa Diocesana
Praça Carlos Alberto
Lounge
Rua do Alamada
Av. Dos Aliados
CATARINA
Bolhão
rua de Sá da Bandeira
Campanhã
Aeroporto
B.V. (Bombeiros)
Sagres
Aliados
Paulista
Duas Nações
Guarany
Praça João I
S.Catarina
Downtown 8
rua do Fábrica
Intl.
Bonjardim
Grande
Carmo
França
Nasoni
Cristal
Universal
Passos Manuel
Majestic
Paris
Praça Liberdade
Brasileira
7 Livraria Lello & Irmão
Douro
Wine 7
Chic Dream
Praça Lisboa
Linha Aeroporto
Linha 500
S.Ildefonso
rua 31 de Janeiro
Caminho por Braga
Jardim Cordoaria
6 Torre dos Clérigos
5 Yes
CORDOARIA
Academia Fotografia
dos Caldeireiros
Bragança
8 Estação São Bento
Poets Inn 6
Triunfo
Rua das Taipas
Best G 4
Caminho por Braga
Rua Chã
Tattva Design
Misericórdia Museu 5
rua das Flores
rua Mouzinho da Silveira
Caminho da Costa
Virtudes
S. Miguel
VITORIA
Oriente
Ig.Vitoria
Taipas
Caminho Central
WC
Bathala
As 7 Maravilhas
r/Belmonte
1 Catedral Sé
Being Porto 3
Bolsa
rua
S.Lourenço
Museu Guerra Junqueiro
< Matasinhos
Comercio
r/Bolsa
Paço Episcopal
Bolsa 4
Túnel
Av. V. Peres
2 Bluesock
Francisco 3
rua Infante D. Henriques
rua Nova da Alfândega
2 Casa do Infante
Pousada Juventude
[+ 4.4 km
Senda Litoral
Funicular
S.Nicolau
Praça Ribeira
Ribeira
Bebobos
Pestana
Bars / Cafés
Cais de Ribeira
Barca
RIBEIRA
Rio Douro
House of Sandeman 1
Jardim do Morro
Mosteiro da Serra do Pilar
Caves do Vinho do Porto
VILA NOVA DE GAIA

Arriving in Porto: ✆ **+351**. Mobile [m] commence with **9.** If you start in Porto and arrive by air there is a tourist counter in the arrivals hall ✆ 229 432 400 (08:00 – 23:00) with a map of the city and hotel information. A regular bus operates to the city centre and takes around an hour for the 14 km trip. Or take the efficient metro from the station in the airport itself. If you arrive by train note there are 2 rail stations. The main station *Estação de São Bento* is in the centre. The modern *Estação de Campanhã* is a few kilometres east and the old *Estação de Trindade* has now been revamped as the ultra modern hub of the efficient metro.

❶ ***Turismo Central***: *(09:00–18:00)* top end Av. dos Aliados *rua Clube dos Fenianos 25 (*adj. *câmara).* ✆ 223 393 472. www.visitporto.travel ❶ ***Ribeira***: 63 Rua do Infante D. Henrique *(down near the river)* ✆ 222 060 412.❶ ***Cathedral*** Terreiro da Se ✆ 223 325174 (10:00 – 18:00). ❶ For information outside Porto city: ✆ 927 411 817 Praca D. João I, 43.

● ***Albergues:*** *[distances from cathedral].* ●✪*Alb.* **Peregrinos do Porto** *Priv. [26÷4]* €12+*4* €22-44 ✆ 912 591 321 [m] Óscar Miguel 220 140 515 www.albergueperegrinosporto.pt r/Barão de Forester, 954 [+**2.6** km]. ●**N.S. do Rosário de Vilar** *Asoc.[12÷2] €7 +8* €22-38 ✆ 226 056 000 Casa Diocesana, r/Arcediago Vanzeller, 50 [+**2.0** km]. ●**ViaPortuscale** *Asoc.[20÷2]* ✆ 960 227 134 r/Vasco Santana, 264, Senhora da Hora [+**6.9** km]. ●**Pousada de Juventude** *[124÷4]* €13-15 ✆ 226 177 257 r/Paulo da Gama, 551 [+**4.4** km]. **Bombeiros** *BV. [2÷1]* ✆ 222 055 845 r/Rodrigues Sampaio, 145 [+**0.9** km].

● ***Hostales Centro:*** *www.hostelworld.com / www.booking.com (all these hostals are on or near the camino and have bunks-beds from €12 as well as private rooms).* ❶ **House of Sandeman** (see previous page). ❷ **Bluesock** *[80÷7]* €20 *+8* €60+ ✆ ✆ 227 664 171 *www.bluesockhostels.com/hostel-porto* r/S. João 40 (Ribeira). ❸ **Being Porto** *[12÷1]* €15 *+30* €50-60 ✆ 222 011 977 r/Belomonte, 13. ❹ **Best Guest** *[16÷3]* €18 *+8* €46 ✆ 967 116 157 r/Mouzinho da Silveira, 257. ❺ **Yes Porto!** ✆ 222 082 391 *www.yeshostels.com* r/Arquitecto Nicolau Nazoni 31. ❻ **Poets Inn** €20 *+12* €50 ✆ 223 324 209 r/Caldeireiros, 261. ❼ **Porto Wine** *[40÷7]* €17 *+10* €60+ ✆ 222 013 167 *www.winehostel.pt* Campo dos Martires da Patria 52 (popular). ❽ **Downtown** *[28÷4]* €12 ✆ 223 234 729 Praça Guilherme Gomes Fernandes 66. ❾ **Gallery** *[24÷5]* €27 *+2* €120 ✆ 224 964 313 r/Miguel Bombarda 222. ❿ **Invictus** *[20÷3]* €12 +€44 ✆ 222 024 371 r/Oliveiras 73.

● ***Hoteles Centro: (€35-55)*** •**Flor Bragança** ✆ 222 082 974 r/Arquitecto Nicolau Nazoni 12. •**Oporto Poets** ✆ 222 026 089 Trv.Ferraz 13. •**França** Praça de Gomes Teixeira,7 ✆ 222 002 791. ***Rua Galeria*** *(Near Lello books)* ***@Nº82*** •**Nasoni** ✆ 222 083 807 & ***@Nº48*** •**Cristal** ✆ 222 002 100. ***Rua Cedofeita*** (on the camino) ***@Nº159*** •**Casa Carolina** *€85+!* ✆ 912 088 249. ***@Nº193*** •**Estoril** ✆ 222 002 751. ● ***Hoteles Centro: (€55-95)*** •**Internacional** ✆ 222 005 032 *www.hi-porto.com* r/Almada 131. •**Grande Hotel Paris** ✆ 222 073 140 r/Fábrica 27 *(olde-world garden) www.stayhotels.pt/grandehotelparis*. •**Paulista** ✆ 222 054 692 Av. dos Aliados 214. •**Aliados** ✆ 222 004 853 r/Elísio de Melo 27 *(above ☕ Guranay with entrance off side road)*. For old-fashioned luxury •*H**** **Grande Hotel do Porto** ✆ 222 076 690 *www.grandehotelporto.com* r/Santa Catarina 197 (near café Majestic). Downtown value at •*H**** **da Bolsa** ✆ 222 026 768 r/Ferreira Borges and by the river •*H**** **Carrís** ✆ 20 965 786 r/Infante D. Henrique 1. •*H**** **Riberia do Porto** ✆ 222 032 097 *www.ribeiradoportohotel.com/en* Praça da Ribeira Nº5 or €100+. •*H***** **Pestana** @ Nº1 ✆ 223 402 300.

Cais da Ribeira with river *Barcos Rabelos* and **Catedral *Sé*** *(top left)*

❑ **Eating Out:** A tourist menu on the riverside piers *Cais de Ribeira* will cost €30+ fish restaurants abound such as 🍴 *Taberna de Bebobos* or 🍴 *Adega S. Nicolau* r/S. Nicolau with views of the river or adj. O Gancho where the view is rated more highly than the food! or for value try the basic 🍴 *O Muro* on Muro dos Bacalhoeiros 88 a pedestrian walkway above the river. If you want to experience the haunting Portuguese music *fado* try the adj. 🍴 *Mal Cozinhado* r/Outeirinho, 13 © 222 081 319 who will try and sell you an pricey dinner but it's possible to prop-up the bar instead and drink overpriced wine while you listen to the melancholy voices accompanied by the Portuguese guitar. For economy you can still find a basic menu in the old town away from the main tourist areas for around €15. Like many reasonably priced eateries in the *cidade velha* the former *Clerigos* r/Fabrica, 73 has changed its name to 🍴 *Ostras e Coisas* now offering excellent seafood and prices to match. 'Local' eateries have been pushed further back. Try the atmospheric 🍴 *As 7 Maravilhas* on rua das Taipas,17 while nearby in rua de S. Miguel 19 is a rare vegan option 🍴 *V O Oriente no Porto*. Up near Trindade Metro find 🍴 *Churrasqueira Lameiras* r/do Bonjardim 546 which still retains a local atmosphere... and prices. On the corner beyond, the elegant 🍴 *Ginjal* in the Ramos family since 1948.

At the other end of the scale is Art Deco ☕ *and* 🍴 *A Brasileira* r/do Bonjardim 118 (corner of Sá da Bandiera). Here you *might* start with an aperitif in the café dine in its restaurant and then, perhaps, make your way the ☕ *Majestic Café* on r/de Santa Catarina 112 for liqueur and coffee. One of the best known Belle Epoque cafés in Portugal with beautiful interior and live piano music, but don't expect much change out of €60 for the evening's entertainment.

❑ ***Self-service Lavandaria*** Rua da Conceição, 23 (off Rua Cedofeita). ***Backpack and Luggage Transfers:*** from €5 per day to Santiago via central or coastal route www.pilbeo.com email: contact@pilbeo.com © +34 670 648 078. *Also:* Top Santiago www.topsantiago.com ✠ ***credenciales***: Catedral / Porto Pilgrim Albergue / Tourist offices. Midsummer festival (June) *Festa São João.*

Historical Sketch: Porto is beautifully situated on the 'River of Gold' *Rio Douro*. A city full of vitality and authenticity and justifiably proud of its long history. It was here in the 12th century that Portugal took its name as an independent nation. By the 14th century it had well-established trade links and we begin to see the emergence of a wealthy merchant class and the building of substantial civic structures. Henry the Navigator was born here in 1394 and we can still visit his house below the square bearing his name. By the 15th century the city was playing a leading role in the maritime discoveries of the New World. The historical centre was declared a World Heritage site in 1996 and in 2001 Porto was chosen as the European City of Culture. In 2004 it proudly hosted the European football championships – Porto and football are synonymous! Today the city has a population of around ½ million with 1½ million in the greater catchment area. All this grew out of a modest Celtic settlement atop what is now Cathedral Hillock *Colina da Sé,* a rocky promontory from which the old quarter tumbles down to the river at the *Cais da Ribeira.*

❑ **Historic Buildings and Monuments: City Excursion:** Allow time to visit the historic city centre and absorb some of its magnificent sights. From the west door of the Cathedral (the start of stage 14 to Santiago) in the old medieval quarter known as the *Bairro da Sé* to the beginning of the pedestrian street rua Cedofeita in the quarter known as *Cordoaria* is less than 2 km (see city map). You can walk this stage in under an hour. However, if you intend to visit the interior of any of the buildings along the way then you need to allow more time. Indeed to soak up the atmosphere of the Cathedral and its cloisters would require at least an hour in itself. Several further options are available from the Cathedral. You can take the tourist tram for a 90-minute tour of Vila Nova do Gaia. If you shudder at the notion, for around €10 you can rattle instead over the cobblestones and over the famous bridge Ponte de D. Luís I. Your money buys you a visit to one of the oldest port wine lodges in Portugal, including a tasting session where you get to sample a ruby and perhaps a less familiar white port. The tour then returns to the Cathedral via the lower section of the bridge, past the old customs hall *Alfândega Nova* and up past the main rail station *Estação de São Bento.*

If a port wine lodge is not of interest, then just behind the cathedral at 32 rua Dom Hugo (around the back of the Archbishop's Palace) is the beautiful former house and museum (mostly Islamic art and artefacts) of the Portuguese poet *Guerra Junqueiro.* The office of the tour company *Porto Tours* is situated in the medieval tower 50m below the Cathedral. Here you can book for any of the extensive city and river Douro tours operated by the company. These include bus tours of the city and environs and a one-day cruise up the Douro, returning by train. There are also tours to the prehistoric rock art valley at Vila Nova de Foz Côa, off the river Douro. The following Porto 'excursion' follows the waymarked route from the cathedral to the start of the pedestrian street rua de Cedofeita (1.6 km) – and then loops back to the river – mopping up the remaining 'must see' sights on the way!

Praça da Liberdade *& Rua dos Aliados leading to* **Paços do Concelho** *(centre)*

❶ **Cathedral** *Sé* overlooking the city and river Douro. Like most medieval cathedrals it has been altered and embellished many times since its inauguration in the 12th century, most notably in the Baroque period. However it never lost its austere Romanesque form of fortress-church. Enter the west door below its fine rose window and just inside is the ⓘ information desk where you can obtain a *credencial* (€2) or have your existing 'passport' stamped. €2 secures a ticket to visit the 14th century Gothic cloisters and provides access to the Chapter House *Casa do Cabido* and the cathedral treasury on the first floor. Many visitors never discover the wonderful notary chamber room on the second floor (immediately above). Richly adorned with hand painted tiles *azulejos* and a stunningly beautiful painted ceiling, with St. Michael making up the central panel over-lighting proceedings below. But, most significantly, here you will find a delightful 16th century statue of Santiago Peregrino, pilgrim staff in hand – an opportunity, perhaps, to obtain a blessing on your own pilgrimage ahead. To the rear of the cathedral is ***museu de Guerra Junqueiro*** with courtyard café in peaceful courtyard garden.

Pick up the first waymark opposite the cathedral west door and proceed down the cobbled ramp past the offices of Porto Tours located in the medieval tower (right) and down the steep steps into the Largo Dr. Pedro Vitorino with the imposing 16-18th century Mannerist façade of *Igreja de S. Lourenço* (*St. Laurence* with museum of religious art) built into the steep rock-face (left) and down again to cross the busy rua Mouzinho da Silveira and up into Largo São Domingos turning right into rua das Flores passing ❺ ***Igreja da Misericórdia*** 18th century Church of Mercy *interesting museum* and on to the imposing edifice of the former Companies office *Casa da Companhia* on the corner of rua das Flores 69 and rua do Ferraz. ***Note***: [!] This is the point where the alternative route, *caminho interior* via Braga separates from the main way *caminho central* – don't confuse them.

The main central route turns up sharp <left into rua do Ferraz past the tiny chapel dedicated to Saint Catherine of the Flowers *Capela de Santa Catarina das Flores. [Formerly the pilgrim office* Associação Dos Amigos do Caminho de Santiago *whose Djalma de Sousa e Correia did so much to waymark the modern camino.]* At the top of rua do Ferraz turn right> into rua dos Caldeireiros and up to the large open area at the top *Campo Mártires da Pátria* that merges into the *Jardim de João Chagas* and here on the left is the façade of the former remand prison *Cadeia da Relação* which is now a refurbished arts centre. On our right is one of Porto's most emblematic buildings ❻ ***Torre dos Clérigos*** Clergymen's Tower an impressive 18th century baroque tower and, at 75m high, the city's main landmark and worth the €4 entrance fee for the 225 steps and the grand 360 degree vista from the top. After you have stretched your quadriceps, the adjoining church *Igreja dos Clérigos,* built in a beautiful elliptical shape, is a delightful environment in which to flex your soul

muscles. The architect, Nicolau Nasoni, is buried in the church in recognition of his dedication and skill in, 'creating such a beautiful and towering monument to God'. Pick up the waymarks again at the *Jardim de João Chagas* and cross diagonally over the park past the former Polytechnic Academy *Antiga Academia Politécnica* to the blue and white tiles *azulejos* of the 18th century *Igreja do Carmo (see photo)*. It is separated from the neighbouring Carmelite convent church *Igreja das Carmelitas* by one of the narrowest building in the world – barely a metre wide! It acted as a physical barrier between the monks and the nuns who, by convention, could not live in adjoining buildings. The waymarked camino now continues straight on (s/o) into rua de Cedofeita.

To continue this excursion of Porto's main sites head down towards the city centre, past the statue of the Lions and into rua das Carmelitas where at number 144 is the *Livraria Lello (see photo)* described as, 'the most beautiful bookstore in the world'. it really is an architectural delight but now has an entry charge (summer). Have a browse or a cup of coffee atop the sweeping staircase. Continue down to join the rua Clérigos just below the church and s/o into Liberation Square *Praça da Liberdade* with its impressive statue of D. Pedro IV. At the top end is the imposing façade of the town hall *Paços Concelho Câmara*. No need to walk up the intervening Avenida dos Aliados unless you want to visit the main tourist office *Turismo* on the left side of the Câmara. It is now only a short hop *under* the Praça de Almeida Garrett to ❼ ***Estação de São Bento*** Main rail station named after the Benedictine monastery built here in the 16th century. Step inside its grand entrance hall with magnificent display of *azulejos* (over 20,000) depicting transport scenes and historical events including the battle of Valdevez in 1140 when the king of Portugal *Afonso I (Afonso Henriques)* defeated the Spanish under king Alfonso VII of Leon thus securing Portugal's independence from Spain. Other panels show the Conquest of Ceuta in 1415 and the arrival in Porto of D. João I and Philippa of Lancaster.

At this point we can return to the cathedral now visible up Av. Vimara Peres or head down the wide rua Mousinho da Silveira towards the river into Praça do Infante Henrique where we find a statue to this most famous son of King D. João I – Henry the Navigator (1394 – 1460) who was a major force in the Portuguese discoveries of the New World. He looks down to the harbour and the house where he was born ❷ ***Casa do Infante*** (also referred to as House of the Navigator) and museum in the rua Infante Dom Henrique. Perhaps it's time to cool off by the harbour and quench your thirst at any of the numerous bars, cafés, restaurants and fado houses that surround this historic and lively riverside area *Cais da Ribeira* or take a river trip on one of Porto's iconic river barges *Barcos Rabelos* now converted to transport tourists rather than Port wine. Around €10 will secure a memorable 1 hour boat ride under 6 of the city's bridges and down to the river mouth. If you have time or energy head back up to Praça do Infante Henrique to visit the fabulous interior of ❸ ***Igreja de São Francisco*** now de-consecrated and turned into a museum but well worth the €2 entry fee to soak up some of its quiet and cool interior bedecked with gilded carvings (some of the most impressive in Portugal). A combined ticket provides access to a small museum opp. the church entrance and the sombre catacombs below. A short walk back into Praça do Infante Henrique and we arrive at the city's splendid stock exchange building ❹ ***Palácio da Bolsa***. You can see the vast inner courtyard at the entrance without having to take the €7 guided tour, although you will miss the magnificent Arab Hall (worth the visit).

Starting Out – ***Options for Stage out of Porto***. This stage can be confusing and there are arrows pointing in every direction placed by different pilgrim associations, municipal authorities and even hotel owners with little or no cooperation between them! Don't panic, just read this carefully (maybe twice!) – you have 3 basic options (ignoring the little used *caminho por Braga*). The map is necessarily detailed but shows the following options:

❶ **Caminho Central:** ● ● ● ● 252.4 km to Santiago and the route chosen by around 60% of pilgrims. Well waymarked and served with excellent pilgrim hostels and facilities. However, the first stage through Porto is mostly on city pavements, main roads or the traditional cobblestone lanes *Calçada* with granite setts *paralelos /adoquín pavés* which are hard underfoot and carry fast moving traffic. The route has been improved by eliminating hazardous sections and waymarking via the Monastery in Vairão which has been restored as a pilgrim hostel (and museum) and makes a welcome first stage stop-over. From Vairão / Vilarinho onwards the route is a delightful mix of quiet country lanes, agricultural tracks and forest paths that undulate over gentle hills separated by wide river valleys and coastal inlets *rias*.

❷ **Caminho da Costa** ● ● ● ● 273.8 km to Santiago and growing in popularity now accounting for around 35% of pilgrims. However, the first stage out of Porto has been cobbled together by local authorities with scant knowledge of the needs of the modern pilgrim. It skirts the airport runway and is *all* by road. While generally well waymarked there are stretches with no signposts. **Note** this refers ***only*** to the first stage out of Porto; the rest of the Coastal way is a delightful mix of small country lanes and forest paths in the hills above the coast dropping down to stretches of sandy paths and boardwalks by the sea. It crosses over the Minho river estuary into Spain and reconnects with the Camino Central in Redondela. ***Both routes*** involve a long slog through the suburbs of Porto and, like any stage through a major city, there will be challenges and these include the difficulty of spotting waymarks with competing signs and street advertisements. The routes *are* well waymarked but you have to stay focussed and this attentiveness must also be directed towards the fast moving city traffic. The following alternatives are worth considering.

❸ **Senda Litoral (alt.):** ● ● ● ● This makes a good alternative for the first stage out of Porto, depending on prevailing weather as onshore winds can make walking difficult with sea-spray and wind-blown sand. A tourist vibe replaces the camaraderie of the main route but the majority is on boardwalks *paseos de madera* which makes for pleasant walking alongside the beaches and sand dunes which are protected on account of their fragile habitat. Several new albergues and campsites now offer pilgrim lodging en route and the historic town of Vila do Conde makes a good stop-over for this stage from where it is possible to reconnect with the Camino Central via Arcos (see next stage for details). Official waymarks have been removed in order to discourage this option with local organisations encouraging pilgrims to commit to one or other route before leaving Porto. If you are comfortable with 'finding your way' switching routes remains a viable option...

...otherwise continue on the main Coastal route *Caminho da Costa* or the largely unwaymarked seashore path ❹ **Senda Litoral** ● ● ● ● which, from this point on, is shown with brown dots. It is generally *not* waymarked with yellow arrows but follows the coastline. This is sometimes difficult in practise as pathways often peter out on some remote beach requiring a hard walk on soft sand or retracing steps. There are also countless local PR & GR paths providing a bewildering array of options. In those situations where a coastal stretch connects easily with the main Caminho da Costa a tick ✓ suggests a good optional alternative; otherwise it makes sense to stick with the main waymarked route.

All routes start at the **Cathedal in Porto** Ⓐ Routes 1 & 2 effectively follow the same waymarks until Pedrão de Légua where they split. ***Note the maps in this guide cover an average of 26 km per stage but this has been designed for page layout purposes only. We each have a different pace and level of fitness so decide where YOU wish to start and end each day.*** The first day on the Senda Litoral covers a total distance of 33.9 km from the cathedral to Vila do Conde. Pilgrims choosing this option can stopover en route (lodging is limited and often full during the tourist season). Alternatively start in **Matosinhos** Ⓑ (bus 500 from Praça Liberdade / tram #1 Praça Ribeira or metro from Trindade to Mercado... or walk along the Douro estuary from the cathedral and overnight in Matosinhos.

Most pilgrims commit to walk the entire route from the cathedral but those with time limitations or wishing to skip the rigours of the road out of the city have various options (see map next page). Metro from Trindade *direction* Póvoa de Varzim and alight at **Vilar do Pinheiro** Ⓒ. Turn right> (east) for *Camino Central* continue s/o over N-13 to join waymarked route in ***Mosteiró [1.5 km].*** Or turn <left (west) to *Caminho da Costa,* waymarking starts at end of *airport runway [+0.7 km]*. After 2.5 km there is another option to turn left to the Senda Litoral via Labruge (Albergue) or s/o to Mindelo. See map next page .

14 PORTO – VILARINHO *VILA do CONDE*

--- --- 0.5 --- --- *2%*
--- --- 16.8 --- --- *61%*
--- --- 10.3 --- --- *37%*
Total km **27.6** km *(17.2 ml)*

Total ascent **250**m +**25** *minutes**
Alto *m* Igreja Maia **125**m *(410 ft)*
<A H> Moreira da Maia **14.9** km. Vairão **24.4** km.

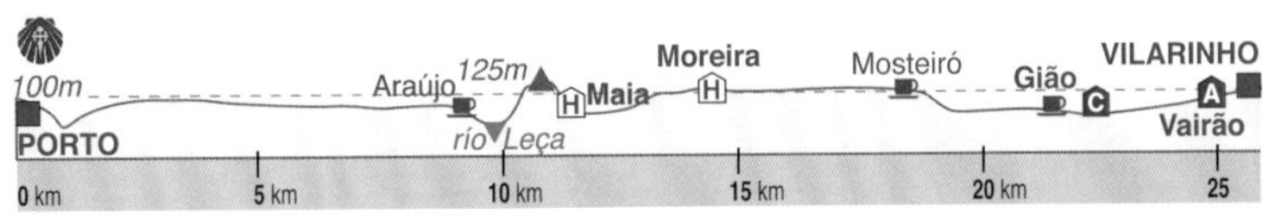

Practical Path: *(*Allow ±8 hours to walk 32.2km at average pace of 4 kph [32.2 ÷4] +25 mins for cumulative ascent of 250m = ±8 ½ hours total. See p.21).* Despite comprehensive waymarking out of Porto street signs etc compete for our attention and if we get distracted it is easy to get lost – stay very focused! Study the map opposite as it covers a wide range of options but everything will become clear 'on the ground'. The various waymarked routes also require us to cross busy main roads [!]. The city pavements and cobbled laneways are hard underfoot and there is little respite from the noise of traffic. While the highest point of this stage is Maia at only 125m there are sections of undulating terrain. All grist for the mill and remember – things can only get better... and they do!

Look at every path closely and deliberately. Then ask yourself, and yourself alone, one question, 'Does this path have a heart?' If it does, the path is good; if it doesn't, it is of no use. *The Teachings of Don Juan*

Mystical Path: Have you found the inner waymark that points in the direction of our true Destination? One thing is certain, it will only be found by following the wisdom of the heart. We have become intoxicated with the things of this world and fallen into a deep stupor. We search for relics housed in stone buildings that mask the true home of spirit. In our delirium we have forgotten the way Home... and yet feelings of alienation and loss stir us to awaken.

Personal Reflections: *"...in the distraction of the city I forgot the waymarks to the inner path. I pause to clear my mind of the anger I directed towards a dangerous driver. Psychic rubbish is every bit as noxious as the physical rubbish that I now observe all around me... I start to pick up litter and, feeling momentarily self-righteous, remind myself of the times in the past that I have littered the landscape. I suddenly become aware of a bright red rose just above my head – still part of the sense-perceptible world but reflecting, perhaps, a symbol of a higher truth. Yet in my initial anger I so nearly missed it..."*

0.0 km **Cathedral** we pick up the first waymark opp. the entrance and zigzag down (as described on p.112) and cross the busy rua Mouzinho da Silveira up into Largo São Domingos veering right> into rua das Flores passing the museu Igreja da Misericórdia and turn up sharp <left into the narrow **rua do Ferraz [0.5** km] [!] *(**Note** the route to Braga 'caminho interior' continues s/o into rua do Almada.*

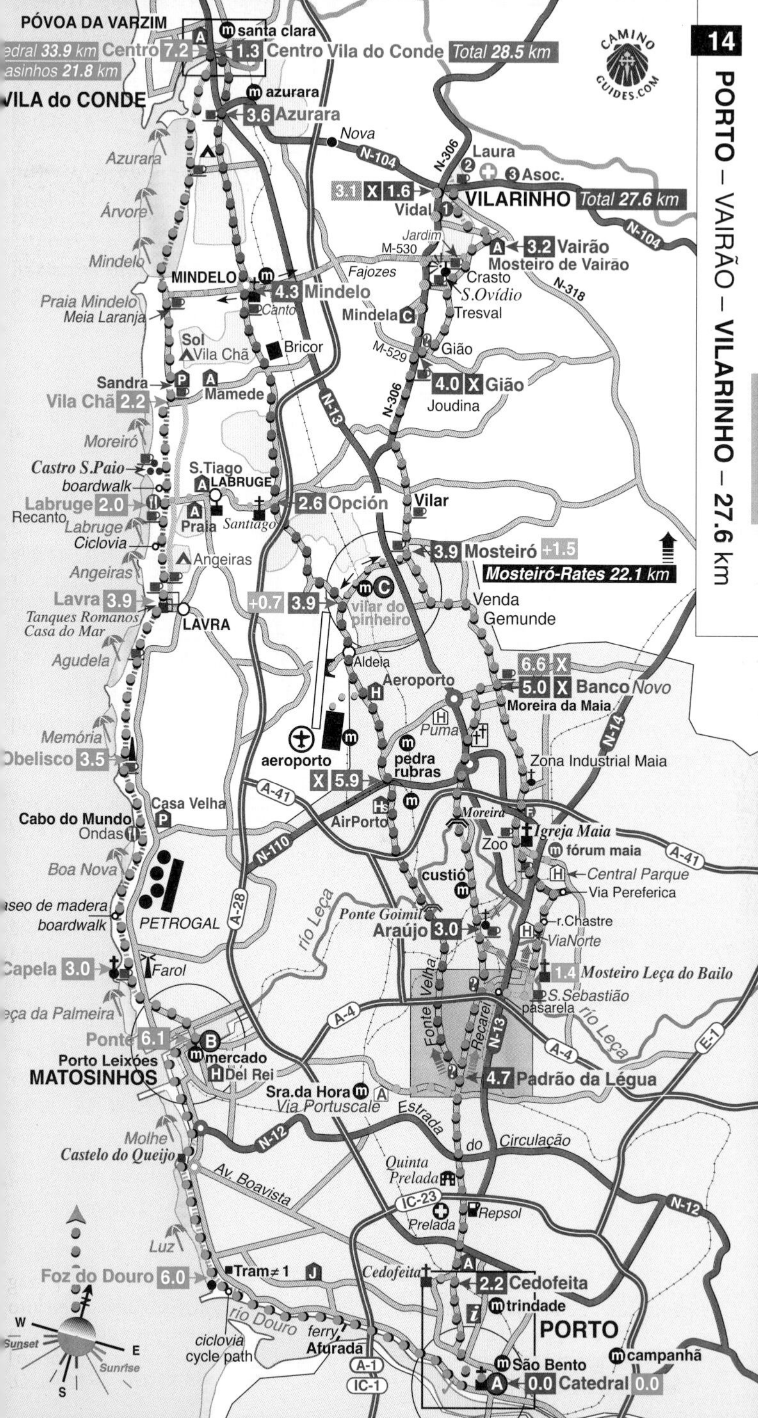

14
PORTO – VAIRÃO – VILARINHO – 27.6 km
CAMINO GUIDES.COM
PÓVOA DA VARZIM
santa clara
edral 33.9 km
asinhos 21.8 km
Centro 7.2
1.3 Centro Vila do Conde
Total 28.5 km
VILA do CONDE
azurara
3.6 Azurara
Nova
N-104
N-306
Laura
Asoc.
3.1 X 1.6
VILARINHO
Total 27.6 km
Vidal
Azurara
Árvore
Mindelo
Jardim
M-530
3.2 Vairão
Mosteiro de Vairão
N-318
Fajozes
Crasto
S.Ovídio
MINDELO
4.3 Mindelo
Canto
Praia Mindelo
Meia Laranja
Mindela
Tresval
Sol
Vila Chã
Bricor
M-529
Gião
Sandra
Mamede
4.0 X Gião
Vila Chã 2.2
N-13
N-306
Joudina
Moreiró
Castro S.Paio
boardwalk
S.Tiago
LABRUGE
Labruge 2.0
Recanto
Labruge
Praia
Santiago
2.6 Opción
Vilar
Ciclovia
3.9 Mosteiró +1.5
Mosteiró-Rates 22.1 km
Angeiras
Angeiras
Lavra 3.9
LAVRA
+0.7 3.9
vilar do pinheiro
Venda
Gemunde
Tanques Romanos
Casa do Mar
Agudela
Aldeia
6.6 X
5.0 X Banco Novo
Aeroporto
Moreira da Maia
N-14
Puma
Memória
aeroporto
pedra rubras
Zona Industrial Maia
Obelisco 3.5
X 5.9
A-41
Casa Velha
Moreira
Cabo do Mundo
Ondas
AirPorto
Igreja Maia
Zoo
fórum maia
A-41
N-110
Boa Nova
custió
Central Parque
Via Pereferica
aseo de madera
boardwalk
PETROGAL
A-28
río Leça
Ponte Goimil
Araújo 3.0
r.Chastre
ViaNorte
Capela 3.0
Farol
Fonte Velha
Recarei
1.4 Mosteiro Leça do Bailo
S.Sebastião
pasarela
A-4
eça da Palmeira
N-13
río Leça
Ponte 6.1
A-4
E-1
mercado
Porto Leixões
MATOSINHOS
Del Rei
4.7 Padrão da Légua
Sra.da Hora
Via Portuscale
Estrada do Circulação
Molhe
N-12
Castelo do Queijo
Quinta Prelada
Av. Boavista
IC-23
Repsol
Prelada
N-12
Luz
Foz do Douro 6.0
Tram≠1
Cedofeita
2.2 Cedofeita
trindade
PORTO
rio Douro
ferry
Afurada
ciclovia
cycle path
A-1
IC-1
São Bento
campanhã
0.0 Catedral 0.0
W
E
S
Sunset
Sunrise

Be careful not to confuse these waymarks at this early stage). Continue up steeply to the top and turn right> into rua da Vitória and then sharp <left into rua dos Caldeireiros and up to the expansive plaza at the top *Campo dos Martires da Patria* with Torre dos Clerigos (right) and the imposing former remand prison **Cadeia da Relação** *(left)* [**0.5** km]. Cross over to the park past the neoclassical building (right) part of the university's science faculty *faculdade de ciências* into Praça de Gomes Teixeira. On the corner (left) is the Carmelite church *Igreja do Carmo* evident from its distinctive blue and white tiles *azulejos (see photo top of p.113)*. From here we pass into the Praça de Carlos Alberto and the start of the pedestrian shopping street **rua de Cedofeita [0.2 km]** which now runs in a straight line to the crossroads at rua de Álvares (Sacadura) Cabral [**1.0** km]:

2.2 km **Cedofeita *Option.*** Crossroads and optional short detour 250m *down left* into rua de Sacadura Cabral to Cedofeita church. (Note: Praça da Republica is *up right* rua de Alvares Cabral 500m for those accessing the route from there):

Detour 250m ● ● ● ● **Igreja de Cedofeita** *site* of one of the oldest Christian places of worship in Europe. The foundations of the Igreja de Cedofeita were laid in the middle of the 6th century, viz. 555 A.D. by the Suevian king Theodomir. What remains is, in most part, a 12th century Romanesque building constructed over the original foundations.

S/o over crossroads into rua do Barão de Forester under rail to Nº 954 (right) welcoming ●✪ **Porto pilgrim albergue** [**0.5** km] *(2.6 km from the cathedral)*. Continue up to the chapel at largo da Ramada Alta veer <left into rua de Nove de Julho. Cross the rua de Egas Moniz *under* block of apartments over rua da Constituição under more apartments veer <left to pass pilgrim cross (left) and up to the crossroads at **Igreja de Carvalhido** [**1.1** km] its exterior adorned with *azulejos*. Continue s/o into rua do Carvalhido merging into rua do Monte dos Burgos past the Hospital da Prelada (left) and Repsol station (right) under city bypass *Via de Cintura Interna* A-20 past entrance (left) of Quinta da Prelada *(formerly city camping now equestrian centre)*. S/o over [**!**] city ring road **Estrada Circunvalação** [**1.5** km] into rua Nova do Seixo to pass Clínica Médica Padrão da Légua and taxi rank (right) to crossroads and option point [**1.6** km].

4.7 km **Padrão da Légua *¡Opción!*** ▼ Roadside cross ***cruceiro***. option ❶ for: *[+**1.5** km ●Alb.* **ViaPortuscale** *Asoc.[20÷2] €7 ✆ 960 227 134 Abel (phone in advance). Directions: s/o over r/Fonte Velha into r/São Gens and r/Vasco Santana 264 (Senhora da Hora)]*. Option ❷ for Camino Costa.

➠ **Caminho da Costa** ● ● ● ● turns <left into Rua do Senhor and Rua Fonte Velha (one-way) from *café Magnólia*. S/o through Santiago de Custóias at Jardim largo do Souto under A-4 into r/do Cal over medieval Ponte Goimil into r/das Carvalhas. The route continues over the A-41 into r/da Estrada past pilgrim ●*Hs* **AirPorto** *[20÷2]* €13-17 ✆ 229 427 397 at Nº244 and up to the N-107 at the roundabout for the **Airport** **5.9 km** Several hotels incl. •*H**** **Aeroporto** €46+ ✆ 229 429 334 w*www.hotelaeroporto.com.pt* r/Pedras Rubras (en route). The camino is now well waymarked all the way to Vila do Conde.

▼ Main **Camino Central** keep s/o Rua do Recarei under **A-4 flyover** [**1.6** km].

Optional Route via ● ● ● ● Mosteiro Leça do Balio 1.4 km: with option to continue s/o to **Moreira da Maia** (Banco Novo): This newly waymarked route replaces the dangerous section over the Ponte de Barreiros and the leap of faith over the N-13! It adds 1.5 km to the main route via Igrexa Maia (8.0 km-v-6.5 km). Directions: (not waymarked) just beyond the A-4 underpass turn right into Rua Dr. Silva Santos (Escuela Básica) and take the footbridge pasarela over the rail line and then over the N-14 and take the cobblestone lane through Largo S. Sebastiao down to the monastery and park. Return the same way, or continue via Igrexa Maia:

***Mosteiro Leça do Balio:** Romanesque monastery founded by the Order of St. Benedict and dedicated to San Salvador in 986 AD. In the 12th century the monastery was donated by queen D. Teresa to the Military Order of St. John and it became the burial place of various Hospitaller knights. In 1372 King Fernando I married Dona Leonor Teles in secret at the monastery. In a complex and gruesome plot Leonor's sister Maria was also subsequently married secretly to Dom João, son of King Pedro and Inêz and thereby heir to the throne. The tumultuous love affair threatened the power of Leonor who falsely accused her sister of infidelity and arranged for her gruesome murder in the Palace at Coimbra (see Coimbra).*

To continue directly to **Moreira da Maia + 6.6** km carry s/o past the Monastery and pick up the waymarks which run between the brewery (left) and shopping complex (right) along Rua da Lionesa and over the **rio Leça [1.0** km] up to Rua do Chartre. *[**Note:** Back sharp left 300m* off *route on the N-14 •H*** **ViaNorte** €35+ ✆ *229 448 294]*. Continue s/o to the new Maia bypass and turn left along the **Via Pereferica [1.0** km] (Av. de João Paulo II) down across the valley and N-14. When the Pereferica ends turn up sharply **right> [1.1** km] past and at the T-junction turn up <left. *[**Note:** the connecting route from Metro Fórum Maia joins from the right 700m* off *route. Also •H*** **Central Parque** €50 ✆ *229 475 563 Av. Visc. Barreiros]*.

Continue up past the **Igreja da Maia** *Capela de Na. Sa. do Bom Despacho* with its façade of *azulejos* and the high point of this stage at 120 m. Just past the church is the shaded *Zoo do Maia* with (left). Turn right at the crossroads by Quinta de Santa Cruz past *Saloã de Jogos* over the new eco-camino ciclovia to pass **Fonte do Godim [1.1** km] fill up with its invigorating waters (often a queue of locals filling up on its high chemical quality!). Now it's up again under the motorway underpass in the direction of Gemunde. Veer <left by shaded park in Guarda with its tiny chapel dedicated to S. António. Follow sign for the industrial zone (Z.I. Maia 1) up to another high point 120m passing sports *Leões* the road (no margin!) continues through woodland and maize crops to the next major crossroads and option point [**2.4** km]:

Moreira da Maia 6.6 km ***Cruce*** crossroads with bank *Espirito Santo* and adjoining. This is where pilgrims taking the main road route join from the left. See main route for accommodation options ½ km (left) at the main crossroads at *Cruz das Guardeiras* on the N-13.

For the main waymarked route (from option at **A-4 flyover 1.6** km see bottom of p. 118▼) Keep s/o Rua de Gondivai over railway to **Araújo** [**1.4** km].

3.0 km **Araújo** with small chapel *Capela* (right) adj. the Sacred Oak ☕ *Carvalho Santo* and shaded park with seating. The café is named after a miraculous event 200 years ago when a hurricane tore through Araújo and demolished everything in sight, save the ancient oak that stood here. Wood from the tree is used in the pulpit in the adjoining 19thc chapel of St. Peter *Igreja de São Pedro de Araújo*. A tiny statue of St. Peter is embedded in the oak which still occupies the centre of the square. Note the ancient *curceiro* with scallop shells and other pilgrim motifs on the shaft. *[Note also: The route down adj. D. Frei Manuel Vas Concellos and over ponte de Barreiros and the dangerous N-13 is now permanently closed].*

Continue s/o Rua de Custío, cross metro line down to the Río Leça and **Ponte de Moreira** [**2.0** km]. Continue s/o over the IC-24 A-41 and turn right> onto Av. do Aeroporto (N-107) and s/o over new roundabout with the A-13 (Quinta do Mosteiro left) veer right> by **cemetery** [**1.4** km].past ☕ *Mosteiro* and turn right> at T-junction *(hotels left 300m see below)* into Rua Eng. Frederico Ulrich to rejoin alt. route from *Leça do Balio* at crossroads [**1.6** km].

5.0 km **Moreira da Maia** ***Cruce*** Traffic lights and Banco Novo and ☕. *[If you need accommodation at this point there is a selection ½ km back down Rua Eng. Frederico Ulrich on the N-13.* •*H*** **Puma** *x36* €40 ✆ 229 482 128 r/Cruz das Guardeiras 776. Other possibilities +½ km adj. airport (see p.122 Camino da Costa). We now leave behind the asphalt and city pavements and head onto quieter cobblestone laneways *calçada portuguesa* which are attractive but the granite setts *paralelos* are hard underfoot and make up much of Portugal's rural road network. Lack of maintenance compounds the problems as missing setts are a hazard to walkers and walking poles stick in the gaps.

Continue s/o between industrial buildings past ☕ *CL5* to crossroads **Gemunde** [**2.6** km]. Keep s/o (signposted Mosteiró) passing ☕ *Beira Campo* in Venda past Rua Mirante (Metro Pinheiro left) into **Mosteiró** [**1.3** km]:

3.9 km **Mosteiró** with pleasant shaded square ☕ *Mosteiró. [pilgrims from the Metro option at Vilar do Pinheiro join here. See p.115* **C** *for details].* S/o past ☕ *Vinte 29* up into **Vilar** s/o over crossroads along the busy N-306 past ☕ *Ramiro* to crossroads in **Gião / Joudina** ☕ *pastelaria*.

4.0 km **Gião /Joudina** ***Option.*** **A** turn right (sign Tresval) for quiet country road to **Mosteiro de Vairão** along r/da Igreja to ☕ *Lemos* and **Capela S. Ovidio** [**2.0** km] with viewpoint over the coast (worth the short 150m climb to the chapel in a sheltered grove of ancient oak trees left). Continue s/o past ☕ *Jardim* into r/do Convento to Largo do Mosteiro in **Vairão** [**1.2** km]. **B** keep s/o along busy N-306 past •*CR* **Casa Mindela** [**0.5** km] *x6* €49-60 ✆ 914 118 018 (Helena Duarte) *www.casamindela.pt* r/da Joudina 427 (N-306). Continue s/o to crossroads in **Vilarinho** [**2.6** km] with albergues cafes and bars (see next page).

3.2 km **Vairão** Monastery founded in the Xth century and recently renovated to provide popular lodging with meditation room & museum. ●*Alb.* **Mosteiro de Vairão** ✪*Asoc.[72÷12]+* €-donativo © Eduardo 915 240 661. *Reiki massage Carla* © 966 431 916. *www.mosteirodevairao.blogspot.com* Kitchen/ *communal dining / local restaurants (deliver from €6!)* 🛒*Teixeira 300m.* The hostel & pilgrim museum is the inspiration of Pedro Macedo and a dedicated team of volunteers who have created this peaceful oasis at the end of this first stage out of Porto city. Continue via rua das Oliveiras over N-104 and N-318 to rejoin main waymarked route in **Vilarinho**.

1.6 km **Vilarinho** small but busy town at junction of the N-306 and N-104 *(The latter links Vila do Conde on the coastal route (left/west) with Trofa (right on the Braga route.)* The town has a welcome shaded central park off which are several bars and cafés incl. ☕ *Nova Aurora* adj. 🍴 *Castelo (Ivo)* at the far end (right) of the square. Vilarinho has 3 albergues. ❶ **Casa Família Vidal** *Priv.[9÷3]* €12 © 252 661 503 m: 966 766 092 rua Salterio 87 (adj. Gelataria Paulos). ❷ **Casa da Laura** *Priv.[8÷1]+* €12 © 917 767 307 rua Estreita 112 with peaceful garden adj. to ☕ *CJ's* with pilgrim menú. The original hostel is located ½ km east ❸ **Escuela *Polidesportivo*** *Mun.[4÷1]* © 252 661 610 along Rua D. Ildefonso past the helpful chemist *Farmácia Rei* © 252 661 610 (09:00 – 19:00) who hold a key. *Next albergue Rates (11.4 km – allow 4 hours at end of day pace) or detour to Vila do Conde (6 km – allow 2 hours or take a taxi (10 mins c. €10) or the bus. See alternative coastal route for lodging in this attractive seaside town.*

Personal Reflections:

Seashore *Senda Litoral* ● ● ● ● (**Not** the Coastal Way *Caminho da Costa*). **Porto Cathedral – Vila do Conde 33.9** km. Popular alternative to the busy road routes out of the city. [Starting in Matosinhos reduces the distance to Vila do Conde to only **21.8** km].

0.0 km Cathedral Turn left diagonally over Cathedral Square *terreiro da sé* down Escades das Verdades (orange arrows) into Rua do Barredo under niche to the Lord of Good Fortune *Senhor da Boa Fortuna* into the ancient Rua dos Canastreiros and out into **Praça da Ribeira** [**0.4** km]. From here we essentially follow the Río Douro and the coast by pavements, cycle tracks *ciclovia* and boardwalks *paseos madera* all the way to Vila do Conde. Continue past the museu dos Transportes (left) and do Vinho (right) and out under the **suspension bridge** [**2.9** km] passing the mini ferry port where €1.50 buys you a ticket to cross the river to visit Afurada on the far side. We pass a bird observatory and park (detour to Pousada de Juventude right) and s/o along the estuary to the #1 **tram terminus** [**2.7** km]

6.0 km Foz do Douro we now leave the river estuary and traverse the shaded gardens along the coast to pass Castelo S. João •*H**** **Boa-Vista** *x70* €78-88 ✆ 225 320 020 *www.hotelboavista.com* Esplanada do Castelo, 58 & **Queijo Castle** [**3.1** km] Boavista roundabout and into **Matosinhos** *Posto de Turismo* ✆ 229 386 423 Av. Gen. Norton de Matos into the busy port of Leixões to **Mercado** [**3.0** km].

6.1 km Matosinhos *Ponte Móvel* ***Lodging***: •*P.* **Leão de Ouro** *x15* €35-45 ✆ 229 380 673 r/ Conde São Salvador, 162 [+150m]. •*Hs* **Fishtail** *x24* €20pp-40 ✆ 229 380 345 *www.fishtail-seahouse.pt* r/Godinho, 224 [+250m]. **Rua Brito Capelo Nº169** [+200m] •*H**** **Porto-Mar** *x33* €56-70 ✆ 229 382 104. **@Nº843** •*Hsr* **D'el Rei** *x20* €30-40 ✆ 229 372 914. **@Nº599** •*P.* **Central** *x24* €35+ ✆ 229 380 664 *www.pensaocentral.net* Cross the bridge over Río Leça a symbolic start as we leave Porto city behind. Waymarks direct us down Rua Hintze Ribeiro to the promenade at **Praia Leça da Palmeira** and we head North by Av. Liberdade towards the lighthouse *farol da Boa Nova (visible ahead)* built to alleviate the shipwrecks along this notorious stretch of the Black Coast *Costa Negra.*

3.0 km Capela *Boa Nova* ☕ we now join the extensive network of wooden boardwalks *paseos de madera.* Providing welcome relief from the hard pavements and soft sand with information panels all along the coast to Vila do conde. We leave behind the giant Petrogal plant (right) and pass through Adeia Nova & **Cabo do Mundo** •**Casa Velha** *x5* €35+ ✆ 965 072 203 r/de Almeiriga Norte 2510. to arrive at Remembrance Beach and Obelisk *Praia da Memória e Obelisco.*

3.5 km Obelisco *da Memória* ☕ we cross Ribeira da Agudela separating praias de Agudela ☕ *Pedras do Corgo* W.C. and Marreco in the area of **Fontão** site of megalithic remains from the 3rd millenium BC and Roman artefacts of 3rd Century AD to traditional stone fisherman's houses *Casas do Mar de Angeiras.*

3.9 km **Lavra** *Angeiras replica* Roman salt tanks *tanques romanos salga* used for salt collection and salting fish. The area was also used to harvest seaweed *Sargaço* to fertilize the sterile sandy soil. *[Detour ½ km Alb.* ▲ **Angeiras** ***Orbitur*** ✆ *229 270 571 (open 24 hours) r/Angeiras.* Bungalows pilgrim price €8-20 pp.(excl. Aug). Keep s/o past *Praia dos Pescadores* and take wooden bridge over Río Onda which separates the parishe of **Lavra** (Matosinhos) from **Labruge** (Vila do Conde) to Praia Labruge:

2.0 km **Labruge** ***Opción*** ☕ *Novo Rumo [Detour Av. Liberdade •CR* **Praia** *x7* €38-45 ✆ 910 894 591 @N°439 [+400m]. *Labruge town centre +0.5 km* ●*Alb.* **São Tiago** *Mun.[18÷2] €-donativo* ✆ *229 284 686. Renovated school with all mod. facilities. Parish church is dedicated to Santiago].* Continue on boardwalks that skirt the next sandy cove and wind our way around the S. Paio headland past **Capela S. Paio** [**1.0** km] ☕ *S. Paio*. Archeological investigations continue and panels explain the rich history and geology of the ancient area. Continue past Praia de Moreiró and into the fishing village of **Vila Chã** [**1.2** km].

2.2 km **Vila Chã** *Largo dos Pescadores* W.C. •*P* **Sandra** *x6* €30+ ✆ 919 254 629 behind ☕ *Tony'.* ●*Alb.Mun.[**20**÷2]* **São Mamede** €10 ✆ 934 379 460 Trv. do Sol, 40 [+250m]. Continue along Rua Facho to turn off right ▲*Parque* **Campismo Sol** €7+ ✆ 229 283 163 www.campingvilacha.com r/do Sol [+200m]. Keep s/o to boardwalks into **Praia Mindelo** [**2.2** km] ☕ W.C. Large expanse of beach continuing to the Ave estuary. New boardwalks skirt the dunes and the beaches of **Praia Árvore** [**2.3** km] ▲ **Camping Árvore** ✆ 252 633 225. **Azurara** ☕ where we turn inland at the round tower (ruins) over small stream turning <left into Rua Francisco Goncales Mosteiró past the shipyards through the suburbs of Azurara up to the main road A-13 where we join pilgrims from the Caminho da Costa to cross the bridge over the estuary of the Río Ave [**2.7** km] into:

7.2 km **Vila do Conde** ***Centro*** *Praça da República* the heart of this delightful town with its medieval quarter built around the harbour and dominated by the prominent white dome of the *Capela do Socorro.* This tiny circular chapel was built in 1603 in the Moorish style with *azulejos* displaying the adoration of the Magi. Nearby is the maritime museum and replica of a Portuguese caravel *(Vila do Conde was a major centre of boat building activity in Portugal's great exploration period).* The narrow cobbled alleyways wind around the ancient fishing quarter and central square with the XVIth parish church *Igreja Matriz.* If you want to swim in the sea head west past to the sandy beach around St. John the Baptist Fort (15 minutes from the town centre). Overlooking the town is the impressive *Convento de Santa Clara (background in photo above).* The walk up to the top is rewarded with fine views of the town and coastal area and the remains of a remarkable aqueduct built in the early 18th century that fed the entire complex with water from the nearby hills.

ⓘ ***Turismo*** ✆ 252 248 473 rua 25 April town centre by taxi rank ✆ 252 631 933. ■ **Lodging *Centro*:** ●*Alb.* **Santa Clara** *Mun.[25÷3]* €7 ✆ 252 104 717 adj. camino shop & *Loja do Caminho* on plaza Mercado. •*Hs* **Bellamar** *[10÷2]* €12 *+9* €38 ✆ 252 631 748 Praça da República,84. ***Riverside*** Cais das Lavandeiras: •*P* **Patarata** *x10* €40+ ✆ 252 631 894 + adj. •*Hs* **Erva Doce** *x6* €16-45 ✆ 919 058 715. •*R* **Princesa Do Ave** €30-40 ✆ 252 642 065 Rua Dr António José Sousa Pereira 261. •*Hs* **Venceslau** *x15* €20-50 ✆ 252 646 362 r/Mós 13 (+500m). •*H**** **Brazão** *x36* €39-56 ✆ 252 642 016 www.hotelbrazao.pt Av. Dr. João Canavarro. ●*Pousada* **HI Vila do Conde** *[56÷5]* €13 *+10* €40+ ✆ 926 739 229. Youth hostel *Pousada* on Av. Bento de Freitas, 460. Selection of restaurants along the river and trendy *Barcearia* in courtyard opp turismo. **Azurara:** •*H***** **Spa Santana** *x75* €64+ ✆ 252 640 460 www.santanahotel.pt r/Santana. •*H***** **Villa C Spa** *x43* €85+ ✆ 252 240 420 on the N-13. The town merges into its modern neigbour **Póvoa do Varzim** which offers additional lodging (see Coastal route p.208).

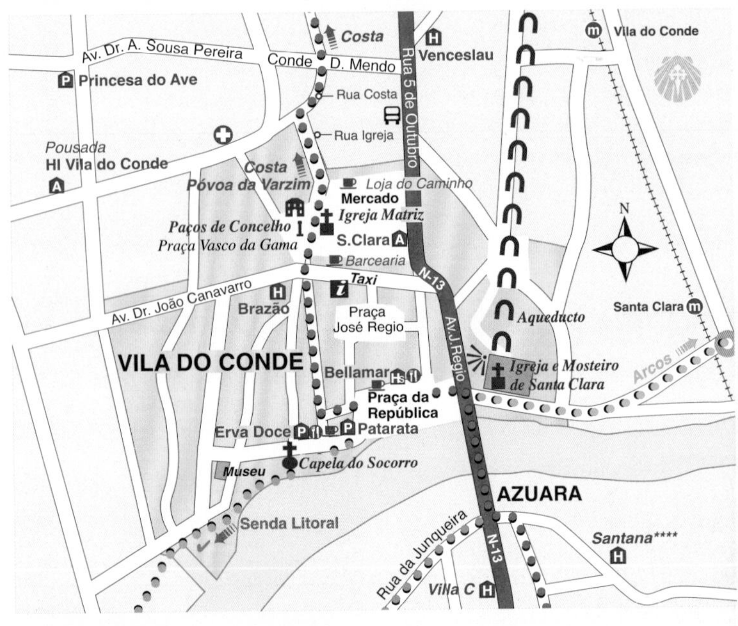

▲ To continue to **Esposende / Marinhas** on the **Caminho da Costa** go to page 208 for stage 15a.
▼ To return to the **Caminho Central** continue to Arcos via Junqueira - see next stage, details page 128.

Personal Reflections:

15 VILARINHO – BARCELOS

(dotted)	7.7	*26%*
(light)	17.1	*58%*
(dark)	4.8	*16%*
Total km	**29.6** km *(18.4 ml)*	

Total ascent **210**m +½ *hr*

▲ Alto *m* Goios **150**m *(492 ft)*

< A H > ➲Arcos **8.5** km ➲Rates **13.3** km ➲Pedra Furada **21.0** km.

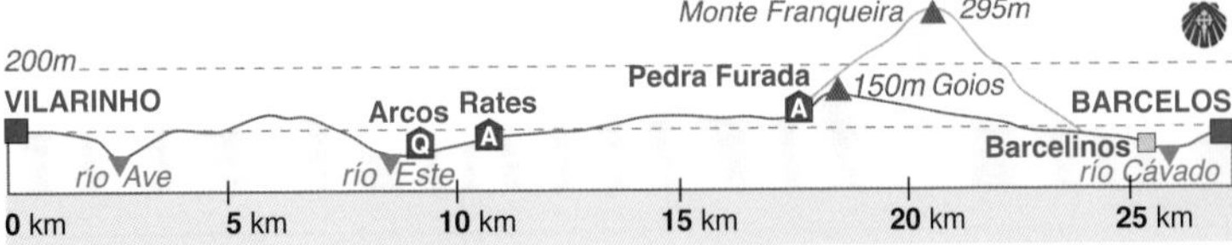

Practical Path: A varied day where we encounter our first delightful woodland paths around Arcos. While the majority is on asphalt this is somewhat kinder underfoot than the traditional granite cobblestones and this is mostly along quiet country lanes screened by eucalyptus and pine woods, offering shelter from wind and shade from sun. There are also some stretches along the N-306 with poor sight lines that require extra vigilance. Improvements are ongoing including a new woodland path around Monte Franqueira. If you are setting out from Vila do Conde see page 128 for directions to rejoin the camino central in Arcos.

The Path around our home is also the ground of awakening. *Thich Nhat Hanh*

Mystical Path: We have mastered how to travel to the moon but we don't know how to find inner peace. *Charity begins at home* is an old adage containing much wisdom. The breakdown of relationships is endemic in our affluent western world – we don't need to switch on the television to witness war. We are at war with ourselves, with our families, our own society... If we want to create peace in our world we don't need to step outside our own home – we just need to develop an open door, an open mind and an open-heart right here and now.

Personal Reflections: "...I was covered in dirt and sweat and suffering from heat exhaustion and dehydration and nearly missed the café entrance. The cool interior and the smile on the patron's face embraced me in welcome. Before I had spoken a word he guided me to a table and poured a fresh orange juice – it was unasked for and tasted like nectar. But the greatest gift was the spontaneous display of generosity. Before I left this haven of hospitality António had pressed the key of his apartment into my hand, *'treat my home as if it were your own,'* he said simply... I write these notes in his apartment overlooking the broad sweep of the river Cávado. He is at work in his restaurant till late but I look forward to having breakfast with him. I want to understand what makes one man open his home to a total stranger while another bars it to his own family..."

0.0 km Vilarinho From the central crossroads continue s/o in the direction of Fontaínhas. Stay on the N-306 and turn **right>** down to the beautiful medieval bridge over the río Ave **Ponte D. Zameiro [1.8 km]** with old mill buildings. The bridge has been damaged on several occasions in recent years. *(If the bridge is*

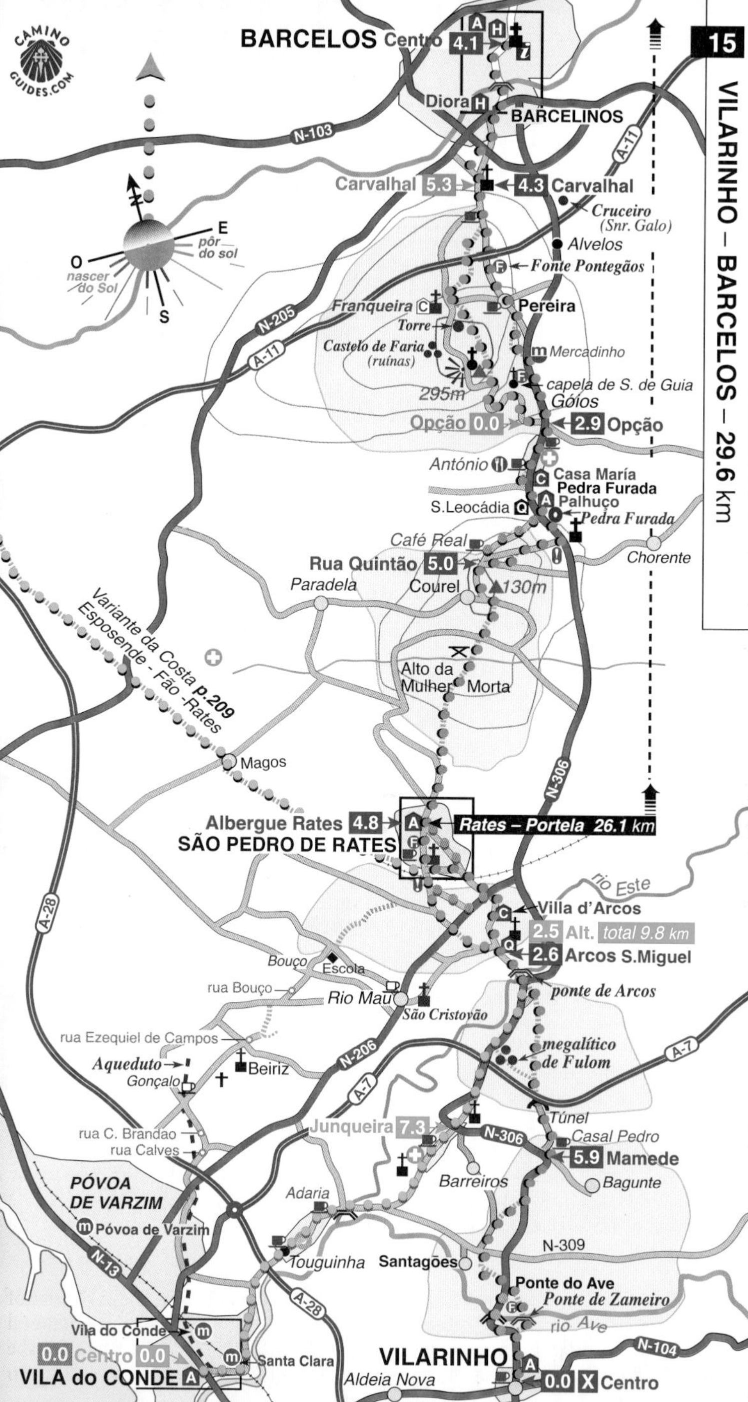
15
VILARINHO – BARCELOS – 29.6 km
CAMINO GUIDES.COM
BARCELOS Centro 4.1
Diora
BARCELINOS
N-103
A-11
Carvalhal 5.3
4.3 Carvalhal
Cruceiro (Snr. Galo)
Alvelos
Fonte Pontegãos
E
pôr do sol
O
nascer do Sol
S
N-205
Franqueira
Pereira
Torre
Castelo de Faria (ruínas)
Mercadinho
capela de S. de Guia
295m
Góios
Opção 0.0
2.9 Opção
António
Casa María
Pedra Furada
S.Leocádia
Palhuço
Pedra Furada
Café Real
Chorente
Rua Quintão 5.0
Paradela
Courel
130m
Variante da Costa p.209
Esposende - Fão -Rates
Alto da Mulher Morta
Magos
N-306
Albergue Rates 4.8
SÃO PEDRO DE RATES
Rates – Portela 26.1 km
rio Este
Villa d'Arcos
2.5 Alt. total 9.8 km
2.6 Arcos S.Miguel
A-28
Bouço
Escola
rua Bouço
Rio Mau
São Cristovão
ponte de Arcos
rua Ezequiel de Campos
N-206
megalítico de Fulom
A-7
Aqueduto
Gonçalo
Beiriz
Túnel
Junqueira 7.3
N-306
Casal Pedro
5.9 Mamede
rua C. Brandao
rua Calves
Barreiros
Bagunte
PÓVOA DE VARZIM
Póvoa de Varzim
Adaria
N-309
N-13
Touguinha
Santagões
Ponte do Ave
Ponte de Zameiro
rio Ave
Vila do Conde
0.0 Centro 0.0
Santa Clara
VILARINHO
N-104
VILA do CONDE
Aldeia Nova
0.0 Centro

impassable continue along river bank and veer up to rejoin the main road and proceed over the modern bridge ½ km down river (see photo) and continue until you join the waymarks again). Proceed past [🚰] (left) up to the crossroads and *Capela de N.S. da Ajuda*. Continue up into woodland back onto **main road** *(alt. bridge route joins here).* Turn right> and imm <left at **camino signboard** [**1.1** km]. (This new detour avoids a busy and dangerous section of the N-306). Continue along quiet tracks and laneways in the direction of **Santagôes** which we skirt around via rua São Miguel onto buys secondary road (☕ by filling station Agrivil 200m off route right). Continue to cross back over the N-306 at **Mamede** to ☕ *Casal Pedro* in **Mamede** [**3.0** km].

5.9 km **São Mamede** continue along N-306 passing ☕ *Moreira* up to the **Casa do Alto** (high point at 125 m) passing the ruins of the old pilgrim and coaching inn *Estalagem das Pulgas* and down under the A-7 motorway where Arcos opens to view straight ahead. *[Optional detour here adds ½ kilometre to the waymarked route: a forest track to the left runs alongside the motorway to the megalithic burial mound* ***Megalítico do Fulom*** *described under alternative route from Vila do Conde].* We now make our way s/o down the rough path to the **rio Este** A sandy riverbank makes a good place for a picnic, or a swim? Proceed s/o over the Ponte de Arcos and up the cobbled lane with the walls of the Quinta São Miguel (right).

2.6 km **Arcos** •*CR* **Quinta São Miguel** *x11* €50+ incl. ✆ 919 372 202 *www.quintasaomiguel.com* (adj. church). Delightfully restored 18th century manor with 2 swimming pools! Owner António Rodrigues speaks English and is very supportive of pilgrims.

●●● **Vila do Conde – Arcos *via Junqueira* 9.8** km:

Follow the river Ave past Convento de Santa Clara and over **metro S.Clara** [**0.4** km] and turn right> at **T-Junction** [**1.6** km] under the A-28 into **Touguinha** ☕ up and s/o over the **roundabout** [**1.3** km] and down to join the N-309 in **Touguinhó** passing ☕ to bridge over the **Río Este** [**1.4** km] (tributary of the Ave). Cross the bridge (cascades upstream *cascatas de Touguinho*) into rua Rio Este past Quinta da Espinheira (right) to turn <left off the N-309 up into rua Central [**0.9** km] veering <left past Centro Médico ☕ (right) s/o past *Igreja Matriz* [**1.2** km] and down past school (right) ☕ *Panidoce* (left) to crossroads with ☕ and central cruceiro at **Junqueira** [**0.5** km]: **7.3 km**

Continue s/o to monastery church ahead *Igreja de São Simão da Junqueira* (statue of Santiago Peregrino in the right-hand niche). Narrow road [**!**] to cross the A-7 motorway [**1.5** km]. ***Megalítico do Fulom*** *(Mamoa do Fulão)* prehistoric Megalithic mound located in the pine forest (right). The burial chambers date back to 3,000 B.C.E. The west-facing opening is discernible in the second of the two mounds. It is little visited which adds to the mysterious atmosphere that pervades this peaceful glade despite is proximity of the new motorway. Continue along the road down to join the main waymarked route from Vilarinho at the bridge over the **Rio Este** [**0.7** km] and up into **Arcos** [**0.3** km]. 2.5 km

Option: ▲ We now have a choice of two waymarked routes to Rates. Original scenic route (left) has had the arrows erased at this point so most pilgrims blindly follow the road route along the busy N-206.

① The original route via woodland path as follows: Turn <left at *cruceiro* 'triangle' (opp. quinta side entrance) and veer right along quiet country lane *(Rua do Caminho do Porto)* which meanders around the edge of the village onto an earth **track** [**0.5** km] into eucalyptus woods and over busy main road **N-206** [**!**] [**1.1** km] by timber yard (route via Rio Mau joins from left). Continue via country lanes down over abandoned **railway** [**2.0** km] [**!**] **N.B.** do not confuse waymarks (left) here which lead to the coastal route *caminho da costa* at Esposende *(pilgrims have found themselves, unintentionally, beside the sea!)*. Keep s/o to parish church in **São Pedro de Rates.** Continue up to the **albergue** [**0.4** km] for a total distance of 4.0 km (versus 3.6 km).

② For road route (detour *desvío*) in Arcos continue s/o past church ☕ *Barbosa* and •*H* **Villa d'Arcos** €60+ ✆ 252 652 041 r/Alegria 38 [**0.5** km] down to N-206 at **crossroads** [**2.0** km] [**!**] (waymarks also point left along the N-206). Keep s/o to roundabout with statue of Santiago in the centre. To visit the historic centre (recommended) veer left here otherwise veer right direct to the albergue. Continue to the church in the centre of Rates **Igreja de S. Pedro** [**2.0** km]. ☕ *Macedo (left)* and continue on past the drinking font *Fontenário de S. Pedro* into rua Direita past •**Casa de Mattos** *x5* €40 ✆ 919 822 398 directly on the camino (not well signposted). At T-junction •**Casa Anabela** *x4* €15-35 incl. ✆ Anabela 919 578 642 *casanabela@gmail.com* r/Padrão da Vila 9 or turn up <left past 🍴 *O Pergrino menú* to Rates albergue [**0.7** km].

4.8 km São Pedro de Rates ●*Alb Asoc.* **Rates** *[50÷4]* €-donativo r/S. António 189. The first dedicated pilgrim hostel to open in Portugal – St. James Day 2004. Renovated & extended in 2009 now with 50 beds in small dormitories & good facilities including a cosy living room, laundry room and kitchen. An extensive courtyard for clothes drying and relaxing and also provides access to a small museum displaying objects typical of rural life in the area. If the hostel is closed you can obtain the key from the well-stocked and welcoming shop located 100m further on opp. *Capela de S. António* where *Dª Lurdes* and her family are usually open until 21:00 (it may look closed!).

The town is a delightful blend of old and new with the parish church dedicated to

St. Peter *São Pedro* a local saint much revered in the area and reputedly ordained by St. James himself on his evangelization of the peninsula. Beheaded in Rates his body later transferred to Braga. Originally built as a monastery church by the Order of Cluny (a powerful influence on the camino) in the 11th century over the remains of earlier pagan temples of Roman and pre-Roman origins. The church belfry is a separate structure to the rear. ❶ **Museum** (09:00-13:00/14:00-17:00) displays some artefacts found during excavation, most dating from 12th century but some exhibits from the Roman period. Adj. public toilets. Just beyond the church an extensive square opens up *Praça dos Forais* with the diminutive Chapel to Our Lady of the Square the *Capela do Sra. da Praça* (see photo p.4) with the historic Town Cross *Pelourinho*. At the far end, by the clock tower, is *Macedo* to •**Casa da Vila** *x2* €35-50 © Pedro 913 317 842 Rua Senhor dos Passos 135.

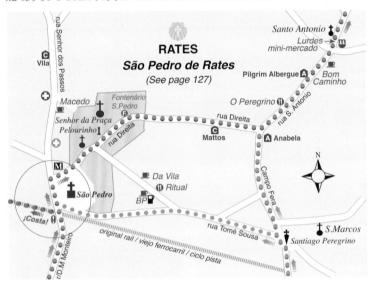

Continue up past the *Da Lurdes* veering right onto short stretch of asphalt road and turn right> onto earth track down to stream bed (wet) up through overhanging vines into eucalyptus woodland continuing along forest tracks up to a high point at Dead Woman's Peak *Alto da Mulher Morta* entering the administrative area of Barcelos. The natural path now undulates gently to cross over a road close to the village of Courel (left) s/o up through woodland ahead along a walled lane up to asphalt road around high walls of a Quinta into rua Quintão.

5.0 km Quintão *Real 100m left. [Alt. quiet road to Pedra Furada. Grey on map].* Turn right> and then <left onto short track that winds back to the main road turn <left along the busy N-306 [!]. Stay alert – the road has poor margins for the fast moving traffic & several blind bends[!]. Pass *Quinta da Sa. Leocádia* (left) and **Igreja Pedra Furada** (right)

with the perforated stone *pedra furada* that gives this area its name. Pass *Alb.* **Palhuco** *Mun.[24÷2]* €8 ✆ 252 954 331 (top photo) . Next •**Casa Dª Maria** €45 (floor space *suelo* from €10. ✆ 913 207 459 directly on main road. Take the shortcut (left) along rua Santiago which brings us to **Pedra Furada** [**2.4** km] with the ever popular ☕-🍴 *Pedra Furada* on rua Santa Leocadia. António Martins (see photo>) and his family have been welcoming pilgrims for many years. Continue up past various ☕ & 🍴 *Portela* adj. ⊕ farmacia *Dias Felix* to crossroads at **Góios** [**0.5** km] and **option:**

2.9 km **Cruce** ***Pedra Furada / Góios / Opção.*** **Option** ① Continue s/o along the main 'lower' route via **Pereira** or ② Turn left uphill to **Monte Franqueira.**

This alternative route has been waymarked through woodland around the slopes of Monte Franqueira *(Alto 290m)* with opportunity to visit Ⓐ **Capela de Sta. da Franqueira** and viewpoint. [**b**] remains of Roman castrum and [**c**] the Manueline Convento da Franqueira adj. Quinta da Franqueira (luxury accommodation). ***Note***: This is a strenuous uphill climb (+140m) and adds 1.0 km but it makes a delightful path through woodland. An annual pilgrimage to Monte Franqueria is held 2nd Sunday in August. Turn up <left at the crossroads and imm. right> by side of timber yard on asphalt road and turn off right [**2.1** km] onto forest path ❖.

[to access the chapel and viewpoint continue s/o along road for a further 800m to the top [a] ***Capela de Sta. da Franqueira*** *XVIII.* ☕ *(summer only) adj. panoramic balcony with good views west over the Atlantic and, allegedly, east to Spain! If you take this option then continue down the far side by steps to rejoin road 300m where there is an option to visit* Ⓑ ***Castelo de Faria*** *a short detour 100 metres (left) along a sandy track to this ancient fortress built over a* **Roman Castrum** *and before that over a prehistoric settlement* **Citania**. *A brief climb up through woodland brings you to the peaceful and little visited ruins built around a rocky outcrop. Continue back down the road to rejoin the waymarked route by the medieval tower 300m].*

❖ For the waymarked route veer right onto the forest path that maintains this contour line *below* Monte Franqueira to cross the road down ancient granite steps past the healing waters of the Fountain of Life *Fonte da Vida* back to road and exterior Ⓒ **Convento da Franqueira** [**1.4** km] built in the 16th century in the Manueline style (left) adjoining •**Quinta da Franqueira** €60-90 ✆ 253 831 606. The convent is under the guardianship of the Gallie family who own the Quinta which also acts as a starting base for pilgrims riding by horseback to Santiago.

To continue take the waymarked path back into the woodland over **A-11** [**0.6** km] steeply down through Monte de Cima to rejoin the main route in **Fulões** [**0.7** km] and then to **Carvalhal** [**0.4** km].

5.3 km **Carvalhal** ***Igreja*** ▲ church and albergue *(see next page)*

To continue on main *lower* route keep s/o at crossroads along **N-306** past ***Capela Senhora da Guia*** [**0.3** km] (left) [🚰]. Turn <left opp. 🛒 *da Vila* onto **track** [**0.3** km] through woodland onto cobblestone road into **Pereira** [**1.6** km]:

S.Salvador small hamlet with shop and chapel at crossroads. Continue past *S.José* along maze of small roads but the route is well waymarked as we pass the ancient [ ] **Fonte de Pontegãos** (right) under motorway and veer right> at T-Junction *[-mercado 50m left alt. route from Monte da Franqueira joins from left]*. Past ●*Alb.* **Casa Brasil** *Priv.[4÷1]* €10 + €20 private ✆ 924 069 382 dinner €5! to parish church in **Carvalhal [2.1 km].**

4.3 km Carvalhal ***Igreja*** **▲.** Turn <left at church & 50m right> into Portocarreiro over stream up to Holy Cross chapel ***Capela da Santa Cruz*** **[1.3** km] into industrial area of Barcelinhos s/o **roundabout** [**0.6** km] to rear of car showrooms & underpass (N-103) to rejoin the main road on the outskirts of **Barcelinhos**. Turn right> along main road passing (left) ●*Hs* **Diora** *Casa da Pombas [12÷3]* €10 *x5* €15-30 ✆ Casimiro 919 448 839 www.diorahostel.pt all facilities on r/São Miguel-O-Anjo, 42. Continue to crossroads and turn down <left into r/Custódio José Gomes Vilas Boas opp. ancient drinking font. *Note* access to *Alb.*❶**Amigos da Montanha** *Asoc.[16÷1]* €5 ✆ 253 830 430 hostel with access on Largo dos Penedos, 39. Pass *Cantinho do Peregrino* menú €5 (07.00–24:00) & s/o down to the medieval bridge *Ponte Barcelos* in **Barcelinhos [1.2** km]. Chapel of Our Lady of the Bridge built in 1328 to provide shelter for pilgrims (the stone benches and basins for washing feet can still be seen). On the corner is the modern •*Hs* **Barcelos Way** €45 ✆ 253 825 090. and along the riverside past the **Bombeiros** *Alb.*❷ **Residência Senhor do Galo** *Folclórico Asoc.[20÷2]* €5 ✆ 918 967 968 Rua da Carniçaria also serves as residence for folk-dance groups.

❶ ***Capela de Nª Sª da Ponte*** *[● Numbers refer to historical monuments on town plan, those with an asterisk* are national monuments. From the bridge to the central square is 800m.]* Cross over the medieval bridge ❷ ***Ponte Medieval*** built by *D. Pedro* Earl of Barcelos in 1328. This acted as a great spur to the development and prestige of the town and facilitated early pilgrims to Santiago.

Note: by taking your time along the following route you will pass most of the historic sites along the way. You can take time to visit them as you pass or return, perhaps, when you have found a place to stay for the night.

Turn <left then first right> up past the 15th century ❸ ***Solar dos Pinheiros**** manor house of the Pinheiro family (left) with its gargoyles of the bearded one *Barbadão*. Next we come to the remains of the 15th century Palace of the Counts ❹ ***Paço dos Condes*** now an open air archaeological museum ***Museu Arqueológico*** with the Pillory ***Pelourinho**** (see photo>) portraying the legend of the Cock *lenda do Gallo* (see later) with the 14th century parish church ❺ ***Igreja Matriz**** fronting onto the municipal square *Largo do Municipio.* This Romanesque church, with later Baroque additions, was built in the 12th century and has a fine display of glazed tiles *Azulejos*. On the opposite side of the square is the sumptuously restored town hall and council office ❻ ***Câmara e Paços do Concelho**** formerly a pilgrim. Continue into ❼ ***Largo do Apoio*** the original town square around which the nobility built their houses with central fountain

(1621) and popular Historial. *[At this point you can take a shortcut direct to the popular pilgrim hostel in rua Miguel Bombarda by continuing s/o past* Três Marias *into rua da Barreta].* Turn right> into rua S. Francisco to small plaza to rear of the church with statues and •*Hs* **In Barcelos** *[16÷2]* €15 *+9* €45-65 ✆ 938 308 290 *www.inbarcelos.com* r/Infante Dom Henrique Nº64. Continue s/o into main pedestrian shopping street, rua D. António Barroso to town centre [**1.0** km]:

4.1 km **Barcelos** ***Largo da Porta Nova.*** The main square is the hub of this lively town with the helpful tourist office located by the 15th century granite tower ❽ ***Torre da Porta Nova**** the only remaining medieval entrance into town. At the other end of the square is a fine stone fountain with 18th century Baroque church dedicated to Good Jesus of the Cross ❾ ***Templo do S. Bom Jesus da Cruz**** *(Igreja de Senhor das Cruces)* built in 1704 in an octagonal shape over an earlier chapel. The interior has outstanding display of *azulejos* and a beautiful statue of N.S Peregrina. This is the venue of the 500-year-old Feast of the Crosses that takes place annually on 3rd May and is named after the miraculous appearance of a cross in the soil of the adjoining market square in 1504. By the church is the central •*Hr* **Arantes** *x12* €20-40 ✆ 253 811 326 above Arantes on Av. da Liberdade 35.

BARCELOS: Opening out from the Largo da Porto Nova is the extensive market square *Campo da Feira* otherwise known as Campo da República. The whole area becomes one of Portugal's best-known and liveliest markets *Feira de Barcelos* every Thursday.

At the top end of the square is the ❿ ***Igreja do Terço*** built in 1707; its plain façade belies its rich interior and ceiling depicting the life of Saint Benedict *São Bento.* To the rear is the shopping centre and hotel in the *Centro do Terço* built around the original Convent of that name. To the rear of the Hospital Santa Maria in Largo dos Capuchinos is ***Igreja de Santo António*** where the Capuchin Franciscans offer a pilgrim blessing *Bênção do peregrino* every evening at 19:00.

Barcelos makes an excellent stopover and there are several parks and squares in which to rest and enjoy the local scene and a municipal swimming pool if you want to cool off. If you have walked from the new albergue in Rates you will have plenty of time to explore. However the next stage to Ponte de Lima is a long day so you need to be refreshed and ready for an early start although intermediate lodging is now available. The tourist office has a list of accommodation, which includes the following (see town map overleaf for locations).

❶ ***Turismo:*** ✆ 253 811 882 Largo Dr. José Novais helpful staff (also handicraft centre + internet). Normal hours: 09.30-18.00. •*Hs* **Casa da Ana** *x6* €60+ ✆ 936 018 008 www.casadaana.pt Rua Visconde Leiria, 37. ◖***Albergues:*** popular *Alb.*❸ **Cidade de Barcelos** ✪*Asoc.[26÷3]*.€-donativo www.alberguedebarcelos.com r/Miguel Bombarda **Nº36** adj. *Araujo* where Emília serves *menú peregrino €6+* nearby@**Nº41** •*Hr* **Kuarenta & Um** *x7* €40+ ✆ 932 117 730 & nearby •*H* **Art'Otel** *x9* €50-60 ✆ 934 024 180 rua da Madalena 29. ***Other central lodging:*** & •*H*** **Bagoeira** *x54* €45+ ✆ 253 809 500 Av. Dr. Sidónio Pais, 495. •*H*** **Terço** *x37* €35-45 ✆ 253 808 380 www.hoteldoterco.com rua de São Bento (pedestrian entrance via shopping mall) modern hotel on upper floors. ***Towards rail station:*** •*H* **Dom Nuno** *x27* €35+ ✆ 253 812 810 r/Dr. Francisco Torres, 141 modern hotel. •*HsR* **Solar da Estação** €25+ ✆ 933 056 887 Largo Marechal Gomes da Costa opp. the rail station.

◖**Restaurants:** Wide range of and snack bars around the main squares. For good value and atmosphere try *Solar Real* Praça de Pontevedra first floor with interesting interior and fading murals. ◖**Transport:** Rail station ✆ 253 811 243 with rail services along the Porto – Santiago line. Bus Av. Dr. Sidónio Pais (Campo da Feira) ✆ 253 808 300.

Barcelos is a delightful town occupying an elevated site above the river Cávado and was the first Portuguese County established by D. Dinis in 1298 but its origins go back to the Roman period. The town retains much of its medieval atmosphere, the oldest remaining structure being the original town walls and Torre da Porta Nova, which date back to the 15th century and to the first Duke of Bragança. There are several museums including the Ceramic Museum *Museu de Olaria* housed in the 19th century *Casa dos Carvalhos Mendanhas* which contains a large collection of ceramics from around the world, especially from this region and particularly of the famous brightly coloured cockerel which has become a national symbol of Portugal and logo for Portuguese tourism.

The Barcelos cockerel is based on the same storyline of the cock in Santo Domingo de Calzada on the Camino Francés. The cross in the Paço dos Condes portrays the miraculous story of the roasted cock that rose from the table of the judge who had wrongly condemned a pilgrim to Santiago to hang from the nearby gallows. The pilgrim had proclaimed his innocence and stated that if he were wrongly condemned to hang then a dead cock would rise from the judge's table in proof of his righteousness. The innocent lad was hanged and sure enough a roasted cock stood up on the judge's plate as he sat for dinner that night. The bewildered judge hurried from his table to find the pilgrim alive on the gallows – saved by the miraculous intervention of St. James and the Barcelos cockerel! *(see photo page 132)*.

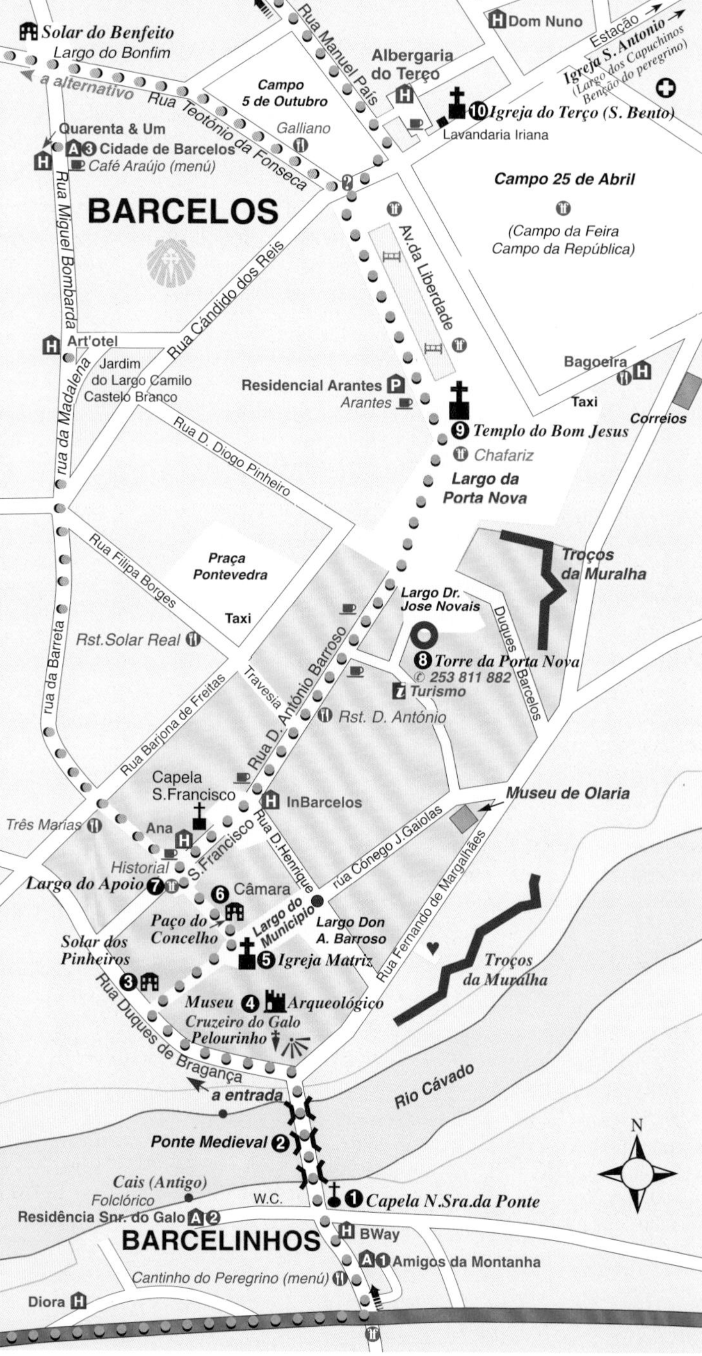

Solar do Benfeito
Largo do Bonfim
a alternativo
Rua Teotónio da Fonseca
Rua Manuel País
Campo
5 de Outubro
Galliano
Albergaria
do Terço
Dom Nuno
Estação
Igreja S. Antonio
(Largo dos Capuchinos
Benção do peregrino)
10 Igreja do Terço (S. Bento)
Lavandaria Iriana
Quarenta & Um
A3 Cidade de Barcelos
Café Araújo (menú)
Campo 25 de Abril
(Campo da Feira
Campo da República)
BARCELOS
Rua Miguel Bombarda
Rua Cândido dos Reis
Av.da Liberdade
Art'otel
Jardim
do Largo Camilo
Castelo Branco
Residencial Arantes
Arantes
Bagoeira
Taxi
Correios
rua da Madalena
Rua D. Diogo Pinheiro
9 Templo do Bom Jesus
Chafariz
Largo da
Porta Nova
Rua Filipa Borges
Praça
Pontevedra
Taxi
Troços
da Muralha
Largo Dr.
Jose Novais
Duques Barcelos
Rst.Solar Real
8 Torre da Porta Nova
© 253 811 882
Turismo
rua da Barreta
Rua Barjona de Freitas
Travesia
Rua D. António Barroso
Rst. D. António
Capela
S.Francisco
InBarcelos
Museu de Olaria
Três Marias
Ana
S.Francisco
Rua D.Henrique
rua Cónego J.Gaiolas
Historial
Largo do Apoio 7
6 Câmara
Paço do
Concelho
Largo do
Município
Largo Don
A. Barroso
Rua Fernando de Margalhães
Solar dos
Pinheiros
3
5 Igreja Matriz
Troços
da Muralha
Rua Duques de Bragança
Museu 4 Arqueológico
Cruzeiro do Galo
Pelourinho
a entrada
Rio Cávado
Ponte Medieval 2
N
Cais (Antigo)
Folclórico
W.C.
1 Capela N.Sra.da Ponte
Residência Snr. do Galo A2
BARCELINHOS
BWay
A1 Amigos da Montanha
Cantinho do Peregrino (menú)
Diora

Detour – Braga

If you plan to visit Braga and nearby Bom Jesus (the most popular tourist site in Portugal) allow a full day. Regular bus & rail journey time ± 40 mins with *www.transdev.pt* from €5 return or 25 mins with *www.rede-expressos.pt*

Best to book an extra night in Barcelos and then travel to Braga without rucksack (bus stop is 10 minutes walk from city centre). Braga is a city with a host of outstanding monuments. Sometimes referred to as the 'Rome of Portugal' it is the country's ecclesiastical capital with a somewhat pompous atmosphere to match.

Its name derives from the original Bracari Celts but Romans, Visigoths and Moors have all occupied it. Amongst the many historic buildings conveniently grouped around the city centre is the Romanesque cathedral *Sé XI* whose foundations go back to 1070 when they replaced an earlier mosque built by the occupying Moors and later underwent Gothic and Baroque embellishments. Access to the museum of sacred art is off a small cloister just inside the main entrance.

Braga has more than 30 churches and several national monuments. The ***Turismo*** is housed in a prominent Art Deco building on Av. da Liberdade, 1 / corner of *Praça da República* © 253 262 550 and provides a useful map of the town and list of accommodation together with details of how to get to the famous ***Bom Jesus do Monte*** overlooking the city from its hilltop perch surrounded by ancient woodland and terraced gardens.

Ponte Medieval Barcelos: •Paço dos Condes •Igreja Matriz •Paços do Concelho
Personal Reflections:

Nuestra Senhora de la Peregrina – Templo do S. Bom Jesus da Cruz

16 BARCELOS – PONTE DE LIMA

(path)	16.5	*48%*
(track)	15.8	*45%*
(road)	2.4	*7%*
Total km	**34.7** km *(21.6 ml)*	

Total ascent **440**m +¾ *hr*

▲ **Alto** *m* Alto da Portela **170** m *(558 ft)*

< A H > ➲Portela **9.8** km ➲Aborim **11.4** Balugães **16.2** ➲ Lugar do Corgo **20.0** ➲ Vitorino dos Piâes **22.5** ➲ Facha **25.2**

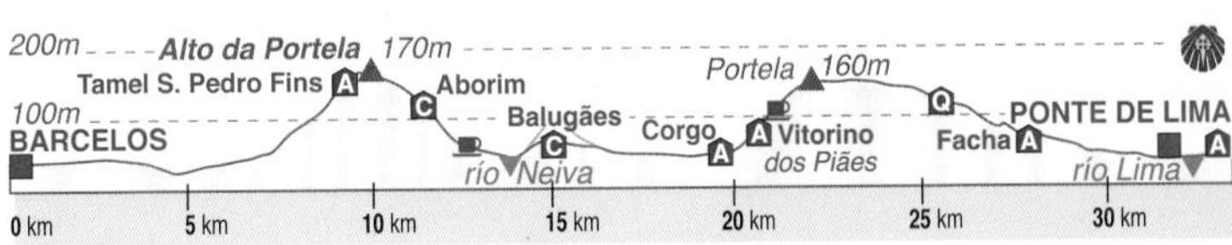

Practical Path: This is the longest but arguably the most beautiful stage. It includes two hill passes *portelas* separating the river valleys of Neiva and Lima and we have the natural landscape to lift our spirits and nearly half the route (48%) is on pathways through vineyards and woodland through the peaceful Neiva valley. From Portela (Vitorino) all the way is downhill into the beautiful Lima valley. The opening of several new albergues and casa rurales provide additional options if tiredness or nightfall overtakes.

I only went out for a walk... and finally concluded to stay out till sundown, for going out, I found, was really going in. *John Muir*

Mystical Path: The word hospitality comes from medieval Latin *hospitare; to receive a guest*. From this root we also find host, hospice, hospital and Hospitaller. The Knights Hospitaller provided welcome to the increasing numbers of pilgrims struggling across the remote landscape and now, centuries later, it is no different. The garb of the knight may have changed but the hospitality can still be found, "... ask and it will be given to you; seek and you will find; knock and the door will be opened unto you." *Matthew 7.*

Personal Reflections: *"I heard there was the possibility of a place to stay in the area but had no idea where to start looking, it was getting late and I was exhausted. As if on cue 3 delightful children appeared 'out of nowhere.' Language was no barrier to their enthusiasm and insistence that I follow them... I sit under the starry sky and scribble these notes by the light of the fire lit from resinous pine needles. The fragrance now overtaken by the smell from food sizzling on the griddle. Framed in the light of the kitchen doorway is Mariana while her mother and father prepare the table in the background. The generosity of spirit that flows from this family leaves me humbled and filled with deep gratitude for the spontaneous hospitality offered to a total stranger."*

0.0 km **Barcelos** ***Centro*** Igreja Bom Jesus continue up Av. da Liberdade by fountain to busy roundabout with *Centro Commercial Terço (right).* ***Option***▼ An alternative (historic) route veers off left via **Abade de Neiva** (Romanesque church *Santa Maria XII)* to loop back and rejoin the main route in **Vila Boa**.

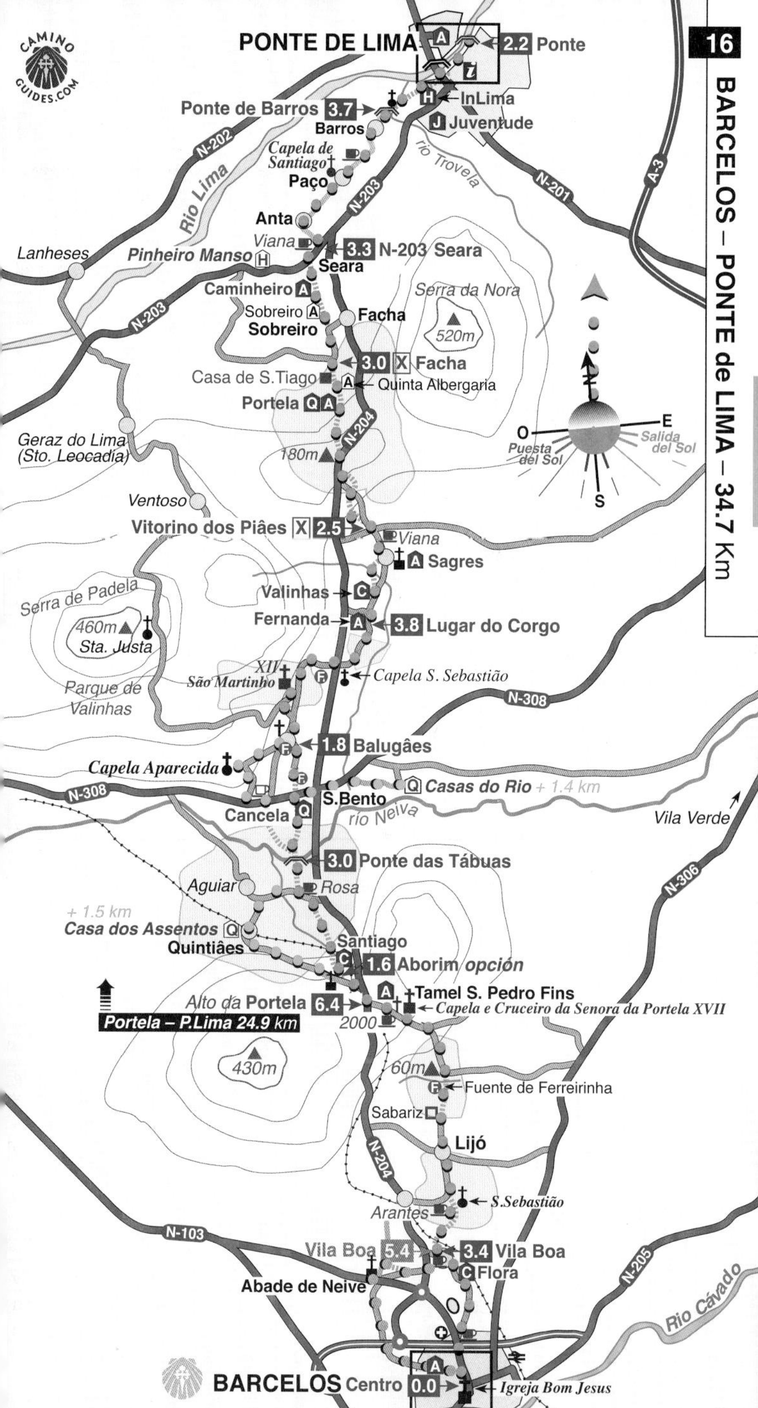

PONTE DE LIMA
2.2 Ponte
InLima
Juventude
Ponte de Barros 3.7
Barros
Capela de Santiago
Paço
Anta
Viana
3.3 N-203 Seara
Lanheses
Pinheiro Manso
Seara
Caminheiro
Sobreiro
Sobreiro
Facha
Serra da Nora
520m
3.0 Facha
Casa de S.Tiago
Quinta Albergaria
Portela
180m
Geraz do Lima (Sto. Leocadia)
Ventoso
Vitorino dos Piães 2.5
Viana
Sagres
Valinhas
Serra de Padela
460m
Sta. Justa
Fernanda
3.8 Lugar do Corgo
XII
São Martinho
Capela S. Sebastião
Parque de Valinhas
1.8 Balugães
Capela Aparecida
Casas do Rio + 1.4 km
S.Bento
Cancela
rio Neiva
Vila Verde
3.0 Ponte das Tábuas
Aguiar
Rosa
+ 1.5 km
Casa dos Assentos
Santiago
Quintiães
1.6 Aborim opción
Alto da Portela 6.4
Tamel S. Pedro Fins
Capela e Cruceiro da Senora da Portela XVII
2000
Portela – P.Lima 24.9 km
430m
60m
Fuente de Ferreirinha
Sabariz
Lijó
S.Sebastião
Arantes
Vila Boa 5.4
3.4 Vila Boa
Flora
Abade de Neive
Rio Cávado
BARCELOS Centro 0.0
Igreja Bom Jesus
N-202
Rio Lima
N-203
rio Trovela
N-201
A-3
N-204
N-308
N-306
N-103
N-205
O
E
S
Puesta del Sol
Salida del Sol
CAMINO GUIDES.COM
BARCELOS – PONTE de LIMA – 34.7 Km

Detour: ● ● ● ● ***via Abade de Neiva*** (2 km longer + climb. Not recommended as waymarking is poor and a variant to Lanheses creates added confusion)**:** At the top of Av. da Liberdade in Barcelos fork left by restaurante Galliano into rua Dr. Teo' da Fonseca into rua do Bem Feito (Solar do Benfeito right Albergue Cidade de Barcelos rua Miguel Bombarda left) and over the **dual carriageway** [**0.4** km] Av. Sao José (use pedestrian crossing) onto local road CM 1069 which merges onto path up and over city bypass [**1.0** km] veering right> into rua do Areal past **Capela S.Amaro** [**0.9** km] over crossroads and turn <left on **N-103** [**1.4** km]. *[½ further up the N-103 is: •**CR Casa do Monte** €70 © 967 057 779 Rua de Santa Maria, 640 Lugar do Barreiro].* Turn up imm. right> to the romanesque church of ***Santa Maria de Abade do Neiva*** [National Monument] founded by D. Mafalda, wife of D. Afonso Henriques in the 12th century with niche in the form of a scallop shell connecting it to the camino de Santiago. Take the road imm. above the church that descends gently and then sharply down woodland path to cross the N-204 (pedestrian crossing) ☕ (left by service station) and down to rejoin the main route in **Vila Boa** [**0.5** km].

5.4 km **Vila Boa** *Lugar do Espirito Santo.*

▼ For the main route take rua Dr. Manuel Pais cross over city **bypass** past *Casa de Saúde São João de Deus* to **roundabout** [**1.3** km] veer right> by ☕ into rua de S. Mamede and right> again (city football stadium ahead left) turn up <left past **school** ●*Alb* **Flora** *Priv.[10÷3]+4* €18 €30-60 Menú €7 © 967 721 290 Rua Travessa Igreja, 24 to **Igreja de Vila Boa** [**1.6** km] with open porch, past concelho and turn right> into rua do Espírito Santo into **Vila Boa** [**0.5** km] *Lugar do Espirito Santo* where alternative route via ***Abade de Neiva*** joins from main road 100m up left *[☕ on main road].*

3.4 km **Vila Boa** village green with cruceiro *Lugar Espirito Santo* [🚰] adj. •*Quinta São João*. Keep s/o under **railway** onto a lengthy stretch of sand road through eucalyptus woods on the original caminho de Santiago over bridge **Ponte de Pedrinha** through Lugar de Ribeira with ☕ *Arantes* [**1.7** km] and chapel of St. Sebastian *Capela de S. Sebastião*. We then pass another chapel **Capela de Santa Cruz** in the area of Lijó and s/o over road onto a short stretch of cobblestone then onto track into mixed woodland back to road passing **Casa do Sabariz** [**2.1** km] (left) © Fernanda Cunha 964 751 844 quinta-style country house with 2 double apartments available for weekly let but may be available for overnight stay. Proceed down gravel track to wayside **Fonte da Ferreirinha** [🚰]. Track meanders through vineyards over stream past the gates of *Quinta de Revorido* to join asphalt road in the parish of *Tamel S. Pedro Fins.* We now a steep climb past [🚰] *Rua da Cruz (quality no longer monitored)* and continue the climb to junction with the main road and wayside cross *cruceiro*. We have another steep climb up past the parish council offices *Freguesia de Tamel São Pedro Fins* and *Capela Sra. da Portela* with ancient wayside cross with interesting pilgrim motifs of staff and gourd on the shaft and, adjoining is the pilgrim hostel [**2.6** km]:

6.4 km **Portela** ***Tamel S. Pedro Fins*** ●*Alb. Mun.[42÷4]* **Casa da Recoleta** €5 © 253 137 075 [m] 935 136 811 restored parish house adj. the church (see photo) with excellent modern facilities. Opp. *-2000.* Continue up to a high point of today at the Portela (195m) junction with the main Barcelos to Ponte de Lima road [**!**] **N-204** and turn right> along the crest of the pass (caution on the dangerous bend in the road [**!**]) as we now start heading downhill into the Rio Neiva valley past Fonte da Portela (dry) and first <left (signposted *Quintiâes*) and then right> onto track over river and past the modern parish church down steps and turn right over the rail line in:

1.6 km **Aborim / Option:** ▲ The main waymarked route now turns right> and imm. <left onto rua Santiago •**Casa de Santiago** €20pp © 914 463 272 at Nº78. **Note:** take care around Aborim as there are several other waymarked paths in the area. One is an alternative route in case the main camino is flooded (it is low lying). The Camino del Norte via Lanheses is also close by and you don't want to inadvertently stray onto it. The safest way to avoid confusion is to make sure you enter Aborim by the modern parish church and leave over the railway line. *[Oliveira 100m (s/o) along the rail line opp. the Estação Aborim Tamel].*

Detour: Quintiâes [+1.5 km] ● ● ● all by asphalt road (signposted s/o left before crossing the railway). The House of Agreements •**Casa dos Assentos** €70+ © 919 640 742 (Sra. Julia Machado) www.casadosassentos.com historic 16th century manor house. On the way you pass by the old parish church of Aborim *Igreja Velha de Aborim* (right). *[The dense woods (right) just before crossing the railway at Quintiâes hide the ruins of a medieval castle and chapel. A visit is only recommended for the seriously adventurous as the area is very overgrown and close to the steep rail cutting].* Waymarks (to the Northern route) will lead you behind the cemetery (right) but the Quinta is located behind the parish Church located at the end of the road to the left. and adjacent.

To rejoin the main route make your way down past the bar to the T-junction and shop in ***Gândara [0.8 km]*** and veer right> signposted Barcelos (Note: this is the opposite direction to the arrows which are for the Camino do Norte via Aguiar, Vilar Nova and the Ponte de Nova). Continue to the bridge over the small stream ***[0.6 km]*** and veer <left immediately over the *Ribeiro do Pico* to rejoin the waymarked route from Aborim by drainage pipe factory.

▲ From Aborim the path continues along alternating stretches of sand-tracks and cobblestone laneways (often wet as this is a low lying area) turning right> on asphalt road [**1.0** km] (winter route in wet weather left) to T-Junction [**0.5** km]. Turn <left onto the *Caminho de Santiago* in Quintiâes district passing *Rosa (right).* The route now meanders through ancient hamlets turning sharp right> by store [**0.5** km] *(here the alternative route from Quintiâes joins from left)* onto a cobble lane leading to the beautiful medieval bridge over the river Neiva [**1.0** km].

3.0 km **Ponte das Tábuas** 'Bridge of Boards' a reference to an earlier wooden bridge over the rio Neiva dating to the 12th century. The present medieval stone structure is very emblematic of the pilgrim way. Up ahead, just visible in the distance, is Capela da Aparecida (see detour). On the far side of the bridge is a small sandy beach by the weir, an idyllic spot for a picnic or perhaps a swim? **Option**: Several optional routes through Balugâes commence at this points:

❶ ● ● ● ● For the main route veer right> along this low-lying area through vineyards veer <left at fork up to main road [!] **N-308** [**1.2** km] with the delightful •*CR* **Quinta da Cancela** *x6* €45+ ✆ 258 763 079 www.quintacancela.pt directly en route *[see photo>] (At this point ☕ on route 2 is 400m up left while the main crossroads at São Bento is 200m down right with shops and café).* Continue s/o onto track which leads into Balugâes and [🚰] and up to junction [🚰] and **signboard** [**0.6** km].

1.8 km **Balugâes Cruce** ▲ ***caminho tabuleta*** all routes converge at this point.

❷ ● ● ● ● **São Bento** Follow the main route veering right to crossroads at **São Bento** (300m) ☕ 🛒 *farmacia* ✚ +1.1 km off route in Lugar de Navió, Cossourado •*CR* **Casas do Rio** *x6* €50+ ✆ 969 312 585 (José Lúis Amaro). Former pilgrim hostel with peaceful gardens fronting the original camino real *[see photo>]* ***Directions:*** from the crossroads head east along the N-308 and veer right> 300m and continue a further 800m.

❸ ● ● ● ● **Capela da Aparecida** 18thc sanctuary of the Apparition of the Virgin *Santuário da Senhora da Aparecida,* site of a miracle where a devout deaf and dumb penitent regained his hearing and speech after the appearance of the Virgin. The sanctuary is the venue for a pilgrimage held annually on 15th August. Detour 1 km off the waymarked route but allow time to refresh by the drinking font and to visit the chapel and delve underneath to wash away your sins forever, according to the local tradition! Not a bad exchange for one hour of your time? However, if you started in Barcelos and intend making it to Ponte de Lima tonight you may need to leave remission for some future date. ***Directions***: turn up <left on main road past timber yard and ☕ *Tamira* [200m] then right> [400m] and wind up past [🚰] and up the steep steps to the Sanctuary [400m]. Access to the tunnel under the chapel is at the side by iron railings. Climb underneath and out the other side – if you can't make it around the boulder you will have to back-out and reflect some more on the errors in your life! Return downhill by the asphalt road ahead (no need to return to the main road) ignore any side roads and rejoin the main route at camino signboard [600].

▲ ***caminho tabuleta*** Continue down along the Stations of the Cross (that lead back up to the sanctuary) to modern fountain cascade (left). The camino is now waymarked via the XII century romanesque church of ***São Martinho*** with covered portico *[see photo>]* set in peaceful park with cruceiro. Rejoin the road onto path through pine woods back onto minor road down to crossroads **N-204** [🚰] (right) by bus shelter. Cross over by wayside chapel *capela de S. Sebastião*. The route now follows peaceful laneways along a small river valley *ribeira de Nevoinho* that flows into the Neiva just above the Ponte das Tábuas. We finally enter a small hamlet at crossroads:

3.8 km **Lugar do Corgo** in the parish of *Vitorino dos Piães* (2.5 km before the village of that name). On the left is the ever popular ●*Alb.*♥ **Casa Fernanda** *Priv.[10÷1]* donativo (*€20 suggested incl.B&B, dinner, wine & song!)* ✆ 914 589 521 home of Fernanda & Jacinto Gomes Rodrigues who have welcomed pilgrims for many years providing authentic hospitality and now extended to accommodate 10 pilgrims in adj. timber chalet. This is a long day's stage and if you started in Barcelos you have already walked 20 kilometres (before adjusting for height climbed and possible detours) and have another 14.7 kilometres before we reach Ponte de Lima. A night at Casa Fernanda will refresh body and soul.

Continue s/o in Lugar do Corgo turn off <left onto track as we crisscross over several roads to the renovated 'stables' **Estábulo de Valinhas [1.0** km] •*CR.***O Estábulo de Valinhas** *x10* €35 ✆ 910 021 180. Continue and turn right along avenue up to the parish church [🚰] [**1.4** km] *Centro Paroquial* in *Vitorino dos Piães* with collection of sarcophagi in the forecourt. Imm. behind the church is ●*Alb.* **Casa Sagres** *Priv.[9÷1]* €15 ✆ João 962 916 441 on Rua do Latão. Continue up to the **crossroads** [**0.1** km].

2.5 km **Vitorino dos Piães** *Cruce* *Viana* + (50m down right). At the crossroads continue s/o *up* the hill turning <left past [ ] onto series of steeply undulating lanes onto woodland path emerging at the main road at **Portela N-204** [**1.1** km]. We now turn right> by cement works along main road [**!**] and turn off <left onto delightful **woodland track** [**0.3** km]. The Rio Lima valley now opens to view as we proceed steeply down through the woods onto cobbled laneway in the **Facha area** [**1.1** km] passing firstly •**Quinta da Portela** *Priv.[6÷3]* €20 *x2* €45 adj. annex menú €15 (vegetarians catered for) ✆ Han 964 257 171 manor house directly en route. Just beyond is •**Casa de SanTiago** (S.Tiago niche and fonte) where a bed may be available from Ceu ✆ 919 216 557 €35+ (phone in advance). Opp *Quinta de Albergaria (long stay)*. Proceed down to asphalt **road** [**0.5** km] at:

3.0 km **Facha** Short track with [ ] onto lane to ***capela de S. Sebastian*** & wayside cross with tile image of Santiago. S/o past *Quinta do Sobreiro (long stay)* through vineyards to turn off (left) 100m detour to •*Alb.* **O Caminheiro** *[4÷1]* €15 menú €7.50 ✆ 968 408 882 private house with basic accommodation. Continue through vineyards to:

3.3 km **N-203 Seara** *[+400m left* •*Hr.* **Pinheiro Manso** *x20* €30-40 ✆ 258 943 775 *modern hotel on main road,]*. Cross busy N-203 [**!**] by *Lotus* and adj. *O Farinheiro* turn <left and follow quiet country lanes through the sleepy hamlets of ***Anta, Bouça, Paço, Periera, Barros*** which all merge one in to the next. Pass Wayside shrine to S. Antonio and at the top of the gentle rise ahead in **Lugar do Paço** [**2.6** km]. Here in the townland of Correlhã we come to the only chapel dedicated to San Tiago on the route in Portugal ***Capela de Santiago*** now renovated (2023). It lies imm. left of the mural to D. Teresa on horseback. The chapel lands were bequeathed to the city of Santiago de Compostela in the year 915, this bequest being ratified by D. Henrique and D. Teresa on their pilgrimage to Santiago in 1097. It is hoped that the fine 18thc statue of *Santiago de Peregrino* will be re-installed in the chapel niche. Proceed s/o along the quiet country lane through ***Pedrosa*** with the ancient *Cruceiro da Pedrosa* (left) and adj. the tiny *Capela de S. Francisco* and sign Ponte de Lima 1.0 *(note it is 2.8 km to the albergue!)*. S/o into Barros to **Ponte de Barros** [**1.1** km]:

3.7 km **Ponte de Barros** medieval bridge over the rio Trovela. We now turn <left by bandstand and chapel to Our Lady of the Snows *capela da Sra. das Neves* continue s/o and pick up the pathway parallel to the river Lima *Ecovia* to junction with viewpoint and boulders [**1.1** km] *(Note: If you plan to stay in the Youth Hostel •Pousada da Juventude* or •*Hotel InLima take the short-cut up the narrow lane (right) to the main road. The YHA is on the opp. side of the main road – 250m)*. Or continue s/o under road bridge ahead past the *Capela de N. Sra. da Guia* and along the shaded tree-lined Av. D. Luis Filipe past the newly renovated •*H* **Império do**

Minho s/o past the medieval tower now the **Tourist office** along the river front to the central square Largo de Camões and medieval bridge Ponte de Lima [**1.1** km].

2.2 km **Ponte de Lima** ***Centro*** For the pilgrim hostel cross the bridge past the church to the hostel entrance [+400m] ●*Alb.* **Casa do Arnado** in a wonderful location. Ponte de Lima is a delightful market town that retains a sleepy medieval atmosphere. Take time to amble around its narrow cobbled streets and historic buildings. This is an ideal place to take a rest day if your schedule allows. The town has several museums and there are lovely walks along the Rio Lima itself. It prides itself on being the 'oldest' town in Portugal and there is certainly little doubt that it occupies one of the most beautiful riverside settings to be found anywhere. The Lima valley is outstanding in its natural surroundings and even the A-3 motorway is far enough away not to disturb its tranquillity. However, a fortnightly market, reputedly the oldest extant market in Portugal (Barcelos claims to be the most popular!) spreads itself along the sandy beach and creates a great deal of activity and several annual fiestas add to the action such as the *Vaca das Cordas* where a roped cow is led around the parish church before being maddened by darts and led down to the beach for slaughter to become part of this annual feast. It all harks back to ancient pagan fertility rites (whatever one thinks about animal rights) and takes place in June, the day before Corpus Christi *Corpo do Deus* when the town streets are covered with incredible floral displays. August generally sees a 'medieval' market arrive with juggling, jousting and joviality. The *Feiras Novas* takes place during the second weekend in September when a sea of humanity floods the town in the biggest party of the year that goes on 24 hours a day for 3 days.

○ **Historic Buildings and Monuments:** The main sites of historic interest are clustered around the town centre and therefore easy to visit (listed from the way in): ❶ **Igreja de S. Francisco e S. António dos Capuchos** *XVI* adj. **Museu dos Terceiros** with baroque façade and museum of religious art and artefacts. ❷ **Torre da Cadeia** *XIV* the original prison now *Turismo* and library with internet access. Intimate square to the rear and statue of woman with water jar *cantareira* and steps to upper ramparts. Along the wide main street ❸ **Igreja Matriz** *XV* parish church with statue of bull in the plaza (see photo) & **Igreja da Misericórdia** *XVI*. At the top end of the old town ❹ **Paço do Marquês** municipal offices with rooftop viewing gallery. Back down by the river: ❺ **Torre de S. Paulo** part of the original defensive walls of the town *[Note the flood levels recorded high up on the wall, just below the azulejos!]* and occupying pride of place in the centre of the main square *Largo de Camões* overlooking the river is the beautiful fountain **Chafariz** fashioned in 1603 surrounded by lively *cafés and bars* and public w.c.'s. ❻ **Medieval stone bridge** rebuilt in 1368 on earlier Roman foundations. This handsome bridge is 300 metres in length and 4 metres wide. It forms the pedestrian link between the busy southern town and the quieter northern quarter with ❼ **Capela do Anjo da Guarda / S. Miguel** open vaulted shrine dedicated to the Guardian Angel with on the riverbank adj. **Capela de Sto. António da Torre Velha** *XIX*. Just beyond the church is the pilgrim hostel and to the rear the beautiful ● **Thematic Gardens** *Jardims Temáticos* with their peaceful well maintained sections each having a separate theme adj. the Arnado riverside park *Concerto*. Further

downstream near the road bridge is ● ***Clube Náutico*** canoe hire 🍴 & festival gardens. Ponte de Lima is the base for *Solares de Portugal* part of the TURIHAB organisation that offers over 1,000 luxurious beds in historic Quintas and Manor houses in Northern Portugal where the Friends of the Portuguese Way to Santiago *Associação dos Amigos do Caminho Português de Santiago* is also housed. • Last year 1,564 pilgrims commenced their pilgrimage in Ponte de Lima.

ℹ ***Turismo:*** *Torre da Cadeia Velha* © 258 942 335 / 258 240 208 *(9:30-13:00 14:00-17:30) Paço do Marquês* Praça de República © 258 900 400.

▮**Lodging:** ***Entrance:*** ●**Pousada de Juventude** *[50÷12]* €12 r/João Paulo II © 258 943 797. Nearby ultra-modern •*H**** **InLima** *x30* €50-70 © 258-900 050 r/Agostinho José Taveira. •*H*** **Império** *x46* €55+ © 258 009 008 www.hotelimperiodonorte.com Rua 5 de Outubro, 97 (on camino by river).

▮***Central:*** •*CR.*Pinheiro *x7* €50+ © 258 943 971 r/G. Norton de Matos, 40. •*H* **Mercearia da Vila** *x6* €60 © 925 996 366 Adj. church on main street r/Cardeal Saraiva: opp: •*Hs* **Casa Abadia** *Ophis* © 960 403 345 r/Souto 2/3. •*P* **Morais** €20-30 basic rooms r/Matriz 8 (opp. church entrance). •*CR.***Pereiras** © 258 942 939 access off r/Fonte da Vila. •*P** **São João** €35 © 258 941 288 above 🍴 *Gula* Largo de S. João entrance r/do Rosário 6. •*P* **Beira Rio** €25 © 258 944 044 Passeio 25 de Abril. ***Suburbs:*** •*P* **O Garfo** © 258 743 147 r/Arrabalde S.João Fora Crasto +0.5 km. •*Hs* **Old Village** *[16÷4]* €15 *x2* €40 © 961 574 929 www.oldvillagehostel.pt v/Foral Velho de D. Teresa, 1415 (N-203) + 1.2 km.

▮***Across bridge*** ●*Alb.* **Casa do Arnado** *Mun.[60÷3]* €5 © m: 925 403 164 (peregrino S.O.S. m: 925 403 162) Largo Dr Alexandre Herculano / Alegria (see photo>). Opp: •**ARC'otel** *x15* €45-60 © 966 506 744.

▮**Restaurants:** wide variety to suit all pockets. Overlooking the river on Passeio 25 de Abril 🍴 *Encanada* with terrace above the road or just behind (half the price) *Katekero* menú from €6 (open all day). On the passeio (outside tables & evening sun: *Taberna Cadeia Velha* & set back on rua Bonfim 🍴 *Manuel Padeiro.* Also *Parisiense* with ground and first floor tables, pizzeria 🍴 *Beira Rio* and 🍴 *Catrina.* Various snack bars spill out onto the central square *Largo de Camões* with its lovely central fountain *Chafariz* and behind the square in *Largo de S. João* 🍴 *Convento da Gula* and 🍴 *A lameda* overlooking the river.

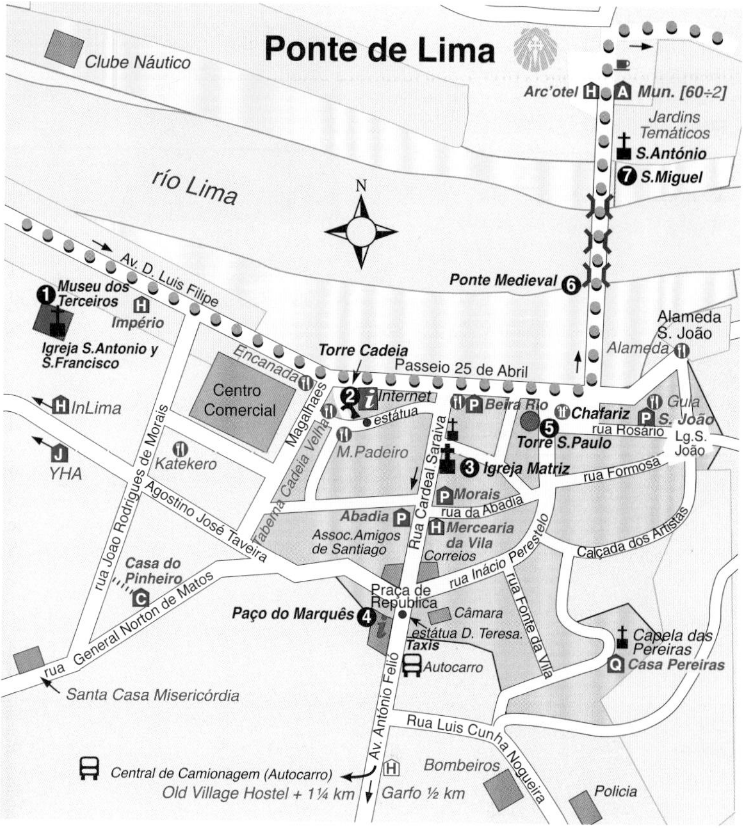

Ponte de Lima

Clube Náutico
río Lima
N
Arc'otel
Mun. [60÷2]
Jardins Temáticos
S.António
7 S.Miguel
Ponte Medieval 6
Av. D. Luis Filipe
1 Museu dos Terceiros
Império
Igreja S.Antonio y S.Francisco
Alameda S. João
Alameda
Torre Cadeia
Passeio 25 de Abril
Encanada
Centro Comercial
InLima
YHA
2 Internet
estátua
Beira Rio
Chafariz
5 Torre S.Paulo
Guia
S. João
rua Rosário
Lg.S. João
Magalhaes
Taberna Cadeia Velha
M.Padeiro
Katekero
rua Joao Rodrigues de Morais
Agostino José Taveira
Rua Cardeal Saraiva
3 Igreja Matriz
rua Formosa
Morais
rua da Abadia
Abadia
Assoc.Amigos de Santiago
Mercearia da Vila
Correios
Calçada dos Artistas
rua Inácio Perestelo
Casa do Pinheiro
rua General Norton de Matos
Praça de Republica
Câmara
Paço do Marquês 4
estátua D. Teresa.
Taxis
Autocarro
rua Fonte da Vila
Capela das Pereiras
Casa Pereiras
Santa Casa Misericórdia
Av. António Feijó
Rua Luis Cunha Nogueira
Central de Camionagem (Autocarro)
Old Village Hostel + 1¼ km
Garfo ½ km
Bombeiros
Policia

Personal Reflections:

17 PONTE DE LIMA – RUBIÃES

Ponte romano *Agualonga*

	--- ---	10.7	--- ---	*58%*
	--- ---	7.9	--- ---	*42%*
	--- ---	0.0	--- ---	*0%*
Total km		**18.6** km *(11.6 ml)*		

Total ascent **760**m *+1¼ hr*

▲ Alto *m* Portela Grande **405**m *(1,329 ft)*

< A H > Labruja **10.1** km Cabanas **15.8** km

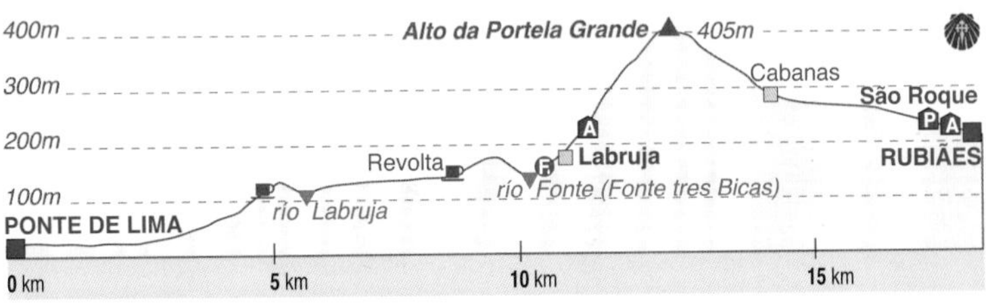

Practical Path: We now have our first glorious day where natural paths account for over half the route and there are no main roads at all. This stage also marks our steepest cumulative climb almost entirely encountered in the one ascent up the Labruja valley to the high pass through the mountain ridge and into the Coura valley via the Alto de Portela Grande. Facilities along the way are limited but there is reasonable shelter amongst the pine woods on either side of the pass and a number of drinking fonts along the way.

I dwell in the high and holy place, with they who have a contrite and humble spirit. ***Isaiah 57:15***

The Mystical Path: With all the great discoveries made within the sense-perceptible world of science we have never been able to see the super-sensible. Not even the most powerful telescope on earth has been able to glimpse the tiniest fragment of God. Knowledge of Higher Worlds does not come from exploring the physical universe but in diving into the mysteries. Paradox is at the heart of the spiritual quest and so the top of the mountain becomes a symbol of the wisdom often found at the lowest point of the journey and within the humblest of hearts.

Personal Reflections: *"The steep climb is rewarded by stunning views over the beauty of the Lima valley. I drink deeply from the clear cool waters that flow from the mountain spring. I like the idea that high places reflect Higher Mind – where clutter and the things of the world seem to evaporate in the rarefied air of the mountains. While fog hangs in the valleys, clarity abounds amongst the peaks.*

0.0 km **Ponte de Lima** ***centro*** Cross bridge past **albergue [0.4** km] on north side of the river Lima turn right> past ☕ (signposted Quinta do Arquinho) around the back of the themed gardens *Jardims Tematicos* veering <left and <left again past **Quinta do Arquinho** ✆ 913 110 347 (2 night min.) and follow the low-lying path to cross over the **N-202** onto a cobbled lane past the fading opulence of **Casa de Sabadão [1.3** km] ✆ 258 941 963 (2 night min.) Lugar de Sabadão *(In winter this whole area can become marooned from the overflowing rivers Lima and Labruja).*

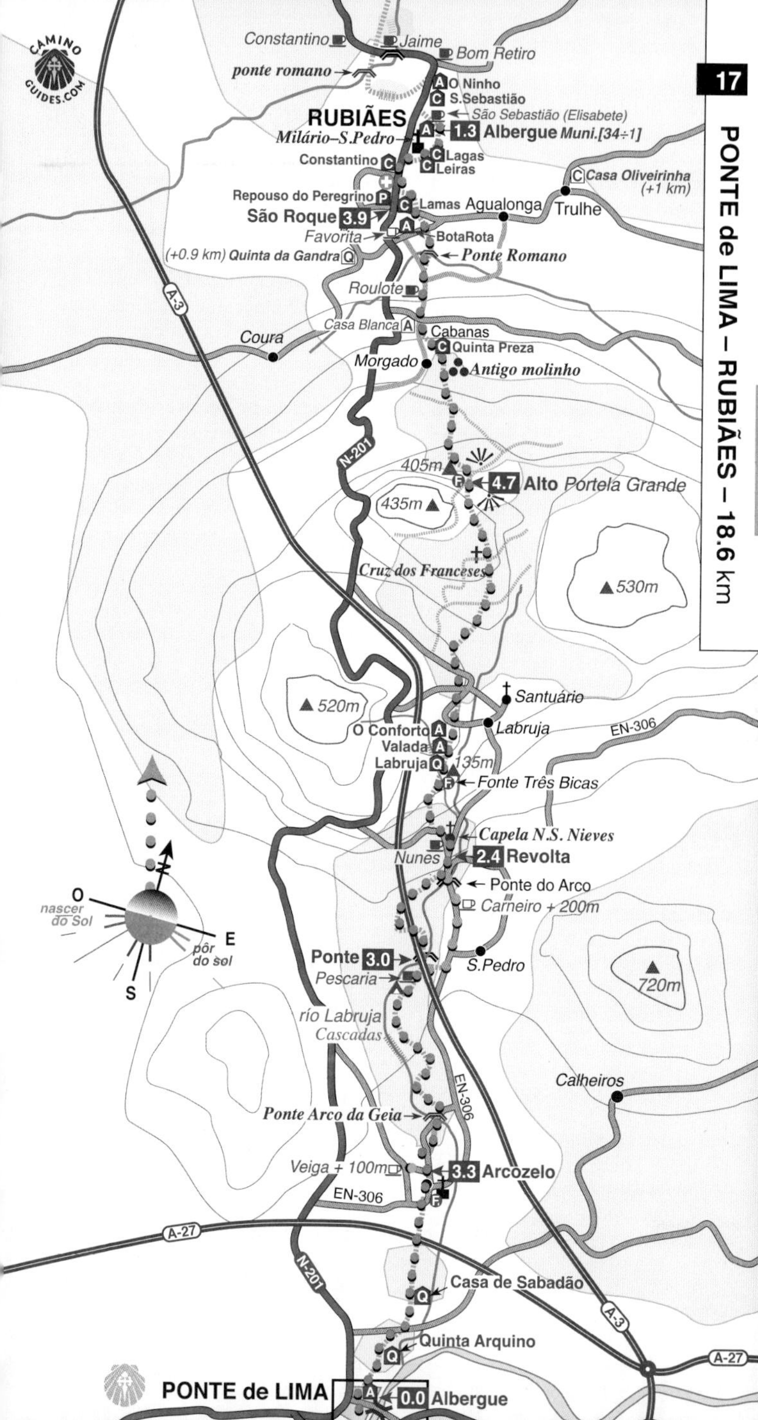

CAMINO GUIDES.COM
17
PONTE de LIMA – RUBIÃES – 18.6 km
Constantino
Jaime
Bom Retiro
ponte romano
O Ninho
S.Sebastião
São Sebastião (Elisabete)
RUBIÃES
1.3 Albergue Muni.[34÷1]
Milário–S.Pedro
Constantino
Lagas
Leiras
Casa Oliveirinha (+1 km)
Repouso do Peregrino
Lamas
Agualonga
Trulhe
São Roque 3.9
Favorita
BotaRota
(+0.9 km) Quinta da Gandra
Ponte Romano
Roulote
A-3
Casa Blanca
Cabanas
Coura
Quinta Preza
Morgado
Antigo molinho
N-201
405m
4.7 Alto Portela Grande
435m
Cruz dos Franceses
530m
520m
Santuário
Labruja
EN-306
O Conforto
Valada
Labruja
135m
Fonte Três Bicas
Capela N.S. Nieves
Nunes
2.4 Revolta
Ponte do Arco
Carneiro + 200m
O
nascer do Sol
E
pôr do sol
S
Ponte 3.0
Pescaria
S.Pedro
720m
río Labruja
Cascadas
Calheiros
EN-306
Ponte Arco da Geia
Veiga + 100m
3.3 Arcozelo
EN-306
A-27
N-201
Casa de Sabadão
A-3
Quinta Arquino
A-27
PONTE de LIMA
0.0 Albergue

We now head out under the A-27 **motorway** [**0.7** km] along quiet country lanes to pass the Centro Social in Arcozelo [**0.9** km] in:

3.3 km **Arcozelo** church [ ] *Veiga (+100m+)* take track over Rio Labruja by ***Ponte arco da Geira*** *(orginally part of the Roman military road between Braga and Astorga).* Turn <left along the río Labruja with lovely cascades (left). We now meander up through the natural environment of the Labruja valley along earth tracks passing **trout farm** [**2.3** km] and *Pescaria* (left) r/Borralhos adj. ▲**Oasis do Caminho** *[10÷1]* €15 ✆ 912 057 420 Italian connections (summer only). We now climb above the A-3 motorway with [ ] (right) and then descend to option point underneath the motorway [**0.7** km].

3.0 km **Pasarela** ***A3 Underpass.*** A new pedestrian bridge over the río Labruja makes a safe passage but during severe flooding use the alternative road route: ▲

For the alternative road route ● ● ● ● take the track to the right that climbs above the A-4 to the asphalt road [0.5 km] turn <left and continue along this road turning off <left [1.3 km] (signposted Labruja/ Sanctuario do Socorro) and cross the rio Lubruja over the Ponte do Arco [0.3 km].

▲ For the direct route take the pasarela over the rio Labruja which flows rapidly through a narrow gorge at this point. Scramble up the far side underneath the A-4 flyover onto a path that climbs up through scrubland at the edge of pine woods away from the A-3 as it flattens out and follows the contours around the side of the *Vale do Inferno*. Rejoin the asphalt road at ***Ponte do Arco*** [**1.8** km] at the point where the road route joins from the right. Continue past the capela de São Sebastião [ ] (left) in the area of Devesa veering <left (signposted Valinhos Valada) to in **Revolta** [**0.6** km]:

2.4 km **Labruja** ***Revolta*** *Cunha Nunes* and shop run by Marcia and Manuel adjoining the chapel to Our Lady of the Snows *Capela de N. S. Das Neves* with statue of pilgrim saint *São Roque* and wayside cross. This is the last chance to acquire food or drink (apart from water at drinking fonts) on this stage. We now start climbing alternating between paths and lanes with the village of Labruja and its distinctive parish church visible over the valley to our right. Lodging now available in this tranquil valley as follows: ❶ Rua dos Valinhos •*B&B* **Quinta Labruja** *x2* €48-68 ✆ 935 268 485 www.quintalabruja.pt ❷ ●*Alb.Hs* **Casa da Valada** *Priv.[4÷2]* €20 +5 €55 ✆ 967 742 694... and nestled under the A-3 viaduct (see photo> ❸ ●**Conforto** *[10÷2]* €15 incl. ✆ 935 883 131 oconforto.wixsite.com/albergue *(Note Quinta da Enxurreira is a holiday let).* Continue up steeply passing ***Fonte des Três Bicas*** [**0.5** km] [ ] where clear water gushes from 3 channels *três bicas (see photo>).* Fill up with the cool water for the long climb ahead. Continue up sharply to **crossroads** [**0.6** km] and take track through pine woods ahead *(Capela Santa Ana visible below in the valley floor)*. The path continues up steeply through woodland and crosses over several forest tracks and while the waymarking is reasonable keep a sharp focus. We pass the remote *cruceiro* ***cruz dos Franceses*** [**1.6** km] where pilgrims have placed stones to mark their passage and prayers (see photo under reflections next page). *[This wayside cross is otherwise referred to as cruz dos Mortos a reference to the ambush that took place here on Napoleon's troops during the peninsular war 1808 – 1814]*. Continue up steeply through pinewoods *[harvested for their resin]* to the high point with wonderful views back over the Lima valley to the south. We make our way around the paddock ahead to finally reach our **high point** [**0.6** km] at:

4.7 km **Alto da Portela Grande** (405m) [ ] 50m adj.forester's lodge. A view north over the wooded rio Coura valley now opens up as we start our descent over a rough stony path [**!**] through pine woods, the terrain flattening-out as we cross a small stream with a series of ancient mills running above and below the path **Moinhos de Cabanas** [**1.1** km] (see photo>) unusual mechanism used to mill mainly maize (for the local bread found in these parts). The path drops down into the hamlet of **Cabanas** onto asphalt road •*CR*.**Quinta da Preza** *x6* €60+ © 960 268 724 r/Cabanas, 845. Pass *cruceiro* to **Carreira crossroads** [**1.0** km] *[Detour left 200m •**Casa Blanca** €15 © Trevor (UK+44) 7867288870 basic albergue bunk beds + priv. €15-30]*. Keep s/o along track past *Roulote* down to roman bridge *Ponte Águalonga*. Cross over road ***option:*** **▌Águalonga:** +100m left ●*EcoAlb.***BotaRota** *Priv.[10÷1]* €15 *+2* €35 Marianne © +44 7804656388. *[**Detour up right +1.5** km Águalonga / Trulhe **+1** km to •CR **Oliveirinha** x3 €55+© 917 600 160 Rua Trulha de Cima. **Detour down left** to •CR **Quinta da Gandra** x5 €45+ © 938 310 855 [**+0.9** km]*. Keep s/o over road onto track to pass rear entrance to new lodging at •*CR* **Casa de Lamas** *Priv.[6÷1]* €15 *+4* €40. © 251 010 282 (Maria Madalena e Josíno) with spacious rooms and all mod-cons. Continue to T-Junction on the main Ponte de Lima / Valença **N-201** / **São Roque** [**0.3** km] with hostel opposite:

3.9 km **São Roque** •*Hr* **Repouso do Peregrino** €15pp *+8* €35 incl. © 251 943 692 (Silvia) newbuild rooms to rear adj. *farmacia Sousa* and •**Constantino** *Priv.[6÷1]* €15pp +25 *+6* €28 © 968 432 059 modern house with various rooms *(also own Constantino by Ponte Nova – shuttle service to local restaurants)* Continue downhill past *Quinta S. Roque* (long-term let) and veer right> onto path past •*CR* **Quinta das Leiras** *x5* €25+ incl. pp © 967 813 689 (Helmut & Heidi) *www.quintadaleiras.com* modern home with laundry, games room & swimpool – adj. •**Casa das Lages** *x3* €15 pp incl. (shared bathrooms) © 964 936 366 (Sophia).

Continue s/o through woodland to ancient ***cruceiro*** **Detour** 100m down to visit the interesting Romanesque church dedicated to St. Peter ***Igreja de São Pedro de Rubiães XII*** and *miliário* the historic Roman mile marker on the Via XIX has been hollowed out to form a sarcophagus (see photo). Continue down the path to **Rubiães Abergue.**

1.3 km **Rubiães** ●*Alb.* **Escola** *Mun. [34÷2]* €5 ✆ 917 164 476 m: 251 943 472 spacious conversion of former schoolhouse with kitchen and dining area and extensive lounge and outside patio. One large dormitory sleeps 26 in bunk beds with additional room for 8 on top floor. Ample ladies and gents toilets and showers. Adj. is ☕ *São Sebastião* operated by the enterprising Elisabete. Simple food available or for more substantial fare make your way down the main road N-201 passing •*CR.* **S Sebastião** *x8* €15-30 ✆ 251 941 258 (Maria Pereira) adj. ●*Alb.*♥ **O Ninho** *(The Nest) Priv. [17÷4]* €15 ✆ 251 941 002 / 916 866 372 (Marlene & Dª Maria Pequena) welcoming lodging in traditional stone family house with outside garden area. (see photo>). [+200m] 🍴 *Bom Retiro* ✆ 251 941 245 popular pilgrim haunt – menú from €7.

On the far side of the road bridge [+500m] is the newly extended shop 🛒 and ☕ *Jaime* on Ponte Nova and just beyond that is 🍴 *Constantino* run by André from albergue Constantino in São Roque. behind Cafe Jaime is a beautiful stretch of river and a weir where pilgrims have swum (with care!). If you are staying in either of the albergues you can return via the roman bridge (rather than the busy main road). We pass this area on the next stage.

Personal Reflections:

Cruz dos Franceses:

18 RUBIÃES – VALENÇA / TUI

|||||||||||||||||	--- --- 9.6	--- ---	*47%*
	--- --- 9.3	--- ---	*46%*
	--- --- 1.4	--- ---	*7%*
Total km	**20.3** km *(12.6 ml)*		

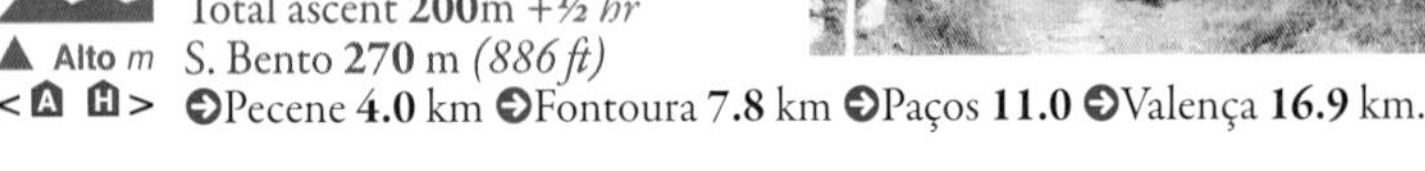

Total ascent **200**m +½ *hr*

▲ Alto *m* S. Bento **270** m *(886 ft)*

<A H> ➲Pecene **4.0** km ➲Fontoura **7.8** km ➲Paços **11.0** ➲Valença **16.9** km.

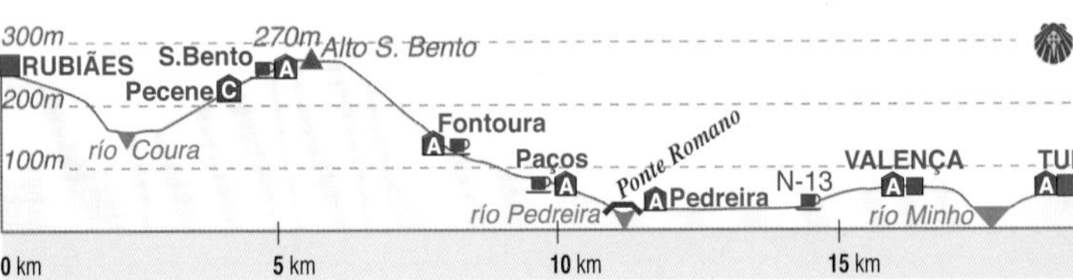

Practical Path: Apart from the short stretch of main road into Tui the rest of this stage is split between natural pathways and quiet country roads through woodland affording shelter and shade. With the exception of a modest climb out of the Coura river valley into the Minho basin the majority of this stage is downhill from São Roque. The Minho now becomes the Miño and our clocks will also need adjusting one hour as we make our way over the border from Portugal into Spain. Most pilgrims head straight for Tui. However you have an option to visit the historic old walled town of Valença and / or stay in the atmospheric *cidade velha* or the modern hostel and hotels just outside it.

Seek not to follow in the footsteps of the men of old; Seek what they sought.
16th century Japanese pilgrim poet. ***Matsuo Basho***

The Mystical Path: '*All roads lead to Rome*' was a truism in the time of the Caesars but now we begin to understand that '*All roads lead Home*' and are assured that all we need to do to realise this truth is to: 'Render unto Caesar the things which are Caesar's; and unto to God the things that are God's.' *Matthew 22:21*. To whom do you pay tribute? Whose footsteps do you follow? What do you seek?

Personal Reflections: *"The dark clouds had been gathering all afternoon but nothing could have prepared me for the downpour the moment I set foot in Galicia! The ensuing deluge was so powerful that within minutes I was wet from head to foot; the road a river... The hot shower restored some heat to my body. Only one other pilgrim in this spacious hostel – who walked to Santiago and then just kept going! Now following the blue arrows towards Fátima but with no destination in mind. What is the hidden force that drive us on, through the blistering heat, the bitter cold, the torrential rain?*

0.0 km **Albergue** turn right> downhill & sharp <left (opp. albergue O Ninho) onto path (often wet) that follows bed of a stream to Roman bridge *Pons Romana II* (see photo next page) over rio Coura to follow the original Roman road and s/o over N-201 **Ponte Nova [1.2** km] ☕ *Jaime* and shop. Continue along track by river Coura with old millrace and weir. The camino now alternates between quiet country lanes and earth tracks up through a wooded valley to **Pecene-Cossourado**

CAMINO GUIDES.COM
(Pop. 17,000) TUI
Turismo © + 34 677 418 405
3.4 Catedral Centro
rio Minho
ESPAÑA
GMT + 1
A-55
N-552
VALENÇA (Pop. 14,000)
Fortaleza
Turismo © + 351 251 823 329
3.4 ? Valença Rotunda
A-3
Valença do Minho
Bonfim
Casa Diego
A Toca
PORTUGAL
< Monte Tecla
N-552
Lido
Maritone
2.3 Tuido N-13
rio Minho
N-13
S.Pedro da Torre
Quinta da Bouça
Quinta do Caminho
Pedreira
Ponte da Pedreira 3.4
ponte medieval
< Caminha
N-13
Padre Cruz
rio Pedreira
Quinta Estrada Romana
Paços
N-201
A-3
Fonte d'Ouro +450m!
Taberna da Igreja
3.3 Fontoura
Pilger Pause
Cruzeiro
S.Julião
Real
O
Puesta del Sol
E
Salida del Sol
S
N-201
365m
Café Castro
4.5 São Bento da Porta Aberta
N-303
Casa Capela
Cossourado Pecene
380m
rio Coura
A-3
Constantino
Ponte Nova
Bom Retiro
ponte romano
RUBIÃES
0.0 Albergue

[**2.8** km] & luxury •*CR.* **Casa da Capela** *x7* €60 © 251 782 005 (Margarida) 917 907 736 quinta with adj. chapel. Continue s/o up to crossroads at high point of this stage 270m [**0.5** km].

4.5 km **São Bento da Porta Aberta** major crossroads ●*Alb.* **Café Castro** *Priv. [12÷3]* €12.50 © 251 782 210 (Pedro Martins) popular café & shop now has beds available. The camino crosses *behind* Santuario São Bento *XVII* onto path with distant views over the Minho valley as we begin our descent towards Valença along delightful woodland paths through pine, eucalyptus, holm oak and the occasional cork tree (Portugal is one of the world's largest producers of cork). The path alternates between these paths and laneways into:

3.3 km **Fontoura** •*Quinta* **Real** *x6* €55 © 969 844 495 (+ 100m). ☕ *Central* & new •*CR.* **Quinta do Cruzeiro** *[4÷2]* €30pp *x4* €38-49 © 937 625 011 menú & swim-pool. ●*Alb.* **Pilger Pause** *Priv.[14÷1]* €13 © Verena **+49** 178 1848 141 Ronald **+49** 1577 0699 249 menú €6 (Reiki + canoes from Tui) opp. village park [⛪] (left) parish church *Igreja de São Miguel* opp. *Taberna da Igreja*. Keep s/o down road and left onto track through woodland into **Paços** [**2.2** km] *(bar Daniel closed)* to ☕ *&* ●*Alb.* **Quinta Estrada Romana** [**0.5** km] *Priv.[18÷3]* © 933 736 078. Traditional farmhouse offering dinner, bed and breakfast in bunk room suggested €25 incl. Similar arrangement in private room €30-50 Canadian links. Keep s/o to rio Pedreira and medieval bridge a Lugar da **Pedreira** [**0.7** km].

3.4 km **Ponte da Pedreira** ●*Alb.* **Quinta do Caminho** *Priv.[18÷1]* €13 *+10* €40 menú €8. Hugo © 251 821 183 *www.quintadocaminho.com* with terrace on river & swim-pool! *[Note: H Padre Cruz* ***4.5*** *km via N-201! free pick-up © 968 660 895].* S/o up past Quinta da Bouça through woods to N-13.

2.3 km **Tuido** cross N-13 [**!**] ☕*(s)* the camino continues via cobblestone road (signposted Araõ) parallel to the busy N-13. pass ☕ *A Toca* and turn <left at **Capela do Senhor de Bonfim** past *CR Diogo* (long let) **Arão** [**1.1** km] turn down right> by lavadero cruceiro [⛪] (left) into r/da Cruz continuing along asphalt road past *café Martins* under **rail** to veer right across the modern outskirts of Valença past the main **bus station** [**1.6** km] *[****+0.4*** *km •H*** ***Valença do Minho*** *x36* €28!-40 © 251 824 211 *Av. Miguel Dantas]* and turn up <left into Valença past rail station (right 200m) to main **roundabout** [**0.7** km] *Largo da Trapicheira*:

3.4 km **Valença** ***Fortaleza options* — Ⓑ *The bridge into Spain*** lies s/o and the first Spanish hostel in Tui only 3.1 km across the río Minho *or* Ⓐ turn up left along Av. Bombeiros Voluntários for the last pilgrim hostel in Portugal (see photo) ●*Alb.* **São Teotónio** *Mun.[85÷4]* €5 © 961 168 501 m: 251 826 286 *(not to be confused with luxury Pousada São Teotónio in the fort).* The Portuguese hostel adjoins the fire station *Bombeiros* on the roundabout opp. *Portas da Coroada* top gate to the Fortaleza *or* Ⓒ follow the follow the waymarked route via ***Portas do Sol***. A visit to the

magnificent Fortaleza and old quarter is recommended. The waymarked route takes in all the main sites but allow time to soak up some of the atmosphere with a stroll through the colourful narrrow laneways. The tourist buses tend to leave around 5 p.m. when the old fort reverts to a more relaxed mode and is a pleasant place for a drink or supper in the evening sunshine. An eletric 'tourist train' connects with the old quarter in Tui.

▮ **VALENÇA *DO MINHO*:** ❶ ***Posto de Turismo*** Portas do Sol ✆ 251 823 329 & ***museu do Bombeiro*** & café. ***Táxis*** ✆ 252 822 121. ***Estação Caminhos do Ferro*** ✆ 252 821 124. Bus ***Autocarro*** ✆ 251 809 588.

▮ **Lodging:** Several hotels in modern ***suburbs*** close to the albergue & entrance to the Fortaleza on Av. dos Bombeiros Voluntários. •*H**** **Lara** *x54* €35-40 ✆ 251 824 348 adj. 🍴 *Cristina* pilgrim menú. •*H** **Val Flores** *x32* €25-32 ✆ 251 824 106 €30 •*Hr.* **S. Gião** *x10* €19-27 ✆ 251 030 040 Av. S.Teotónio 17 (mixed reports). Within the old fort ***Fortaleza:*** ●*Hs* **Bulwark** *[20÷2]* €19 ✆ 251 837 022 *www.hostelbulwark.com* beautifully renovated building XVIIc. on Tv. do Cantinho, 7-11. •*Hr* **Portas do Sol** *x8* €30-70 ✆ 964 607 915 r/Conselheiro Lopes da Silva 51. •*Hs* **Vila** *x9* €45+ ✆ 251 826 080 r/José Rodrigues, 34. The enchanting •**Casa do Poço** *x7* €60-€80 ✆ 251 010 094 'hidden' down Calçada da Gaviarra, 4 adj. •*H***** **Pousada de S. Teotonio** *x18* €80-90 ✆ 251 800 260 disappointing in its stark modernity. At the other end of the scale you may find a bed *camas* to let above the bars and shops in the old quarter.

All this activity is encompassed within the huge fortress *Fortaleza* that stands guard over the Rio Minho. The cobbled streets are lined with souvenir shops, bars and restaurants. It is very busy during the day with bus tours but you could stay the night and take a whole day to explore both Valença and Tui. There is much of interest in both towns and pleasant walks along the Minho. A ferry operated between these border towns until the rail and road bridge was opened in 1886.

Valença Occupies an elevated position on the border of Portugal & Spain and has been a major military defensive from the earliest times and more recently modelled on the design of the 17th century military architect Vauban. In 1262 The town received a royal charter from D. Afonso III and was renamed Valença (formerly Contrasta). In 1502 D. Manuel I stayed in the town on his royal pilgrimage to Santiago. **Historic monuments**: (see town map next page): ❶ **Portas da Coroada** main entrance to the fortress opposite the pilgrim hostel. This leads directly to the tiny ❷ **Capela de São Sebastião** on the wide Largo Dr. Alfredo Guimarães. Next we come to ❸ **Capela do Bom Jesus** with its harmonious proportions in front of which is the statue to the illustrious son of Valença, S. Teotónio and in the square is the popular Bom Jesus serving food throughout the day with outside terrace that gets the last of the evening sun. We now pass over the dry central moat and inner gate ❺ **Portas do Meio** leading to the lower part of fortress and main entrance 'Sun Gate' ❹ **Porto do Sol *(Turismo)*** also known as Porto de Santiago and point the waymarked camino starts. Next is the busy main square ***Praça do Republica*** with Town Hall *Paços do Concelho (right)* and ringed with shops and cafés, *Vira da Esquina 'Turn the Corner'* is popular with pilgrims. Continue out the square via the narrow r/Mousinho de Albuquerque past (visible up right 50m detour) ❻ **Igreja de Santo Estevão** XIIc. with adj. ❼ **Roman Miliário** dating to Emperor Claudius 47 CE (National Monument). Continue up the narrow street to the venerable ❽ **Igreja Santa Maria dos Anjos** fine XIIc. Romanesque church adj. ❾ **Capela da Misercórdia** XVIIIc. with sculpture by master Teixeira Lopes *'O Senhor Morto.'* Beyond this church is •**Pousada de S. Teotonio** and beyond it a viewpoint over the Minho ❿ **Baluarte do Socorro.** The waymarked route now drops down steeply below the Pousada / Capela da Misercórdia & Casa do Poço (now up to our right) and out through ***Portas da Gaviarra*** *(Cisterna)* a little used side exit leading to steps directly down to the international bridge. *[Last year 8,726 pilgrims arrived in Santiago having started their journey in Valença].*

Portugal – GMT + 0 / © internacional **+351** (telefone fixo: 2 ou 3 / móvel: 9)
Proceed over the bridge into *Galician* Spain veering right> by police station *or:*

Option ✓ instead of the waymarked route along main road take the path **PRG-19** imm. (right) down steeply to the river and follow it for a delightful 1.3 km past rowing club until you reach the steps opp. the marina. Ascend to the Praza da Estrela and on up rua Bispo Castañon to intersection with rua S. Telmo and turn <left under arch to Church of S.Telmo and then up right> to the entrance to the albergue (situated just below the cathedral 0.3 km). The distance is the same as the waymarked route but you enter Tui along the river instead of the main road.

For waymarked route continue on main road and turn right> at crossroads passing Tui •**Parador** down to the Rio Miño & rowing club *Remo* Xunta da Galicia to the first official waymark *mojón* in Spain – PK 115.454 *(the camino is changing constantly so distances cannot be relied on but the mojónes are useful as waymarks)*. It was at this point *Praia de Fábrica* that the ferry carrying pilgrims and merchants from Valença would land and this is the Camino 'starting' point in Spain. You also have an option here to continue along the riverside route (right) ▲

Note: *Spanish time + 1 hour ahead of Portugal and switch from Portuguese to Spanish. Note many signposts will now appear in a mixture of Spanish* Castellano & *Galician* Galego. *Last year 21,308 pilgrims started their journey in Tui.*

Spain – GMT + 1 / ✆ internacional **+34** (teléfono fijo: 9 / número de móvil: 6).

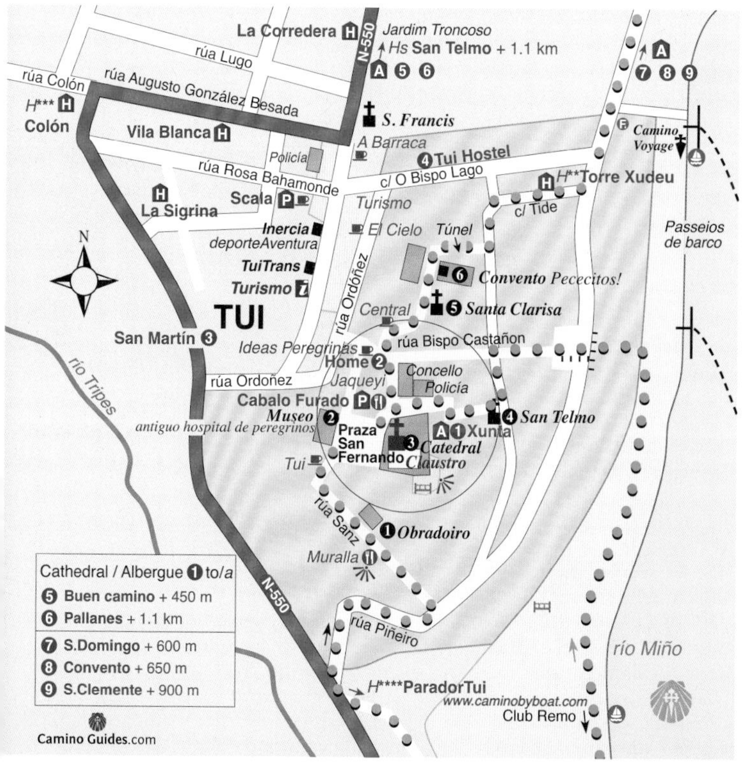

The main waymarked route (left) winds its way up to the cathedral passing *Fonte* [] built into cliff (left). There is now a steep climb up to the cathedral square in Tui past *Rst. A Muralla* onto main road to turn off right> into the medieval heart of this border town passing the 16th century prison (now the school of Restoration *Obradoiro*) up into Plaza San Fernando to the west door of Tui Cathedral.

3.4 km **Tui *Catedral*** also on the main square we find the helpful ❶ ***Turismo*** (original pilgrim hospital) and to rear of the cathedral *off Praza do Concello* and past the police station is *Alb.*❶ *Xunta [36÷2]* €8 © 638 276 855. Large lounge, kitchen and pleasant open patio (see photo>). Well restored XIXc. rectory centrally located in the heart of the historic town centre although a nearby nightclub can be noisy at weekends. Preference to pilgrims from Portugal.

TUI: Historical border town with population of 15,000. At its heart is the well-preserved medieval town and the waymarked route conveniently passes the following ***historical monuments:*** ❶ **Obradoiro** *XVIc.* the original prison where the date of construction 1584 can still be seen over the door. ❷ **Museo Diocesano** *XVIIIc.* now the Tourist office and Diocesan museum with acdisplay of Celtic, medieval and religious artefacts and worth the small fee just to savour an original pilgrim hostel with its central courtyard. Here also is the sarcophagus in which lay San Telmo's body after he died at the Bridge of Fevers in 1251 (which we pass on the next stage). On the opposite side of the square is Tui's centrepiece the impressive Romanesque cathedral ❸ **Catedral de Santa María** *XIIc.* dating from 1120 but with later Gothic additions, most notably the fine portico. The cathedral has a handsome cloister, reputedly the only remaining example of a medieval cathedral cloister in Galicia (see photo>). Off the cloister are steps down to a delightful garden overlooking the Miño (photo next page). Overlooking the gardens is the medieval tower with access off the far corner of the cloisters *(light switch on wall to illuminate the spiral staircase)*. The interior of the cathedral itself is no less outstanding with a chapel dedicated to St. James 'the Moor Slayer' *Santiago Matamoros* and a statue to the first black saint from Africa *Sta. Ypiîgenîa.*

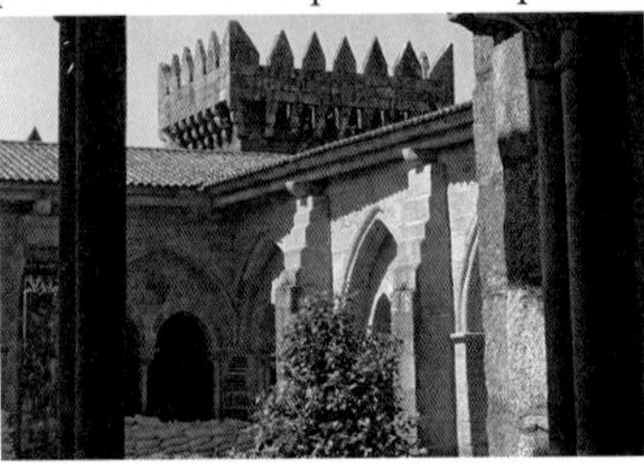

Below the Cathedral (and albergue) is chapel of Mercy *Capela de Misericordia* and ❹ **Igrexa de San Telmo** *XV* built over the crypt that housed the relics of S. Telmo. The waymarked route leaves town via *plaza Concello* with Town hall *Concello.* On the corner at Porta da Pia,1. is popular *Alb.*❷ **♥Home *Ideas Peregrinas*** *Priv. [10÷2]* €13 +*10* €30+ © 986 076 330 Mónica & Silvana www.ideas-peregrinas.com who also stock pilgrim guides, walking poles etc. and ☕ serving delicious organic cakes! The main activity lies down left while the waymarked route out of town continues s/o past ☕ *Central* to ❺ **Igrexa Santa Clarisa** *XVII* (the work of master mason Santiago Domingo de Andrade with fine Baroque altarpiece) adj. ❻ **Convento de Clarisas** *XVIc.* surrounded by the walls of the convent of the enclosed order of nuns of St. Clare *Convento das Clarisas Encerradas* who maintain the delightful tradition of baking biscuits from eggs donated by locals – ring bell by hatch and try the 'little fish symbols' *Pececitos* for a few euros. The waymarked route continues through an the evocative Nuns Way *Rua das Monxas* with arched passage below the convent known as the nuns tunnel ***Túnel das Monxas*** to leave the medieval city through the *Porta Bergana,* today nothing more than a memory.

❶ ***Turismo*** now at Paseo de Calvo Sotelo 16 (prev. by catedral) ✆ 677 418 405 open 9:30–14:00/ 16:00-19:00. ▮ ***Other Central albergues***: ❸ **Jacob's** *Priv. [19÷4]* €13-15 ✆ 644 557 194 c/Obispo Lago, 5. ❹ **San Martín** *Priv.[19÷5]* €12 ✆ 640 616 473 c/ Coruña, 6. ❺ **Buen Camino** *Priv.[20÷1]* €15 incl. ✆ Alba 986 604 052 Av. Concordia, 10 adj. *Liceo* & *Piscina municipal.* ❻ **Pallanes** *Priv.[20÷2]* €13 *+6* €20-35 ✆ 986 682 446 with large garden near railway station on c/Palláns, 11. ***Tui Exit: c/ Antero Rubín: @ Nº20*** ❼ **Santo Domingo** *Priv. [22÷5]* €12-15 ✆ 650 820 685 with rear garden, and just beyond at ***@ Nº30.*** ❽♥**Convento del Camino** *Priv.[43÷6]* €13-15 ✆ 690 328 565 Jorge & Ainoa have lovingly restored this historic convent with mod-cons, courtyard & peaceful botanical gardens to the rear *www.conventodelcamino.com*. ❾ **Villa San Clemente** *Priv.[20÷3]* €15 *+3* €40+ ✆ 678 747 700 & rear garden c/Canónigo Valiño, 23.

▮ ***Hotels:*** •**O Novo Cabalo Furado** *x8* €30-60 ✆ 986 604 445 c/Seijas, 3 (adj. cathedral). •*Hs* **La Sigrina** *x10* €45-65 ✆ 654 396 782 *www.lasigrinahostal.es* r/ Foxo 8. •*P* **La Corredera** *x14* €40-50 ✆ 629 879 730 (refurbished *La Generosa*) *www.pensionlacorredera.com* Paseo de Calvo Sotelo 37. •**Scala** €15+ ✆ 986 601 890 c/Rua Rosa Bahamonde, 5 (adj. cafe Scala). Boutique hotel •*H*** **Villa Blanca** *x10* €45-60 ✆ 986 603 525 Rúa Augusto González Besada, 5. •*H**** **Colón** *x66* €48-60 ✆ 986 600 223 modern hotel c/Colón. Historic Jewish Tower •*H*** **A Torre do Xudeu** *x8* €50-60 ✆ 986 603 535 *www.atorredoxudeo.es* c/Tide 3. A walk around the old quarter may reveal discreet signs for beds *camas* from €15. ***Tui Outskirts:*** •*H***** **Parador de Tui** *x32* €70+ ✆ 986 600 300. •*Hs*** **San Telmo** *x27* €15-40 ✆ 986 906 116 Av. Concordia,84 (opp. rail station on N-550). •*H**** **Alfonso I** +2.2 km free pick-up *(see next stage).*

▮ ***Cafés:*** Take a stroll along *Paseo de Calvo Sotelo* with lively pavement *A Barraca* & *El Cielo* with evening sun. Midway along is ***Iglesia de S.Francisco*** *XVIIc.* and far end 'wild horses' statue overlooks Troncoso gardens built around the old medieval city walls. *Scala* on c/Rua Rosa Bahamonde serves food all day. Adj. cathedral on Praza do Concello *Novo Cabalo* & *Jamonería Jaqueyi.* Entering Tui on the camino you pass *A Muralla Demetrio* ✆ 606 910 323 heavenly terrace (eve sun). ▮ ***Backpack transfers*** *transporte de mochilas* **Tuitrans** ✆ 638 555 253 *www.tuitrans.com* Paseo de Calvo Sotelo 19. Outdoor gear *deporte aventura at* ***Inercia*** *(10:00-20:00)* Calvo Sotelo 31. ***Canoe trips*** to Caminha from ***Club Remo do Miño*** (adj. parador) *www.caminobyboat.com*

19 TUI – PORRIÑO

------	4.1 ------	*24%*
------	9.5 ------	*57%*
------	3.1 ------	*19%*
Total km	**16.7** km *(10.4 ml)*	

Total ascent **340**m *+½ hr*

▲ Alto *m* Capela La Guia **75** m *(246 ft)*

<A H> *S.Telmo* ***5.8 km+1.3*** km Orbenlle **9.5** km.

100m TUI S.Telmo Opción Orbenlle S.Campio 75m PORRIÑO
rio S.Simón rio Louro rio Louro
0 km 5 km 10 km 15 km

Practical Path: A challenge today is the stretch of main road entering the industrial town of Porriño. However, a new route along the rio Louro avoids the slog through the main industrial area. This recommended alternative is longer and so the original stage to Redondela has been split to allow for two more relaxed stages. Many pilgrims start their pilgrimage in Tui *(**120.4** km from Santiago entitling the bona fide pilgrim to apply for a Compostela)* so a stopover in Porriño allows those starting out, time to acclimatise body and soul to the rigours of the way. If you started further back in Lisbon or Porto and decide to continue to Redondela note there is a very steep climb *up* and *down* Monte Cornedo at the end of a long day. Porriño now has several modern pilgrims hostels and good facilities serving the industrial town of 18,500 largely employed in granite products.

Death – the last sleep? No, it is the final awakening. Walter Scott

The Mystical Path: When we live as though each day is our last we start to fully live in the present. "Our priorities change; our hearts open, our minds begin to clear and what really matters becomes instantly apparent: the transmission of love, the letting go of obstacles to understanding, the relinquishment of our grasping, of our hiding from ourselves.' Who Dies? *Stephen Levine*

Personal Reflections: "... around me everything is silent but for the babbling brook. The isolated cross marks the spot where a saint died and my inner silence is broken with thoughts of death. Like the busy waters of the little stream, I too, will return to the Source. My body, like the Earth's, is already half way through its life-span. Body and Earth, both will dissolve back into the dust from which they were made. Only what is perfect and formless is eternal and created by the Source of Love. All else is impermanent and ephemeral. Even the sun will die..."

0.0 km **Tui *Catedral*** Proceed via Praza do Concello s/o at *Ideas Pergrinas* past *Central* into rua das Monxas & *Convento das Clarisas* through the nun's tunnel *Túnel das Monxas* down c/Tide into r/Antero Rubín to the ancient [ ] (below the overpass) past •Alb. **S. Domingo** (right) to **Convento Sto. Domingo** XIVc. *[the Dominicans have been associated with this site since 1330]* now •Alb. **Convento** s/o under archway (access to public gardens overlooking the river) past **•Alb. S. Clemente** (left) and turn right> (sign Praia da Areeira) into Praza San Bartolomé one of the oldest suburbs of Tui with the XIc Romanesque monastic church of St. Bartholomew **San Bartolomé de Rebordáns [1.1** km**]**. *(Recent excavations in*

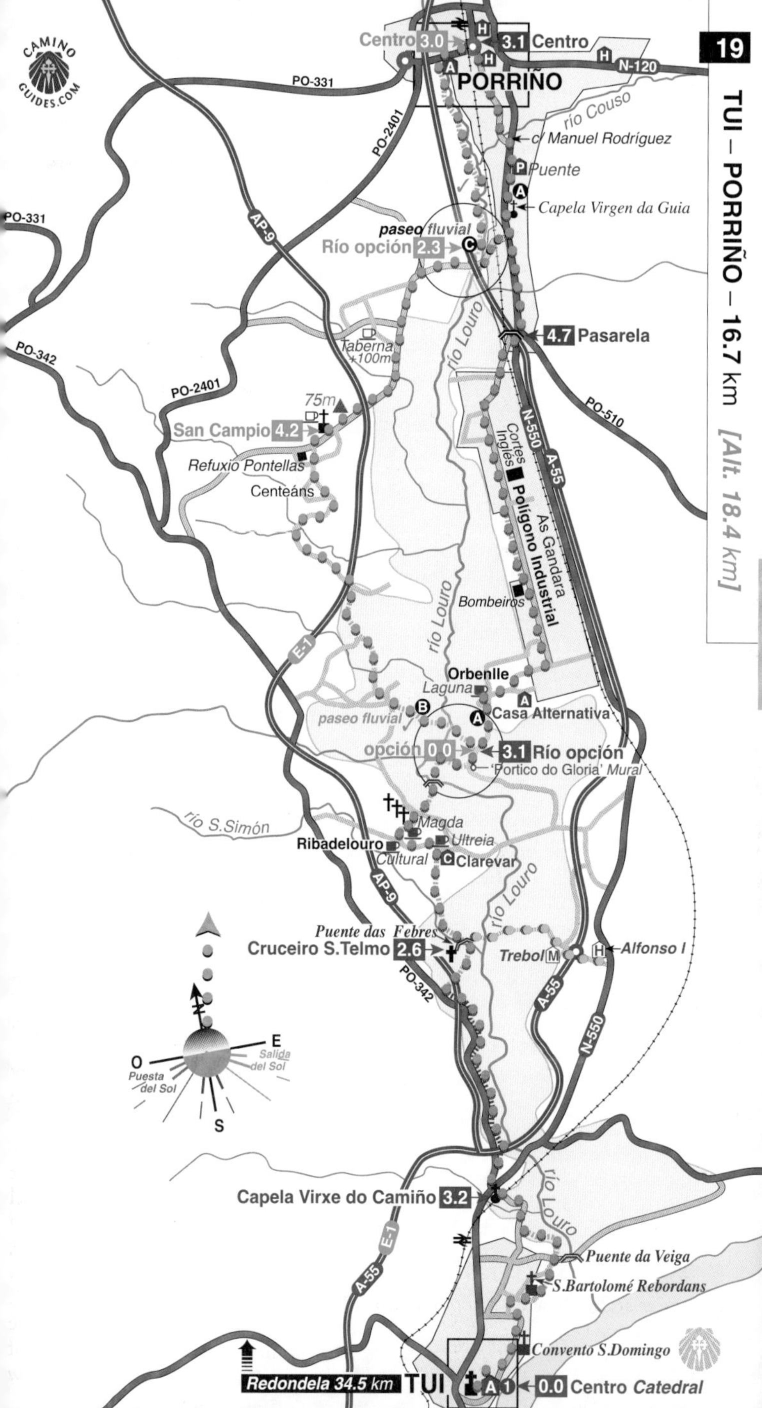
19
TUI – PORRIÑO – 16.7 km [Alt. 18.4 km]
CAMINO GUIDES.COM
Centro 3.0
3.1 Centro
PORRIÑO
N-120
PO-331
PO-2401
río Couso
c/ Manuel Rodríguez
Puente
Capela Virgen da Guia
PO-331
AP-9
paseo fluvial
Río opción 2.3
Taberna +100m
4.7 Pasarela
PO-342
PO-2401
río Louro
PO-510
75m
San Campio 4.2
Refuxio Pontellas
Centeáns
Cortes Inglés
Polígono Industrial
As Gandara
N-550
A-55
Bombeiros
río Louro
E-1
Orbenlle
Laguna
Casa Alternativa
paseo fluvial
opción 0.0
3.1 Río opción
'Portico do Gloria' Mural
río S.Simón
Magda
Ribadelouro
Ultreia
Cultural
Clarevar
AP-9
río Louro
Puente das Febres
Cruceiro S.Telmo 2.6
Trebol
Alfonso I
PO-342
A-55
N-550
E
Salida del Sol
O
Puesta del Sol
S
Capela Virxe do Camiño 3.2
río Louro
Puente da Veiga
S.Bartolomé Rebordans
E-1
A-55
Convento S.Domingo
Redondela 34.5 km
TUI
0.0 Centro Catedral

the area have unearthed Roman and Visigothic ruins. The finely cruceiro dates from 1770). We now leave the town and turn down onto path to the medieval bridge over the rio Louro **Ponte da Veiga** which we do *not* cross but turn <left along the ancient Via Romana XIX. The camino has been realigned (to avoid crossing rail tracks) and meanders in a wide loop *under* the railway and over the main road [**!**] **N-550** to the Virgin of the Way **Chapel** [**2.1** km].

3.2 km **Capela da Virxe do Camiño.** We crosses the motorway A-55 along a dedicated pilgrim track with timber safety barrier. We follow this all the way *under* the AP-9 [**1.9** km] and 200m later we turn right> [**0.2** km] [**!**] back *over* the motorway to enter a densely wooded section that is low-lying and can be wet and muddy after rain to emerge at a glade by the river and wayside **cross** [**0.5** km].

2.6 km **Cruz de San Telmo** also known as bridge of Fevers *Ponte das Febres.* Here San Telmo fell sick and died of a fever in 1251 on his way back from a pilgrimage to Santiago de Compostela. A cross marks this mournful spot *Aqui enfermo de Muerte San Telmo Abril 1251.* ▲

*[**Detour 1.3** km* ● ● ● ● **•Hotel Alfonso I** *x64* €35+ pilgrim price © 986 607 060 ***Directions:*** *From S. Telmo cross río S.Simón by pasarela [0.0 km] and turn imm. right* ***off*** *waymarked camino onto grass path and over río Louro & turn right again on woodland track and s/o to asphalt road and turn right to* **•Motel Trébol** *[0.8 km] x30* €35 © 986 607 087. *And over motorway to Hotel Alfonso I [0.5 km] return the same way].*

▲ Turn <left over *pasarela* on waymarked route along forest track (several local walking routes in the area – stick to yellow arrows). We wind our way up into **A Magdalena** [**1.1** km] •*CR* **Clarevar** *x3* €30+ © 626 203 738 Rúa Farrapa, 24 adj. popular ☕ *Ultreia* up to crossroads **Ribadelouro** [**0.4** km] ☕ *Cultura* (left) keep s/o past ☕ *La Magda* (right) and turn <left past *Calvario* and imm. right> down onto path through woodland over stone bridge ***Ponte Romana de Orbenlle.*** Shortly afterwards the open cast mines of Porriño appear on the horizon heralding the intense industrial activity ahead. Continue up to road to ***mural of the Portico de Gloria*** [**1.4** km] (see photo>) and just beyond is **option** [**0.2** km] for an alternative *complemetario* route that avoids the soulless slog through the Industrial estates ahead.

3.1 km **Opción Ⓐ *Orbenlle.*** Original route s/o through the industrial suburbs or new scenic route left along the course of the rio Louro (1.7 km longer).

Note: These optional routes are often disputed for commercial or other reasons and waymarks may have been obliterated. An unfortunate but common attempt to disguise or remove these quieter options. We come across it again as we enter Porriño at option **C** *which would deprive you of a delightful riverside path into the centre of Porriño.*

For original road route keep s/o at option **A** and follow waymarks into **Orbenlle** [**0.6** km] *Chimay* and *Laguna* last café break before the industrial estate *polígono industrial* A Gandara. Also popular ●*Alb.* **Casa Alternativo** *Priv. [8÷2]* €30 incl. Dinner B&B ✆ Dries 622 900 377 with access to either route. Take the grass verge where possible – there is a section of wide track just after *Bombeiros Galicia*. Continue to footbridge ***pasarela*** [**4.1** km] over the railway.

4.7 km **Pasarela** across railway (under A-55) onto the N-550. Keep s/o over río Casavella *Louriña (first of many bars and cafes along the N-550)* to the tiny pilgrim chapel ***Capela A Virxe da Guía*** (1640). Pass •*P* **Puente** turn <left at next traffic lights over rio Couro into c/ Manuel Rodríguez. Waymarks now take us past *Pinzas* to San Sebastian roundabout [ ] right 50m ***Capela San Sebastián*** *XVI* up into r/S. Sebastián past Capela S. Benito *[left – leads to* •*P.* ***Maracaibo****]* and turn down left past ***Igreja Santa María*** and right into main street *calle principal Ramón González* past the impressive stone façade of the Town Hall *Casa Consistorial* and Minerals Museum *Museo Municipal de Minerals* to the central fountain and park *Fonte y Parque do Cristo [steps leading up to the Igreja Bom Cristo (right)]* to central **roundabout**:

3.1 km **Porriño** ***centro*** alterative route joins from the left. See next page for list of accommodation and other facilities in Porriño.

B For new alternative *complementario* route over the rio Louro (avoiding the industrial area *As Gándaras)* turn <left at option point. Once you enter the woodland waymarks become obvious and appear at every turn on the maze of paths and country lanes ahead. To take this more scenic route turn <left onto woodland path over rio Louro *puente Baranco (see photo>)* and up to a series of quiet country roads that wind their way over the **AP-9** to pilgrim 'rest' area *Refuxio Pontellas* (often closed) adj. Capilla de San Campio.

4.2 km **Capilla San Campio** 'high point' a mere 75m! the rear of the church (weekends only): The route now heads back over the AP-9 to the *Velodromo Municipal* [**1.3** km]. *Here up left 200m off route is* *Taberna.* Continue over roundabout and under A-55 to ***option*** **C** [**1.0** km].

2.3 km **Opción Ⓒ** *Puente*. As we emerge under the A-55 turn imm. <left *[**not** s/o over pasarela to join road route along the N-550]*. Waymarks left to the join the recommended river path ✓ may have been removed –you can't get lost if you simply follow the river path *paseo fluvial* keeping the river always on your right all the way to municipal albergue in **Porriño** [**2.4** km] *see map opposite*.

*Alb.*❶ **Peregrinos** *Xunta.[52÷2]* €8 ✆ 986 335 428 purpose built hostel on the river Louro (15:00–22:00) *see photo*. Detour 100m left (visible under the A-55 bridge) *Alb.*❷ **Camino Portugués** *Priv.[54÷6]* €10-12 ✆ 886 133 252 (Alex) Av. Buenos Aires 40 (opens 10:30–22:00) all mod cons and massage facility. Continue into town with detour 100m right to new build *Alb.*

❸ **Senda Sur** *Priv.[48÷2]* €10+ *+8* €25+ ✆ 886 129 569 www.sendasur.es Rua da foz 3. Continue past •*H*** **Louro** *x11* €28-48 Raquel ✆ 669 683 476 www.hostallouro.com Av. Buenos Aires, 6 (above Froiz) & *Sendasur* •*P* **Cando** *x4* €18-36 ✆ 986 333 471 r/Progreso, 1 *(above Paso Nivel)*. and keep s/o over rail line to *Banco Santander*, taxi rank and central roundabout [**0.6** km].

3.0 km **Centro** ***Rotunda*** main road route joins from the right.

Central Roundabout: ☕ *Central* & *A* ☕ *Francachela* (with large shell) operates *Alb.* ❹ **Camino Santiago** *Priv.[28÷2]* €12 ✆ 623 161 267 occupying 3 upper floors (lift) of mod. building to the rear access r/Servando Ramilo N°17 *(check in A Francachela (same owner – mixed reports)*. *Alb.*❺ **Rincón** *Priv.[21÷1]* €13 ✆ 886 319 533 Opp. railway at r/Cando 3 rear of ☕ *Rincon*. ▮ **Other Lodging:** •*H******Parque** *x43* €40 ✆ 986 331 504 www.hotelparqueporrino.es Parque Cristo. •*H****Azul** *x16* ✆ 986 330 032 www.hotelazul.es c/ Ramirás,38. •*P*****Maracaibo** €22-48 ✆ 986 330 901 c/ Manuel Rodríguez, 50. ❻ **Fonte dos Aloques** *Priv.[10÷1]* €14 ✆ 695 493 838. ❼ **Casucho da Peregrina**.*[30÷2]* €23incl +2 ✆680 665 498 Jesús & Pili. ***Outskirts*** *(+0.5km)* •*H*****Internacional** *x50* €45-58 ✆ 986 330 262. c/ Antonio Palacios 99. •*P****Puente** €40 ✆ 986 348 094 Av. Domingo Bueno, 67.

Porriño: A sprawling industrial town of 18,500 sandwiched between the río Louro and the A-55 motorway and the steep cliffs to the east where granite quarries provide much of the raw material for the intense industrial activity in the mining and finishing of granite for building and decorative purposes. *Museo Municipal de Minerals* opposite the Town Hall. A Variety of bars and restaurants around the Plaza del Cristo in the centre).

Note: *Porriño is **103.7** km from Santiago and provides the last chance for a bona fide pilgrim to commence their journey and apply for a Compostela.*

Camino Guides.com

PORRIÑO

Estación

Salida

Azul

El Patio

4 Camino Santiago

Paso Nivel

Cando

Sendasur

Louro

Taxi

Central

Francachela

2 Camino Portugués

Plaza del Cristo

Parque

Municipal 1

Av. Buenos Aires

rua da Foz

3 Sendasur

Malloserá

Concello

Rúa Antonio Palacios

6 Fonte

Internacional

Casucho 7

Rua Pio XII

5 Rincón

Maracaibo

S. Maria

Puente

Rua do Progreso

rua Estación

Ramiranes

Rua do Cando

Ramón González

Trv. Matadero

río Louro

A-55

N-550

N-120

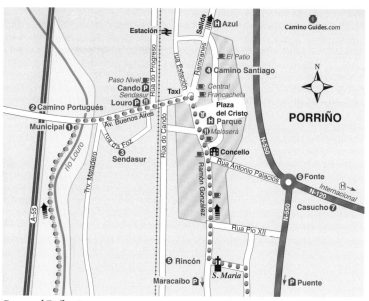

Personal Reflections:

Ponte da Veiga & Via Romana XIX

20 PORRIÑO – REDONDELA

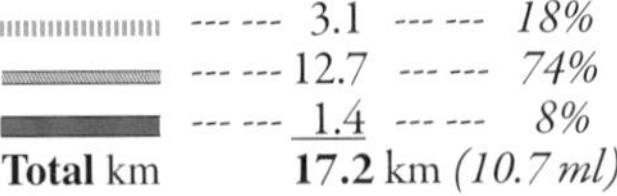

--- --- 3.1 --- --- *18%*
--- --- 12.7 --- --- *74%*
--- --- 1.4 --- --- *8%*

Total km **17.2** km *(10.7 ml)*

Total ascent **850**m +*1½ hr*
▲ Alto *m* Monte Cornedo **250**m *(820 ft)*
<A H> ➲Veigandaña **4.2** km ➲Mos **6.8** km ➲Saxamonde **13.5** km

Marco Miliário Via XIX Monte Cornado

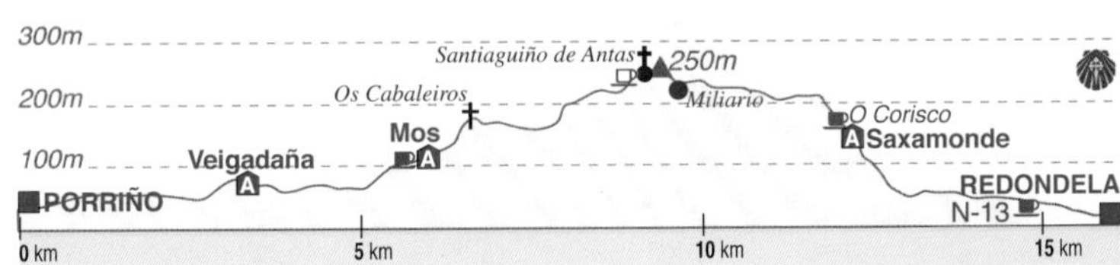

Practical Path: Don't be deceived by the short distance this is a challenging stage with a steep climb up and *very* steep climb *down.* The equivalent distance allowing for the cumulative ascent is 21.4 km and ¾ on asphalt which is hard underfoot. Our destination is delightful Redondela where the coastal route from Vigo joins – adding to the liveliness and pilgrim vigour in town. Porriño marks the last chance to obtain a Compostela beinbg just over 100 km from Santiago.

There are two ways of spreading light: to be the candle or the mirror that reflects it.
***Edith Wharton** novelist*

The Mystical Path: The Light, while obscured, lies hidden in our memories. We need to re-member and re-light the flame of love. While we remain in darkness we fail to see the angelic realm that surrounds us. It is time to let go our irrational fear and false humility and step into the light of our Divine Essence. We can continue in ignorance and remain hostage to the ego or become Host to God. The choice we make will affect everything around us... and within us.

0.0 km **Porriño *centro.*** At central roundabout keep s/o r/ Ramiranes past rail station & Lidl (left) and over [!] N-550 roundabout *capela das Angustias* [ ] (right). A new detour takes a short forest track right> on a 1 km loop *over* the A-52 [many still take the original route s/o over access road and *under* the A-52]. Pass *Tía Albina* to hamlet of **Fonte do Chan** [ ] *[rest area and granite boulder with dedication to first Galician to summit Mount Everest]*. **Option** ▲

2.5 km **Chans *opción.*** The route has recently been re-waymarked at this point.

The original route continues s/o here (waymarks at the start have been obliterated) along a tranquil river path by the rio Louro. To take this 'green' route keep s/o and take *next* turn left and cross the **N-550 [0.3** km] [!] turn right and veer left (50m) to cross **rail line [0.2** km] [!] Continue parallel to rail track past timber yard and turn left to cross **Ponte Loura [0.5** km]. Take the river path right and continue along the river bank crossing several country lanes until the path ends at childrens play area [**3.0** km] with the church of Santa Eulalia clearly visible above. Take the road up steeply to join the waymarked route at Mos [**0.2** km]. **Total 4.2** -v- **4.3** km.

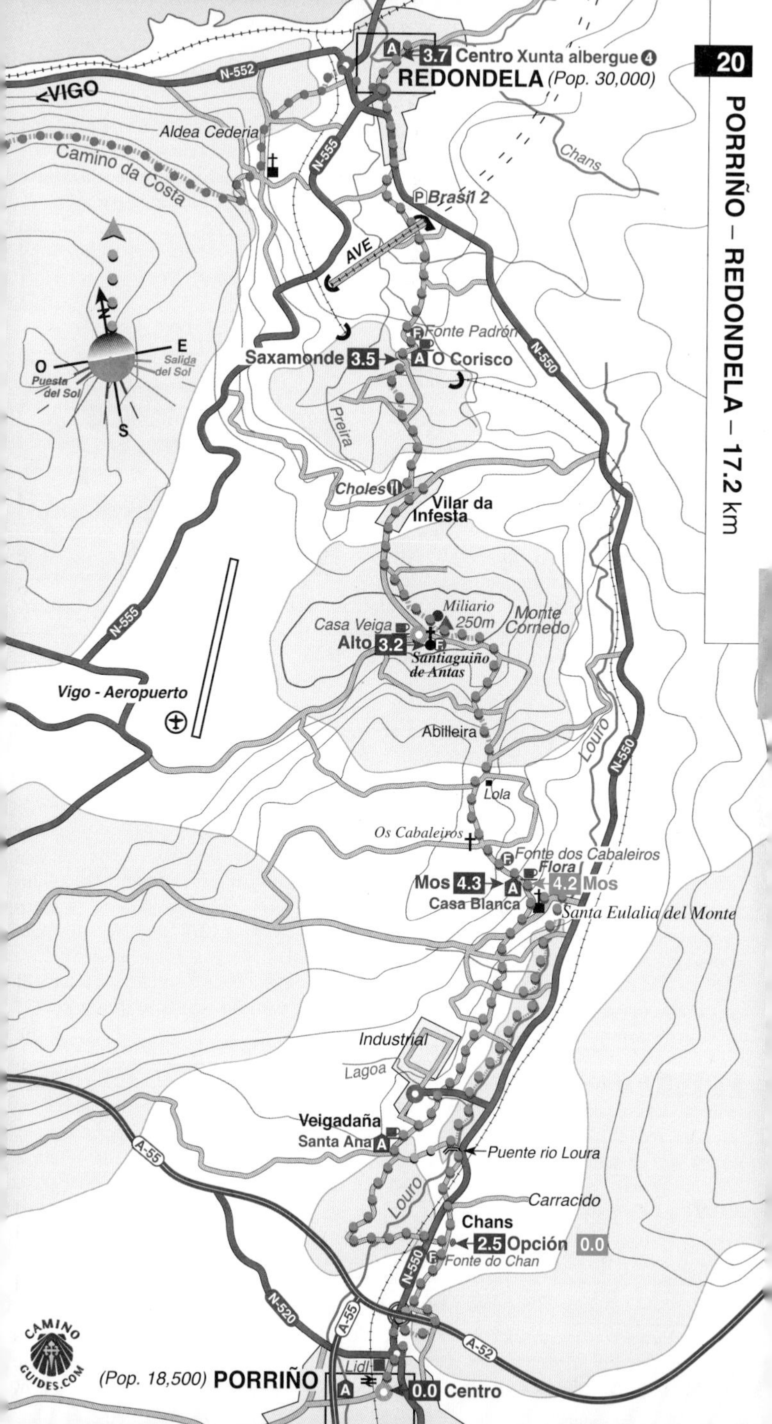
PORRIÑO – REDONDELA – 17.2 km
3.7 Centro Xunta albergue 4
REDONDELA (Pop. 30,000)
<VIGO
N-552
Aldea Cederia
Camino da Costa
N-555
Chans
Brasil 2
AVE
Fonte Padrón
Saxamonde 3.5
O Corisco
N-550
E
O
Salida del Sol
Puesta del Sol
S
Preira
Choles
Vilar da Infesta
Miliario 250m
Monte Cornedo
Casa Veiga
Alto 3.2
Santiaguiño de Antas
Vigo - Aeropuerto
Abilleira
Louro
Lola
Os Cabaleiros
Fonte dos Cabaleiros
Flora
Mos 4.3
4.2 Mos
Casa Blanca
Santa Eulalia del Monte
Industrial
Lagoa
Veigadaña
Santa Ana
Puente rio Loura
A-55
Carracido
Chans
2.5 Opción 0.0
Fonte do Chan
N-520
A-52
Lidl
CAMINO GUIDES.COM
(Pop. 18,500) PORRIÑO
0.0 Centro

For the newly waymarked route at **Option** ▲ Turn left opp. granite boulder and s/o over N-550 [!] under rail and over río Louro. Turn right and continue parallel to río Louro to **Veigadaña [1.6 km]** & ●*Alb.* **Santa Ana de Veigadaña** *Asoc. [16÷1]* €7 ✆ 986 094 277 Petelos-Mos. Keep s/o over rivulet *Lagoa* and under new road bridge (access to industrial estate left) past ***Fonte Magdalena*** & school *Concello de Mos* where we start our climb up to Mos over crossroad into the pedestrianised village of Mos *Iglesia de Santa Eulalia del Monte* (right) *O Alpenore* & *Bo Camiño* opp. newly renovated *Pazo* ***Pazo de Mos*** *(original XVII residence of the Marquis of Mos)* to **albergue [2.7 km]**.

4.3 km **Mos** ●*Alb.* **Casa Blanca** *Asoc. [16÷1]* €8 ✆ 986 348 001 Check-in Pazo de Mos. Opp. •*Alb./* **Flora** *[13÷3]* €10 *x3* €30 *menú* ✆ Flora 986 334 269. Continue up steeply the road of the Knights *rua dos Cabaleiros* passing *Fonte Os Cabaleiros (right)* to crossroads ***Cruceiro Os Cabaleiros*** wayside cross *[Santísimo Cristo da Victoria e Virxe das Dores – erected 1733 and site of local pilgrimage]*. S/o past *florista Lola* in Abilleira to climb again alternating between road and path through woodland past *Vending* at *Parque Cerdeiriñas* to our high point *Alto Cornedo* 235m at **Monte de Santiago de Antas** (left).

3.2 km **Parque** ***Alto Os Valos*** laarge park and chapel dedicated to *Santiago Caballero* his mounted image carved above the door ***Capela de Santiaguiño de Antas.*** 100m off route (left) *Casa Veiga* on the airport road Estrada Peinador. We now start our long descent towards the Ria Vigo which lies hidden by woodland around Monte Cornedo but we can hear aeroplanes landing at Vigo airport only 2 km to the West. We pass a Roman milestone *Marco Miliário* marking the military route Via XIX evidence that we are directly on the original pilgrim way to Santiago. Shortly afterwards we pass O Loureiro and enter the main road at **Vilar da Infesta [2.2 km]** *Pastelería O Parque* (right) and turn off sharp <right at the far end of village to *Churrasquería Choles* **[0.7 km]**. We alternate between path and road through woodland around *Chan das Pipas* and *Casal do Monte* and continue our descent past rest area *Área de Descanso* and follow a maze of small country lanes *very* steeply down [!] along camiño Romano in the area of Padrón (Saxamonde) to Albergue **[0.6 km]**.

3.5 km **Padrón** ***Saxamonde*** & ●*Alb.* **Corisco** *Priv.[12÷1]*+ €12 + €25 ✆ 986 402 166 camiño Romano 49. We now descend (virtually vertically!) and level out to cross under new **rapid rail [1.7 km]** ***Ave*** (Vigo –A Coruna) *[off route (up right)* •*H* **Brasil** *2 x10 €27+✆ 986 402 251].* S/o to **N-550 [0.6 km]** turn <left *Novo Regueiro* and right> at sign 'town centre' into **Redondela Praza Ponteareas [0.8 km]** ***Convento de Vilavella*** *XVI Apt.de época* €90+ ✆ 986 460 913. Rotunda (left 150m) on Rúa Rabadeira Canabal,1 new albergue ❶**A Rotonda** *Priv.[11÷1]* €17 ✆ 657 805 988. Continue into **rúa Pai Crespo** ***@Nº55*** *Alb.*❷ **Santiago de Vilavella** *Priv.[46÷1]* €15 ✆ 673 414 752 & ***@Nº60*** ❸**A Conserveira** *Priv. [40÷1]* €10 ✆ 676 667 293 with air-con. Veer right under rail viaduct (off main road) past •**Alvear Suites** €40+ ✆ 986 400 637 to central **rotunda [0.6 km]**.

3.7 km **Redondela** ***Centro*** ❹ **Casa da Torre** *Xunta [42÷2]* €8 ✆ 986 404 196

Plaza Ribadavia ***Casa da Torre*** *XVIc.* renovated as the original pilgrim hostel with all mod cons and to compensate for its tiny kitchen, it has an enormous lounge! Council library upstairs with well preserved Roman Miliário. Located just off the main paseo by culvert of río Pexeiro its atmospheric environment somewhat diminished by the proximity of the busy traffic roundabout.

▮ **Other Lodging**: Near Casa da Torre ❼ **Alfonso XII** *Priv.[8÷1]* €15 *+2* €35 ✆ 676 167 672 / ✆ 648 745 287 r/Alfonso XII, 22. ***Rua Isidoro Queimaliños Nº44*** •*P* **A Boa Estrela** *x6* €20-40 ✆ 663 292 196 www.aboaestrela.com @***Nº35*** (corner Praza de Alfóndiga): ❺ **A Casa da Herba** *Priv.[24÷3]* €12-15 *+2* €40-50 ✆ 644 404 074 www.acasadaherba.com **@Nº33** ❻ *Hs* **Rosa D'Abreu** *Priv.[6÷1]* €15-20 ✆ Rosa 688 422 701. **@Nº10 •Casa Virginia** house sleeps 8+ from €87-€200 ✆ 660 589 515. **@Nº9** •*Apt.* **O Descansino Pilgrim Rooms** *x3* €30+ ✆ 666 260 651 www.descansino.com + other apartments nearby also in ***Calle Telmo Bernádez*** *(opp. Igrexa Santiago)* **@Nº11** ❽ **El Camino** *Priv.*[24÷3] €10-12 ✆ 650 963 676. **&@Nº15** ❾ **Santiago Apóstol** *Par.*[30÷2] €10 ✆ 627 748 802. *Alb.* ❿**Avoa Regina** *Priv.[32÷2]* €15 ✆ 986 125 297 r/ Picota, 23. 666 260 651 on the way out of town. ***Turismo*** ❶ ✆ 986 400 300 Concello r/ Alfonso XII 11-14 / 15-19. ***See next stage for additional lodging.***

Redondela Town built at the top end of Ría de Vigo but not visible from the town centre. However a 200m walk past the bus-stop under the city bypass brings us to a boardwalk alongside the estuary. The Xunta albergue is located in the centre adj. 🍴 *Casa Consejo* with pilgrim *menú*. The town has a lively atmosphere with numerous cafés bars & restaurants off rua Alfonso XII and the paseo passes along the river and town park. The 15th century ***Iglesia de Santiago*** is located up the cobbled rua do Adro and just 50m off the waymarked route (opp. Casa Virginia). The church is very emblematic of the camino with a statue of Santiago Matamoros above the fine rose window and other Santiago motifs. Pilgrim mass 20.30 (times may vary).

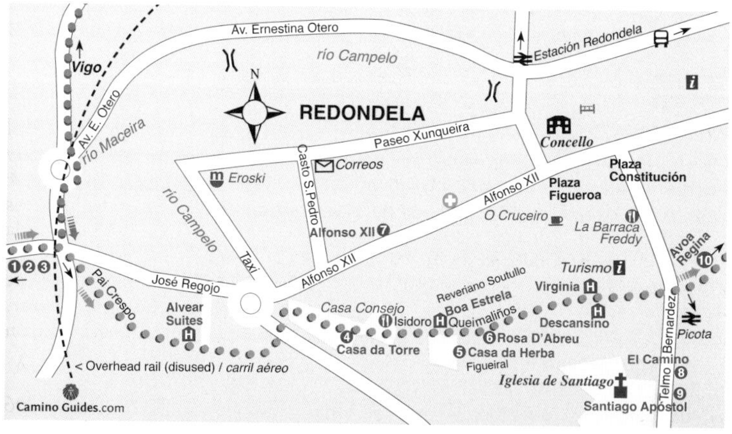

21 REDONDELA–PONTEVEDRA

Centro

	6.2	*32%*
	11.4	*58%*
	2.0	10%
Total km	**19.6** km *(12.2 ml)*	

Total ascent **360**m *+½ hr*

▲ Alto *m* Alto da Lomba **153** m *(502 ft)*

< A H > ➲Cesantes (Jumbolí) **3.1** km ➲Arcade **6.7** km

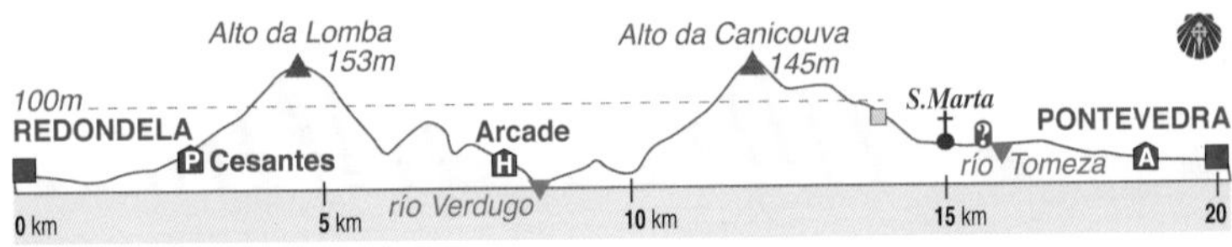

Practical Path: Refreshing coastal stage around Rías Vigo and Pontevedra. We start at sea level then climb up through mixed forest around Alto de Lomba before dropping down again to the sea at Arcade which offers safe swimming (beach showers). We then start the 2nd uphill stretch to climb the ancient stone path *Vella da Canicouva* to the next high point around *Cruceiro Cacheiro* before descending finally to the provincial capital of Pontevedra. The route is varied with several drinking fonts and cafés. If you take the river option into Pontevedra 48% of this stage is via woodland paths offering shade and tranquillity; the remainder along quiet country lanes apart from a brief but dangerous uphill stretch of the N-550 into Arcade. Note that the main well-equipped pilgrim hostels are 1½ kilometres *this* side of the town centre in Pontevedra.

Words are but symbols of symbols and therefore twice removed from reality. ***ACIM***
The Mystical Path: 'Words will mean little now ... we seek direct experience of truth alone. For we wait in quiet expectation... we have come far along the road, and now we wait... we look ahead, and fix our eyes upon the journey's end.'

Personal Reflections: *"I surround myself in the silence of nature endeavouring to empty my mind of its constant stream of thought. To write these reflections I must engage my mind. I now close this notebook and will wait... and see?"*

0.0 km **Albergue** Leaving the central roundabout (Xunta albergue) head up into rua Isidoro Quemalinos past rua do Adro (right/ Church of Santiago). Pass under rail viaduct and over N-550 [!] [**0.7** km] by Capela de Santa Mariña *XVIII*. We now follow a narrow asphalt road into r/ Zacande [**1.0** km] ●*Alb.* **A Dársena do Francés** *Priv.[31÷5]* €20 incl. *+1* €45-60 ✆ Tito 663 911 233 trad. stone house with large garden. Continue into **rua de Torre *Option*** [**0.4** km] ▲

Detour Cesantes ●●●● seaside resort ***+1.5** km via camiño do Picho left sign Hotel Antolín (full description p.251):* •*H* **Antolín** €35+ ✆ 986 459 409 Paseo da Praia also 🍴 •*P.* **O Regato** €20+ ✆ 653 794 740. •*CR* **A Vella** €25+ camiño da Vella, 4 ✆ 658 535 935 Jesús, also runs taxi. ***Continue to Arcade +4.3** km by coast via* ***Soutoxusto*** •*H* **Santo Apóstolo** *x16* €28-47 ✆ 986 495 136 *on* N-550 & ●*Alb.* **O Recuncho do Peregrino** *Priv. [12÷1]+* €10 ✆ 617 292 598 Miguel. Continue down side of albergue over rail and up through woodland into Arcade.

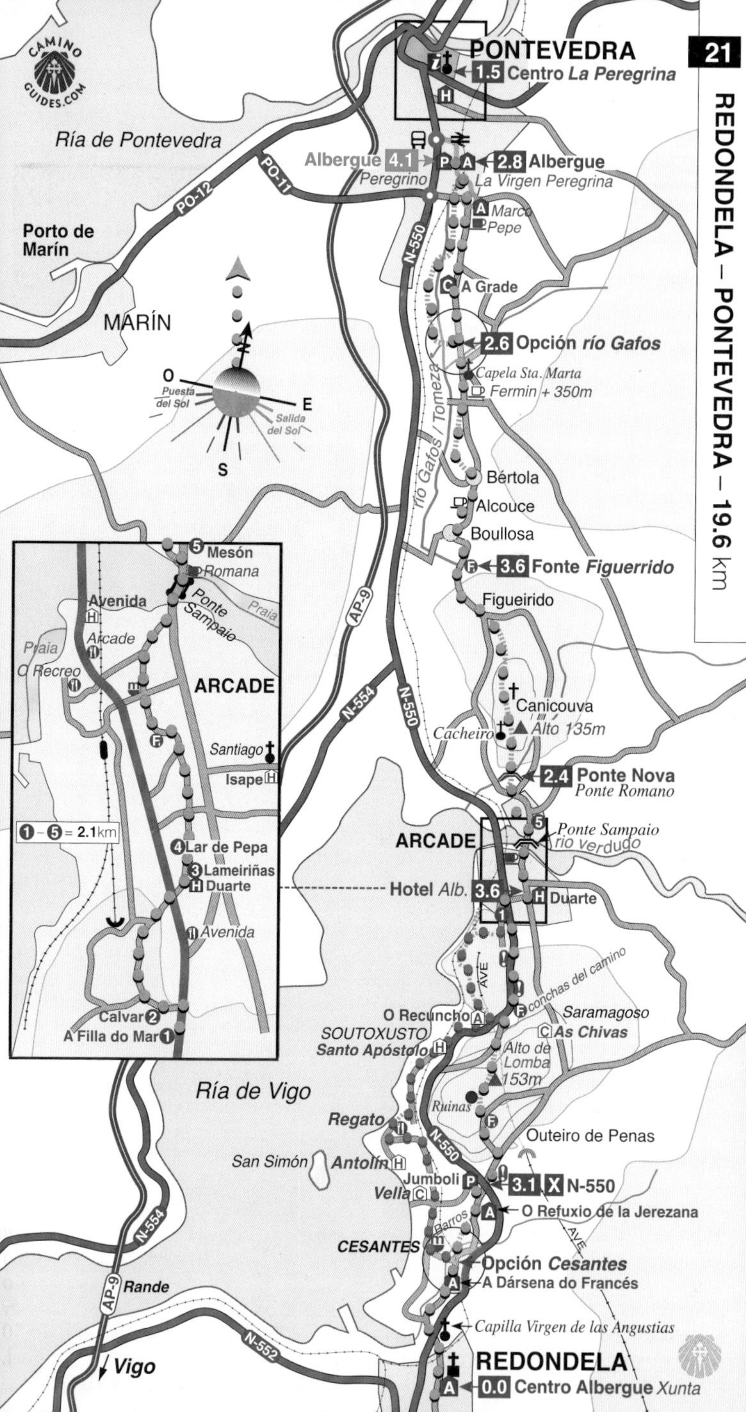
CAMINO GUIDES.COM
PONTEVEDRA
1.5 Centro La Peregrina
Ría de Pontevedra
PO-12
PO-11
Albergue 4.1 Peregrino
2.8 Albergue La Virgen Peregrina
Marco Pepe
Porto de Marín
MARÍN
N-550
A Grade
2.6 Opción río Gafos
Capela Sta. Marta
Fermin + 350m
O
Puesta del Sol
E
Salida del Sol
S
río Gafos / Tomeza
Bértola
Alcouce
Boullosa
3.6 Fonte Figuerrido
Figueirido
AP-9
N-554
Canicouva
Cacheiro
Alto 135m
2.4 Ponte Nova
Ponte Romano
5 Mesón
Romana
Avenida
Ponte Sampaio
Praia
Arcade
Praia O Recreo
ARCADE
Santiago
Isape
1 – 5 = 2.1km
4 Lar de Pepa
3 Lameiriñas
Duarte
Avenida
Calvar 2
A Filla do Mar 1
Ponte Sampaio
río Verdugo
Hotel Alb. 3.6
Duarte
AVE
conchas del camino
Saramagoso
O Recuncho
As Chivas
SOUTOXUSTO
Santo Apóstolo
Alto de Lomba 153m
Ría de Vigo
Ruinas
Regato
Outeiro de Penas
San Simón
Antolín
Jumboli
3.1 N-550
Vella
O Refuxio de la Jerezana
Barros
CESANTES
Opción Cesantes
A Dársena do Francés
Rande
N-552
Capilla Virgen de las Angustias
REDONDELA
Vigo
0.0 Centro Albergue Xunta

▲ At option continue s/o and turn <left onto path just over rail line. We now make our way up to the **N-550 [1.0** km] at Cesantes:

3.1 km **N-551 *Cesantes*** •*Hs &* ☕ **Jumbolí** €33 ✆ 986 495 066 Note some beds in separate location. *[200m down right on N-550 welcoming* ●*Alb.* **O Refuxio Jerezana** *Priv. [24÷3] €12-15 +2 €40* ✆ 601 165 977 *www.orefuxio.org*

Cross N-550 [**!**] and turn up steeply <left [**0.4** km] past [⛲] O Viso. Turn <left onto forest track through eucalyptus woods *Outeiro de Penas* past ruins of ancient wayside Inn *Hostal da Malaposta* to reach the high point of this stage *Alto de Lomba* (155m). ***[Saramagoso** Detour 1.3 km off route* •*CR* **As Chivas** *x7* €45 ✆ 986 496 853 *www.aschivas.com]*. The otherwise peaceful surroundings disturbed by occasional air traffic on the flight path to Vigo. Views over the distant ría de Vigo and its iconic bridge now open up as we descend back to the **N-550 [2.0** km] [⛲] *Conchas del camino! [Alb.O Recuncho 300m left]*. Continue up dangerous 700m stretch of the N-550 [**!**] to *Alb.* ❶ **A Filla do Mar** *Priv. [28÷5]* €35 ✆ 986 841 522 + *terraces, pool & menú.* *www.albergueafilladomar.com* Turn <left off the main road by Park to *Alb.*❷ **Casa Calvar** *Priv. [26÷2]* €15 ✆ 986 401 754 *www.casacalvar.com* Campo da Feira, 1. Continue on short circuitous route past *Fonte do Lavandeira* and cross main road into Arcade with hotel & albergues [**1.2** km].

3.6 km **Arcade** •*H*** **Duarte** *x20* €25 ✆ 986 670 057 *www.hotelduarte.com* c/ Lameriñas 8 adj. *Alb.*❸ **Lameiriñas** *Priv. [28÷1]* €10-12 ✆ 616 107 820. Pass ☕ *O Camino* opp. ❹ **O Lar de Pepa** *Priv. [12÷5]* €10 ✆ 986 678 006 c/Ribeiro 1. Continue down narrow r/ Barronoas through Cimadevila [⛲]to crossroads ***r/ Rosalia de Castro*** [**0.8** km] and ❖ ☕ *Acuña* + 🛒 at this point the waymarked route proceeds s/o. *[Turn left for ⊕farmacia & main road with ☕s/🍴s /hotels and beach!].* ▮**Other Lodging** *(see map)*: •*H*** **Isape** *x18* €30-45 ✆ 986 700 721 r/ Soutomaior,36 (+**0.8** km) opp. *Iglesia de Santiago.* •*H**** **Avenida** *x30* €24-36 ✆ 986 670 100 N-550 (+**0.4** km). To access main beach (+600m *off* route) proceed over main road at traffic lights past taxi rank and over rail line to roundabout with statue *Mariscadora* past the popular ☕🍴 *O Recreo* (*mariscos*) to the sandy beach *Praia do Peirao* with beach showers. Along the main street in Arcade are several seafood restaurants including the Michelin star 🍴*Arcadia* and 🍴 *Marisqueria Avenida* both located on the main road. Oyster festival first weekend in April.

❖ Keep s/o past library *biblioteca* via *A Calle* and over **Pontesampaio.** Historic stone bridge over río Verdugo built in 1795 over earlier foundations *[it was here that local militia inflicted a significant rout on Napoleon's troops during the War of Independence, witnessed by a memorial at the far side].* ☕ *A Romana* lovely position on the bridge (last café before Pontevedra!)

with a fine sandy beach (beach showers just up river 100m). *[**Detour:** ●●●● to view the Romanesque Igrexa Santa María XIII continue up main road for 300m adj.* ❺*Alb.* **O Mesón** *Priv. [26÷1]* €12 *+2* €65 ✆ 687 462 398 (Tomás) all mod cons.

The waymarked route branches off steeply up <left just past the bridge memorial to take a detour away from the main road passing the *cruceiro de Ballota* and winding its way up and down again before crossing over the main road to:

2.4 km **Ponte Nova** ***rio Ulló*** modern metal bridge that replaces the medieval stone bridge built over earlier Roman remains all part of the calzada Romana XIX. Peaceful picnic spot by the river. Continue up the ancient stone paved pilgrim way *Brea Vella da Canicouva* up to the crossroads and wayside cross *cruxeiro Cacheiro.* This section alternates between paths and quiet country lanes and just past the hamlet of Boullosa we begin to descend towards Bértola and Pontevedra to handsome roadside fountain at:

3.6 km **Fonte Figueirido** ***Salgueriño*** Source of delightful río Gafos (Tomeza) which we follow on the alt. scenic path into Pontevedra. Continue through Alcouce *kiosco Oasis* alternating between quiet country lanes and green pathways *[Café Fermin +350m right]* until we enter the Pontevedra municipality *Concello de Vilaboa* at the tiny *Capela da Sta. Marta XVII* at the main road where we turn left over rio Pobo towards Pontevedra and option for riverside walk [**!**]

2.6 km **Río Gafos *(Tomeza) Option*** ▲ The main route is by the soulless EP-0002 into Pontevedra. However, there is a wonderful alternative *C. Complementario* (+ 1.3 km) along tree lined river all the way to the outskirts of the city. This scenic route replaces the noise and hazard of traffic with woodland and bird song.

Alternative River Route 4.1** km -v- **2.8** km:* ●●●● ***Senda Fluvial río dos Gafos** Tomeza.* ✓ *– the extra 1.3 km through woodland alongside the river will refresh body and soul – go with the flow! Note a similar opportunity is offered exiting Pontevedra.* Turn <left off EP-0002 at sign for Ponte Rebón & right> over **bridge** [**0.3** km] along the river which we now follow all the way into Pontevedra. Continue over road at ***Ponte da Condesa [**1.5** km] *[rail bridge left and Casa A Grade (see below) right]*. Pass mill-race *Mar da Presa / Poza da Moura* and cross over the romantic Valentine's bridge ***Ponte Valentín*** [**1.1** km] and under the city bypass via **tunnel** [**0.7** km] (see photo>) to rejoin the waymarked route on the main road [**0.3** km] where we turn <left up to the main albergue in Pontevedra [**0.2** km].

▲ For road route keep s/o along EP-0002 past •*CR* **Casa A Grade** €35 ✆ 696 306 129 Airbnb with extensive gardens onto río Tomeza. Past ☕ *Casa Pepe* and •*Alb*

Marco *[8÷1]* €20 © 658 507 972. s/o over Av. de Marco roundabout at pedestrian crossing. The traffic now intensifies as we enter the suburbs of Pontevedra bearing up <left to •*Hs* **Peregrino** *x15* €35-45 © 986 858 409 *www.hostalperegrino.es* opp. Xunta albergue ramp.

2.8 km **Pontevedra Sur *(South)*** *Alb.*❶ **La Virgen Peregrina** *Asoc.[56÷2]* €8 © 986 844 045 c/Ramón Otero Pedrayo (adj. Estación de tren) opens 13:00. Modern Xunta hostel (photo>) sandwiched between road & rail but good facilities and warm welcome. Keep s/o and cross roundabout (rail station right/ bus station left) into minor road **Rua Gorgullón @ Nº72** *Alb.*❷ **GBC** *[40÷3]* €17 *+6* €21+ ©676 188 664 *www.gbchostel.com* / @ **Nº68** *Alb.*❸ **Aloxa** *Priv.[56÷2]* €12-15 © 986 896 453 *[rear •H*** **Alda Estacion** © 886 300 029 *Av.Pombal 76]*. / **@Nº16** *Alb.*❹ **Dpaso** *Priv.[20÷1]* €19 incl. © 653 548 059 *www.dpasohostel.es* ***opp.*** •*H*** **Avenida** 986 857 784 Av.Pombal 46. adj.**@Nº10** *Alb.* ❺ **Nacama** *[42÷1]* €15 © 644 929 243 *www.nacamahostel.es*

Note: These hostels are located 1½ kilometres *south* of the medieval city centre. Depending on your arrival time you can visit the city centre after a rest and shower in this area or spend time in the centre on the way through in the morning. Another option is to continue to the city centre and find a more central hotel or pension. Allow a leisurely 30-minute walk to the Praza da Peregrina at the start of the old town; alternatively, there are buses or taxis from the rail station or the main bus station opposite. Whatever you do, don't miss savouring this wonderful city with its many fascinating monuments and historic buildings, many of them directly associated with the pilgrimage and most of them directly en route. Cross Rúa Eduardo Pondal into *rua Virxen do Camiño* past •*H* **Virgen del Camino** © 986 855 900 @Nº55. Continue to *Glorieta de Compostela* with fountain and into rua de Peregrina to the 'heart' of the town centre:

1.5 km **Pontevedra Centro *Praza Peregrina*** ❶ ***Turismo de Pontevedra*** Casa da Luz, Praza da Verdura 986 090 890. ***Accommodation includes:*** ▌**Albergues:** ❻ **Slow City** *[6÷1]* €17 *+2* €40 © 631 062 896 (Jorge) r/ Amargura 5. *Alb.*❼ **Acolá** *[16÷1]* €17-20 © 678 680 758 r/Arzobispo Malvar 15. ▌**Hostels:*(€25-35)*** •**Charino** *[24÷6]* © 615 641 432 r/Charino 19. •**Casa O Fidel** © 986 851 234 pulpería Fidel, r/San Nicolás 7. •**Casa Alicia** *x4* © 986 857 079 Av. Santa Mariá 5, adj. Praza España & •*P** **Casa Maruja** © 986 854 901 *www.pensioncasamaruja.com* •**Casa Sara** *x3* €20-40 Mercedes © 686 970 265 r/Alta 17. •**Bulezen Urban** *[54÷4]* © 886 060 247r/García Camba 12. ***(€35-55)*** •*H*** **Room** *(Vedra)* © 986 869 550 c/ Filgueira Valverde, 10. •*H**** **Rias Bajas** © 986 855 100 c/ Daniel de la Sota Valdecilla, 7. •*H*** **Ruas** *x22* €39-61 © 986 846 416 *www.hotelruas.net* c/ Sarmiento,20. •*H*** **Boa Vila** *x10* €40-55 © 986 105 265 *www.hotelboavila.es* r/ Real, 4. ***(€100+)***•**Parador Casa del Barón** © 986 855 800 c/Barón, 19

Pontevedra: Regional capital and university town with an expanding population of 80,000. At the heart of its modern suburbs is a delightful medieval core *zona monumental/barrio antigo* with its intimate *prazas* (photo right). We enter via rua Peregrina & Porta do Camiño and follow the original *Rua Real* through the

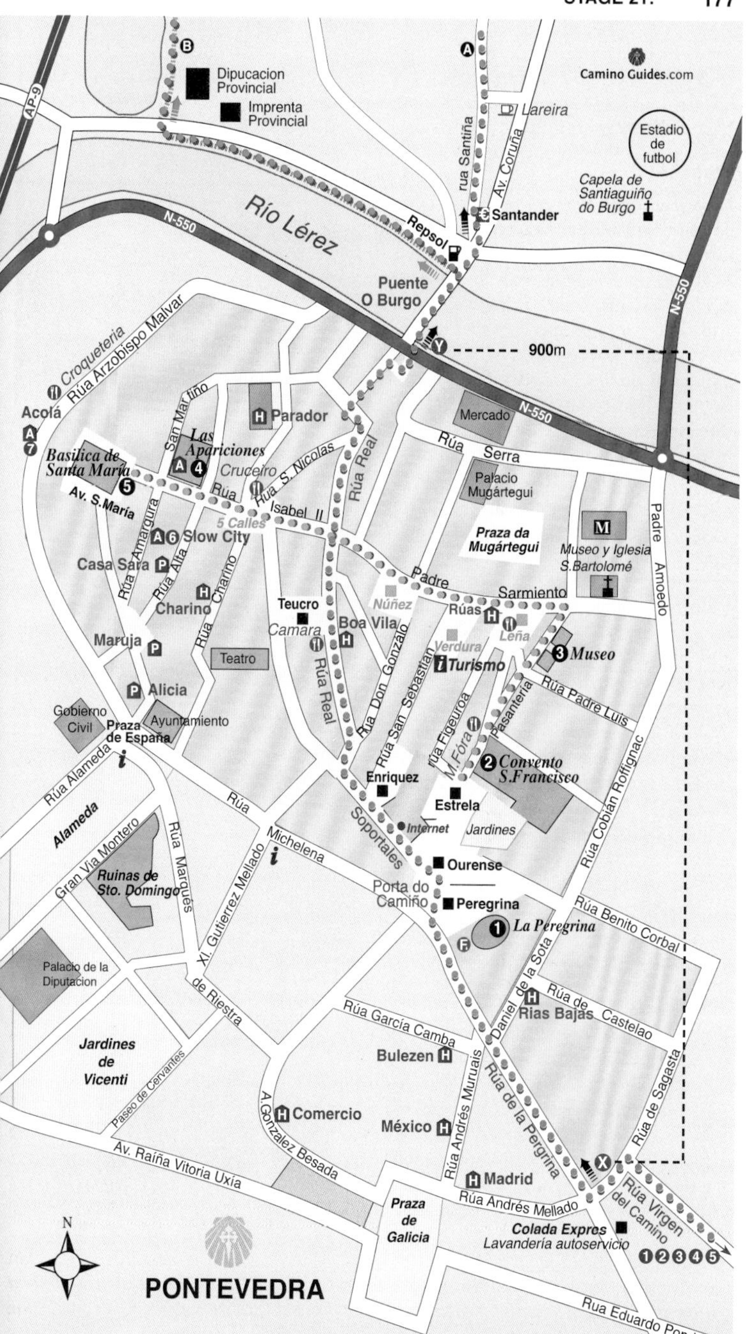

Camino Guides.com
Dipucacion Provincial
Imprenta Provincial
Lareira
rua Santiña
Av. Coruña
Estadio de futbol
Capela de Santiaguiño do Burgo
AP-9
N-550
Río Lérez
Repsol
Santander
Puente O Burgo
900m
Croqueteria
Rúa Arzobispo Malvar
Acolá
San Martiño
Las Apariciones
Parador
Mercado
Basilica de Santa María
Av. S.María
Cruceiro
Rúa S. Nicolas
Rúa Real
Rúa Serra
Palacio Mugártegui
Rúa Isabel II
5 Calles
Slow City
Praza da Mugártegui
Museo y Iglesia S.Bartolomé
Padre Amoedo
Rúa Amargura
Rúa Alta
Casa Sara
Charino
Rúa Charino
Padre Sarmiento
Teucro
Camara
Boa Vila
Núñez
Rúas
Leña
Verdura
Turismo
Museo
Maruja
Teatro
Rúa Don Gonzalo
Rúa San Sebastian
Alicia
Rúa Padre Luis
Pasantería
Gobierno Civil
Praza de España
Ayuntamiento
rúa Figueroa
M. Fóra
Convento S.Francisco
Rúa Cobián Roffignac
Rúa Alameda
Enriquez
Estrela
Rúa Michelena
Soportales
Internet
Jardines
Alameda
Gran Via Montero
Rúa Marqués
XI. Gutierrez Mellado
Ourense
Ruinas de Sto. Domingo
Porta do Camiño
Peregrina
La Peregrina
Rúa Benito Corbal
Palacio de la Diputacion
de Riestra
Daniel de la Sota
Rias Bajas
Rúa de Castelao
Rúa García Camba
Jardines de Vicenti
Bulezen
Rúa Andrés Muruais
Rúa de la Pergrina
Rúa de Sagasta
Paseo de Cervantes
A.Gonzalez Besada
Comercio
México
Madrid
Av. Raíña Vitoria Uxía
Rúa Andrés Mellado
Rúa Virgen del Camino
Praza de Galicia
Colada Expres
Lavandería autoservicio
PONTEVEDRA
Rua Eduardo Pondal

Santuario de la Virgen Peregrina

centre of the ancient quarter beginning at ● ***Praza de la Peregrina*** site of the beautiful 18th century pilgrim chapel conceived by the architect Arturo Souto and built in the Baroque style to a floor plan in the shape of a scallop shell! ❶ **Santuario da Peregrina**. One of the great treasures of the camino (see photo next page). The route leads directly into ● ***Praza de Ourense*** with its delightful gardens *Xardíns de Castro San Pedro* and cheerful cafés and bars forming part of the nightly *paseo* with the imposing edifice of the 14th century ❷ **Convento de San Francisco** in the background. The lower section of this extensive open area is known as ***Praza Ferraría*** (from the iron grills used in the square) and provides an optional detour:

Praza da Leña

Detour ● ● ● ● (see city plan) Make time to soak in the atmosphere of this quintessential Galician city and explore its emblematic squares and museums as follows: Continue from the *Santuario da la Peregrina* via Praza Estrela down rua Pasantería into the city's most emblematic squares ● *Praza de Leña (former firewood market)* with its squat granite arcades and central *cruceiro* so typical of Galicia and museum ❸ **Museo de Pontevedra** in adj. historic buildings connected by stone bridge *Casa García Flórez* houses exhibits of the famous jet-black jewellery from Santiago and an interesting collection of images of St. James dating from as early as 12th century. There is also an entire floor dedicated to the famous Galician writer and philosopher Alfonso Castelao who, along with Rosalía de Castro, did so much to preserve the unique Galician culture that we can enjoy today. Continue via rua Padre Sarmiento into ● *Praza da Verdura* ❶ ***Turismo*** with its lively cafés that link into ● *Praza Méndez Núñez* also accessible off the waymarked camino via the colourful rua de Don Gonzálo or continue along rua Padre Sarmiento to rejoin the rua Real.

Rua Don Gonzalo – Rua Sarmiento

To visit the Cathedral continue up into rua de Isabel II to ● *Praza das Cinco Ruas* the meeting point of five of the timeworn cobbled laneways. A magical spot with an intriguing *cruceiro* depicting the temptation of man with a snake coiled around the shaft watching a naked Eve offering the apple to Adam. Continuing up rua de Isabel II to pass ❹ **Santuario da Aparicións** where the Blessed Virgin also appeared to sister Lucía and at the top of the street we arrive at ❺ **Basílica de Santa María A Grande** the celebrated 16th century Basilica. Either side of the main entrance are statues of the founding fathers of the church, St. Peter and St. Paul, while the rose window portrays the Assumption and Coronation of the Virgin Mary. But the real celebration is the southern façade and the mystery and mastery of Flemish sculptor *Cornielles de Holanda* and the Portuguese artist *João Nobre* together with the stonemasons who created this 'storybook in stone' displaying the unfolding drama of the church ending with the Passion of Christ and the promise of redemption – reminiscent of the craftsmanship that created the Pórtico da Gloria in Santiago cathedral. If you have followed this itinerary you are probably in need of refreshment. Help is at hand as the cobbled lanes of the old quarter are bursting with *tapas* bars and cafés. If you head back towards Praza España from the cathedral along Av. Santa María you come to a triangular 'square' site of a medieval Jewish cemetery *Lampán dos Xudeus* around which are several restaurants and hostals leading to ● *Praza España* the main square that divides the modern city from its ancient heart. Here we find the main government buildings, town hall and Alameda with its array of statues to modern and ancient heroes of Spain and the ruins of the 13th century Igrexa de Santo Domingo. Head back towards the old centre down any of the myriad narrow paved streets or back to the Praza das Cinco Ruas with its tempting *Taperías* watched over, in case you had forgotten, by the cross of temptation and a direct route to the heavenly Parador down rua do Barón... or pick up the waymarks at ***Praza de la Peregrina*** and proceed down the waymarked Rua Real via *rua dos Soportais* with its ancient arcaded cafés into bustling ● ***Praza Curros Enríquez*** passing ● ***Praza do Teucro*** to the junction of Rua Real and Padre Sarmiento. The two main (busy) festivals in town are: *Festas da Peregrin*a 2nd week in August and period inspired *Feira Franca* 2nd week in September.

Basílica de Santa María A Grande

Personal Reflections:

La Virgen de Peregrina

22 PONTEVEDRA – CALDAS de REIS

▒	7.6	34%
▒	13.7	62%
▬	0.9	4%
Total km	**22.2** km *(13.8 ml)*	

Ascent **160**m ±¼ *hr*

▲ **Alto** *m* San Amaro **135** m *(443 ft)*

<A H> *Portela* ***10.3 km +0.5*** *Briallos* ***17.0 km +0.2*** Tivo **20.0** km.

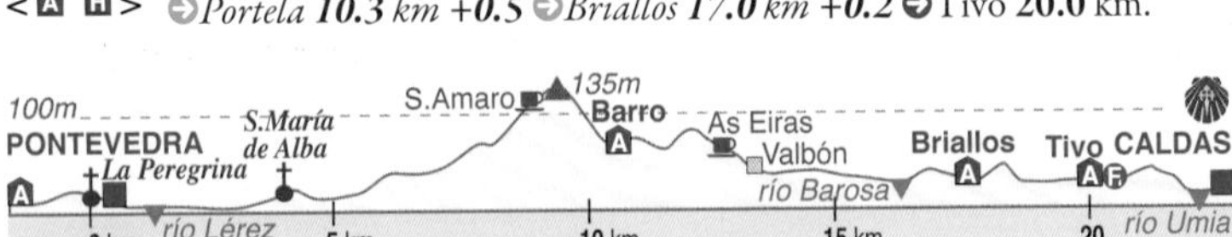

If you want to become full, let yourself be empty.
If you want to be reborn, let yourself die. ***Lao Tzu***

Practical Path: 1/3 of this stage is on natural pathways through woodland offering shade along gentle river valleys which we share with the rail line. Facilities are good with cafés, drinking fonts and several interim hostels. Recent improvements to the route now bypass the busy N-550 and Caldas de Reis has greatly expanded its pilgrim facilities and bedroom capacity during the past year and now offers a wide selection of albergues, hostels and hotels.

0.0 km **Pontevedra Centro** ***Praza Peregrina*** The camino is waymarked down rua Real *rua dos Soportais* into *rua da Ponte* emerging from the old quarter at the riverfront **río Lérez** [**0.6** km]. *[Here we can see the excavations of the foundations of the original Roman bridge and a replica miliário]*. Cross over the city ring road [!] and Ponte do Burgo *río Lerez* ***Option:*** **A** Main route keep s/o into Av. Coruña and turn <left and imm. right> into rua Da Santiña winding our way out through the city suburbs past bird observatory and wetlands ***Marismas de Alba*** [**1.8** km] by [ ] *Communidades Montes* where 'green' route joins from the left.

Option: **B** ● ● ● ● instigated during repairs to Ponte O Burgo and offering a delightful alternative along woodland trails. No longer 'officially' waymarked but it follows the river. ***Directions:*** Turn left over the bridge along the Rio Lerez and cross the road by the Diputación Provincial depot 300m onto sandy track alongside the lagoon and follow the rio Granada over road 900m and onto boardwalks to rejoin the main route 700m at [ ] *Montes* 300m. ***2.1 km -v- 1.8 km.***

Continue on Rua Gándara *[part of original Via Romana XIX]* to bridge [**0.9** km].

3.2 km **Puente** ***option*** *[Here the* ***Variante Espiritual*** *along the ria Arousa turns left over the río Gándara –see p.252 for route details]*. Main route turns right under rail up through the hamlet of **Pontecabras** to ***Iglesia Santa de María de Alba*** [ ] and pilgrim monument. Continue up past wayside cross and turn <left onto the busy main **road** [!] *narrow verge [!]* through **Cayetano** ***Capela San Caetano (right)*** veer right> off main road by **factory** [**1.6** km] *(off route on main road 300m* *Bubela & Cañota)*. Continue up past *Vending machine San Cayetano* and pick up path alongside rail line through dense woodland. In the low-lying sections the

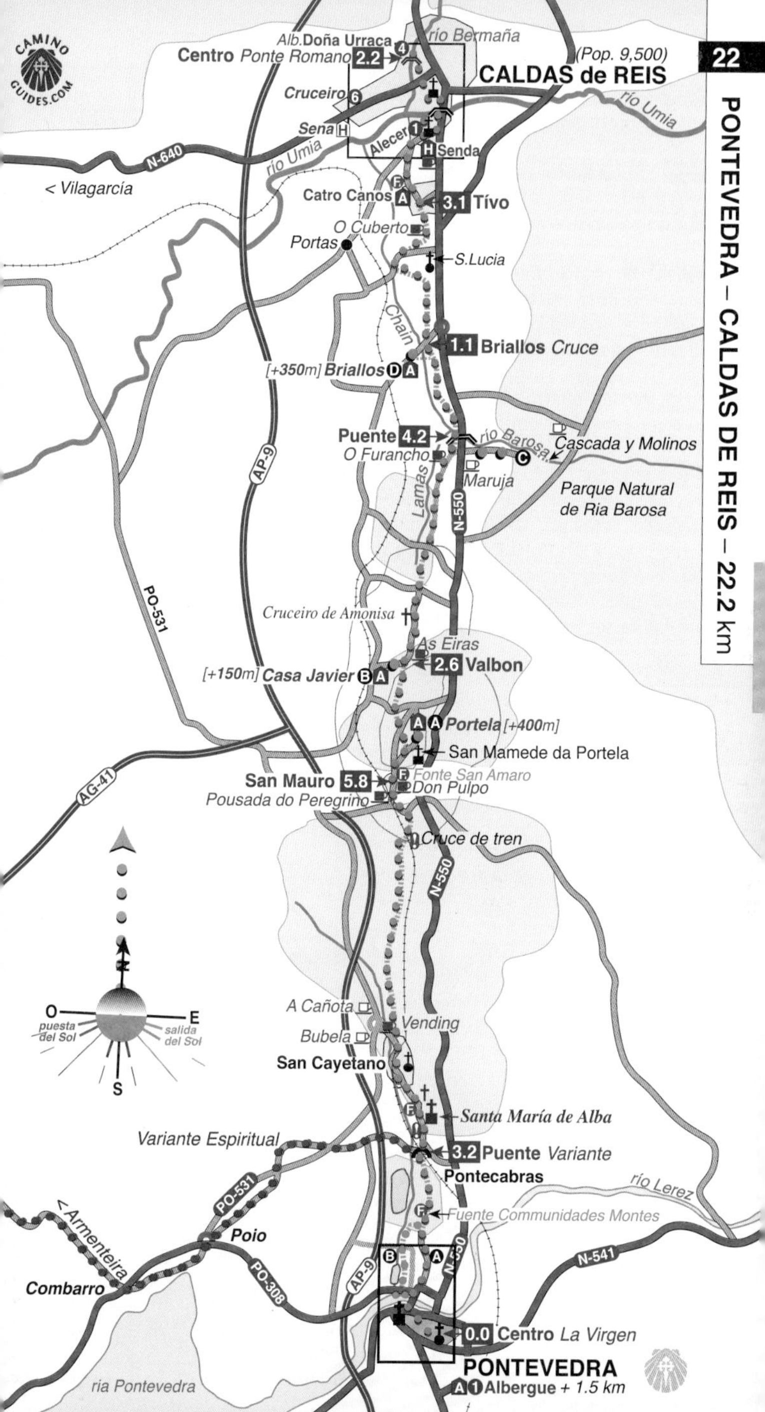

22
PONTEVEDRA – CALDAS DE REIS – 22.2 km
CALDAS de REIS
(Pop. 9,500)
Alb. Doña Urraca
Centro Ponte Romano 2.2
río Bermaña
Cruceiro
Sena
Alecer
Senda
río Umia
N-640
< Vilagarcía
Catro Canos
3.1 Tívo
O Cuberto
Portas
S.Lucia
Chain
1.1 Briallos Cruce
[+350m] Briallos
Puente 4.2
O Furancho
río Barosa
Cascada y Molinos
Maruja
Parque Natural de Ria Barosa
Lamas
N-550
AP-9
PO-531
Cruceiro de Amonisa
As Eiras
2.6 Valbon
[+150m] Casa Javier
Portela [+400m]
San Mamede da Portela
San Mauro 5.8
Fonte San Amaro
Don Pulpo
Pousada do Peregrino
AG-41
Cruce de tren
O
puesta del Sol
E
salida del Sol
S
A Cañota
Vending
Bubela
San Cayetano
Santa María de Alba
Variante Espiritual
3.2 Puente Variante
Pontecabras
río Lerez
Fuente Communidades Montes
< Armenteira
Poio
Combarro
PO-308
N-541
0.0 Centro La Virgen
PONTEVEDRA
Albergue + 1.5 km
ria Pontevedra
CAMINO GUIDES.COM

path can be wet, the tranquil setting disturbed only by the proximity of the rail and AP-9 / E-1 motorway. Cross over **rail** [**!**] in San Amaro up to **Portela** [**4.2** km]:

5.8 km **San Amaro** ***Portela*** popular break-fast *Peregrino* after this long stretch; if busy step around the corner to *Meson Pulpo*. Just beyond this tiny hamlet we pass rest area [ ] and *cruceiro* to **option** [**0.9** km] Detour to Portela ▲

Detour Ⓐ ● ● ***Alb. Portela,*** *A Cancela, Concello de Barro* ***+400****m* keep right> on road and imm. <left past Iglesia San Mamede Portela to ●*Alb.* **Portela** *Par. [16÷2]* €8 © 655 952 805 with welcome from Jorge who can arrange dinner. Small renovated school building in quiet location with no shops or other facilities.

▲ From detour junction turn left down track to rejoin secondary road and keep s/o to track through woodland over *rego do Areal* and up to option **road** [**1.7** km].

2.6 km **Valbon** ***[Detour*** Ⓑ ● ● ***Alb. Pilgrim House +150****m turn left for* ●*Alb.***Casa Javier** *[6÷1]+ €-donativo + private rooms © 617 058 348 dinner & swimpool].* Turn right at option point past *Vending* & *Meson As Eiras* with garden terrace **Valbón** [**0.2** km]. Keep s/o past the ancient ***Cruceiro de Amonisa*** *[St. James looking pensively north to Compostela].* Veer <left by granite blocks onto a series of quiet country lanes and earth tracks past *O Furancho Vinos y tapas* just before emerging onto the **N-550** [**4.0** km] *Cascadas* opp. and option.

4.2 km **Puente** *N-550* ***[Detour*** Ⓒ ● ● ***Parque Natureza / Muíños Río Barosa +500****m Cross main road to visit the impressive cascades, swim area, mill buildings and riverside cafés Muiñada de Barosa all joined by woodland pathways].* To continue on the camino turn <left along alongside N-550 over río Barosa turning <left onto one of several short sections of pathways through vineyards that run parallel to the road. Continue to crossroad in **Barros** [**1.3** km].

1.1 km **Briallos** *cruce* ***Detour*** Ⓓ ● ● ***Alb. Briallos +350****m turn left for detour direct to* ●*Alb.* **Briallos** *Xunta.[27÷2] €8 © 986 536 194 (Pilar) Lugar San Roque +Cantina].* Keep s/o at Barros crossroads onto short woodland path *[Capela Santa Lucia now off route right +100m]* past *Cuberto* (left) in Areal *Vending* (right) into the hamlet of Tivó.

3.1 km **Tívo** ●*Alb./* **Vintecatro** *Priv.[18÷4]* €15 *José* © 696 582 014 garden adj. [ ] & wayside cross. Continue on concrete path to rejoin **N-550** [**1.3** km] •*P* **A Senda** *[4÷1]* €11 *x6* €30 © 986 091 485 new-build on main road opp. •*CR* **Casa Herreria** €70 © 658 780 098 Fernando. Continue into Caldas veering left past ***Iglesia de Santa Maria*** *XVIIc.* to *Alb.*❶ **Alecer** *Priv.[12÷5]* €12 © 630 105 582 Av. Doña Urraca. ❷ **A Queimada** *Priv. [72÷4]* €12 © 986 189 194 *www.alberguaqueimada.com* modern building on N-550 adj. ❸ **Timonel** *Priv.[18÷1]+* €8-10 © 986 540 840 with lodging in

separate building to the rear (see photo on previous page). We now pass over the **bridge in CALDAS DE REIS [0.2** km] *Alb.*opp. *balneario* •*H*** **Acuña** *x62* €43-60 ✆ 986 540 010 opp. *Policía Local.* Cross the busy road bridge [!] over río Umia into Caldas de Reis with renowned riverside local taverna 🍴 *Taberna O Muiño* (right). The waymarked camino turns <left at Banco Pastor into rua Laureano Salgado *Apt.* •**Caldas de Reis** €50 ✆ 698 163 832 apts. with balcony on river adj. *balneario* •*H*** **Dávila** *x26* €45-65 ✆ 986 540 012 by thermal fountain ***fuente de las Burgas*** *XIXc.* where the famous hot waters issue forth and health and safety regulations now prohibit bathing tired feet! (see photo). Overlooking the central park with ☕ is the parish church of St. Thomas ***Iglesia parroquial de Santo Tomás*** *which effectively* marks the **CENTRE OF TOWN [0.4** km] *decide here where to stay for the night*!

The waymarked camino continues along pedestrian street ***Rua Real*** *(original Via XIX)* with its ancient granite colonnades passing **@Nº19** •*Apt.* **Real Atico** *x1* €50+ &**@Nº23** (by Bonsai) •*Apt.***Garden** *x1* €75+ ✆ 722 487 820 on the corner of r/Fornos 13, is •*H*** **Via XIX** *x6* €75+ ✆ 986 541 425 opp. **@Nº49** •*Apt.* **Real** €48+ ✆ 630 982 488 and •*H*** **Roquiño** €70+ ✆ 886 251 020 c/ Fornos,8. ***[Cross [!] busy N-640 c/Juan Fuentes]*** where at **@Nº58 Rua Real** •*H**** **Pousada Real** *x11* €55+ ✆ 986 189 910 www.hotelpousadareal.com Opp. **@Nº63** *Alb.*❹ **Albor** *Priv.[35÷5]* €15-18 ✆ 600 351 157 www.alberguealbor.com keep s/o to the iconic medieval stone bridge [🚰] over río Bermaña with several pleasant ☕ *cafés* overlooking the river which get the last of the evening sun and original pilgrim hostel [**0.3** km].

2.2 km **Caldas de Reis** ***Puente Romano*** close to all amenities incl. ❺ **Caldas de Reis** *Priv.[26÷4]* €814 ✆ 683 605 335 *(Previously Doña Urraca now under private maanagment)* c/ Campo de la Torre 1 adj. •*Hs.* **Torre** €25 ✆ 6656 648 309.

CALDAS DE REIS (Reyes) population 9,500 is neatly contained between the ríos Umia and Bermaña. The history of Caldas is inextricably linked to its thermal waters that have gushed from its ground source at a constant 40 degrees for millennia. Inhabited by early Celtic tribes it became a major spa *Aquae Celenae* on the Via Romana XIX. Under Christian authority it became the bishopric of Celenis, transforming itself into Rex Calda during the *Reconquista*. King Alfonso VII, son of Queen Doña Urraca was born here – it was later to become the birthplace of hydro electricity in Galicia during the industrial era. Today Caldas de Reis continues to benefit from its waters as a major health spa. It also has delightful botanical gardens *xardín botánicas* planted along the banks of the river Umia.

The parish church commands a central position in town ***Igrexa parroquial Sto. Tomás*** dedicated to Saint Thomas à Becket Archbishop of Canterbury (1118-

1170) who made the pilgrimage to Santiago 3 years before his assassination. The church consecrated in his name was built in 1890 using stones from the medieval tower of Queen Doña Urraca (birthplace of King Alfhonse VII) which stood near the roman bridge *Campo de Torre*. The Patron Saint of Caldas de Reis is ***San Roque*** *Roch Rocco [Born a nobleman's son he gave his inheritance to the poor to wander Europe as a mendicant pilgrim so he became patron saint of pilgrims, dogs, and plagues. His feast day is August 16th. San Roque is associated with miracle cures wrought during the plague that ravaged medieval Europe. He himself contracted the plague but was saved by the intervention of a dog who licked his wounds and brought him bread every day. Indeed he is invoked against all contagious diseases so appropriate for our Covid-19 pandemic and also cures knee problems to boot which may be particularly helpful for his pilgrim brethren!*

❶ ***Turismo:*** limited tourist information. Biblioteca Municipal Av. Roman Lopez ✆ 986 530 604 (adj. Centro Saude).

▮ **Other Lodging:** ***Along N-550 / Av. Pedro Mateo Sagasta:*** •*P.* **Río Umia.** €15-30. •*P.* **La Moderna** €20-30 ✆ José 986 540 312 above corner *Droguería.* ❻ **Agarimo** *Priv.[17÷5]+* €18+€35 ✆ 677 333 703. •*H** **Lotus** *x30* €35-55 ✆ 670 466 063 reception in *Café Lotus* opp. (rear rooms overlook Ponte Romano). ***Along N-640 / c/Juan Fuentes (Echevarría)*** ❼ **Celenis** *Priv. [44÷1]* €16 ✆ 613 116 894 www.alberguecelenis.com r/Silgadas, 16. ❽ **O Cruceiro** *Priv.[34÷8]* €14 ✆ 986 540 165 www.ocruceiroalbergue.com also adj. •*H** **O Cruceiro** €30-52. ❾ **As Pozas Termais** *Priv. [26÷1]* €20 ✆ 986 070 731 r/Carlos García Bayón. *[+**300m** •H** **Sena** €35 ✆ *986 540 596].* •*P* **As Burgas** *x6* €25-35 ✆ 615 033 297 **@Nº21**. •*P* **Caldas** *x3* €18-48 ✆ Adolfo 607 020 402 **@Nº19** also owns •*H* **Villa Galicia** €20-45 Rua Gaioso, 16 with rear garden.

▌***Apartments***: €20–110 *depending on number of bedrooms / people sharing.* **Rua Porto Rio:** •*Puerto del Rio* 2 bed apt. @Nº15 ✆ 722 487 820 & •*Habitacion del Peregrino* 1 bed apt. **Along N-640** •*Sarnadela* 2 bed apt. @Nº45. •*Marvera* 3 bed apt €70-100 @Nº52 (opp. Hotel Sena).

Caldas de Reis: Cafes & restaurants sprawl out along the town pavements and riverbanks. Adj. Puente Romano (evening sun) *Number 2* and *Varadoiro* . On high street (N-550) *Roquiño* opp. pedestrian Rua Loureiros *Loureiros* and just beyond is the 'hidden' gem *Convido*. For an authentic *Galego Taberna* try your luck in the *Taberna O'Muiño* where you can eat with the locals (and flies!) on the river. The *camarero* is won't to wipe the sweat from his brow with the self-same cloth that wipes the plates but if you've made it this far you should survive and even enjoy the experience.

Personal Reflections:

23 CALDAS de REIS – PADRÓN

--- ---	8.4 --- ---	*44%*
--- ---	10.3 --- ---	*54%*
--- ---	0.4 --- ---	*2%*
Total km	**19.1** km	*(11.9 ml)*

Total ascent **260**m ±½ *hr*

▲ Alto *m* Cortiñas **165**m *(525 ft)*

<A H> Carracedo **1.0** km Valga **9.6** Pontecesures **16.0** km

*Herbón **16.0 km +3.1***

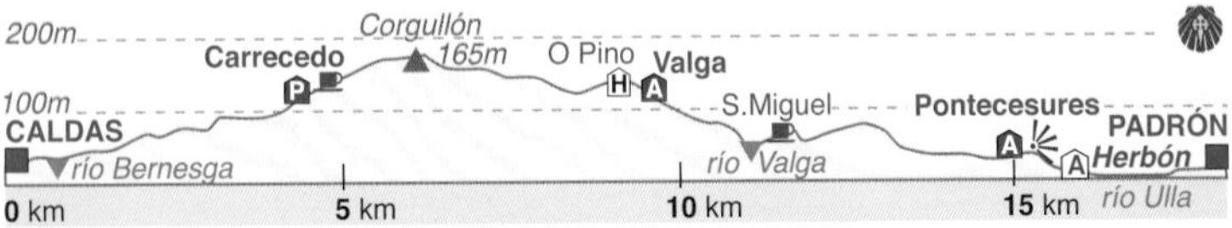

200m Corgullón 165m O Pino Valga Carrecedo 100m S.Miguel Pontecesures CALDAS PADRÓN río Bernesga río Valga Herbón 0 km 5 km 10 km 15 km río Ulla

Emptiness, which is conceptually liable to be mistaken for nothingness, is in fact the reservoir of infinite possibilities. ***Daisetz Teitaro Suzuki***

The Practical Path: Almost half this stage is on natural pathways through extensive woodland. Facilities are limited but there are a choice of hostals and cafes just *off* route – fill up with water as you pass the few drinking fonts. The route takes us along two river valleys, firstly *Bermaña* then a gentle climb up Cortiñas (the high point of this stage) before dropping down sharply into the *Valga* valley. From there we have another gentle climb up to a viewing point above the industrial suburbs of Pontecesures before descending to cross the río Ulla to join a tributary of the río Sar into Padrón. There are only two short stretches of main road, firstly leaving Caldas de Reis and entering Padrón over the bridge at Pontecesures. Otherwise the route is split between natural pathways and quiet country roads – *buen camino...*

0.0 km **Caldas de Reis** ***Puente Romano*** cross bridge s/o past *Capilla de San Roque* turn up <left on the main road and right> onto path. *[**+100m** •Hs* **Estrella Do Camiño** €32-50 ✆ 655 011 315*]*. Continue under viaduct along delightful Bermaña river valley through woodland to [!] N-550 in ***Carracedo.***

5.1 km **Carracedo** ***N-550*** *Esperón [**+200m** •P* **Sevi** €20-40 ✆ 986 534 260 and *Antonio]*. Keep s/o to ***Iglesia S. Mariña de Carrecedo*** with plaza and cruceiro (see photo>). Continue up through ***Gorgullón*** and back over **N-550** [!] at ***Casalderrique*** onto gravel track *Vending 'museo' Labrego (toilets) [O Castro on N-550* ***+100m****]. Continue on track* cross motorway **Puente AP-9** [**3.2** km] *[Pardal s/o* ***+50m****]* turn right> down path between N-550 and AP-9 into woodland up to ***Valga / O Pino:***

4.5 km **Valga** ***O Pino Option*** *Los Camioneros* and sign for ●*Alb.* **Valga** *Xunta*.*[78÷3]* €8 ✆ 638 943 271 (Mª Teresa) Lugar O Pino / N-550 (+200m) purpose built hostel (see photo top next page) located opp. *El Criollo* with *menú peregrino. [Hs Mosteiro 200 off route in Cernadas O Pino on N-550 remains closed].* This marks the high point of this stage at 160m and the camino now descends a steep path through dense woodland to the río Valga and bridge with viewing terrace over the river to join the country lane into the village of ***San Miguel de Valga*** [ ]*(right)* passing parish church.

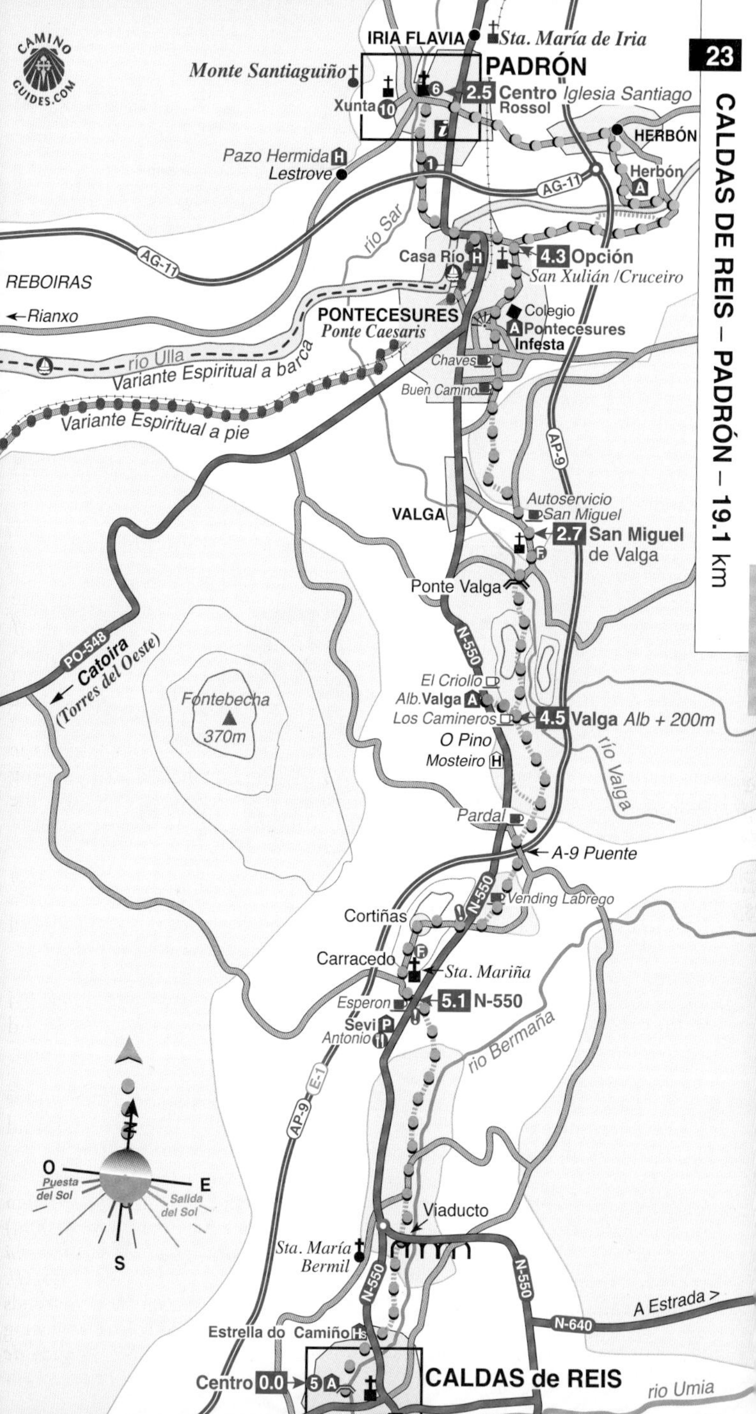

23
CALDAS DE REIS – PADRÓN – 19.1 km
CAMINO GUIDES.COM
IRIA FLAVIA
Sta. María de Iria
Monte Santiaguiño
PADRÓN
6
2.5 Centro
Iglesia Santiago
Rossol
Xunta
10
i
HERBÓN
Pazo Hermida H
Lestrove
1
Herbón
A
AG-11
río Sar
Casa Río H
4.3 Opción
San Xulián /Cruceiro
REBOIRAS
AG-11
←Rianxo
PONTECESURES
Ponte Caesaris
Colegio
A Pontecesures
Infesta
río Ulla
Variante Espiritual a barca
Chaves
Buen Camino
Variante Espiritual a pie
AP-9
Autoservicio
San Miguel
VALGA
2.7 San Miguel
de Valga
F
Ponte Valga
PO-548
Catoira
(Torres del Oeste)
N-550
Fontebecha
370m
El Criollo
Alb. Valga A
Los Camineros
4.5 Valga Alb + 200m
O Pino
Mosteiro H
río Valga
Pardal
A-9 Puente
N-550
Vending Labrego
Cortiñas
Carracedo
F
Sta. Mariña
Esperon
5.1 N-550
Sevi P
Antonio
río Bermaña
AP-9
E-1
O
Puesta del Sol
E
Salida del Sol
N
S
Viaducto
Sta. María Bermil
N-550
N-550
A Estrada >
N-640
Estrella do Camiño Hs
Centro 0.0
5
A
CALDAS de REIS
río Umia

2.7 km **San Miguel de Valga** *San Miguel (Autoservicio)*. The camino is well signposted as we re-enter woodlands and cross and re-cross a series of country lanes through the hamlets of ***Pedreira***, ***Cimadevila*** [ ] ***Fontelo*** and ***Condide*** with *vending Buen Camino* + **w.c.'s** [**2.4** km] s/o over PO-214 [**1.0** km] *Chaves* / N-550 (left). Up past *Mesa de Pedra Ales + menú peregrino* to arrive at ***Mirador Pontecesures*** [**0.3** km] views over río Ulla and Padrón (río Sar). Just behind the Colegio (+50m) purpose built hostel ●*Alb.* **Pontecesures** *Xunta.[54÷2]* €5 ✆ 699 832 730 Estrada das Escolas, Lugar de Infesta. Continue down past the Romanesque church of ***San Xulián*** *XII* [ ] *[adj. historic* ***Cruceiro de San Lázaro*** *XIV site of a medieval leper colony]* to **Herbón option [0.6** km]. •*P.* **Casa do Hórreo** *x3* €25-35 incl. ✆ 609 155 607 *www.casa-do-horreo.negocio.site* r/Cantillo 10.

4.3 km **Cruce** ***Opción*** Turn <left for the main route directly to Padrón ▲ *[or turn right> for the alternative route to the monastery in Herbón].*

Detour Herbón 2.9 km: ●*Alb.***Herbón** *Conv.[22÷1]* €-donativo lodging in the ancient and tranquil surroundings of the Monasterio Franciscano de Herbón for pilgrims seeking a more contemplative experience. Communal dinner following mass at 20:00. Breakfast at 07:30. The hostel is run by volunteers from the Galician pilgrim association (AGACS) and is temporarily housed in a block at the rear with entrance from a discreet door in the top terrace. 22 individual bunk spaces (no groups) in one dormitory with basic facilities. ***Directions***: Follow ***red*** arrows to **Cortiñas** [**1.0** km] *[option to take path - often overgown- down left along river]* or keep s/o under AP-9 and turn down left to river and cross over bridge [**1.2** km] *[note the weirs* pesqueiras *used since Roman times to trap fish, primarily Lamprey]*. Turn back along far side of river past back gate and up to monastery [**0.7** km] ***(Total 2.9 km). Note:*** Yellow arrows mark the way back to ***Padrón*** by road to town centre a distance of ***2.6 km.***

▲ For Padron turn <left at option cross rail and take tunnel under N-550 to the bridge **Pontecesures** over río Ulla (separating the province of Pontevedra from A Coruña). Statue of Santiago in wall niche (left). *[Detour* ***+200m*** •**A Casa do Rio** *x15* €40+ ✆ 986 557 575 *www.hotelacasadorio.es c/Dr. Victor García turn left* ***this*** *side of river]*. Cross bridge *Farrucan (left)* and continue s/o left (*not* main road). Continue along quiet country lane and right> along **río Sar** under motorway to first of Padron's many **albergues [1.6** km] ***(listed sequntially)*** *Alb.*❶ **Camiño do Sar** *Priv. [20÷1]* €13-15 ✆ 618 734 373. Next +100m mod. apt bldg. ❷ **O Pedrón** *Priv. [43÷3]* €13 ✆ 881 121 266 & *La Hacienda* and to the rear ❸ **O da Meiga** *Priv. [50÷1]* €13+ ✆ 639 994 048 r/Noirmoutier 16. +200m ❹ **Flavia** *Priv. [22÷5]* €12 *+7* €25-38 ✆ 981 810 455 *(Isabel)* Campo da Feira + *Flavia (50m right)*. •*B&B.* **Ecorooms** *x5* €35+ ✆ 639 818 229 Trav. Campo da Feira, 19 adj.

☕ Noroeste. Keep s/o into Padrón's market square (toilets left) along río Sar with shaded *paseo* lined with plane trees (replica *Padrón* on opp. bank). ❺ **A Barca de Pedra** *Priv.[22÷5]* €15-18 incl. ✆ Rebeca 679 199 770 *www.abarcadepedra.es* c/ Vidal Cepeda 6 and into to the centre of Padrón with the statue of her most famous daughter and illustrious poetess ***Rosalía de Castro*** see photo> with door to ***Igrexa de Santiago*** [**0.9** km].

2.5 km **Padrón** ***Centro*** the heart of Padrón and legendary landing place of St. James with the original stone bollard that secured his boat *padrón* located under the high altar. Opp. main door ❻ **Rossol** *Priv.[18÷1]* €13-16 ✆ 981 810 011 *www.alberguerossol.com* + popular ☕ *Rossol* (see photo>) that spills out onto the central plaza in front of the church *Plaza Rodriguez Cobián.* Also ☕ *Pepe's* on the corner of rua Nova *[The colourful Pepe may offer 'rooms' in flat ¾ km away!]* ❼ **Murgadán** *Priv. [32÷1]* €14 *x3* €45 ✆ 638 298 437 r/Corredoira da Barca, 5. ❽ **Corredoiras** *Priv.[18÷1]* €14-17 ✆ 981 817 266 c/ Corredoira da Barca, 10.

For the original Xunta hostel proceed over bridge [!] (narrow medieval bridge also used by traffic) and cross road [!] (blind bend) to ***Fuente del Carmen*** below ***Convento do Carmen*** which is perched on the rocky promontory above. ❾ **D'Camiño** *Priv. [15÷3]* €15+ ✆ 615 046 723 *www.baralberguedcamino.com* r/Peregrinos, 3 *Alb.*❿ **Padrón** *Xunta. [46÷1]* €8 ✆ 673 656 173 Costanilla do Carmen *(see photo>)*. The impressive edifice of the adjacent 18th century Carmelite monastery lie above and the climb up offers good views over the river Sar and town beyond.

Nearby are the access steps and *Via Crucis* to ***Monte Santiaguiño*** (cover photo of this guide). This witnesses the start of St. James ministry on the Iberian peninsular thus initiating the whole Camino de Santiago story. ***Directions:*** while only ½ km to the mount this is a steep climb up the Stations of The Cross. From the *Fuente del Carmen* take the *rua Peregrinos* for 50m and turn <left by no 17 up steeply along *Escaleras Santiaguiño* to *Santiaguiño Mount* situated behind the small chapel of Santiaguiño with motif of the apostle baptising a pilgrim with water poured from a scallop shell.

Padrón: ❶ ***Turismo Kiosco*:** 10:00-14:00 / 16:15-19:00 ✆ 646 593 319 Av. Compostela N-550 List of accommodation/ town plan and issues the Pedronía.

▮ **Hoteles:** •*H*** **Chef Rivera** *x17* €35-46 +🍴 ✆ 981 810 413 *www.chefrivera.com* r/ Enlace Parque (opp. turismo). •*P*** **Casa Cuco** ✆ 981 810 511 Av. Compostela (modern building opp. Jardín Botanico). •*P**** **Jardín** *x7* €35+ ✆ 981 810 950 *www.pensionjardin.com* period town house opp. Jardín Botanico corner of Av. da Estación. •*H*** **Rosalia** *x21* €25-40 ✆ 981 812 490 *www.hotelrosalia.es* modern hotel r/ Maruxa Villanueva (adj. estación de tren and museo de Rosalia de Castro). •*P*** **Grilo** *x9* €19-39 ✆ 981 810 607 Av. Camilo José Cela (N-550). Wide variety of restaurants most serving the local speciality *Pimientos de Padrón.*

Padrón Town: 20 kilometres South of Santiago is where we find the legendary starting point of James ministry in Spain and also the subsequent return of his mortal remains following his martyrdom in Jerusalem that lie in the reliquary at the heart of Santiago cathedral. Padrón is built along the banks of the rivers Sar and Ulla and essentially an 'extension' of Iria Flavia. The latter being the original seat of the bishops of Galicia before it was transferred to Santiago de Compostela. The varied attractions of this historical town include: ❶ **Igrexa de Santiago.** This Romanesque church dates back to the time of Bishop Xelmírez but has been extended many times since and the present structure is rather sombre in appearance. Inside is one of the great Jacobean treasures for here, below the altar, is the original stone *O Pedrón* from which the town takes its name. You may need to ask for the partition to be rolled back and the light switched on for you to see the stone itself (see photo above).

While legends abound, the most consistent is that this is the mooring post to which the boat carrying James the Apostle tied up to the quayside along the river bank here. And, just as St. James relics in Santiago were covered over with the basilica church, so too this sacred spot is covered over with the present church. The stone was also, allegedly, a Roman altar dedicated to Neptune. *[A replica by the river – far side of the bridge – may evoke a more authentic response to the legend. It is certainly easier to imagine a boat coming alongside here to tie up with its sacred cargo].* Inside the church we find a fine 16th century Gothic pulpit with an image of Santiago Peregrino, while a glass case houses the image of Santiago Matamoros, slaying the Moors as the spearhead of the Reconquista. A recently restored 18th century oil painting has a more peaceful image of St. James' body being carried across the sea accompanied by his faithful disciples (see photo>).

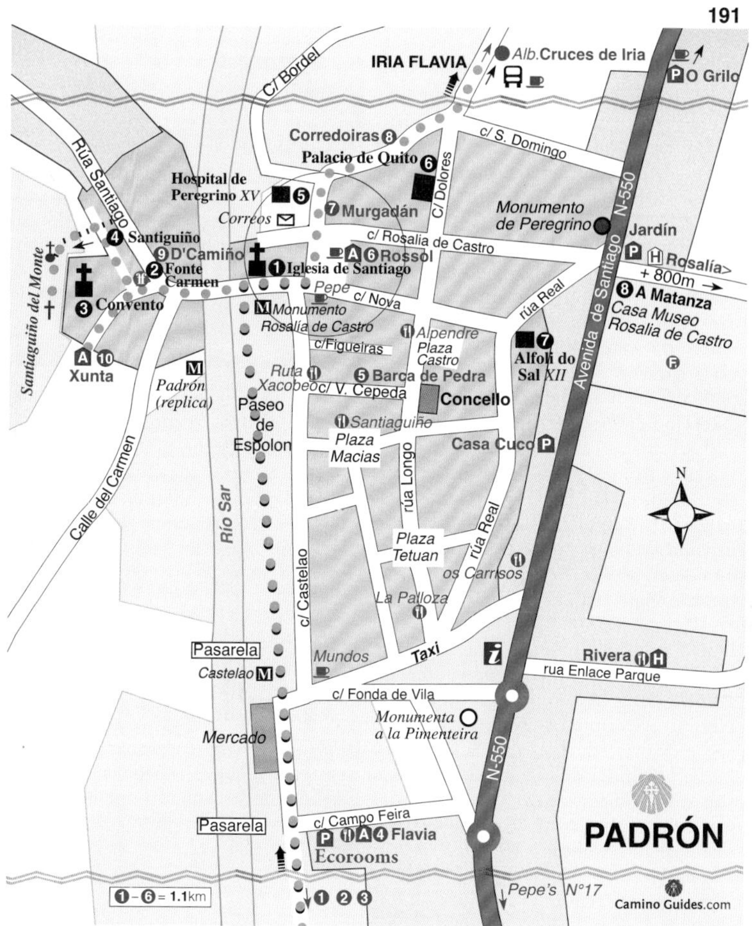

On the far (western) side of the river is the emblematic drinking font and roadside monument ❷ **Fonte do Carme** *XVI* displaying the arrival of the sarcophagus of St. James with his disciples Theodore and Athanasius and the scene of the conversion and baptism of the pagan Queen Lupa. And standing prominently above is the imposing facade of ❸ **Convento do Carme** *XVIII* with its extensive balcony with fine views over the town. Nearby is one of the best kept Santiago secrets and little visited ❹ **Monte Santiaguiño** here, legend tells us, is where St. James first preached the gospel message. Standing imposingly above the river it is not difficult to envisage him delivering Christ's message of unconditional love and forgiveness from this remote and peaceful place. *(See directions page 189)*. Make time to visit this most significant of Jacobean sites.

Just as the vast majority of pilgrims believe there is only one camino de Santiago they also mistakenly believe that St. James arrived in Spain dead – not alive. They therefore miss, perhaps, the most important part of the Santiago story – his life and teaching rather than his death and burial. See statue of Santiago above the main altar under *reflections* next page.

❺ **Hospital de Peregrinos** *XV*. The medieval pilgrim hostal adjoining the church of St. James. ❻ **Palacio de Quito** *XVIII* century Palace of the Bishop of Quito. *(see next stage for* ***Colegiata de Santa María de Iria Flavia*** *and* ***Museo de Cela****).* ❼ **Alfoli do Sal** *XII* century former salt depot and one of the oldest extant building in Padrón (now a café). While not connected directly with the Santiago story, don't miss the most visited museum in Galicia ❽ **A Matanza** *Casa Museo Rosalía de Castro* (see photo>) the house where she lived and died (1837–1885) and wrote some of her exceptionally beautiful prose. It is lovingly maintained in its original condition and set in peaceful and delightfully shaded gardens. Some of her works are available from the museum shop (with translations from Gallego into Castellano and English). The house is situated outside the town centre 700m from the main road. *Directions:* Take c/ Salgado Araujo between the Botanical Gardens and Pensión Jardín, continue over the river cutting (connecting ríos Sar and Ulla) and immediately over the railway turn left and the museum is on your right after 100 meters. Daily 10.00-13.30 / 16.00-19.00 €2

Don't miss sampling a plate of the famous Padrón Peppers ***pementos de Padrón*** cultivated exclusively in nearby Herbón a delicious combination of sweet and piquant flesh with only one in every 20 being chilli-hot – The added fun is you never know which one! This has given rise to the saying, 'Padrón peppers, some are hot, some are not' *Os pementos de Padrón, uns pican e outros non!* 🍴 *O Alpendre (formerly O'Pementeiro)* in Plaza do Castro specialises in them (see photo above) but you can find them in any of the myriad cafes around town in season which runs from May to October (*Fiesta de pementos* in August). Traditionally fried in oil and served as tapas. The seeds were imported by the Franciscan monks of Herbón during their missionary work in Central and South America which adapted to the soil conditions found locally. Also at 🍴 *Ruta Xacobea (Guinness sign)* spills out onto paseo de Espolon and gets the last of the evening sun.

El Excelentísimo Ayuntamiento de Padrón
concede la credencial de

PEDRONÍA

"HIC FUIT CORPUS BEATI JACOBI"

Pedronía: Padrón now has its own *certificado*. Ostensibly issued to anyone who has walked any stage into town and visited the major sites incl. *Monte Santiaguiño, Iglesia Santiago & Iria Flavia.* Obtain the Pedronía at the tourist kiosk ❶ *Turismo* on N-550 ✆ 646 593 319 or *Concello* ✆ 981 810 451 c/Longa,27. Also available from the municipal albergue Additional info: *www.concellodepadron.es*

Personal Reflections:

24 PADRÓN – SANTIAGO

(natural path)	8.2	32%
(quiet road)	13.8	54%
(main road)	3.6	14%
Total km	**25.6** km *(15.9 ml)*	

Total ascent **340**m +½ *hr*
▲ Alto *m* Monte Agro **260**m *(853 ft)*
< A H > ➲Iria **1.0**. ➲Escravitude **6.4** km.
➲Picaraña **9.5** km. ➲Faramello / Teo **10.8** km. ➲Miladoiro **18.6** km.

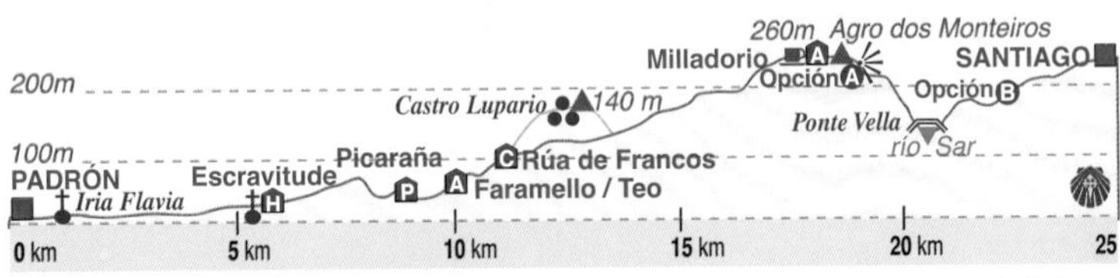

The eye with which I see God, is the same eye with which God sees me.
Meister Eckhart

Practical Path: This final stage into Santiago provides us with a varied day's walking and the inevitable stretches of main road that gets increasingly busy as we near the city. However, we still manage 30% on natural pathways through oak, pine and eucalyptus woodlands offering shade and respite from the traffic. There are plentiful cafés and alternative lodging along the N-550 and drinking fonts at regular intervals. This stage also has the detour to Castro Lupario, so if you want to push through the undergrowth and sit atop the pile of stones (all that remains of Lupa's hill fortress) allow yourself an extra two hours. Alternatively stay in nearby accommodation around Teo and visit this remote location at your leisure and make your way into Santiago in the morning for the pilgrim mass at noon.

0.0 km Padrón *Centro* Leave the town centre ***Iglesia Santiago*** / *Alb.*❻ **Rossol** and make your way through the streets of the old quarter of Padrón along rua Corredoira da Barca into rua Dores emerging onto open ground with the river on your (left) and the main road over to your (right). We pass the bus station [**0.4** km] with regular services to Santiago throughout the day and ☕ (opens early). Next we cross a tributary of the Sar and modern ☕ ●*Alb.* **Sant-Yago** *Priv.[10÷1]* €15 ✆ 686 961 793 Trav. Iría, 131. S/o up to main road [!] **N-550** [**0.4** km] with several ☕ on either side *(open early for breakfast)* to enter the ancient bishopric of ***Iria Flavia*** [**0.2** km] **with** and ●*Alb.***Cruces de Iria** *Priv.[16÷2]* €13-15 ✆ 649 602 092 N-550.

1.0 km Iria Flavia ***Colegiate church of Santa María de Iria*** and adj. cemetery of Adina mentioned in Rosalía de Castro's melancholy poetry. It was here in 1885 that, as she had wished, she was buried. You can see her grave*stone* along the wall adj. the main road. *[In a cruel twist of fate, her fame led to her body being exhumed and moved to the Pantheon in Santiago]*. The medieval church was originally dedicated to Santa Eulalia and was ransacked by Almanzor in 997. Later reconstructed and re-dedicated to the Virgin Mary, a sign of increasing Marian devotion along the Camino at this time. Xelmírez of Santiago further embellished the church in the

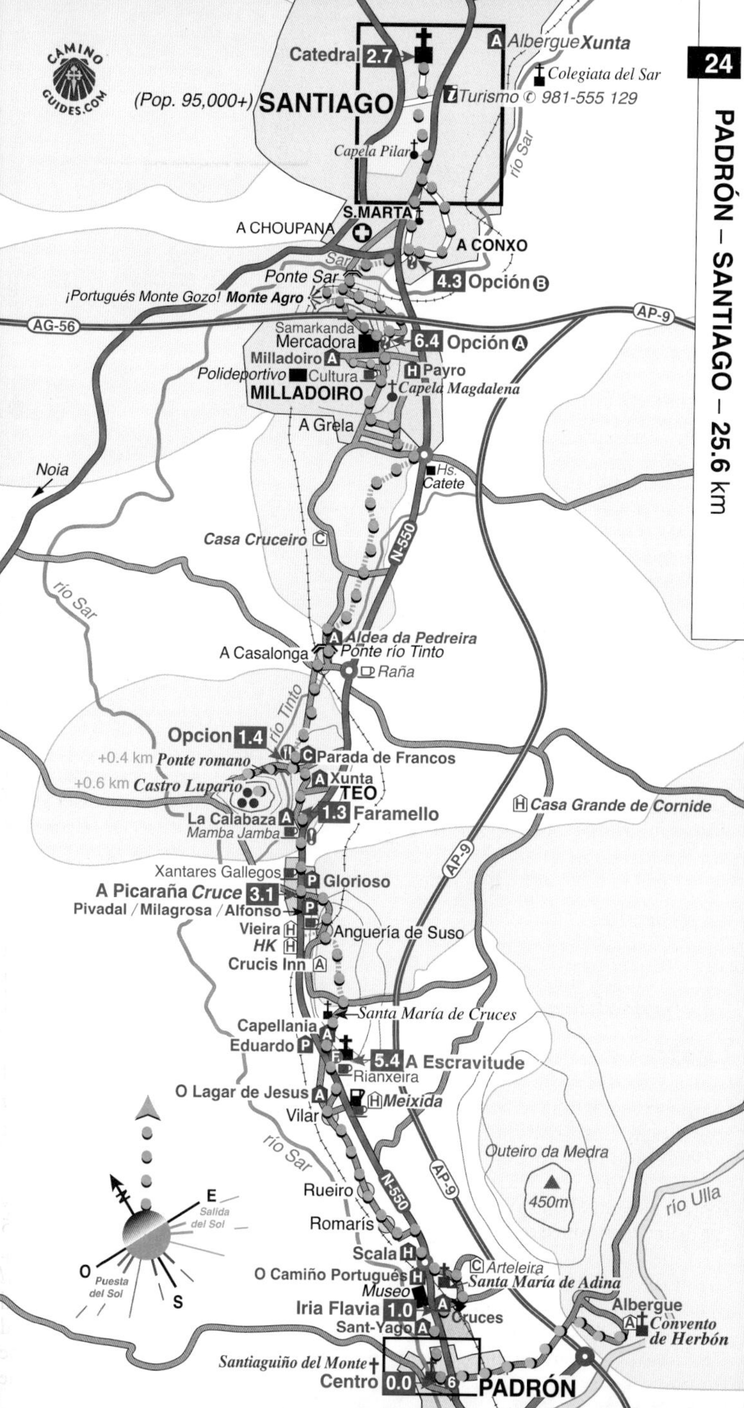
24
PADRÓN – SANTIAGO – 25.6 km
CAMINO GUIDES.COM
Catedral 2.7
(Pop. 95,000+) SANTIAGO
Albergue Xunta
Colegiata del Sar
Turismo © 981-555 129
Capela Pilar
río Sar
S.MARTA
A CHOUPANA
A CONXO
Sar
Ponte Sar
4.3 Opción B
¡Portugués Monte Gozo! Monte Agro
AG-56
AP-9
Samarkanda
Mercadora
6.4 Opción A
Milladoiro
Polideportivo
Cultura
Payro
MILLADOIRO
Capela Magdalena
A Grela
Hs. Catete
Noia
Casa Cruceiro
N-550
río Sar
Aldea da Pedreira
A Casalonga
Ponte río Tinto
Raña
río Tinto
Opcion 1.4
Parada de Francos
+0.4 km Ponte romano
+0.6 km Castro Lupario
Xunta
TEO
La Calabaza
1.3 Faramello
Mamba Jamba
Casa Grande de Cornide
AP-9
Xantares Gallegos
Glorioso
A Picaraña Cruce 3.1
Pivadal / Milagrosa / Alfonso
Vieira
HK
Anguería de Suso
Crucis Inn
Santa María de Cruces
Capellania
Eduardo
5.4 A Escravitude
Rianxeira
O Lagar de Jesus
Meixida
Vilar
río Sar
Outeiro da Medra
450m
N-550
AP-9
Rueiro
Romarís
río Ulla
E
Salida del Sol
O
Puesta del Sol
S
Scala
Arteleira
O Camiño Portugués
Santa María de Adina
Museo
Iria Flavia 1.0
Cruces
Albergue
Convento de Herbón
Sant-Yago
Santiaguiño del Monte
Centro 0.0
6
PADRÓN

Romanesque style in the 12thc and accorded it collegiate status. During the 13th century it was expanded along the lines of a basilica and was changed again during the Baroque period by the locally born Bishop of Quito. He commissioned architect Melchor de Velasco to build the chapel of San Ildefonso. Open sarcophagi line the wall of the church and provides the whole with a final flourish of morbidity [].

On the opposite side of the main road is the house of the cannons, now a museum and office of the Camilo José Cela Foundation. Like Rosalía de Castro, lived in Padrón and wrote some of his famous works here. He was awarded the Nobel Prize for Literature in 1989, *'for a rich and intensive prose, which with restrained compassion forms a challenging vision of man's vulnerability.'* He died in 2002. Adjoining is the Cela Railway Museum also housed in this fine 18th century terrace. Cela's maternal grandfather, John Trulock, was a Scot and built the first railway in Galicia.

The route now passes *under* rail up to **Lugar Pedreda [0.5** km] *[Detour + 200m •CR **Arteleira** © 636 931 524]* back down to cross the N-550 [!] past *& Hs.* **O Camiño Portugués** *x8* €45 © 981 810 250 to ***rotunda*** **[1.1** km] and modern •*H**** **Scala** *x190* €40-75 © 981 811 312. S/o along N-550 past *Fogar de Brogán* and turn off <left by a garage ***Talleres Casal*** **[0.4** km] to join quiet country lanes *(between railway and N-550)* as we pass through a series of hamlets ***Romaris***, ***Rueiro*** with overhanging vines and granite horreos over *regos Pastoriza* and *Tarrio* into ***Tarrio*** and ***Vilar*** to **T-junction [2.3** km] *[Detour (right **+300m**) N-550 O Descanso and behind Repsol (+200m) •CR **Meixida** x5 €45-60 © 981 811 113 A Escravitud].* We now take a short stretch of track by the rail line to pass **entrance [0.3** km] ●*Alb.&* **O Lagar de Jesús** €16 © José 881 060 708 www.olagardejesus.com beautifully restored finca in peaceful gardens We now emerge back onto the busy **N-550** [!] past *Rianxeira* in **A Escravitude [0.8** km]:

5.4 km **A Escravitude** [] Another famous Marian shrine built in the early 18th century over a fountain, site of a miracle that took place in 1732. A rather gloomy Baroque sanctuary, and like the church at Iria, has the N-550 built hard up against both the fountain and the church. Not a peaceful place to pray or slake the thirst. •*H** **Grande da Capellania** *x7* €46-51 © 981 509 854. •*P** *&* **Buen Camino** €15-30 © 616 228 775. Proceed around small park at the side of sanctuary and up steep country lane past Romanesque church of ***Sta. María de Cruces*** and turn right at T-jct (temporary detour) and <left onto **path** through pine woods **option [1.1** km] *Detour left **+200m** to* ●*Alb.* **Cruces Inn** *Priv.[22÷2]* €13+ © 646 596 573 Lugar de Cruces. Continue under rail line at **Picaraña Abaixo.** *[Detour left **+400m** N-550 •P* & **HK** x5 €18-35 © 981 803 210 &* ●*Alb.***Camiño da Vieira** *Priv.[13÷1]* €17 +2 €40 © 696 790 965*].* Continue through **Anguería de Suso** and **Areal [1.5** km]. ***+200m*** •*P** **Areal** *x5* €15-24 © 650 194 760 and back down to the N-550 at **Picaraña [0.5** km].

3.1 km **Picaraña** *(Areal)* choice of lodging and 🍴's along the main road opp. industrial estate. •*P*** **Pividal** *&🍴 /Milagrosa / Alfonso x14* €25-40 ✆ 981 803 119. •*P** **Glorioso** *x6* €20-33 ✆ 981 803 181. Cross N-550 [!] past 🍴 *Xantares Gallego* alongside N-550 veering left *(sign Faramello)* past ☕ *O Alpendre do Camiño* & ☕ *Mamba Jamba* (Pazo do Faramello – down left) into Lugar del Faramello.

1.3 km **Faramello** ***Teo*** *Alb.&* 🍴 ●**La Calabaza del Peregrino** *Priv.[36÷4]* €14 ✆ 981 194 244 with rear terrace. S/o [🚰] (right) to **Option** [**0.4** km] ▲ ***albergue sign Teo +150m** up right.* ● *Alb.* **Teo** *Xunta.[20÷2]+ €8. [further up* ☕ *Casa Javier & several restaurants along the busy N-550]. Also* ***Casa Grande de Cornide*** €55-80 ✆ *Carlos Feal 981 893 044 off route* ***+2,000m].*** ▲ At fork keep s/o up sharply to ***ermita de San Martiño*** and ***cruceiro do Francos*** [**0.6** km] one of the oldest wayside crosses in Galicia (see photo>). It is here we also join the ancient pilgrim way, which still retains its original name *rua de Francos* and leads to the shaded village green ***Parada de Francos*** [**0.4** km] with •*CR* **Parada de Francos** *x10* €60-80 ✆ 981 538 004 *www.paradadefrancos.com* opp. 🍴*Carboeiro* tranquil location amongst ancient oaks directly on camino with detour to *Castro Lupario:*

1.4 km **Parada de Francos** ***Detour***

● **Detour 1.1 km Castro Lupario** (one of the sites associated with legendary queen Lupa central to the Santiago story): Round trip 2.2 km *(ruins only – no standing buildings).* Access has been improved but you may have to push through the undergrowth. Allow around 2 hours to give yourself time for reflection amongst the ancient stones and to admire the view. This route is not waymarked but a sign on the road points to the start of the track and indicates the hill fort. ***Directions***: make your way diagonally over to the far side of the square and take the asphalt road by the modern house (no. 56). As you turn the corner, a view of Castro Lupario opens up in front of you (see photo). Proceed down to the río Tinto (a tributary of the Sar which in turn flows into the Ulla at Padrón) and cross over on the original and beautifully preserved ***Roman bridge [400m]***. Continue up the asphalt road into Concello de Brión and proceed to the top of the short incline and just where the road begins to drop down again over on the left hand side of the road is a rough ***lay-by [200m]***. Proceed along the track and after ***[150m] turn up right*** onto the ancient stone access route that winds its way up around the ***hill for [350m]***. The fort extends over the entire hilltop which is surprisingly level with a diameter of 100m. Make your way to the stand of oak trees that struggle for a root hold amidst the ruins and let your imagination loose. It certainly evokes a greater sense of mystery than the alternative sites at Castro de Lobeira overlooking the ria Arousa and the Pico Santo. From the ancient ruins here it is not difficult to imagine the pagan rituals, wild bulls and wolves which are all intimately connected with the fabled story of Queen Lupa and Sant Iago's faithful disciples searching for a site in which to bury his mortal remains.

From ***Parada de Francos*** take path by casa rural (see photo>) to join country lane over railway into ***Osebe*** [**1.4** km] with ●*Alb.***Casa Aldea da Pedreira** *Priv. [20÷2]* €20 ✆ 619 544 966. *(just before N-550* ☕ *200m* off *route)* [⛲]. S/o over crossroads onto woodland path cross **road** [**1.8** km] *[**Detour Raíces +400m**: •**Casa do Cruceiro** x7* €62-69 ✆ 981 548 596*]*. Keep s/o wide forest track before emerging onto road by factory and roundabout ***A Grela*** [**1.3** km] *kiosco movil* on **N-550**. A provisional pilgrim track leads up to join quiet lane and take 2nd turn <left up to the road and turn right> up steeply to ***Novo Milladoiro*** [**1.4** km] high point of this stage *alto* 250m. *[**Capela de María Magdalena** looks somewhat out of place amongst the towering modern luxury apartment blocks right]*. Keep s/o past sports centre *Polideportivo (left) &* ☕ *Casa Cultura* [⛲] & **100**m later *[**detour +200**m (left)* ●*Alb.***Milladoiro** *Priv.[62÷3]* €14 ✆ 981 938 382 c/Buxo,6 adj. ☕ *Joy or **detour** (right) **+300**m down Rúa Pardiñeiros on corner of Rúa Anxeriz •H" **Payro** €40 ✆ 881 975 176]*. Continue to shopping centre ***Mercadona*** [**0.5** km].

6.4 km Milladoiro *Mercadona opción* Ⓐ ☕ *Samarkanda* (quiet ☕ to rear *menú*) ***Option:*** ▲ Here on the corner the city 'authority' has decided to re-waymark the route down what looks like a lovely forest path that peters out after only 200m and then meanders up and down steep roads to rejoin the original (now alt scenic) route around the forested *Agros dos Monteiros*).

For alt. route ●●●●(200m shorter mostly on woodland paths) keep s/o along asphalt road past ***Union Fenosa*** to high point *Agro dos Monteiros* 260m with first (distant) views of Santiago cathedral. The road descends over **autovia AG-56** [**1.0** km] turning <left (arrows partially erased) onto a delightful woodland path that winds its way over a secondary road to emerge through a narrow gap between 2 houses (pilgrim graffiti) in *A Rocha Nova.* Keeo s/o and turn right along the railway to join the main route at **rail bridge** [**1.4** km] ***A Rocha Vella***. ❖

❖ **Detour** [+**200**m] ***Castelo de Rocha Vella*** ●●●●site of the city's ancient fortified bishops residence. The area is undergoing excavation by the archeological department of Santiago university and has recently been fenced off so we can no longer scramble (easily) amongst the ruins. However, it is part of the Santiago story and worth a visit for those interested in the historical past. ***Directions***: On the far side of the crash barrier is a path alongside the rail line that leads directly to the ruins [200m] or turn back up the road and take the first left and proceed to the end of the cul de sac *rua do Piñeiro* for a circuitous 800m].

▲ For new waymarked route ●●●● turn down forest track to asphalt road [**0.2** km] continue under motorway viaduct and steeply up to roundabout ***A Rocha Vella*** *[•Hs Balboa* ✆ *981 521 598 N-550 +400m right]*. to ***railway bridge*** [**2.4** km] ❖ *[here the alternative scenic route joins from the left and detour right>]*.

Continue over bridge and down steeply turning right at T-jct. *[Detour +100m left ancient Fonte Velha by río Sar]*. Pass ☕ *A Paradiña! (small stop!)* to the medieval bridge over the **río Sar** [**0.7** km]. A new waymarked route now takes a pleasant path up through woodland under city bypass to option point [**1.0** km].

4.3 km **City Bypass *Option* Ⓑ** ◆ Two waymarks point in opposite directions with no explanation as to what our options are! (see photo>). For the most **direct route *por Santa Marta*** (600m shorter/ better waymarking) keep s/o (left) over bridge through university campus onto rua Santa Marta Arriba which merges into Av. Rosalia de Castro at roundabout where the alternative route joins from the right [**1.6** km]. ◆

*[**Alternative route por Conxo** ● ● ● ● turn right at option point down Travesia de Torrente into rua da Benefica de Conxo into the modern suburbs. Waymarking is poor but keep s/o up past prominent Televes studios (right) up to N.S Merced De Conxo (psicoterapia) ☕ Caiman. S/o over new rounadabout up rua Sánchez Freire over Av. Romero Donallo into Av. Vilagarcia to join the other route in Av. de Rosalia de Castro **[2.2 km]**.*

◆ The two routes join and continue s/o up to enter Santa Susana park by Capilla Pilar (left) as we make our way to *Porto Faxeira* (Traffic lights have replaced the historic south gate into the city!). We now take our final steps towards the fabled cathedral down the narrow ***rua Franco*** lined with restaurants and pause, perhaps, at another of the little known gems of the caminos and one of the most historic of all the buildings in Santiago associated with St. James ❽ ***Capela de Santiago*** *[this tiny chapel is the place where, by tradition, the cart carrying the body of St. James came to rest and his body laid out awaiting its final burial. The discreet shell above the door* ***adj. No.5*** opp. Correos *is easily bypassed].* We have taken our weary body on the self-same road and now we take our last few steps towards the cathedral. By tradition the pilgrim from Portugal turns up right into rua Fonseca into the *Praza das Praterías* to enter the cathedral by the south door. This was the entrance used by the medieval pilgrim travelling the Camino Portugués and remains the oldest doorway to the Cathedral dating back to the 11th century (1078). The magnificent stone carvings surrounding this portal show hardly a hint of the intervening 900 years. St. James is represented in the centre between 2 cypress tress next to Christ [**0.4** km].

2.7 km **Santiago *Cathedral*** Take time to 'arrive'. We each feel different emotions on arriving at our destination after the physical, emotional and spiritual challenges of our journey. Entering the cathedral can bring tears of joy... or disappointment. Whatever our individual reaction it is absolutely valid in that moment so honour it. Gratitude for our safe arrival is a universally appropriate response. However, if you are overwhelmed by the crowds why not return later when you might feel more composed and the cathedral is, perhaps, quieter. Whether now or later and whichever door you entered by, you might like to follow the timeworn pilgrim ritual as follows *(ongoing cathedral renovations allowing)*:

Ⓐ Stand before the Tree of Jesse, the central column of Master Mateo's masterpiece: the Entrance of Glory *Pórtico da Gloria*. Millions of pilgrims, over the millennia, have worn finger holes in the solid marble as they placed their hands there as a mark of gratitude for their safe arrival (a barrier was placed here in 2007 to prevent further wear) but we can breathe in the beauty of this inner portico fashioned by Mateo in the 12th century (the outer porch was added in 1750). The Bible and its main characters come alive in this remarkable marble façade. The central column has Christ in Glory, flanked by the apostles and, directly underneath, St. James sits as intercessor between Christ and the pilgrim.

Proceed to the other side and Ⓑ touch your brow to that of Maestro Mateo, whose kneeling figure is carved into the back of the central column (facing the altar), and receive some of his artistic genius in the ritual known as the head-butting saint *santo dos croques*. Proceed to the High Altar (right hand side) to ascend the stairs and Ⓒ hug the Apostle. Perhaps lay your forehead on his broad shoulders and say what you came here to say. Proceed down the steps to the far side to the crypt and the reliquary chapel under the altar. Ⓓ Here, you can kneel before the casket containing the relics of the great Saint and offer your prayer.

Pilgrim mass currently takes place four times per day; 07:30 / 09:30 / 12:00 / 19:30. The swinging of the giant incense burner *Botafumeiro* was originally used to fumigate the sweaty (and possibly disease-ridden) pilgrims. The ritual requires half a dozen attendants *tiraboleiros* to perform it so has become a more infrequent event, details of special occasions when the *Botafumeiro* will be used can be found on the cathedral website (*www.catedraldesantiago.es*). You may also chance upon the spectacle when a private party has paid for the ritual to be performed, though these dates are not available in advance.

Personal Reflections:

Before a new chapter is begun, the old one has to be finished.
Stop being who you were and change into Who you are. ***Paulo Coelho***

4 squares surround the cathedral, as follows:

■ **Praza do Obradoiro**. The 'golden' square of Santiago is usually thronged with pilgrims and tourists admiring the dramatic west facing façade of the Cathedral, universal symbol of Santiago, with St. James looking down on all the activity from his niche in the central tower. This provides the main entrance to the Cathedral and the Portico de Gloria. To the right of the steps is the discrete entrance to the museum. A combined ticket will provide access to all rooms including the crypt and the cloisters and also to the 12th century palace of one of Santiago's most famous individuals and first archbishop, Gelmírez *Pazo de Xelmírez* situated on the (left). In this square we also find the beautiful Renaissance façade of the Parador named after Ferdinand and Isabel *Hostal dos Reis Católicos* on whose orders it was built in 1492 as a pilgrim hospice. Opposite the Cathedral is the more austere neoclassical seat of the Galician government and town hall *Pazo de Raxoi* with its solid arcade. Finally, making up the fourth side of the square is the gable end of the *Colegio de S. Jerónimo* part of the university. Moving anti-clockwise around the cathedral – turn up into Rúa de Fonseca to:

■ **Praza das Praterías**. The most intimate of the squares with its lovely centrepiece, an ornate statue of horses leaping out of the water. On the corner of Rúa do Vilar we find the Dean's House *Casa do Deán* formerly the pilgrim office. Along the walls of the Cathedral itself are the silversmiths *prateros* that give the square its name. Up the steep flight of steps we come to the magnificent south door to the Cathedral, the oldest extant doorway and traditionally the entrance taken by pilgrims coming from Portugal. The quality of the carvings and their arrangement is remarkable and amongst the many sculptured figures is one of St. James between two cypress trees. Continuing around to the right we pass Pilgrim Backpack storage *Quintana* into:

■ **Praza da Quintana.** This wide square is identified by the broad sweep of steps separating the lower part *Quintana of the dead* from the upper *Quintana of the living*. Opp the Cathedral is the wall of the *Mosteiro de San Paio de Antealtares* (with museum of sacred art). The square provides the eastern entrance to the Cathedral via the Holy Gate *Porta Santa*, referred to as the Door of Pardon *El Perdón* only opened during Holy Years. Adjoining it is the main entrance to the Cathedral shop that has several guidebooks (in various languages) with details of the Cathedral's many chapels and their interesting carvings and statuary and the priceless artefacts and treasures in the museum. Finally, we head up the broad flight of steps around the corner and back into:

■ **Praza da Inmaculada (Azabachería)** to the north facing Azabachería façade, with the least well-known doorway and the only one that *descends* to enter the Cathedral. It has the most weathered aspect, with moss and lichen covering its bleak exterior. Opposite the cathedral is the imposing southern edifice of *Mosteiro de San Martiño Pinario* the square in front gets any available sun and attracts street artists. The archbishop's arch *Arco Arzobispal* brings us back to the Praza do Obradoiro.

Capitulum huius Almae Apostolicae et Metropolitanae Ecclesiae Compostellanae, sigilli Altaris Beati Iacobi Apostoli custos, ut omnibus Fidelibus et Peregrinis ex toto terrarum Orbe, devotionis affectu vel voti causa, ad limina SANCTI IACOBI, Apostoli Nostri, Hispaniarum Patroni et Tutelaris convenientibus, authenticas visitationis litteras expediat, omnibus et singulis praesentes inspecturis notum facit: Dominum

Ioannem Brierley

hoc sacratissimum templum perfecto itinere sive pedibus sive equitando post postrema centum milia metrorum, birota vero post ducenta, pietatis causa, devote visitasse. In quorum fidem praesentes litteras, sigillo eiusdem Sanctae Ecclesiae munitas, ei confert.

Datum Compostellae die 8 mensis aprilis anno Dni 2015

Segundo L. Pérez López
Decanus S.A.M.E. Cathedralis Compostellanae

The **Pilgrim Office** *Oficina del Peregrino* now at rua Carretas *below the parador* ✆ 981 568 846 open daily 08:00-20:00 (10:00-19:00 winter). The new office has tight security procedure (expect lengthy delays). It lacks the informal atmosphere of the former office in rua Vilar with its team of *Amigos.* However, providing you have fulfilled the criteria of a bona-fide pilgrim and walked at least the last 100 km (200 km on bike or horseback) for religious/spiritual reasons and collected 2 stamps per day on your *credencial* you will be awarded the *Compostela* which may entitle you to certain privileges such as reduced entry fees to museums and a free meal at the Parador! If you do not fulfil the criteria you may still be able to obtain a ***certificado*** (€3) which is essentially a certificate of distance travelled. The welcoming Companions meet in a room behind the adjoining pilgrim chapel (see below).

•**The Camino Chaplaincy** offers Anglican services Sundays 12.30 at Igrexa de Santa Susana, parca da Alameda. •**Camino Companions** based within the Pilgrims Office, offer reflective prayer in the pilgrims office *chapel* 11:30 and reflection and integration room 6, 1st floor 15:00 (both daily Mon-Sat). Mass in English daily (excl. Wednesdays) 10:30 also in the *chapel.* •**Pilgrim House** rua Nova 19 also offers a place of welcome and reflection 11:00–20:00 (closed Wed & Sun) under the care of Terra Nova USA.

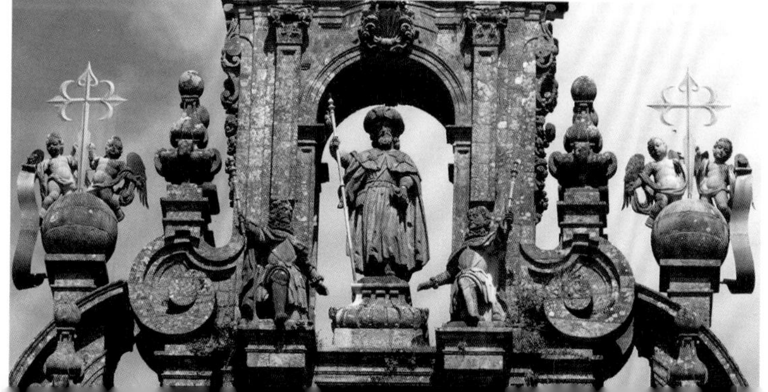

●**Pilgrim's Reception Office** Rúa das Carretas, 33. © 981 568 846 *(09:00-19.00)*
❶ **Turismo** *Centro*: r/ Vilar 63 © 981 555 129 *May-Oct: 09:00-19.00 (winter 17:00)*
● **Laundromat:** 09:00-22:00 **SC18** Rúa San Clemente 18 © 673 753 869.
● **Consignia Praca Quintana** (09:00-21:00) backpack storage €3 per day opp. Cath.
● **Intermodal Central Train/Bus Station** 700m (10 mins) South of Praza Galicia.

● *Albergues: €10-€20 (depending on season / beds per dormitory)* ❶–❾ *(Camino Francés).* ▌**Rúa Concheiros Nº48** ❿ **Santos** *Quijote Priv.[20÷2]* © 881 088 789. **Nº36** ⓫ **La Estrella** *Priv.[24÷6]* © 617 882 529. **Nº10** ⓬ **Porta Real** *Priv.[20÷6]* © 633 610 114.▌**Belvís +500***m* ⓭ **Seminario Menor** *Conv. [173÷12]+81* © 881 031 768 www.alberguesdelcamino.com Av. Quiroga Palacios. ▌**c/ S.Clara** ⓮ **LoopINN** *(La Salle)* © 981 585 667 ▌**c/ Basquiños Nº67** ⓯ **Meiga Backpackers** *Priv.[30÷5]* © 981 570 846 www.meiga-backpackers.es.

■ **Centro Histórico:** ⓰ **Linares** *[14÷2]* © 981 943 253 r/ Algalia de Abaixo, 34. ⓱ **O Fogar de Teodomiro** *Priv.[20÷5]+* © 981 582 920 Plaza de Algalia de Arriba 3. ⓲ **The Last Stamp** *Priv.[62÷10]* © 981 563 525 r/ Preguntorio 10. ⓳ **Azabache** *Priv.[20÷5]* © 981 071 254 c/Azabachería 15. ⓴ **Km.0** *Priv.[50÷10]* (€ 18-26) © 881 974 992 www.santiagokm0.es r/ Carretas 11 (new renovation by pilgrim office) ㉑ **Blanco** *Priv.[20÷2]+ +€35-55* © 881 976 850 r/ Galeras 30. ㉒ **Mundoalbergue** *Priv.[34÷1]* © 981 588 625 c/ San Clemente 26. ▌***Otros:*** ㉓ **La Estación** *Priv.[24÷2]* © 981 594 624 r/ Xoana Nogueira 14 (adj. rail station **+2.9** km). ㉔ **Compostela Inn** *Priv.[120÷30]+* © 981 819 030 off *AC-841 (adj. H Congreso +6.0 km).*

■ ***Hoteles €30–60:*** •*Hs* **Santiago** © 608 865 895 r/Senra 11. •*Hs* **Moure** © 981 583 637 r/dos Loureiros. •*H* **Fonte S. Roque** © 981 554 447 r/do Hospitallilo 8. •*Hs* **Estrela** © 981 576 924 Plaza de San Martín Pinario 5. •*Hs* **San Martín Pinario** *x127* © 981 560 282 www.hsanmartinpinario.com Praza da Inmaculada. •**Pico Sacro** r/San Francisco 22 © 981 584 466. •*H*** **Montes** © 981 574 458 www.hotelmontes.es r/ Raíña 11. ▌**Rúa Fonseca Nº1** •*P* **Fonseca** © 603 259 337. **Nº5** •*Hs* **Libredon** 981 576 520 & •*P* **Barbantes /Celsa** ©981 583 271 on r/ Franco 3. **Rúa Vilar Nº8** •*H**** **Rua Vilar** © 981 519 858. **Nº17** •*H** **Airas Nunes** © 981 569 350. **Nº65** •*Hs*** **Suso** © 981 586 611 www.hostalsuso.com. **Nº76** •*Hs* **Santo Grial** © 629 515 961. •*Hs* **Alameda** © 981 588 100 San Clemente 32. ■ ***€60–90:*** •*H* **A Casa Peregrino** © 981 573 931 c/ Azabachería. •**Entrecercas** © 981 571 151 r/Entrecercas. **Porta de Pena Nº17** •*H* **Costa Vella** © 981 569 530 (+ Jardín) **Nº5** •*P* **Casa Felisa** © 981 582 602 (+Jardín). •**MV Algalia** © 981 558 111 Praza Algalia de Arriba 5. •*H**** **Pazo De Altamira** © 981 558 542 r/ Altamira, 18. ■ ***€100+*** •*H*** **San Francisco** Campillo de San Francisco © 981 581 634. •*H*** **Hostal de los Reyes Católicos** Plaza Obradoiro © 981 582 200.

○ ***Centro Histórico*:** ❶ Convento de Santo Domingo de Bonaval XIIIth *(panteón de Castelao, Rosalía de Castro y museo do Pobo Galego).* ❷ Mosteiro de San Martín Pinario XVIth *y museo* ❸ Pazo de Xelmirez XIIth ❹ Catedral XIIth –XVIIIth *Portica de Gloria, claustro, museo e tesouro* ❺ Hostal dos Reis Católicos XVth *Parador* ❻ Pazo de Raxoi XVIIIth *Presendencia da Xunta* ❼ Colexio de Fonseca XVIth *universidade y claustro* ❽ Capela y Fonte de Santiago ❾ Casa do Deán XVIIIth *Oficina do Peregrino (original).* ❿ Casa Canónica *museo Peregrinaciónes.* ⓫ Mosteiro de San Paio de Antealtares XVth *Museo de Arte Sacra.* ⓬ S.Maria Salomé XIIth.

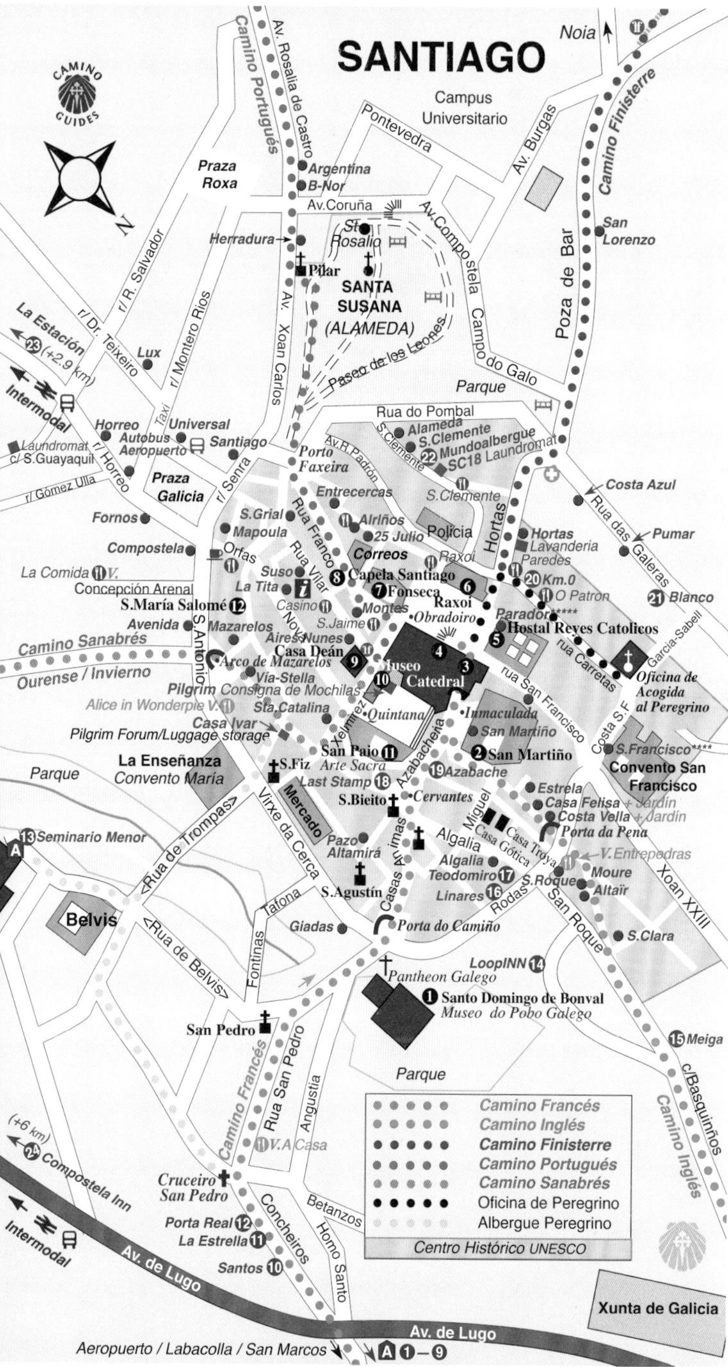
SANTIAGO
Camino Guides
Campus Universitario
Noia
Camino Finisterre
Camino Portugués
Av. Rosalia de Castro
Pontevedra
Av. Burgas
Praza Roxa
Argentina
B-Nor
Av.Coruña
Av.Compostela
San Lorenzo
Poza de Bar
Herradura
St. Rosalia
Pilar
SANTA SUSANA (ALAMEDA)
r/ R. Salvador
r/ Dr. Teixeiro
r/ Montero Rios
Av. Xoan Carlos
Paseo de los Leones
Campo do Galo
La Estación 23 (+2.9 km)
Intermodal
Lux
Parque
Rua do Pombal
Horreo
Autobus Aeropuerto
Universal
Taxi
Santiago
Laundromat
c/ S.Guayaquil
r/ Horreo
r/ Gómez Ulla
Praza Galicia
r/ Senra
Porto Faxeira
Av.R.Padrón
S.Clemente
Alameda
S.Clemente
22 Mundoalbergue
SC18 Laundromat
Costa Azul
Entrecercas
S.Clemente
Fornos
S.Grial
Mapoula
Rua Franco
Alrlños
25 Julio
Policía
Hortas
Hortas
Lavanderia Paredes
Rua das Galeras
Pumar
Compostela
Orfas
Correos
Raxoi
La Comida V.
Suso
Rua Vilar
8 Capela Santiago
6
20 Km.0
Concepción Arenal
La Tita
7 Fonseca
Raxoi
O Patron
21 Blanco
S.María Salomé 12
Casino
Montes
S.Jaime
Obradoiro
Parador*****
Avenida
S.Antonio
Mazarelos
Nova
Aires Nunes
Hostal Reyes Catolicos
5
Camino Sanabrés
Casa Deán
4
3
rua Carretas
Garcia-Sabell
Arco de Mazarelos
9
Museo Catedral
10
Oficina de Acogida al Peregrino
Ourense / Invierno
Vía-Stella
rua San Francisco
Pilgrim Consigna de Mochilas
Alice in Wonderpie V.
Sta.Catalina
Quintana
Inmaculada
Xelmirez
Casa Ivar
San Martiño
Costa S.F
Pilgrim Forum/Luggage storage
San Paio 11
Azabachería
2 San Martiño
S.Francisco****
La Enseñanza Convento María
S.Fiz
Arte Sacra
Convento San Francisco
Parque
Last Stamp 18
19 Azabache
Estrela
S.Bieito
Cervantes
Miguel
Casa Felisa + Jardín
Mercado
Costa Vella + Jardín
Rua de Trompas
Virxe da Cerca
Casa Gótica
Casa Troya
Porta da Pena
13 Seminario Menor
A
Pazo Altamirá
Algalia
V. Entrepedras
Casas Animas
Algalia
Moure
Teodomiro 17
S.Roque
Altaïr
Xoan XXIII
S.Agustín
Linares 16
Rodas
San Roque
Tafona
Belvis
Giadas
Porta do Camiño
S.Clara
Rua de Belvis
Fontiñas
LoopINN 14
Pantheon Galego
1 Santo Domingo de Bonval
Museo do Pobo Galego
San Pedro
15 Meiga
Camino Francés
Rua San Pedro
Angustia
Parque
c/Basquiños
Camino Inglés
Camino Francés
Camino Inglés
Camino Finisterre
Camino Portugués
Camino Sanabrés
Oficina de Peregrino
Albergue Peregrino
Centro Histórico UNESCO
(+6 km)
24 Compostela Inn
V.A Casa
Cruceiro San Pedro
Intermodal
Concheiros
Betanzos
Homo Santo
Porta Real 12
La Estrella 11
Santos 10
Av. de Lugo
Xunta de Galicia
Av. de Lugo
Aeropuerto / Labacolla / San Marcos
A 1–9

PORTUGUESE COASTAL ROUTES: ❶ *Caminho da Costa* ❷ *Senda Litoral*

2 wonderful routes now being discovered by an increasing number of pilgrims. Choice between the 'main' ***Caminho da Costa*** ●●●● which runs parallel to the coast along a mix of country roads and woodland paths. This historic way *Vía Veteris* has the familiar yellow arrows and a sense of camaraderie so beloved of pilgrims. However, there are extensive sections on asphalt. **273.2** km from Porto Cathedral to Santiago – *[**325.2** km to include the **Camino Espiritual** ●●●●].* Commence no later than Vigo (101 km to Santiago) to obtain a Compostela.

The ***Senda Litoral*** ●●●● basically follows the shoreline. It has more of a tourist vibe and wind-blown sand can obliterate paths and boardwalks *pasarelas de madera* and it is difficult to walk in high winds. However, a new pedestrian bridge at Foz de Neiva and other ongoing improvements to the *Ecovia Litoral Norte* has greatly improved this route which is becoming increasingly popular. Where the *senda litoral* connects easily with the main *Caminho da Costa* a tick ✓ suggests a good optional alternative for adventurous pilgrims who have a good sense of orientation; otherwise it makes sense to stick with the main waymarked route.

The addition of these routes is not welcomed by everyone. There are those with investment in the *Camino Central* who are concerned at the increasing popularity of the coastal route and claiming it has no historical basis... and those along the coastal route who endeavour to promote it as their own. But no one need worry for the camino is generous in its embrace and nobody has a monopoly on the caminos which are there to help us create a more loving and inclusive world. Gratitude is due to the voluntary work of pilgrim associations and individuals who have promoted & waymarked the routes over the years so that today we need only the barest information to get us safely to our destination.

Luis Freixo based in Vigo has been waymarking routes along the coast for many years and his detailed maps can be found at ***caminador.es***. Another useful offline mapping app. for the area can also be downloaded from ***maps.me*** In these early formational years of the coastal routes feedback helps towards their improvement. Thanks to David Hamilton for the warning of the danger of crossing the río Nieve in flood and Ian Omnet for permission to reproduce the photograph above. Spate rivers are very unpredictable and we need to assess risks honestly in these situations. While the maps are not designed for going 'off route' in this case steps were retraced to the road bridge that was fortuitously included on the map which allowed rejoining the waymarked coastal route at Santiago do Neiva...

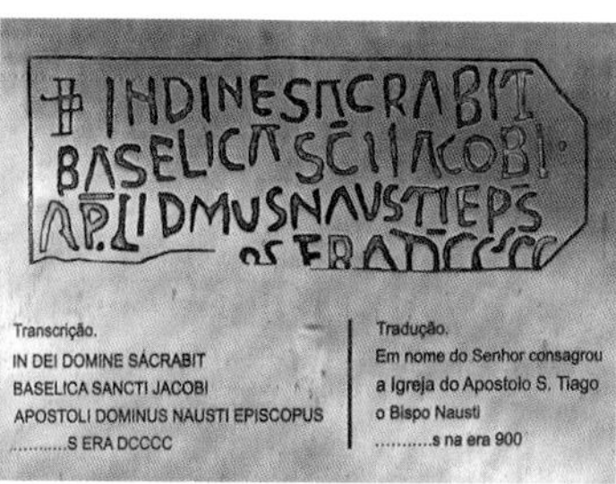

Transcrição.
IN DEI DOMINE SÁCRABIT
BASELICA SANCTI JACOBI
APOSTOLI DOMINUS NAUSTI EPISCOPUS
..........S ERA DCCCC
Tradução.
Em nome do Senhor consagrou
a Igreja do Apostolo S. Tiago
o Bispo Nausti
..........s na era 900

...and this neatly answers those who argue that the coast is not an authentic camino. When renovating the *Igreja Santiago de Castelo do Neiva* directly on the *Camino da Costa* the earliest evidence ever found in Portugal commemorating Santiago was unearthed. A stone carved in the year 900 and dedicated to Sancti Jacobi was found in the wall. Placed there within a few short decades from the discovery of the great saint's tomb and it lies there still... don't miss it!

Little else needs to be said. It is the experience of walking these lovely routes that will inform. Check *updates at **www.caminoguides.com*** for the most recent corrections and additions.

(The following stages begin with 15a from Vila do Conde, if you are setting out on the coastal route from Porto first see stage 14a from page 116).

Bom caminho...

15a VILA do CONDE – ESPOSENDE
Póvoa de Varzim *Marinhas*

Campos de Masseira

(path)	5.6	23%
(minor road)	18.2	75%
(main road)	0.4	02%
Total km	**24.2** km *(15.0 ml)*	

Total ascent **440**m +¾ *hr*

▲ Alto *m* Apulia **20**m *(65 ft)*

<A H> ➲Póvoa Varzim **3.9** km ➲Praia S. Andrés **9.2** km
➲*Praia Estela* ***14.8 km +0.5*** ➲*Apulia* ***17.8 km +0.6*** ➲*Fão* ***21.5 km +0.2***

100m
VILA CONDE — Póvoa Varzim — Praia André — Praia Estela — Apulia — Fão — ESPOSENDE — Marinhas
0 km — 5 km — 10 km — 15 km — 20 km — 25 km

I can't understand why people are frightened of new ideas. I'm frightened of the old ones. *John Cage, composer.*

Inner Camino: Old and new is a recurring theme as we contemplate the re-emergence of the coastal route. Those who are invested in the status quo often feel threatened by fresh initiatives. But we must let go the old ways for new opportunities to arise. Doubtless the seaweed harvesters of Aguçadoura resisted the emergence of the masseira just as, in turn, the masseria is threatened by intense glasshouse horticulture. But we need discernment; not all things new are beneficial. All that glitters is not gold.

Practical Path: Virtually flat as we hug the coast through the *masseiras*. These low-lying market gardens form a unique system of agriculture. The masseiras (troughs) are dug into the sand to protect vines and vegetables from wind and salt air and trap warm air creating a microclimate or greenhouse effect. The troughs are then filled with seaweed as fertilizer. The area between the cape of Santo André and the estuary of río Cávado is protected for this purpose. On the far side of the Cávado we enter the delightful seaside town of Esposende with hotels and new pilgrim hostels in addition to the one in Marinhas 4.3 *beyond* the town.

Senda Litoral: ●●●● Coincides with parts of the Camino do Costa but with additional stretches along the seashore mostly by boardwalks *pasarelas de madera.* **26.9 km -v- 24.4 km** *(see p. 212).*

0.0 km **Vila do Conde** ***centro.*** With option to take the coastal *senda litoral...*
or follow the waymarks along the narrow lanes of Vila do Conde past the Igreja Matriz into the relative bustle of Póvoa de Varzim to the ***Igrexa San Roque y Santiago Maior*** in Praça de Republica (see photo>). This is a modern vibrant town with all facilities.

3.9 km **Póvoa de Varzim** ***centro***

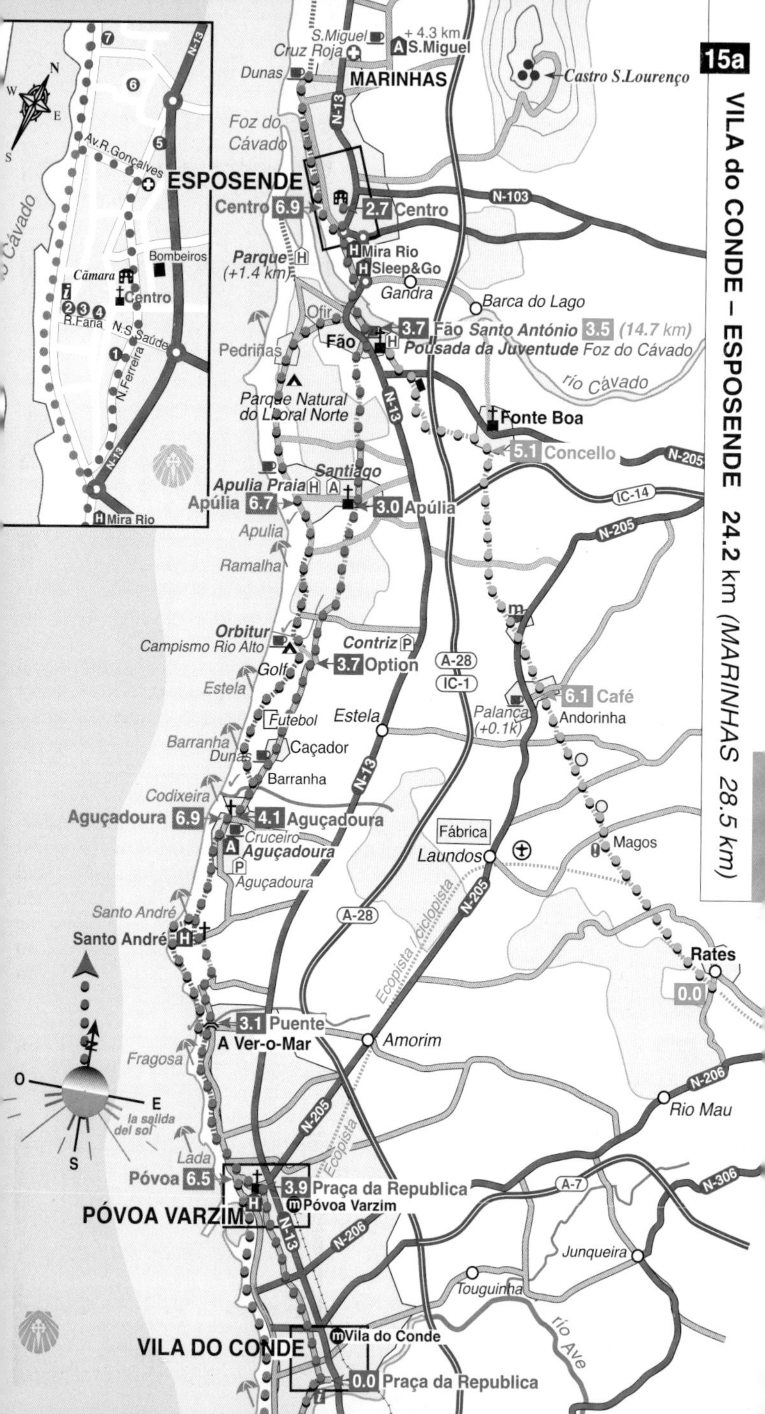
15a
VILA do CONDE – ESPOSENDE 24.2 km (MARINHAS 28.5 km)
S.Miguel
+ 4.3 km
S.Miguel
Cruz Roja
Dunas
MARINHAS
Castro S.Lourenço
Foz do Cávado
ESPOSENDE
Centro 6.9
2.7 Centro
N-103
Mira Rio
Sleep&Go
Parque (+1.4 km)
Gandra
Barca do Lago
Ofir
Fão
3.7 Fão Santo António 3.5 (14.7 km)
Pousada da Juventude Foz do Cávado
río Cávado
Pedriñas
Parque Natural do Litoral Norte
Fonte Boa
5.1 Concello
N-205
Santiago
Apulia Praia
Apúlia 6.7
3.0 Apúlia
IC-14
N-205
Apulia
Ramalha
Orbitur
Campismo Rio Alto
Contriz
Golf
3.7 Option
A-28
IC-1
Estela
Futebol
Estela
6.1 Café
Palanca (+0.1k)
Andorinha
Barranha
Dunas
Caçador
Barranha
Codixeira
Aguçadoura 6.9
4.1 Aguçadoura
Cruceiro
Aguçadoura
Aguçadoura
Fábrica
Laundos
Magos
Santo André
Santo André
A-28
Ecopista / ciclopista
N-205
Rates
0.0
3.1 Puente
A Ver-o-Mar
Amorim
Fragosa
O
E
S
la salida del sol
N-206
Rio Mau
Ecopista
Lada
Póvoa 6.5
3.9 Praça da Republica
Póvoa Varzim
PÓVOA VARZIM
A-7
N-306
N-206
N-13
Junqueira
Touguinha
río Ave
Vila do Conde
VILA DO CONDE
0.0 Praça da Republica
N
W
E
S
Av.R.Gonçalves
ESPOSENDE
Bombeiros
Câmara
Centro
R.Faria
N.S.Saúde
N.Ferreira
Mira Rio
Cávado

ℹTurismo: Praça Marquês de Pombal © 252 298 120. •*Hs* **Sardines and Friends** *[6÷1]* €14 +*7* €35 © 962 083 329 www.sardinesandfriends.com r/Ponte 4. •*Hs* **Junqueira 76** *x7* €25-50 © 918 607 411 r/Junqueira, 76. •*H*** **Luso Brasileiro** *x62* €40+ © 252 690 710 r/ Dos Cafés 16. •*H**** **Grande Hotel** *x88* €65+ © 252 290 400 Largo do Passeio Alegre, 20. ●*Alb.***São José de Ribamar** *Par.[36÷4]* €-donativo © 252 622 314 (paróquia) Av. Mouzinho de Albuquerque N°32 & @N°54 •*H*** **Avenida** *x22* €38-48 © 252 683 222. We join the senda litoral at ☕ *Sol* on the coast road and head out along the Promenade and boardwalks that run alongside the sandy beaches to:

3.1 km **A Ver O Mar** ***puente***. We now leave the asphalt and modern suburbs and enter quieter pathways past the headland at Santo André and •*H* **Santo Andre** *x80* €58-68 © 252 615 666 www.hotelsantoandre.com Av. de S. André. Continue on boardwalks by ☕ *Caminho beach bar!* past Praia Pedra Negra *[***+350**m •*CR.* **Aguçadoura** *x4* €15pp © 252 010 865 + 300m on *r/ Guizos 120]*. into:

4.1 km **Aguçadoura** with ●*Alb* **Aguçadoura***[24÷6]* €15 alberguedeagucadou.wixsite.com Rua da Praia, 186. Route passes ☕ *Cruceiro* over river through Caçador ☕ *Dunas* passing football ground and golf course (left) to option for Praia Estela:

3.7 km **Opción *Praia Estela*** *option [***+500**m (left) ☕ 🍴 ▲ ***Rio Alto (Orbitur)*** *welcomes pilgrims €8-16+ © 252 615 699 continue via 'tunnel' to beach or boardwalks to Praia Apúlia]*. Sign Hotel 1500m= •*H*** **Contriz** *x30* €35-45 © 252 644 473 on r/Estela 2843 – or keep s/o along laneways & tracks into:

3.0 km **Apúlia** ***Igreja Matriz*** *[****Av. Praia N°67 +600****m* ●*Alb.***Santiago da Costa** *Priv.[9÷4]* €12 © 961 885 803. ***N°45*** •*H**** **Apulia Praia** *x44* €40+ © 253 989 290 www.apuliapraia-hotel.com *]*. Keep s/o through *Parque Natural* into:

3.7 km **Fão** ***Igreja do Bom Jesus*** *S.Antonio*. •*Hs* **Spot** *[8÷2]* €14 +*6* €30+ © 934 324 426 r/ dos Veigas 14. ●*Alb./Pousada* **Hi Ofir** *[90÷4] Foz do Cavado* €12+ © 253 982 045 Alameda Bom Jesus. ●*Hs* **Do Alto** *[16÷3]* €23 +3 €37-€45 © 912 652 602 r/ Alexandre Losa Faria, 4. *[Also: off route* **+1.2** *km several resort hotels at* ***Ofir*** *incl. •H***** ***Parque do Rio*** *€40-80 © 253 981 521 www.parquedorio.pt]*.

● ● ● ● **Rates – Fão** *alternativo* 14.7 km. This is the point at which the connecting route from Rates on the central route joins with the coastal way. Pilgrims still arrive here 'by default' as they fail to notice the detour waymarks in Rates. Either return to Rates (by foot or taxi) or continue along the coastal route.

Continue over río Cávado turn <left along estuary past welcoming •*Hs* **Sleep&Go** *[12÷2]* €11 +*2* €36 ✆ 932 005 800 Av. São Martinho (by roundabout + 200m) and •*H*** **Mira Rio** €40± ✆ 253 964 430 r/ Ponte D. Luis Filipe to 2nd roundabout. Here you can continue s/o along the estuary boardwalks to the albergue in Marinhas *or* veer s/o (right) into the main street to pleasant main square.

2.7 km **Esposende** ***Centro.*** *Population 9,000.* New waymarks into the *centro histórico* along rua Narciso Ferreira where at Nº57 is the welcoming new hostal ❶ *Alb.*Eleven *Priv.[12÷2]* €16 + *x1* €45 ✆ 962 651 485 [m] Vitor 253 039 303 + *menú* www.hosteleleven.pt r/Narciso Ferreira, 57 adj. Pelourinho XVIIc. Continue into the intimate main square ***Praça do Município*** *cafes* & *Pastelaria Doce Río* and Igreja da Misericórdia (left) with find statue of Santiago Peregrino (see photo right) and Concello *Paços do Concelho XVIth c.*

❶**Turismo** ✆ 253 960 100. **Other lodging:** ❷ *Hs* **Esposende** *x5* €20-55 ✆ 932 832 818 r/ Conde Agrolongo **Nº29** &@**Nº22** ❸ *Hs* **InnEsposende Sports** *[6÷1]* €14 +*10* €29-44 ✆ 932 466 542 www.innesposende.com ❹ *Hs* **Eskama** *x5* €30-€45 ✆ 916 952 098 Largo Dr. Fonseca Lima 4. •❺ *H**** **Zende** *x25* €30+ ✆ 253 969 090 Av. Dr. Henrique Barros Lima 23. ❻ **Clube Pinhal da Foz** €45-55 ✆ 253 961 098 r/Pinhal da Foz. Continue through town and turn <left down Av. Rocha Gonçalves opp. hospital to the seafront past ❼ *H**** **Suave Mar** *x88* €44-50 ✆ 253 969 400 www.suavemar.com

Note association albergue for Esposende is located at Marinhas 4.3 km the *far* side of town. ●*Alb.* **San Miguel** *Asoc. [34÷2]* €5 (donativo) ✆ 967 611 200. Popular pilgrim hostel with all facilities. Managed by *Via Veteris: Associação Jacobeia de Esposende: Manuel Miranda* ✆ 962 748 657 *e José Costa* 933 561 896 & Cruz Vermelha. The association plan to open a replica 'pilgrim ferry' over the Cávado River by Foz.

● ● ● ● **Detour:** ***Castro de São Lourenço y Mirador*** info: ✆ 253 960 179. [5 km or 10 minute by taxi – equidistant from Marinhas or the centre of Esposende]. Interesting collection of buildings and wonderful panoramic viewpoint of the coast. The site dates back to 4th century BCE and was occupied through the Roman and medieval periods.

15a Practical Path: The development in recent years of the ***Ecovia Litoral de Norte*** has greatly improved these coastal pathways. Extensive areas of new boardwalks *pasarelas de madera* has made the way easier to both navigate and walk. *Note that walking on soft sand makes for very slow progress and the camber of the sand can create stretched muscles. Try where possible to walk on flat areas of sand closer to the waters edge which is harder underfoot.* From Póvoa de Varzim to Aguçadoura the senda litoral coincides with the camino da costa. Beyond Aguçadoura football grounds the camino da Costa turns inland and the senda Litoral continues along the coast on a high level boardwalk skirting the Estela Golf Course into Apulia. The Senda Litoral is 2.5 km longer than the Camino da Costa: **26.9 km -v- 24.4 km**.

0.0 km **Vila do Conde** *centro.* ***Note:*** *All lodging is listed on previous pages.* We can avoid the traffic through ***Póvoa de Varzim*** By continuing from the **Centre of Vila do Conde [0.0** km] down the bank of the río Ave past the replica Caravel to Praia da Senhora da Guia and on past **Forte de São João Baptista [1.8** km] and the **marina** [**3.2** km] to rejoin Camino da Costa *(Alt. Route)* at Diana Bar opp. **Av. Mouzinho de Albuquerque** [**1.5** km]. 6.5 -v- 4.5 km.

6.5 km **Póvoa de Varzim** ***Promenada.*** We continue along the beach front to pasarela at **A Ver-o-Mar** [**3.1** km]. Here the Camino do Costa heads inland but we cross over onto new boardwalks that take us all the way over the high dunes past windmills (see picture top) to *Caminho Beach Bar* and hotel **Santo André** [**2.1** km] *(Alt. Route joins).* Continue to **Aguçadoura** [**1.7** km].

6.9 km **Aguçadoura**. Continue along the sand dunes to the Aguçadoura **football ground** [**1**.7 km] *(Alt. Route goes inland).* Take the narrow path by side of football stand and take high level boardwalk all the way to **Orbitur Camping** [**2.0** km]. The boardwalk continues to **Apulia** [**3.0** km] *(lodging previous page).*

6.7 km **Apulia** ***Promenada.*** The route veers right into **Fão** [**4.1** km] where the main route joins to continue over the rio Cavado into **Esposende** ***Centro*** [**2.**7 km]

6.8 km **Esposende** The Senda Litoral continues along the boardwalks but Esposende is well worth the short detour for its architectural merit and facilities. *(Lodging listed previous pages).* Adj. the main square is the equally delightful Largo Fonseca Lima with its boat fountain representing its maritime history and links to the 'Discoveries' with it's representation of a Caravel *Barca d' Agua (see photo> & above>)*

Personal Reflections:

16a ESPOSENDE – VIANA do CASTELO

Río Neiva

--- --- 7.8 --- --- *30%*
--- --- 15.6 --- --- *61%*
--- --- 2.2 --- --- *9%*
Total km **25.6** km *(15.9 ml)*

Total ascent **300**m *+½ hr*
▲ **Alto** *m* Neiva **140**m *(460 ft)*
<A H> ➲ Marinhas **4.3** km ➲ Antas **10.0**
➲ Castelo do Neiva **13.5** km ➲ Chafé **17.0** km ➲Darque **22.9** km.

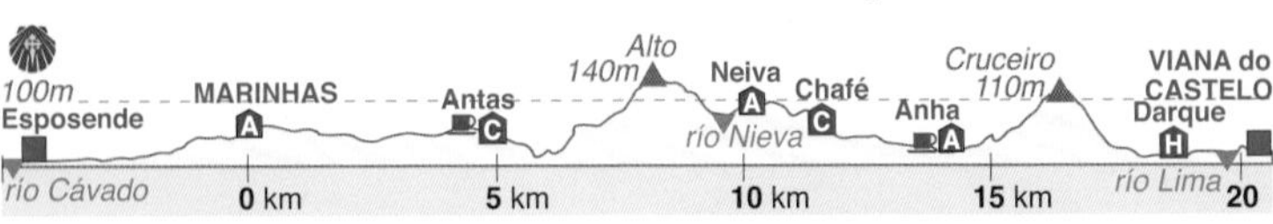

I am not particularly interested in saving time; I prefer to enjoy it.
Eduardo Hughes Galeano – novelist
Our lives are getting busier as we rush around our egoic world going nowhere, fast. Dismissive of those in the slow lane we unconsciously long for more spaciousness in our lives. We find it hard to walk slowly let alone stop to 'stand and stare' or witness the sunset. It takes courage and discipline to slow down. However, if we never move out of the fast lane perhaps we miss the point...

Practical Path: •*Camino da Costa:* quiet country lanes interspersed with stretches of woodland paths and river crossings in the hills parallel to the coast. Take time to visit the oldest extant structure directly related to the Santiago story, *Baselica Sancti Jacobi* in Castelo do Neiva which also has an albergue. We have two short but steep climbs on todays route. *[See page 218 for •**Senda Litoral.**]*

0.0 km **Esposende** ***centro*** s/o past Câmara and over road by Igreja Matriz and turn left opp. hospital to rejoin the **seafront** [**0.9** km]. Turn right past *Farol* & *Forte de São João Baptista* to option point by *Dunas* for **senda litoral** [**1.4** km]. Keep s/o and turn <left into r/Agrela and right> into Av. Praia back over main road N-13 *[!]* by the Red Cross *Cruz Vermelha* © 253 964 720 who hold key to the albergue when closed. S/o past chapel and <left into rua Padre Francisco Cubelo Soares to association albergue [**2.9** km].

4.3 km **Marinhas** pass the *alb* (photo and details p.211) *S.Miguel* (left) Iglesia Marinhas (right) and ●*Hs* **Costa Selvagem** *[6÷1]*+ €15 -€45 © 913 212 250. Follow country lanes passing 'bom caminho' signs from the local school into:

3.8 km **Belinho** several /. Next we enter San Amaro & **Antas** [**1.9** km] *Kabul* (adj. Quinta Paraiso) 200m later at r/Barão de Maracanã, 4 •*CR* **Antas** *x4* €17pp+ © 962 319 979 *www.antasguesthouse.pt* We now begin our ascent to the high point of this stage (140m). A delightful stretch of woodland paths that wind down to the pedestrian bridge *pasarela* over the **river Nieva** [**1.7** km]:

3.6 km **Ponte Neiva** cross river on stepping stones. Note this is a spate river and if in flood you must retrace your steps to take road bridge (see note and photo on p.207). Continue up into woods on onto a country lanes to Capilla N.S.Guadalupe

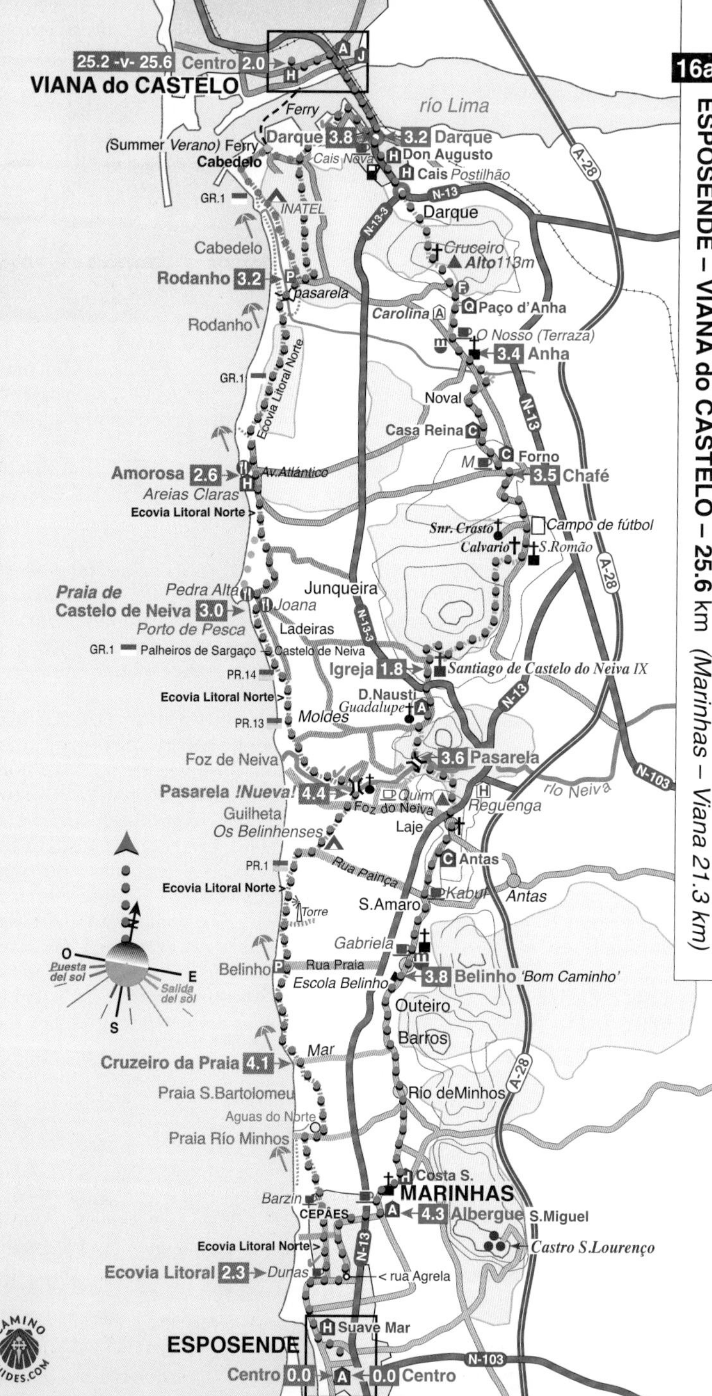

16a
ESPOSENDE – VIANA do CASTELO – 25.6 km (Marinhas – Viana 21.3 km)
25.2 -v- 25.6 Centro 2.0
VIANA do CASTELO
río Lima
Ferry
(Summer Verano) Ferry
Cabedelo
Darque 3.8
3.2 Darque
Cais Nova
Don Augusto
Cais Postilhão
A-28
N-13
GR.1
INATEL
N-13-3
Darque
Cabedelo
Cruceiro
Alto 113m
Rodanho 3.2
pasarela
Paço d'Anha
Carolina
Rodanho
O Nosso (Terraza)
3.4 Anha
Ecovia Litoral Norte
GR.1
Noval
N-13
Casa Reina
Forno
Amorosa 2.6
Av.Atlántico
3.5 Chafé
Areias Claras
Ecovia Litoral Norte
Snr. Crasto
Campo de fútbol
Calvario
S.Romão
A-28
Praia de Castelo de Neiva 3.0
Pedra Alta
Junqueira
Joana
Porto de Pesca
Ladeiras
GR.1
Palheiros de Sargaço
Castelo de Neiva
N-13-3
Igreja 1.8
Santiago de Castelo do Neiva IX
PR.14
Ecovia Litoral Norte
D.Nausti
Guadalupe
N-13
PR.13
Moldes
Foz de Neiva
3.6 Pasarela
N-103
Pasarela !Nueva! 4.4
Quim
rio Neiva
Reguenga
Guilheta
Foz do Neiva
Laje
Os Belinhenses
Antas
PR.1
Rua Painça
Ecovia Litoral Norte
Kabul
Antas
S.Amaro
Torre
Gabriela
O
Puesta del sol
E
Salida del sol
S
Belinho
Rua Praia
Escola Belinho
3.8 Belinho 'Bom Caminho'
Outeiro
Barros
Mar
Cruzeiro da Praia 4.1
A-28
Praia S.Bartolomeu
Río deMinhos
Aguas do Norte
Praia Río Minhos
Costa S.
Barzin
MARINHAS
CEPÃES
4.3 Albergue
S.Miguel
Ecovia Litoral Norte
Castro S.Lourenço
N-13
Ecovia Litoral 2.3
Dunas
< rua Agrela
Suave Mar
ESPOSENDE
N-103
Centro 0.0
0.0 Centro
CAMINO GUIDES.COM

adj. ●*Alb.* **Don Nausti** *Mun.[20÷2]* €6-10 +*1* €20 ✆ 962 471 251 to:

1.8 km **Igreja *Santiago de Castelo do Neiva*.** *[During reconstruction of the church (see photo>) important archaeological items were discovered: a votive altar from the Roman period and an inscription of consecration of the original church dedicated to Santiago dating from the year 862. This is the oldest consecration to the apostle ever found outside Spain].* •*CR.* **Santiago** *x3* €30 ✆ 964 560 104 mod. house just before the church. Our route continues up on woodland path behind the church to emerge at the monastery of São Romão (right) with steps up to the Capela Snr Crasto (left). Continue into:

3.5 km **Chafé Igreja S. Sebastiao** ☕ *M* opp. •*CR.* ✪ **Campo do Forno** *x4* €25-30 Fatima ✆ 934 122 695. Continue past •*CR* **Casa da Reina** *x5* €60+ ✆ 258 351 882 c/Pardinheiro, 122. Continue through Noval into:

3.4 km **Anha** several cafes and shops ☕ *O Nosso+terraza [+**500m** ●Alb. **Carolina** Priv.[8÷2]* €15 ✆ *969 004 514 on main road Av. 9 Julho].* Keep s/o past •*H**** **Paço d'Anha** €30-60 ✆ 258 322 459 www.pacoanha.com quinta and up into woodland past monument and *almina* (left) to Cross of the Fallen *Cruzeiro da Matança* as we begin our descent distant views open up of the río Lima estuary and Viana do Castelo beyond. We cross the busy N-13 over waste ground into Darque industrial park opp. Galp: •*H** **Cais** *x23* €40+ ✆ 258 331 031. •*P.* **Don Augusto** €40 ✆ 258 322 491 parallel to N-13 to roundabout by estuary where pilgrims on the Senda Litoral join for the short stretch into Viana town centre.

3.0 km **Darque** Take the bridge over the río Lima *(pilgrims on the camino central cross 25 km upstream in Ponte de Lima)* into **VIANA DO CASTELO** roundabout ***Praça Dom Afonso III*** and ***option*** (see town plan). Over to the right: ●*Alb.* **São João da Cruz** *Conv.do Carmo [20÷4]* €10 +*6* €27-50 ✆ 258 822 264 Rua do Carmo 1. ●**Pousada de Juventude** *Mun.[40÷2]* €11-13 ✆ 258 838 458 Rua de Limia. •*H*** **Do Parque** *x120* €30+ ✆ 258 828 605 Praça da Galiza. •*H** **Calatrava** *x15* €50+ ✆ 258 828 911 r/Manuel Fiúza 157. For the centre of town and cathedral turn <left into r/Gontim (N°70) •*H**** **Fábrica do Chocolate** *x18* €80+ ✆ 258 244 000 s/o into narrow r/ Mateus Barbosa and up right> into r/ Gago Coutinho (N°26) •*Hs* **Zimborio** *x2* €45 ✆ 938 354 863 into:

2.7 km **Viana do Castelo** ▮***Praça da Republica*** central plaza & fountain *Chafariz* (photo>) adj. council offices *antigo Paços do Concelho* costume museum *museo do Traje* and lively *cafés*. The **cathedral** ***Sé*** *XV*[th]c and *Igreja Matriz* on r/ Sacadura Cabral. Hub of activity continue along r/Picota to Av. dos Combatentes & ▮***Praça da Liberdade*** by the harbour ❶**Turismo** ✆ 258 098 415. 10-13/14-18 (closed Sun/Mon). •*Hs* **Enjoy Viana** *x8* €30-39

✆ 914 668 475 r/M.Romaria, 53 opp.Câmara. Nearby on r/ Cândido dos Reis 45 •*H*** **Laranjeira** *x30* €52+ ✆ 258 822 261. •*P.* **Dona Emília** *x6* €38+ ✆ 917 811 392 www.dona-emilia.com •*Hs* **Senhora do Carmo** *x10* €23-35 ✆ 927 811 099 r/Grande 72. By harbour ▌**Largo 5 de Outubro Nº58** •*H**** **Margarida Da Praça** €57+ ✆ 258 809 630. **Nº68** •*H*** **Jardim** *x20* €40-50 ✆ 258 828 915. ▌**Av. Combatentes Nº49** •*Hs* **Avenida** *x10* €23-35 ✆ 927 811 099 www.avenidaviana.com above ☕ *Paris.* Pilgrim office AACS ✆ 968 523 593 r/General Luís do Rego 149.

Viana do Castelo: Evidence of human settlement dates to the Mesolithic era 10,000 BCE. The Romans established a presence in until the 2nd century CE. Afonso III issued a royal charter in 1258 and Viana was an important port during the Portugese Discoveries in the 16th century and became a cathedral city under the reign of Queen Maria II in 1848 when it reached the height of its commercial activity centred around the export of wine, fruit and cod *bacalhau*. The city population is 88,000 with a strong tourist trade in the summer. **Monte Santa Luzia** is accessible by foot but this requires a very steep climb up innumerable steps. A Funicular makes a pleasant alternative (see plan – easy access via the rail station) or a taxi ride 3.5 km by road. The rather austere neo-Byzantine sanctuary *O Santuário de Santa Luzia* also known as *Templo do Sagrado Coração de Jesus* stands sentinel atop the hill from where there are splendid views over the coastline and up the Lima river www.templosantaluzia.org ●*Alb.* **S.Lucia** *Conv.[38÷5]* €15-25 ✆ 258 823 173 mod. bldg. with excellent facilities and views! adj. basilica. Also •*H***** **Pousada** *x80* €120+! ✆ 2588 00 370. To the rear are the ruins of a Celtiberian fortified village *citânia* dating from the 4th century BC.

Santiago Peregrino is well represented in town with one of the original gates into the medieval city known as *Porta de Santiago* and the original pilgrim hostel *hospital velho* was built in 1468 as a pilgrim inn (until recently used as the tourist office). On rua de Santiago is the old Santiago hall *Recolhimento de Santiago* with image of the saint above the entrance door. All attest to the popularity of the coastal route in the medieval period. Local pilgrimage *Romaria da Nossa Senhora da Agonia* end of August.

16a Interim accommodation:
➲ Amorosa **16.4** km ➲ Cabadelo **23.2**

Practical Path: The ***Ecovia Litoral*** has come up trumps with the building of a fine footbridge *pasarela* over the rio Neiva *(see photo>)* close to its estuary *Foz de Neiva*. This single initiative has transformed this route and made it accessible by coast path from Esposende to Amorosa. There are plans to extend the boardwalks all the way to Cabadelo. In the meantime we head inland to join with the main route to cross the Lima estuary into Viana do Castelo. The entire stage is level.

0.0 km **Esposende *centro*** Exit via Câmara and s/o over road by Igreja Matriz turn <left opp. Hospital to rejoin the **seafront [0.9** km]. Turn right> past *Farol* & *Forte de São João Baptista* to option point by ☕ *Dunas* for **senda litoral** [**1.4** km] (see photo>).

2.3 km **Senda Litoral *option*** We branch off from the Camino da Costa at this point and continue along a new section of the Ecovia past **Praia de Cepães** [**0.9** km] ☕ *Bazin* to **Rio Minhos** [**1.4** km] beach parking [🚰] and marshland. At this point we have to turn inland turning first left past *ETAR Marinhas* water treatment plant to make our way back to the coast at Praia de São Bartolomeu and just beyond **Cruzeiro de Praia de Mar** [**1.8** km].

4.1 km **Cruzeiro de Praia** (no facilities). Waymarks are unclear at this point but we make our way along track parallel to the beach. This peters out at a field and a hand drawn arrow points us to a path onto the beach before veering back onto track to **Belinho Praia *Parking*** [**1.4** km] *(Belinho town is 1.8 km inland).* Continue past turnoff to prominent observation tower **Torre de Observação** [**0.6** km]. Continue to Praia da Carruagem (the old railway carriage *carruagem* has been removed following a fire) and head inland (to avoid the estuary) past **Campismo de Belinho** [**1.6** km] ▲ **Os Belinhenses** ✆ 933 612 546. and s/o (not well waymarked) over **rua Foz do Neiva** [**0.7** km] *(sign for Toca Bar 200m is in fact 700m [1.4 km return!])* onto riverside path to pedestrian footbridge *pasarela* (photo top) over the **rio Nieva** [**0.2** km].

4.5 km **Pasarela *rio Neiva*.** We now take a delightful path around the beautiful river estuary *Estuário do Rio Neiva* (See photo bottom of next page) and turn left up just past the large lodge (children holiday hostel) onto **Rua da Dunas** [**1.7** km] now part of the Ecovia Litoral (variously PR-1 / PR-13 / PR-14) and keep s/o to roundabout in **Praia de Castelo do Neiva** [**1.3** km].

3.0 km ***Praia* de Castelo do Neiva *Rotunda*** *(the town is 1.7 km inland).* Lodging here seems to be limited to week-long holiday lets but there is a range of restaurants. Adj. roundabout 🍴 *Segredos Do Mar* or try the delightful 🍴 *Casa da Joana* adj. 🍴 *Taberna da Laurinda*. Just above the village by the fish market *Posto* *de Vendagem* 🍴 *Pedra Alta*. Until the Ecovia Litoral is extended the route remains poorly waymarked out of the village. Either take the high level sandy path by the fishing boats or take one of the lower tracks that meander back to the seashore at **Praia de Lordelo [1.4** km] *(no facilities)*. At this point we can continue along the beach (no path) or turn right inland to join the waymarks on road into **Amorosa roundabout** [**1.1** km].

2.5 km Amorosa ***rotunda***. •*H*** Areias Claras €35+ ✆ 258 351 014. Various shops, bars & restaurants, shops, chemist, ATM. Head out on Av. Marginal parallel to seashore and s/o to path at ☕ **Pénareia [0.5** km] onto path (boardwalk left peters out on beach) and head s/o over the dunes or veer right onto woodland path (both paths are the same distance and lead to Rodanho car park). Continue to small bridge over the **Ribeira de Anha** [**1.8** km] and either continue s/o over dune paths to turn right over boardwalk bridge to Rodanho (it is not possible to cross the estuary further on) or turn right over the stone bridge turning left on road to **Rodanho Car Park** [**0.7** km].

3.0 km Rodanho ***Car Park*** There are several ways to enter Viana do Castelo. The most direct is to take the road and turn left 200m onto **woodland path** [**0.2** km] (sign Praia Eemiana) and continue past **Orbitur Camping** [**2.0** km] ▲ **Orbitur** €8+ ✆ 258 322 167 r/Diogo Álvares. At this point we can keep s/o to hotels, bars and ferry (summer) in **Cabedelo** (1 km) •*H**** **FeelViana.** •*H*** **Cais** *x46* €120+! ✆ 258 330 330. Turn right to Av. do Cabedelo •*Hs* **Cabedelo** €60-70 (Booking.com only) past the commercial port and onto pedestrian walkway through parkland to Capela de S. Lourenço. Here we turn right around a sea inlet to join the Camino da Costa at **roundabout in Darque** [**1.6** km].

3.8 km Darque ***Rotunda*** We now join our fellow pilgrims to cross the rio Lima via narrow walkway alongside the traffic down to town roundabout. Take the level crossing into Rua do Gontim and keep s/into pedestrian Rua Mateus Barbosa turning right into Rua Sacadura Cabral past cathedral to Praça da República.

2.0 km Viana do Castelo ***Praça da República*** See previous pages for accommodation and other facilities and town map.

17a VIANA do CASTELO – CAMINHA

(path)	--- ---	10.7	--- ---	*40%*
(quiet road)	--- ---	16.2	--- ---	*60%*
(main road)	--- ---	0.0	--- ---	*00%*
Total km		**26.9** km *(16.7 ml)*		

Total ascent **365**m *+¾ hr*

▲ Alto *m* Cruceiro **150**m *(492 ft)*

< A H > ➲Carreço **9.0** km ➲Afife **12.1** km ➲Vila Praia de Âncora **19.0** km.

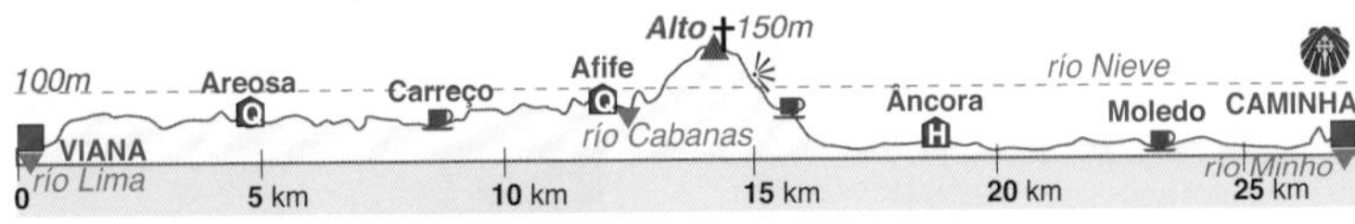

What can we gain by sailing to the moon if we are not able to cross the abyss that separates us from ourselves? This is the most important of all voyages of discovery, and without it, all the rest are useless. *Thomas Merton*

Inner Camino: Adventurers left this harbour in search of new lands that lay over the horizon. This was the age of the 'Discoveries' and Portugal played no small part in this quest. But did these great navigators of old discover anything new? The natives of the Americas already knew their land well and had long harvested its riches. Today we set out on a new quest; to discover Who we really are – beyond the external drama of our human story – to what lies Within. This is the urgent task of our time and we must find the courage to set sail without delay. Our destination is assured and will, perhaps, be familiar when we arrive. We but journey back to the Source from whence we came.

Practical Path: •*Camino da Costa* offers varied terrain with distant views of the coast and several sections through woodland offering shade. However 60% is on asphalt, mostly quiet country lanes. The route out of town is complicated – stay focussed! *See town plan on p.217.* We cross the N-13 to take a steep climb up into Boa Viagem. The route now undulates with another steep climb up to Cruzeiro da Matança before dropping down to Âncora whence our route joins the Senda Litoral and is level all the way to Caminha. It is 2.0 km shorter than the alternative beach paths 26.9 -v- 28.9. See p.224 for •***Senda Litoral.***

0.0 km **Viana do Castelo** ***centro*** From Praça da Republica into r/M da Romaria (Santander) turn <left into Rua Cândido dos Reis (Laranjeira) s/o over Av. dos Combatentes into Rua Gen. Luís do Rego by Red Cross *Cruz Vermelha*. Pass the pilgrim offices AACS at 149/151 and turn right> into Largo 9 de Abril and take the *underpass* N-13 and veer up <left and imm. right> into rua Portela de Cima which leads *over* the N-202 and up onto Rua. Dr. Moisés Alves Pinho where the route levels out and waymarks become clearer, through woodland to Areosa *Alta* and on to the grand old Quinta da Boa Viagem.

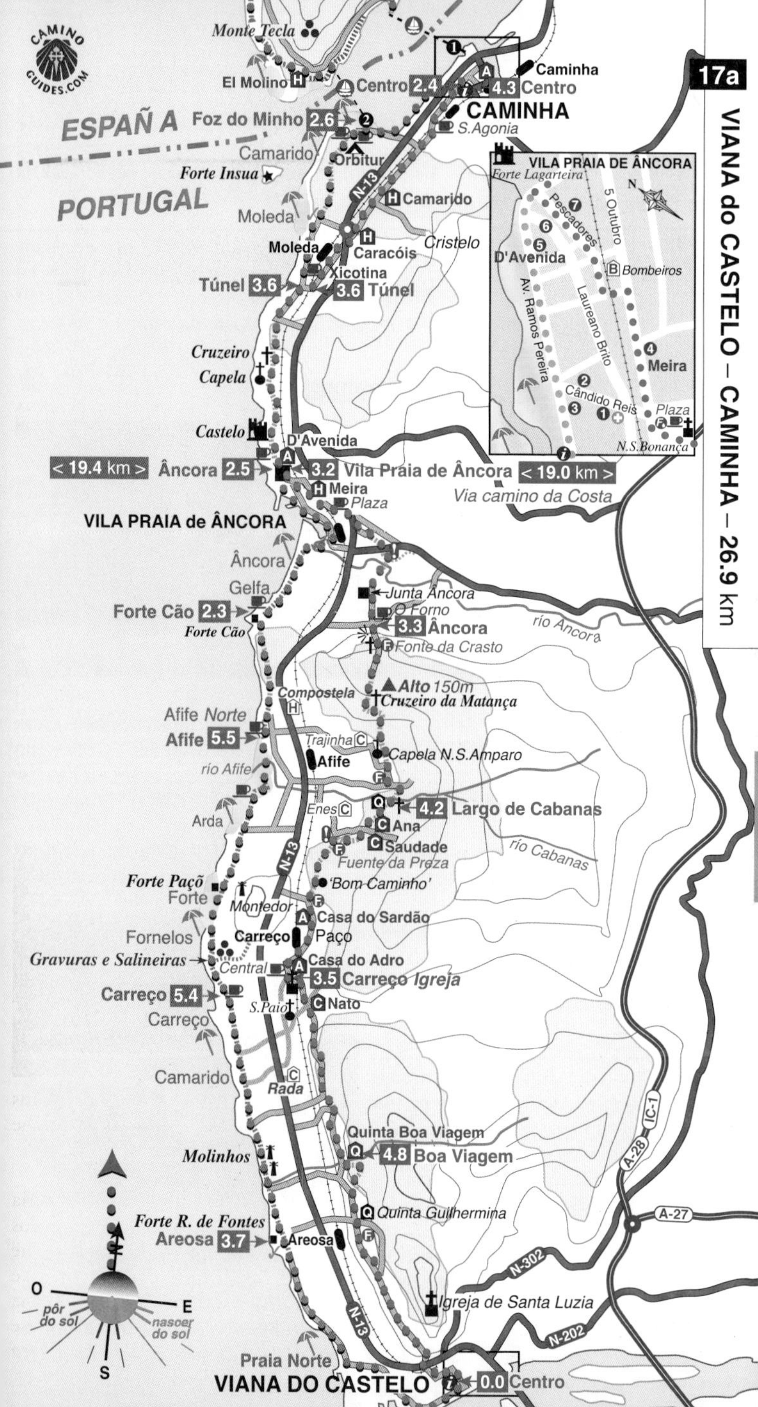
17a
VIANA do CASTELO – CAMINHA – 26.9 km
CAMINHA
Caminha
Centro 4.3
Centro 2.4
Monte Tecla
El Molino
Foz do Minho 2.6
S.Agonia
ESPAÑ A
PORTUGAL
Camarido
Orbitur
Forte Insua
Camarido
Moleda
Moleda
Caracóis
Cristelo
Xicotina
Túnel 3.6
3.6 Túnel
Cruzeiro
Capela
Castelo
D'Avenida
< 19.4 km > Âncora 2.5
3.2 Vila Praia de Âncora < 19.0 km >
Meira
Plaza
Via camino da Costa
VILA PRAIA de ÂNCORA
VILA PRAIA DE ÂNCORA
Forte Lagarteira
Pescadores
5 Outubro
D'Avenida
Bombeiros
Laureano Brito
Av. Ramos Pereira
Meira
Cândido Reis
Plaza
N.S.Bonança
Âncora
Gelfa
Forte Cão 2.3
Forte Cão
Junta Âncora
O Forno
3.3 Âncora
río Âncora
Fonte da Crasto
Alto 150m
Compostela
Cruzeiro da Matança
Afife Norte
Afife 5.5
Trajinha
Capela N.S.Amparo
Afife
río Afife
Enes
4.2 Largo de Cabanas
Arda
Ana
Saudade
río Cabanas
Fuente da Preza
N-13
'Bom Caminho'
Forte Paço
Forte
Montedor
Casa do Sardão
Fornelos
Carreço
Paço
Gravuras e Salineiras
Central
Casa do Adro
3.5 Carreço Igreja
Carreço 5.4
S.Paio
Nato
Carreço
Camarido
Rada
Quinta Boa Viagem
4.8 Boa Viagem
Molinhos
Quinta Guilhermina
Forte R. de Fontes
Areosa 3.7
Areosa
A-28
IC-1
A-27
N-302
O
E
pôr do sol
nascer do sol
S
Igreja de Santa Luzia
N-202
Praia Norte
VIANA DO CASTELO
0.0 Centro

4.8 km **Boa Viagem** •*Apt.***Quinta da Boa Viagem** *x5* €70+ © 258 835 835 historic quinta in quiet suburb of Viana. *[N-13 +**400**m off route •Alb.CR* **Rada** *Priv.[**6**÷1]* €14 *+3* €30+ © *966 211 969 Tv. Vinha Nova].* The route goes down to rail bridge (left) *Capela S.Paio.* Keep s/o right past •*CR* **Nato** *x8* €65-75 incl. © 258 834 041 www.casadonato.com r/Moreno 130 and s/o into **Carreço.**

3.5 km **Carreço** ***Iglesia*** Cross rail line by *Central* & ●*Alb.***Casa do Adro** *Priv.[20÷2]* €14 *+2* €40 © 966 557 617. Recross to station *Estação* and s/o to ●*Alb.***Casa do Sardão** *[**20**÷2]* €12 where Hugo Lopes welcomes © 961 790 759 Av. do Paço 769. Head back up into woodland around **Armada *Afife*.** *[+ 500m off route •CR* ***Trajinha*** *x3* €55 © 918 712 179 c/Tomenga, 438. *+100m* •*CR* **Penedo da Saudade** *x4* €40 © 936 839 698. •*CR* **Santa Ana** *x2* €75 © 258 981 774.

4.2 km **Largo da Cabanas** peaceful riverside oasis overlooked by *Quinta e São João de Cabanas* and its fine Magnolia inspiring poet Alberto D'Oliveira to hyperbole in his praise but the tree is looking somewhat worse for wear like the fading pink of the Quinta itself! We cross the bridge over the río Cabanas up into woodland to the high point of this stage at Cruzeiro da Matança at which point we start our long descent to:

3.3 km **Âncora** [ ] *fonte do Crasto* *Forno* local government offices *Junta De Freguesia* on r/Calvário. Cross the río Âncora and veer s/o left to enter the town via the eastern suburbs (poor waymarking) past municipal swimpool *under* N-13 into *Praça da República* *Praça* into r/ 5 Outubro past ❹ *H****Meira** *x54* €60-70 © 258 911 111 www.hotelmeira.com *&* *Dna Belinha* and turn <left on r/ Celestino Fernandes (by side of fire station *Bombeiros*) and over the rail line onto the promenade with colourful bars and restaurants (see below) to Âncora castle.

3.2 km **Vila Praia de Âncora *Castelo.*** **Lodging: *r/Cândido dos Reis* @Nº23** ❶*Apt.***Quinta Vila Praia** *x20* €40+© 258 950 050 **@Nº32** ❷**Baixinho** *x8* €60. ***Av. Ramos Pereira*** *(beach front)* **@Nº115** ❸**Quim Barreiros** *x26* €40 © 258 959 100. **@Nº 353** ❺*Alb.Hs* **D'Avenida** *[18÷3]* €10 *+20* €40 © 258 407 764 www.hosteldavenida.com ❻*P.* **Farol do Portinho** *x6* €24 © 258 911 542 r/Laureano Brito, 82. ❼*P** **Abrigo Portinho** *x7* €30 © 258 911 577 r/ Pescadores 22. Continue on coastal path with Monte Tecla visible ahead. Caminos Costa & Litoral merge onto a gravel path alongside rail line to the outskirts of Moledo where they separate again (see next page for Senda Litoral).

3.6 km **Moledo *opción.*** Main route turns right under rail. *[s/o for •P.* **Xicotina** *x3* €20-40 © *912 279 889 Av. Santana, 556].* Pass station to roundabout •*Hs* **Caracóis e Borboletas** *x6* €35 © 258 722 104 & take road parallel to N-13

into **Camarido** •*Apt* **Aldeamento do Camarido** €65 ✆ 258 722 130 Lugar da Joaninha, Cristelo. Cross rail past station in **Largo Senhora da Agonia** @N°13 *AL*•*P* **Litos** *x6* €30+ ✆ 938 452 300. ●*Alb.* **Bom Caminha** *[14÷2]* €15 +*3* €45 ✆ 963 528 441 (Vani) r/Benemérito Joaquim Rosas 25-29. Keep s/o into main square in Caminha:

4.3 km **Caminha** ***Centro Praça Conselheiro Silva Torres*** clock tower *Torre do Relogio* (see photo>) & centre of activity with *cafes & restaurants* +❶**Turismo:** ✆ 258 921 952 Open: 9:30–13:00 /14:00–17:30 + ferry sailing times. •*H***** **Design & Wine** *x23* €50+ ✆ 258 719 040 & •*Hs* **Caminha** *x4* €45+ ✆ 968 939 660 www.caminhahostelandsuites.pt **Other Lodging:** •*P* **Galo D'Ouro** *x10* €30-40 ✆ 258 921 160 r/Corredoura 15. •*H* **Muralha** *x7* €50 ✆ 258 728 199 r/Barão S.Roque 69. •*P** **Arca Nova** *Priv.[20÷1]* €14+*12* €20-40 ✆ 935 390 402 Largo Sidónio Pais adj. •*P. Rio Coura* (opp. rail station). ●*Alb.* **Caminha** *Asoc.[30÷2]* €6 ✆ 914 290 431 Av Padre Pinheiro *(adj. Zarcus & piscina municipal* pilgrim hostel on river estuary. **Suburbs: +2.4** km from town centre ▲ **Orbitur** €8-14 ✆ 258 921 295 Praia do Foz do Minho. **+1.5** km on N-13. •*H***** **Porta do Sol** *x110* €100+ ✆ 258 710 360.

FERRY: ❶ **Principal ferry** ✆ 986 611 526 from main harbour in Caminha. ❷ **Taxi Mar** (Marco) ✆ 915 955 827. ❸ **Mário Gonçalves** ✆ 963 416 259 from the beach at Foz do Minho to beach by Hotel Molino €6. *[**Note** ferries are dependent on strong tidal flows of the Minho estuary. It was at this point that the currach carrying Irish pilgrims capsized in 2017. See Camino Voyage www.anupictures.com].* In the event ferries are not running (main ferry closed Mondays) you have the option **[a] Walk:** there is a pleasant riverside route *passeio fluvial / Ecopista* mostly by pedestrian track and pathways. See next page. **[b] Taxi** to A Guarda (27 km via Vila Nova de Cerveira and road bridge over rio Minho into Spain).

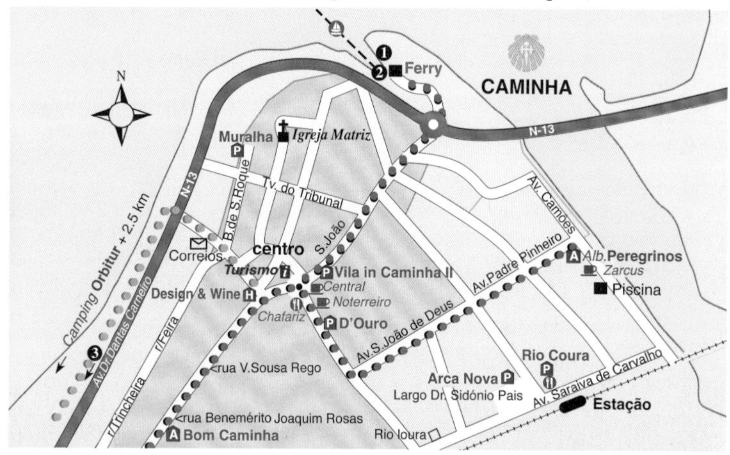

17a *Viana do Castelo – Caminha*

Interim accommodation: ➲ Âncora **16.4** km ➲ Modelo **23.2** km. (see also Camino da Costa). This delightful route hugs the coast with remote beaches and ancient forts. It has several beach cafes (summer) and is almost entirely by tranquil beach paths and sand dunes but exposed to coast with little shelter against sun or wind (see photo above of partly obliterated path). Unlike yesterdays stage from Amorosa it is easy to follow and virtually flat the entire way.

0.0 km **Viana do Castelo** ***centro*** From Praça da Republica head into r/M da Romaria (Banco Santander) turn <left into Rua Cândido dos Reis (Hotel Laranjeira) s/o over the wide Av. dos Combatentes into Rua Gen. Luís do Rego by Red Cross *Cruz Vermelha (right)*. Pass the pilgrim offices AACS at 149/151 and turn right> into **Largo 9 de Abril** [**0.5** km]. This is the point we leave the alternative camino da costa and turn <left into Rua de São Tiago passing *Recolhimento de Santiago* with image of the saint above the entrance door. We pass along the Jardim Dom Fernando and across busy roundabout and s/o down the busy Av. do Atlantico to the seafront at Praia Norte [**1.4** km]. We take the seafront promenade to Forte da Areosa [**1.2** km].

3.1 km **Forte da Areosa** *[•One of several forts we pass between here and Caminha which were built between 1640 – 1668 to suppress the frequent pirate raids on the Portuguese coast]*. We continue along the seafront passing numerous windmill Moinho de Vento all the way to our first refreshment stop at Carreço.

5.4 km **Carreço** ***Praia*** *[Carreço town is located inland on the camino da Costa 1.3 km with various accommodation options see previous page]*. The beach bar is a popular pilgrim pit-stop open most of the year ☕ *Areia*. Good place to contemplate the alternatives ahead at the Iron Age salt pans *Pias Salineiras de Fornelos* chiselled into the rocks at this point. **Option** [0.4 km]. **Ⓐ** ***High level route via Moinos de Montedor 2.4 km to Paços*** part of the revitalised Senda Litoral de Norte. Proceed up Rua de Fornelos to Montedor windmills [**0.5** km] continue to new ecopista through woodland offering shade but with intermittent views of the coastal path below. Follow the waymarks down to beach and carpark at Paços:

2.4 km **Paços** ***Praia*** *Estação da Biodivesidade de Montedor* and romantic ruins of Forte Paços (left). ☕ *Quiosque* (summer).

Option [0.4 km]. **Ⓑ** ***seashore route 2.2 km to Paços.*** We pass the salt pans and various prehistoric carvings *gravuras* on the rocks nearby as we scramble through a gap in the rocky foreshore to pick up a rough path that passes **Torre de Montedor** [**0.5** km]. We follow the seashore to cross a beautiful sandy beach with the ruins of Forte de Paços to join the alternative route to **Paços car park** [**1.3** km].

From Paços we continue onto track veering inland along the Ecovia past Praia da Arda to **Praia Afife** [**2.9** km] (100m left. Bar Summer). Continue onto cobbled road *rua adoquinado* that becomes a rough track through woodland (awaiting Ecovia upgrading) passing (left) Praia Ínsua and then Gelfa (no facilities) to **Forte do Cão** [**2.1** km].

5.0 km **Forte do Cão** Best preserved of these forts on rocky promontory. Closeby is *Camarão* (You'll pay for the seaview). We continue along paths and boardwalks to ▲ **rio Âncora estuary option [1.4** km] by Âncora Praia football grounds: Ⓐ head inland along the Ecovia boardwalks and pathways to railway bridge and then back into the town to pedestrian bridge over the **rio Âncora [1.5** km] (see photo>)and continue along the promenade to **Forte da Largarteira [0.5** km].

3.4 km **Vila Praia de Âncora** ***Forte da Largarteira***

At option point ▲ Ⓑ (1.0 km shorter) make your way down over the sandy estuary and up alongside woodland path at Caldeirões over pedestrian bridge to **Âncora promenade [0.5** km]. continue along the promenade with its colourful Restaurants, Bars, Cafés and variety of Lodging to **Forte da Largarteira [0.5** km].

See previous pages 222/223 for details of facilities and accommodation in **Vila Praia de Âncora**. We continue along the seashore (this stretch coincides with the Camino da Costa) and turn <left by **Capela Santo Isidoro [1.9** km] onto new Ecovia by seashore *[the 'old' route continues s/o past Cruzeiro de Santo Isidoro to rejoin new ecovia just before Moleda]* **Moleda option point** [**2.0** km].

3.9 km **Moleda** ***option point***. *[The Camino da Costa turns inland under the rail tunnel]*. For Senda Litoral continue s/o along the promenade with various cafes and restaurants. Keep s/o after *Mergulho* along cobbled road to enter a delightful woodland path [**1.0** km] [beach bar *Pé Na Praia* left]. The path continues to **Praia Foz do Minho [1.6** km].

2.6 km **Praia Foz do Minho.** Capela N.S. das Areias *Barracuda* ▲ *Camping* **Orbitur Caminha park** from €50 bungalow © 258 921 295. Marina for **Maritime Taxi** © 931 636 360 [m] 967 094 630 with the colourful *Capitão Mário* who will whisk you to the beach on the other side of the estuary for €5 at anytime of day. **Note** the town of **Caminha is 2.4** km around the estuary. See previous pages for facilities and accommodation if you intend to stay the night in Caminha before taking the ferry from the main port in the morning or heading up river on the ecovia to Vila Nova de Cerveira and Valenca and Tui on the camino Cental.

17b CAMINHA – VALENÇA / TUI

	--- ---	10.9	--- ---	*40%*
	--- ---	16.5	--- ---	*60%*
	--- ---	0.0	--- ---	*00%*
Total km		**29.9** km *(18.6 ml)*		

Total ascent **150**m ±¼ *hr*

▲ Alto *m* Valença 95m *(310 ft)*

<A H> V.N. Cerveira **14.4** km. *Loivo / Segirém alt.* ***12.0*** *km.*

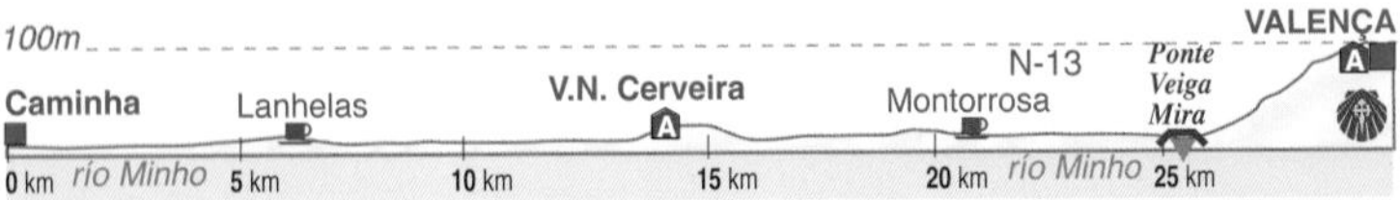

What you are is what you have been, what you will be is what you do now.
Buddha

Inner Camino: *that we reap what we sow is a generally accepted truism and follows closely the concept of karma. Jesus exhorted us to, Do to others as you would have them do to you. This Golden Rule follows closely the Buddhist prayer, May all beings have happiness and the causes of happiness. Every day we are presented a choice of which path to walk but the real question is how do we choose to treat everyone we meet along the way. We might turn to the silent Hindu greeting for help, 'When the God in me greets the God in you, in that we are One'.*

Practical Path: The Minho separates Portugal from Spain and this route provides an alternative link to ❶ A Guarda from Caminha via the bridge in Vila Nova de Cerveira (necessary if the ferries aren't running). ❷ links the *camino da Costa* with *camino Central* in Valença for the crossing into Tui. A new ***Ecopista*** was recently opened alongside the river providing a quiet traffic free path along the riverbank. This river route is the one described here. The original route along quiet country lanes above the N-13 is still well waymarked.

0.0 km **Caminha *Ferry*** From the terminal take road bridge over the río Couro and keep s/o (right) ***off*** the N-13 onto track and over railway and back onto N-13. *[**After 400**m alt. inland route right> by* ☕ *Capital rua Parede Alta* ***•R São Pedro €50*** *✆ 258 727 486 www.residencialsaopedro.com +* ***●Alb.S.Bento*** *p.228].* For river route continue for 150m and turn <left after **cemetery** (opp. BP services).

2.9 km **Cementerio *Capela de São Sebastião*** continue down lane over rail to the Minho which we now follow (more or less) all the way to Valença along a new ***Ecovia*** for pedestrians and cyclists. ***Seixas*** [**0.4** km]. *[access road* rua do Praia *to N-13 several* ☕ *&* ***•Q Villa Idalina €65*** *✆ 258 724 367 its ornate tower clearly visible].* Keep s/o along Av. Marginal to chapel ***Capela de São Sebastião*** [**0.8** km]. *[Access road to N-13* ***•R O Forno*** *€30 ✆ 258 727 757 Av. São Sebastião Seixas].* S/o Ecovia and **over rail** [**1.4** km] onto N-13 (wide margin) which we follow into **Lanhelas** [**0.8** km].

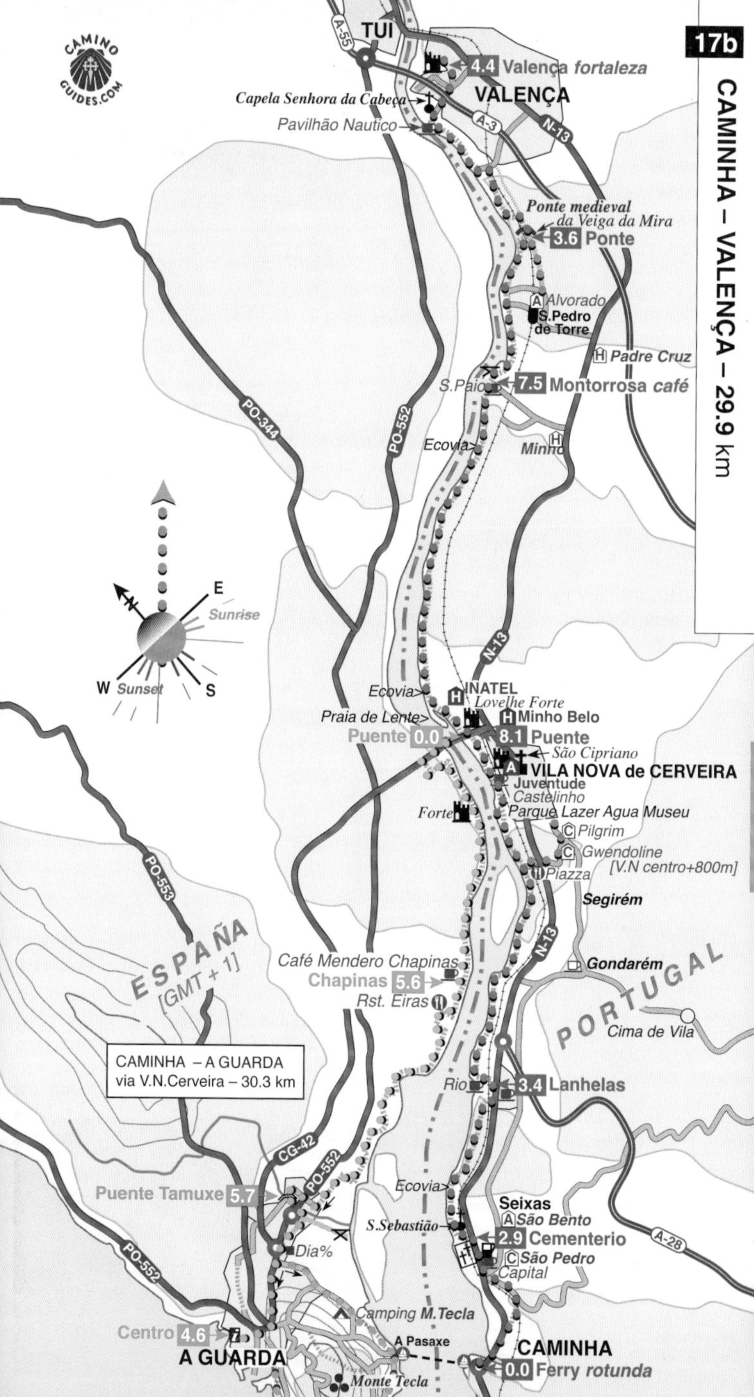
17b
CAMINHA – VALENÇA – 29.9 km
CAMINO GUIDES.COM
TUI
A-55
4.4 Valença fortaleza
VALENÇA
Capela Senhora da Cabeça
Pavilhão Nautico
A-3
N-13
Ponte medieval da Veiga da Mira
3.6 Ponte
Alvorado
S.Pedro de Torre
Padre Cruz
S.Paio
7.5 Montorrosa café
Minho
Ecovia
PO-344
PO-552
E
Sunrise
W Sunset
S
N-13
INATEL
Lovelhe Forte
Minho Belo
Praia de Lente
Puente 0.0
8.1 Puente
São Cipriano
VILA NOVA de CERVEIRA
Juventude
Castelinho
Parque Lazer Agua Museu
Forte
Pilgrim
Gwendoline
[V.N centro+800m]
Piazza
Segirém
PO-553
ESPAÑA [GMT + 1]
Café Mendero Chapinas
Chapinas 5.6
Rst. Eiras
Gondarém
PORTUGAL
Cima de Vila
CAMINHA – A GUARDA
via V.N.Cerveira – 30.3 km
Rio
3.4 Lanhelas
CG-42
PO-552
Puente Tamuxe 5.7
Seixas
São Bento
S.Sebastião
2.9 Cementerio
Dia%
São Pedro
Capital
A-28
Camping M.Tecla
Centro 4.6
A Pasaxe
A GUARDA
CAMINHA
0.0 Ferry rotunda
Monte Tecla

3.4 km **Lanhelas** ▼ ☕*Alvarinho* *[**Note: +100m** Rua S.João da Sa leads to cafes in town centre. **+250m Caminho da Senhora do Norte** from Lanheses (río Lima) joins the inland route from Caminha at this point. **Note also** ●Alb.S. **Bento** Priv.[24÷4]* €10 *+6* €30 ✆ 966 437 532 *adj. Capela de São Bento in Seixas.* ▼Welcoming pilgrim lodgings en route in **Loivo/Segirém** incl. •*CR* **Gwendoline** *€12-30 menú €6+ Shuttle into V.N. Cerveira (1.3 km) €2* ✆ 963 528 441 (Lawrence & Vani) rua da Reguinha 136. •**Pilgrim's Rest** ✆ 927 441 126 r/ de Segirém 359 and •**Moinho17** *x3* €75+ ✆ 969 436 355 r/ do Senhor dos Esquecidos, 117. To continue on the Ecopista take the Estrada do Río over rail to ☕ *do Rio* (summer – see photo above) pass several piers *Cais da Mota* and *Cais de Ligo* and island *Ilha da Boega* to an extensive park ***Parque de Lazer de Castelinho*** ☕ *do Castelinho* and exhibition of Miño river life ***Agua Museu*** €2. S/o into Av. dos Pescadores. *[To access walled town and Praça da Liberdade take passage under rail into rua do Cais].* Continue s/o past swimming pool to bridge over the Minho and option.

8.1 km **Vila Nova de Cerveira** ***Puente Lovelhe Forte*** *XVII* (ruins) overlooking Minho River. The town was established by *Dom Dinis* in 1321 and, despite modernisation, retains its 'old world charm'. The population of 9,000 attends to the lively summer tourist trade. **Lodging:** Hostal Minho ● **Pousada de Juventude** *Mun. [44÷2]+* €8 (+£35) ✆ 251 709 933 Rua Alto das Veigas (N-13). Several casas rurales incl. •**Casa do Cais** €55 ✆ 934 874 367 near river also modern luxury at •*H***** **INATEL Cerveira** r/ do Forte de Lovelhe €70 ✆ 251 002 080. Far side of N-13 •*H* **Minho Belo** Bairro de Lourido €35 ✆ 251 794 690.

To continue to A Guarda – 15.9 km:

0.0 km **Ponte** ***Vila Nova de Cerveira*** take road bridge over Minho into Spain and first turning left onto **track** [**0.7** km] turn left again s/o down to river and follow the yellow /white signs along delightful riverside path passing **Fortaleza** [**1.6** km] and ☕ (summer). Continue to ☕ *Mendero Chapinas* & 🍴 *Eiras* at:

5.6 km **Playa de Eiras** ***Chapinas*** Continue along river paths through ***San Miguel y Pias*** past football ground onto country lane up to and over main road to:

5.7 km **Ponte** ***Río Tamuxe*** Continue to roundabout. Waymarking is poor but it is *not* possible to proceed by the river due to marshland and channels. Take road imm. left of PO-522 to rejoin it (Nissan) and s/o at roundabout (Dia%) to church and ✣ **crossroads** [**2.4** km]. For direct route keep s/o by PO-552 to **town centre** [**2.2** km]. While this is a busy main road it has good sight lines *[✣ An alt. at this point is to turn left and follow signs to* ▲ ***Monte Tecla*** €30 ✆ 986 613 011 *and continue to **A Pasaxe** [5.2 km]. Continue on coast path around headland to **A Guarda** centre [**6.8** km]. Adds 9.8 km (14.4 -v- 4.6) part of PR-G 160.*

4.6 km **A Guarda** ***Centro***
See next stage (p.232) for details

To continue to Valença – 15.5 km: pick up riverside path by the bridge Estrada Inatel past the hotel to picnic area by town beach *Praia de Lente*. We now have an uninterrupted walk along the riverbank to recreation area in Montorrosa.

7.5 km **Montorrosa** ***Área Recreativa*** ☕ *S.Paio (summer)*. Continue along the Ecopista and in the few places where it has not been completed just push through scrubland. Continue past Beco da Pesqueira and isolated ☕ (summer) onto boardwalks and continue to follow riverside path or pass through Sao Pedro de Torre (right) and ●*Alb.****Alvorado Medieval*** *Priv.[****20****÷3]* €16 +€50 ✆ 934 283 297 *[Detour +1.7 km N-13 •H*****Padre Cruz*** *€30 ✆ 251 830 040]*. Both options meet at medieval bridge by railway.

3.6 km **Ponte medieval** ***da Veiga da Mira***. The ancient stone bridge crosses a tributary of the Minho and waymarks suddenly blossom in all directions with red and white blaise of the *Grande Randonnée*, red and yellow of local walks *Pequena Rota...* and the yellow arrows to Santiago. The camino follows the rail line all the way into the outskirts of Valença with the different routes opting for different sides of the line! S/o past water treatment plant *Aguas do Minho* onto asphalt road by *cruceiro* to **rail bridge** [**1.4** km]. We have several routes to the town centre. A good option is to turn down right and take the red pavement paseo *under* the railway which connects back to the river on boardwalks at the ***Pavilhão Nautico*** ☕ as we start our steep climb up past ***Capela Senhora da Cabeça*** ☕🍴 & picnic area past *Cruz Vermelha* to cross **A-3 motorway** [**2.1** km] ◆. Here we have another option.

To proceed direct to the International bridge over the Minho into Tui turn left over second motorway bridge to a pleasant tree-lined walk *below* the citadel.

◆ To continue to the albergue and town centre continue s/o up to top of rise at GNR HQ. *[Albergue São Teotónio 100m down right by Bombeiros]*. For town centre turn up into the main gate of the old citadel s/o down through Portas do Meio to the Câmara Municipal in **Praça da República** [**0.9** km] where the Camino Central joins.

4.4 km **Valença Central** ***Praça da República***. See Stage 18 (p.157) for list of accommodation and town plan.

Sunset over the río Minho

18a CAMINHA – PORTO MOUGÁS
Via A Guarda & O Serrallo

	--- ---	10.1	--- ---	*44%*
	--- ---	13.1	--- ---	*56%*
	--- ---	0.0	--- ---	*00%*
Total km		**23.2** km *(14.4 ml)*		

Total ascent **240**m +½ *hr*
▲ Alto *m* Monte Tecla **100**m *(328 ft)*
<A H> ➲A Guarda **3.8** km. ➲Oia **16.7** km. ➲O Serrallo **20.3** km.

Ferry

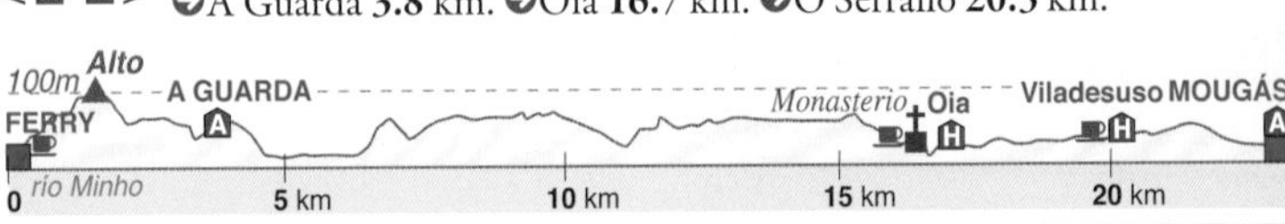

Conscience is one's compass, and though the needle sometimes deviates... one must still try to follow its direction. *Vincent van Gogh*

It is not just our conscience that we are required to navigate; our consciousness also needs to be set a new direction. For too long we have, collectively, set our horizon too low and have foundered on the rocks of the ego world. But the abyss to Higher Worlds has to be crossed to reach the destination that has been set since time began. We will need to jettison all unwanted baggage if we are to make it securely to the other shore. We simply cannot make it to the other side carrying the limiting beliefs of the mundane world. We need fortitude but also foresight to seek the help we need; which is already there ...waiting but for the asking.

Practical Path: The main waymarked route from the ferry port **A Pasaxe** to **A Guarda** is shorter (3.8km -v- 6.8) but the Senda Litoral makes a delightful walk around the headland mostly on pedestrian pathways (see p.233). A variety of lodging in **O Serrallo** (20.3 km) incl. a popular new albergue makes for a more equal split to **A Ramallosa** (19.2 km) the following day or a stopover in beautiful **Baiona** (14.1 km). With an overnight stay in A Guarda it might be possible to reach Baiona (30.6 km) in one full day. The section to Oia is mostly by cycle track *ciclovia (see photo>)* parallel to the busy main road which detracts somewhat from the lovely coastal views. The pathways around Oia offer welcome relief.

0.0 km **Caminha *centro*.** The ferry port is ½ km from the town centre. On the far side of the Minho we enter Spain (clocks + 1 hour) at **A Pasaxe** *estación marítima* *Maritimo* first Spanish *sello*! •*Camping* ***Santa Tecla*** [**+1.4** km] Rua Baixada O Rio Miño *bungalow x10* €40 ✆ 986 613 011. The main route heads up steeply to a woodland path around the flank of Monte Tecla and enters A Guarda at the top eastern end of town passing the entrance to the Monte Tecla Archaeological park (see next page). Continue down into the centre of town:

3.8 km **A Guarda *centro*** The intimate but lively main square ***Praza Relo*** with

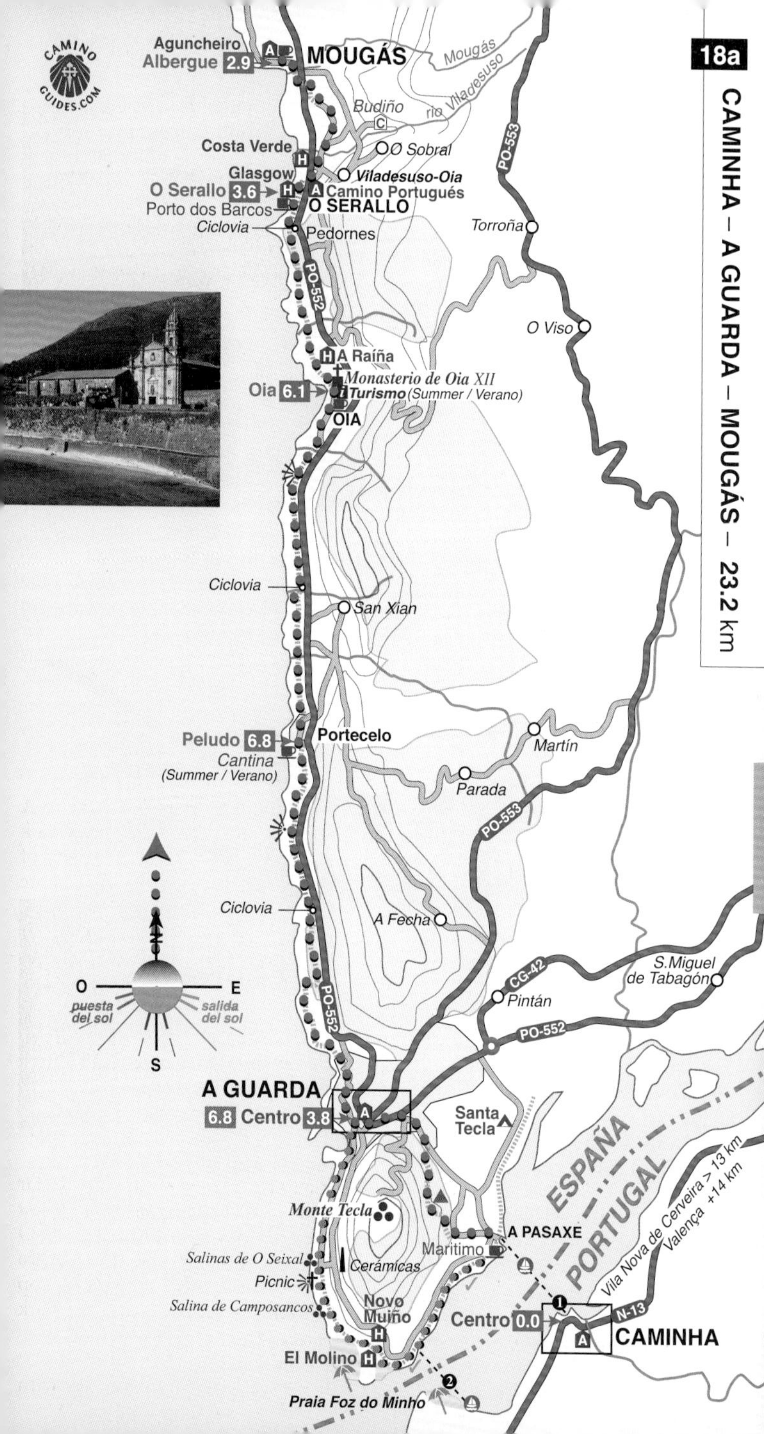

CAMINO GUIDES.COM
18a
CAMINHA – A GUARDA – MOUGÁS – 23.2 km
Agungheiro Albergue 2.9
MOUGÁS
Mougás
río Viladesuso
Budiño
PO-553
Costa Verde
O Sobral
Glasgow
Viladesuso-Oia
O Serallo 3.6
Camino Portugués
Porto dos Barcos
O SERALLO
Ciclovia
Pedornes
Torroña
PO-552
O Viso
A Raíña
Monasterio de Oia XII
Oia 6.1
Turismo (Summer / Verano)
OIA
Ciclovia
San Xian
Peludo 6.8
Portecelo
Cantina (Summer / Verano)
Martín
Parada
PO-553
Ciclovia
A Fecha
O
E
puesta del sol
salida del sol
S
S.Miguel de Tabagón
CG-42
Pintán
PO-552
PO-552
A GUARDA
6.8 Centro 3.8
Santa Tecla
ESPAÑA
PORTUGAL
Vila Nova de Cerveira > 13 km
Valença +14 km
Monte Tecla
A PASAXE
Maritimo
Salinas de O Seixal
Cerámicas
Picnic
Salina de Camposancos
Novo Muíño
Centro 0.0
N-13
CAMINHA
El Molino
Praia Foz do Minho

municipal offices **ⓘTurismo** ✆ 986 614 546 opp. popular ☕ *Art*. Lively town with a population of 10,000 serving a busy fishing fleet and summer tourist trade. The annual Seafood and Lobster Festival *Fiesta de la Langosta* takes place in A Guarda in early July.

Lodging ***central.*** ❶ *Alb.* **Peregrinos** *Mun. [36÷2]* €10 Concello ✆ 986 610 025 [m] 619 258 075 r/Puerto Rico, 7 college building on main road. *Alb.*❷ **O Peirao** *Priv.[16÷1]* €12-15 ✆ 682 190 102 *www.albergueopeirao.com* r/Oliva, 43 'behind' concello, fishermans house with rear garden. •*H* **Celta** *x20* €58 ✆ 986 610 445 *www.hotelcelta.es* r/Galicia, 53. •*H** **Vila da Guarda** *x26* €30 ✆ 986 611 121 c/Tomiño, 8. •*H** **Bruselas** *x16* €25-45 ✆ 986 614 521 *www.hotel-bruselas.com* Rúa Ourense 7. •*H*** **Eli-Mar** *x16* €35-45 ✆ 986 613 000 *www.eli-marhotel.com* r/Vicente Sobrino, 12. •*H**** **Convento de San Benito** *x16* €50+ ✆ 986 611 166 *www.hotelsanbenito.es* Plaza de San Benito. ***Suburbs + 1.0 km*** •*Hs*** **Del Mar** *x10* €18-33 ✆ 986 610 638 Irmáns Noia (Praia Area Grande). + ***1.2 km*** •*H** **Brisamar** *x27* €30-40+ ✆ 986 613 901 main road PO-552.

The harbour area is worth exploring with lively restaurants and bars and the Museo do Mar on Paseo marítimo 986 610 000. **Monte de Santa Tecla** (Galician: ***Trega***) Celtic castro of 1st century BCE (petroglyphs date 2 millennia earlier). Museum open daily ✆ 986 614 546 located 2.5 km up steeply from town entrance (note Monte Santa Tecla viewpoint a *further* 1.2 km at 341 meters. Take a taxi?).

Note there are no facilities between A Guarda and Oia a distance of 12.9 km (excepting a summer cantina in Perludo) so stock up with snacks and water before leaving town. This is a tiring stage mostly on concrete but with splendid sea views providing some relief.

6.8 km **Perludo** *Cantina* (summer). S/o parallel to the PO-552 which we leave to make our way down into the magical seaside hamlet of Oia:

6.1 km **Oia** beautiful seaside hamlet is dominated by the imposing Cistercian monastery dating back to 1185 *Real Monasterio de Oia.* The 18th century church is the only part that can be visited but there are plans to renovate the entire. There are several *bars & restaurants* and the delightful •*CR* **Casa Puertas** *x8* €50+ ✆ 986 362 144 www.casapuertas.es Vicente Lopez,7. •*CR* **La Cala** ♥*A Pilgrims Inn x4* €15-30+ ✆ 617 209 888 Tanya www.lacalainn.com c/ Laurel 22. •*H*** **A Raíña** *x12* €45-55+ ✆ 986 362 908 www.hotelaraina.com r/A Riña. We now have a section of track alongside the rocky coast to make our way back up to the main road at Pedornes into Viladesuso.

3.6 km **O Serrallo** ***Viladesuso-Oia*** ●*Alb.***Camino Portugués** *Priv.[**20**÷1]* €12 +*5* €20-35 ✆ 604 036 290 – sea views & all facilities. Opp. •*H**** **Glasgow** *x60* €50-60 ✆ 986 361 552 www.hglasgow.com •*H**** **Costa Verde** *x23* €44-60 ✆ 986 361 561 www.hotelrestaurantecostaverde.es Cross the PO-552 to take a quiet country lane *[**Serraseca Viladesuso +1.5** km •CR **Budiño de Serraseca** x4* €55 ✆ 986 361 856 www.budinho.com/en *]* back down and over the main road into:

2.9 km **Porto Mougás** seaside hamlet with ●*Alb.***Aguncheiro** *Priv.[**18**÷4]* €12 *x4* €30 ✆ 665 840 774 https://aguncheiro.wixsite.com/alojamientoturistico (Javier y Jorge) with 🍴 & ☕.

•*Senda Litoral:* ● ● ● ● ✓ **A Pasaxe – A Guarda** (**6.8** km -v- **3.8** km)**:** If you take the main ferry from Caminha this lands at the ferry terminal at A Pasaxe. While most pilgrims take the shorter waymarked route inland to A Guarda the Senda Litoral makes a wonderful alternative route around the headland. It is a combination of boardwalks and paths with some shade in the woodland sections. We make our way out along the estuary past *Parque Infantil* and *Praia do Muíño* (the beach where Mario's Maritime Taxi drops off pilgrims). We pass ☕ *Tapería O Forte* & •*H* **El Molino** *x50* €50-70 ✆ 986 627 233 www.hoteleselmolino.com Playa de Camposancos or 300m behind its sister hotel •*H** **Novo Muiño** *x20* €70 ✆ 986 627 169. Continue on boardwalks passing the pre-Roman salt pans *Salina de Camposancos* and picnic area with cruceiro overlooking the Minho estuary and the *Fortaleza e Convento da Ínsua* www.diverminho.pt on its remote island site. We pass Salinas de O Seixal and the chimneys are from the *Cerámicas Técnicas Galegas.*

19a MOUGÁS – A RAMALLOSA *Via BAIONA*

--- --- 2.3 --- --- *14%*
--- ---14.0 --- --- *86%*
--- --- 0.0 --- --- *00%*
Total km **16.3** km *(10.1 ml)*

Total ascent **260**m +½ *hr*
Alto *m* Portela **130**m *(427 ft)*
< A H > Pedra Rubia **2.0** km.
A Ermida **4.1** km Baiona **11.2** km.

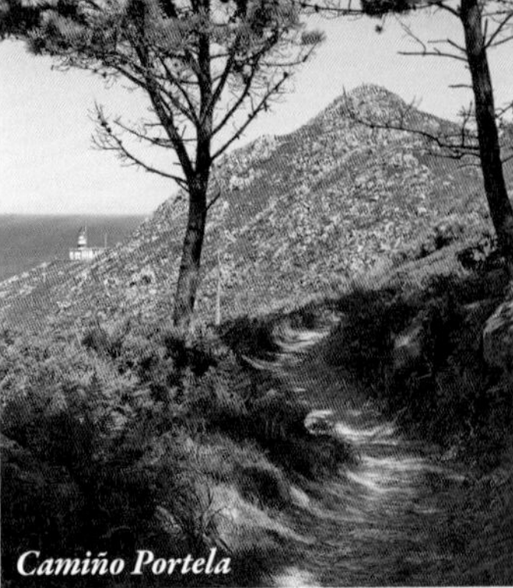

Camiño Portela

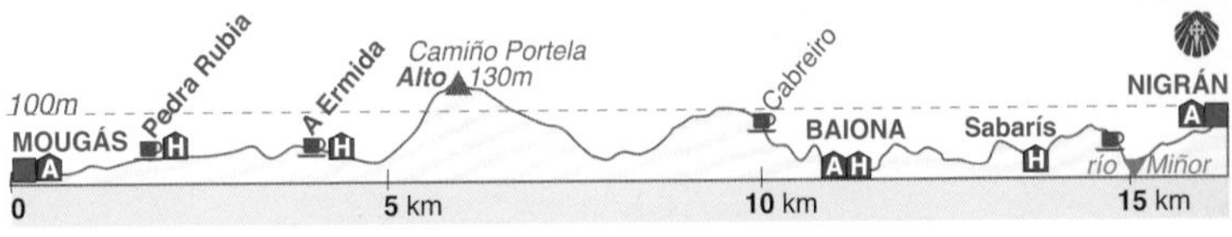

When we give everything to the Divine, we have nothing left to worry about. *We are so preoccupied by our commitments in this world that we forget why we came here in the first place. Our striving to succeed and our attachment to the values of society are so all-encompassing that we fail to ask even the most basic questions; success and values of what? Then comes the real quest – Who am I. Why am I here. Where am I going. When will I arrive. What is the Plan? If we are to reach our Destination we must start an honest dialogue with ourselves. Our immediate goal maybe Santiago but that is not our Objective. We may receive a Compostela but that is not the Purpose of pilgrimage...*

❑ **Practical Path:** We have the option to stop in **Baiona *(11.2 km)*** and take the afternoon to visit its historic sites and narrow medieval streets, enjoy its lively cafes or relax on its beautiful beaches. This would make the next stage into **Vigo** a reasonable 24.9 km. Baiona is an historic town and many pilgrims start their camino here. For those coming from Mougás we can extend this stage by continuing to **A Ramallosa *(16.3 km)*** in Nigrán which would give more time to explore Vigo the following day. The camino da Costa heads inland to take the high level route along the *camiño Portela* which climbs up through woodland (see photo above). There is an option here to stay alongside the road and coast via the *ciclovia* (see Senda Litoral p.238).

0.0 km **Porto Mougás**. Leaving the albergue we connect again with the *ciclovia* with limited lodging and cafes along this stage based around summer tourism.

1.5 km **Pedra Rubia.** ▲ **O Muiño** tent €10 / bungalows €50 ✆ 986 361 600 *www.campingmuino.com* (far side of the PO-552) we find *Bodas* •*H*˚ **O'Peñasco** *x18* €40 ✆ 986 361 565 (PO-550) *[nearest point for detouring to the* castros y petróglifos ***Ruta Máxica de Oia.*** *These ancient Celtic forts are located off remote tracks on the hillside above].* Continue on ciclopista to **A Ermida.**

2.4 km **A Ermida** *Las Mariñas* *O Silleiro* •*H*˚ **Soremma** *x18* €45-€55 ✆ 986 356 067 and ▲ **Mougás** €65 in bungalow ✆ 986 385 011 *[Alb.**Solidario** – closed].* Continue down to option point:

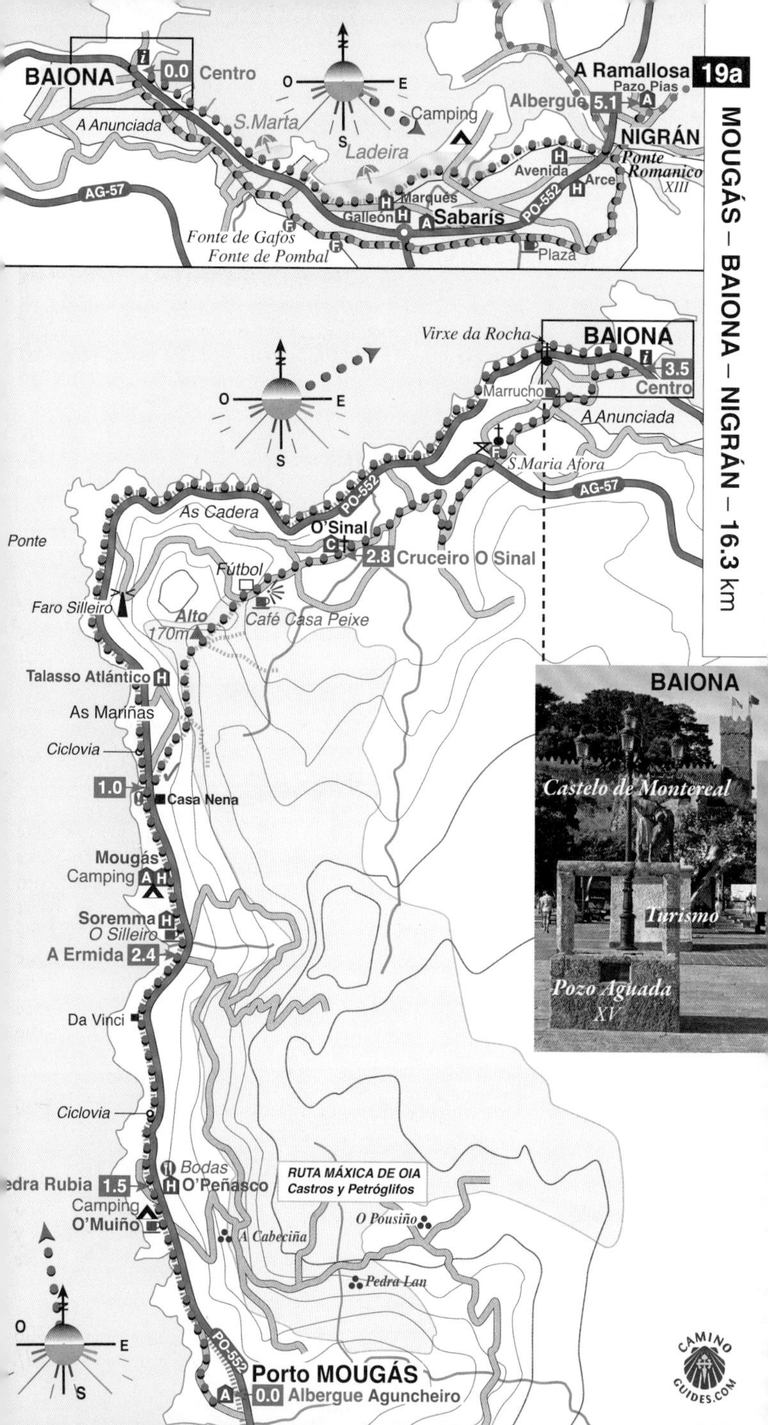

19a
MOUGÁS – BAIONA – NIGRÁN – 16.3 km
BAIONA
0.0 Centro
A Anunciada
S.Marta
Camping
Ladeira
A Ramallosa
Pazo Pias
Albergue 5.1
NIGRÁN
Ponte Romanico XIII
Avenida
Arce
Marques
Galleon
Sabarís
PO-552
AG-57
Fonte de Gafos
Fonte de Pombal
Plaza
Virxe da Rocha
BAIONA
3.5 Centro
Marrucho
A Anunciada
S.Maria Afora
AG-57
PO-552
As Cadera
O'Sinal
2.8 Cruceiro O Sinal
Ponte
Fútbol
Faro Silleiro
Alto 170m
Café Casa Peixe
Talasso Atlántico
As Mariñas
Ciclovia
1.0
Casa Nena
Mougás
Camping
Soremma
O Silleiro
A Ermida 2.4
BAIONA
Castelo de Montereal
Turismo
Pozo Aguada XV
Da Vinci
Ciclovia
Bodas
O'Peñasco
edra Rubia 1.5
RUTA MÁXICA DE OIA
Castros y Petróglifos
Camping
O'Muiño
O Pousiño
A Cabeciña
Pedra Lan
PO-552
Porto MOUGÁS
0.0 Albergue Aguncheiro
CAMINO GUIDES.COM

1.0 km **Option** ***Casa Nena*** Turnoff to take the discreet concrete ramp onto woodland path ***Camiño da Portela*** to rocky outcrop with base of ancient stone cross our high point today Alto 170m. Several forest paths merge at this point but we take the track s/o which leads down to junction of *estrada a Cabo Silleiro* and football ground opp. pilgrim rest house *Casa do Peixe* © 652 821 002 Asoc. Via XX in **Cabreiro [1.8** km]. The camino now winds its way down quiet country lanes too numerous to mention but waymarking is reasonable *stay foccussed!* Continue down to prominent roadside cross in the *centre* of the road **O Sinal** [**1.0** km] ***Cruceiro*** adj. *CR* **Oscar** whole house *x2* €100) shortly after we pass the delightful boardwalks *senda fluvial molinhos de Baredo.* We now begin our steep climb up and over the autopista AG-57 at **Santa Maria Afora** [**2.0** km] with picnic area [ ]. We now commence our steep descent into the rear (inland) suburbs of Baiona past *Taberna Marrucho* to major roundabout. Head over to the far side *Alb.***Baionamar**. The most direct way to the harbour is to continue down Palos de Frontera to the harbour in **Baiona** [**1.5** km].

6.3 km **Baiona** *Centro*. ❶***Oficina De Turismo*** Paseo Ribeira © 986 687 067 (10:00-15:00 + 16:00-21:00) + public toilets. Just beyond is ❶ ***Castelo de Monterreal*** (now a Parador) but there is a lovely walk around the headland past Praia da Barbeira and Baiona Yacht Club along the paseo de Monte Boi. Adj. the tourist office is a memorial plaque and ❷ ***Pozo Aguada*** *XV* which is reputedly the well where the crew of the Pinta took on water for their epic crossing between two worlds. Baiona is also where Martín Alonso Pinzón first made landfall with news of the 'discoveries'. This event is celebrated in the park behind with the modern ❸ ***Monumento Encontro entre dous mundos.*** ❹ ***Caravelle Pinta replica*** on board the museum anchored in the harbour. ❺ ***Collegiate Church of Santa María*** *XIII* on Praza Sta. Liberata. The town centre has several historic manor houses *pazos* incl. ❻ ***Casa da Correa*** *XVI* now the town hall *Concello de Baiona* with tower and ornate balconies on Rúa Lorenzo de la Carrera (see photo>)

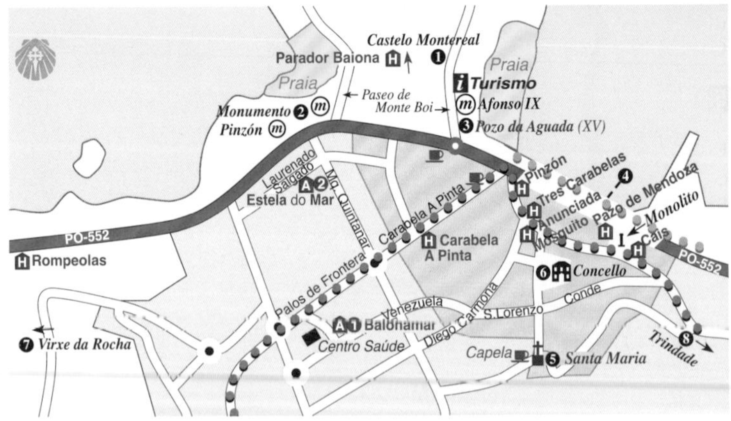

and *Casa Mendoza* with its arcade and Baroque façade – now a hotel.

Outskirts: ❼ ***Virxe da Rocha*** an enormous granite monument on Mount Sansón with 15m statue of the Virgin Mary holding a boat that serves as a viewing deck! ❽ ***Cruceiro da Trindade*** *XV* rare example of a wayside cross under a Renaissance cupola or canopy *baldachin Praza Santísima Trindade.* ● ***Festa da Arribada*** Held in first week in March commemorates arrival of the Caravel Pinta (replica see photo above) from the Americas and is marked by a mediaeval style fair & market.

Accommodation: *Alb.*❶ **Baionamar** *Priv.[24÷2]* €15-18 ✆ 986 138 025 www.hostelbaionamar.com c/ Venezuela, 6. ❷ **Estela do Mar** *Priv.[20÷1]* €15 ✆ 986 133 213 (Ivana) www.esteladomar.com Laureano Salgado, 15. •*H*** **Rompeolas** *x34* €40-55 ✆ 615 140 220 Av. Joselín. •*H* **Parador de Baiona** *x120* €85+ ✆ 986 355 000 Castelo Montereal. •*H* **Carabela La Pinta** *x14* €25-35 ✆ 986 355 107 c/Carabela la Pinta. •*H* **Pinzón** *x18* €25+ ✆ 986 356 046 r/Elduayen, 21.▌**Rua Ventura Misa @Nº61** •*H*** **Tres Carabelas** *x12* €40+ ✆ 986 355 441. **@Nº58** •*H*** **Anunciada** *x28* €33-40 ✆ 986 356 018. **@Nº32** •*P*** **Mosquito** *x12* €40 ✆ 986 385 264. •*H*** **Pazo de Mendoza** *x10* €50-75 ✆ 986 385 014 Elduayen, 1. •*H* **Cais** *x12* €40+ ✆ 986 355 643 c/Alférez Barreiro, 3. Exiting town on Av.Santa Marta: •*Hs*** **Santa Marta Playa** *x8* €25+ ✆ 986 356 045 & •*H*** **Bahía Bayona** *x88* €55-65 ✆ 986 385 004.

Camino da Costa: Baiona – A Ramallosa From the Turismo take the medieval Rúa Ventura Misa by hotel Pinzón past Praza Pedro de Castro with the Monolito da Arribada and up into Rúa Porta da Vila. We then head out into the modern suburbs on secondary roads parallel to the PO-552 into **Sabarís.** ●*Alb.* **Playa de Sabarís** *Priv.[20÷1]* €15 ✆ 986 152 380 Rúa Porta do Sol, 55. Several hotels €35+ on main road: ***Av. Julián Valverde*** *@Nº41* •*H* **Avenida** *x8* €50 ✆ 986 354 728 and ***@Nº40*** •*H* **Arce** *x10* €44-58 ✆ 986 386 060. •*H* **Vasco da Gama** *x10* €55 ✆ ✆ 986 353 350 Av. José Pereira Troncoso, 18. From the plaza in Sabaris the waymarks take us up in a wide loop to the Roman bridge at A Ramallosa. Continue s/o up into Rúa Damas Apostólicas to the albergue:

5.1 km **A Ramallosa** *Nigrán* ●*Alb. Hospedería* **Pazo Pias** *Priv.[60÷30!]* €10-38 ✆ 986 350 654 www.pazopias.org Camiño da Cabreira, 21. XVII th c pazo operated by religious order of nuns. Basic rooms with shared bathrooms or en suite. Meals available. Large garden. Quiet area with several restaurants in the area incl. Antipodas c/ Romana Alta. 4.

19a *Caminha / A Guarda – Baiona / A Ramallosa*

Interim accommodation: *(see Camino da Costa previous page).*

Senda Litoral *entering Baiona*:

0.0 km **Option** ***Camino Portela*** From the option turn off by Casa Nena to the upper route via Camino Portela there is the choice to continue s/o along the *ciclopista*. While we have the Atlantic waves to our left we also have the main road on our right! This is the only option for cyclists wheelchair pilgrims. This coastal route is 400m longer **6.8** km -v-**6.4** km. It passes several viewpoints *Miradoiros* and hotels •*H**** **Talasso Atlántico** *x70 €75+* ✆ *986 385 090* and just before entering Baiona •*H*** **Rompeolas** *x40* €55+ ✆ 986 355 130 Rua Virxe da Rocha with access to the Virxe da Rocha monument and viewing platform and into:

6.8 km **Baiona** ***Turismo*** (see previous pages for accommodation and description). From the Tourist office we can take the seashore path around the base of the Pardor hotel (see photo bottom right>)

Senda Litoral *exiting Baiona*: This makes a delightful alternative to the steep climb of the Camino da Costa inland from **Sabarís**. It is flat and continues along the beaches that line the route out from Baiona.

0.0 km **Baiona** ***Turismo*** From the Turismo head out along the promenade along the harbour front onto boardwalks and pedestrian path veering left along **Praia de Santa Marta** [**1.4** km]. *[Here we have an option to take a short detour 400m around the headland past Ermida de Santa Marta to rejoin main route]* the next beach is tree-lined **Praia Ladeira** [**0.6** km] ***Rúa das Areas***: [+100m •*H* **Casa do Marqués** *x8* €70 ✆ 986 353 150 •**Areas Mar de Baiona** *x20* €90. Cross the rio Guillade to roundabout [+200m •*Hs*** **El Viejo Galeón** €35 ✆ 986 350 207] and the estuary of the rio Miñor (a natural reserve). Finally we make our way over the medieval bridge Ponte Ramallosa [**1.8** km].

4.2 km **Ponte Ramallosa** rio Minor *[For Alb. Pazo Pias on the Camino da Costa keep s/o over roundabout. The distinctive Pazo Pias is 400m up Rúa Damas Apostólicas]*. The Senda Litoral continues left over the bridge past taxi rank and along the estuary (see later for stage 20a into Vigo).

Personal Reflections:

20a A RAMALLOSA *NIGRÁN* – VIGO

------	8.3	38%
------	11.9	54%
------	1.7	08%
Total km	**21.9** km *(13.6 ml)*	

Total ascent **520**m +**1.0** *hr*

▲ Alto *m* Alto Saiáns **180**m *(590 ft)*

<A H> Saiáns **8.9**+*0.3* Freixo **10.2**+*5.5*

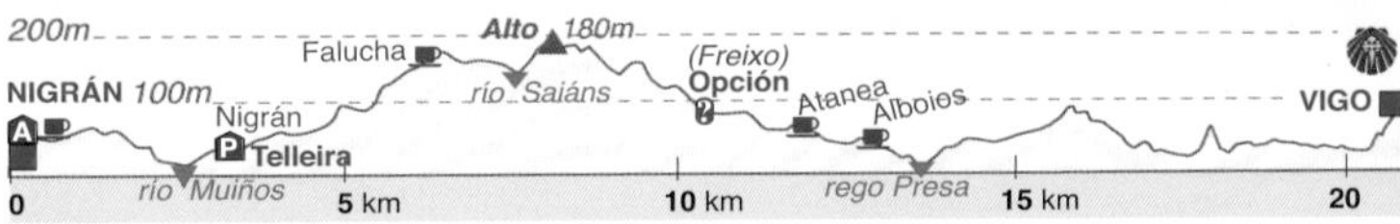

God recognizes how much we love Him by how we treat other people.
The Koran

Every separated heart harbours prejudice. We are taught from birth to separate all experience into good and bad. Pre-judgement and condemnation become second nature. Colour of skin, tone of voice,... every detail becomes a way to categorise a friend or foe. However, at the heart of all true religious practise is the exhortation *'Love your neighbour as yourSelf.'* The Bhagavad Gita tells us *'When we can see the Divine within ourself, we will know perfection in everything.'* The Shawnee say *'Do good to your neighbour and add to his days of happiness as you add to your own'.*

Practical Path •Camino da Costa: ●●●● ❶ The main waymarked route takes us inland into *Parque Forestal de Coruxo* and down into the industrial suburbs of Vigo via *Parque de Castrelos* where two alternatives join. ❷ Riverside path along the río Lagares. ❸ Woodland path from Freixo. All 3 routes start off climbing up through the eastern suburbs of Nigrán before entering the high level forest paths around Monte de Coruxo. Then all 3 routes wind their way down to the pleasant paths through Castrelo park before climbing steeply to Vigo *Alta*.

•Senda Litoral: route ❹ connects to Castrelos along the río Lagares from the sea. ❺ The entire way is along the coast and a largely level walkto enter Vigo *Baja* via the harbour area (see p.244).

0.0 km A Ramallosa *Albergue As Pias Nigrán.* Leave the hostel and head up Camiño da Cabreira through San Pedro and down over motorway and back up to crossroads at A Barxa:

3.4 km A Barxa *Cruce.* •*P* **Nigrán** *x4* €30 ✆ 986 365 613 r/Telleira 33. 600m further out on r/Telleira is •*P* **El Retiro** *x12* €30-40 ✆ 986 367 936 Rúa Telleira, 10. •*H* **7 Uvas** €60 ✆ 986 366 326 r/Lagoiña +300m. Head s/o past *Abacial de Nigrán XVII* onto path and up steeply to junction with the main road PO-552.

3.2 km Priegue *cruce* ☕ *Falucha [100m down left].* We leave the main road after 100m and make our way to the high point today at 185m in Saiáns *alto* onto woodland path around Monte de Coruxo to option point.

3.6 km Opción *Freixo* Detour to Freixo 5.3 km (see next page).

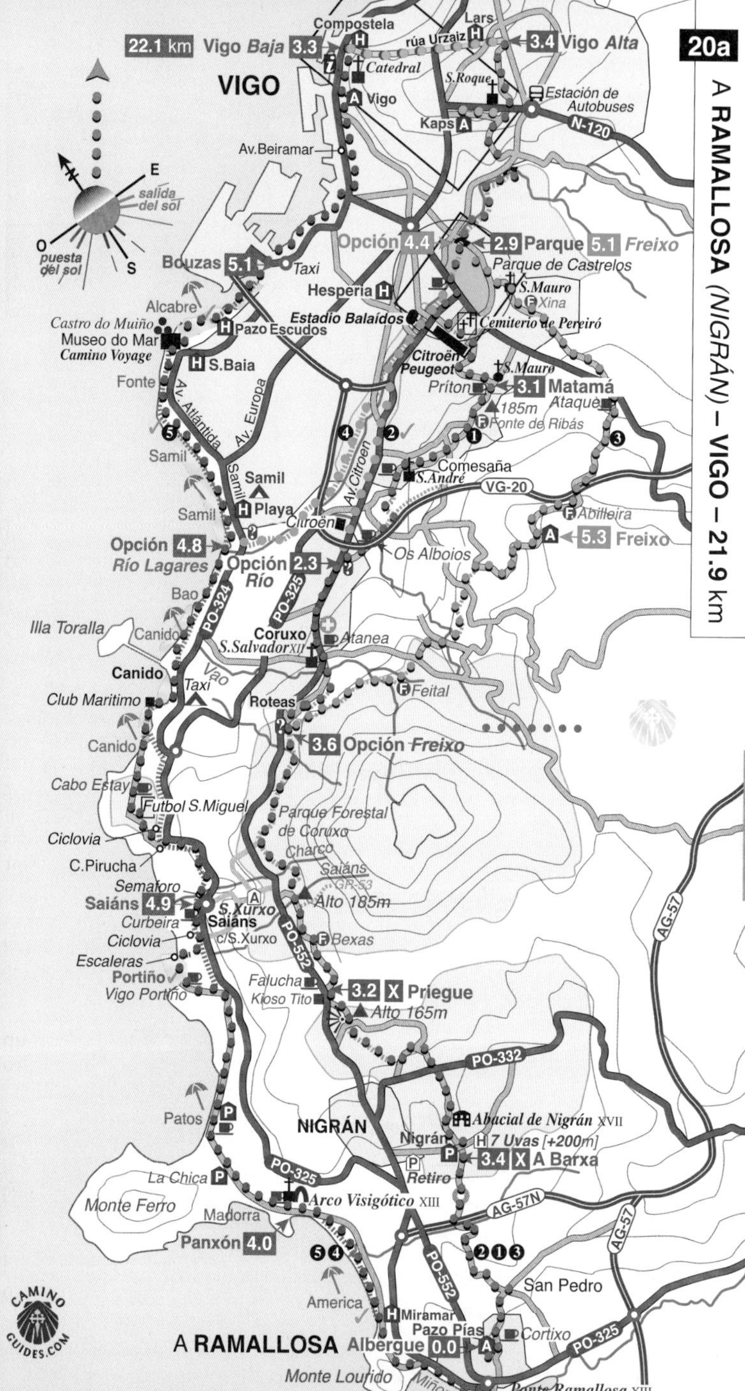

20a
A RAMALLOSA (NIGRÁN) – VIGO – 21.9 km
22.1 km
Vigo Baja 3.3
3.4 Vigo Alta
VIGO
Compostela
rúa Urzaiz
Lars
Catedral
S.Roque
Vigo
Estación de Autobuses
Kaps
N-120
Av.Beiramar
E
salida del sol
O
puesta del sol
S
Opción 4.4
2.9 Parque 5.1 Freixo
Parque de Castrelos
S.Mauro
Xina
Bouzas 5.1
Taxi
Hesperia
Estadio Balaídos
Cemiterio de Pereiró
Alcabre
Castro do Muiño
Museo do Mar
Camino Voyage
Pazo Escudos
S.Baia
Citroën Peugeot
S.Mauro
Príton
3.1 Matamá
Ataque
185m
Fonte de Ribás
Fonte
Av. Atlántida
Av. Europa
Av.Citroen
Samil
Comesaña
S.André
Samil
Playa
VG-20
Abilleira
Citroën
Os Alboios
5.3 Freixo
Opción 4.8
Río Lagares
Opción 2.3
Río
Bao
PO-324
PO-325
Illa Toralla
Canido
Coruxo
Atanea
S.Salvador XII
Canido
Vao
Taxi
Feital
Club Maritimo
Roteas
Canido
3.6 Opción Freixo
Cabo Estay
Futbol S.Miguel
Parque Forestal de Coruxo
Ciclovia
C.Pirucha
Charco
Saiáns
GR-53
Semaforo
Saiáns 4.9
S.Xurxo
Alto 185m
Curbeira
Saiáns
Ciclovia
c/S.Xurxo
PO-552
Bexas
Escaleras
Portiño
Vigo Portiño
Falucha
Kioso Tito
3.2 Priegue
Alto 165m
AG-57
PO-332
Patos
NIGRÁN
Abacial de Nigrán XVII
Nigrán
7 Uvas [+200m]
3.4 A Barxa
La Chica
Retiro
PO-325
Monte Ferro
Arco Visigótico XIII
Madorra
AG-57N
Panxón 4.0
PO-552
AG-57
San Pedro
America
Miramar
Pazo Pías
Cortixo
A RAMALLOSA
Albergue 0.0
PO-325
Monte Lourido
Miñor
Ponte Ramallosa XIII
CAMINO GUIDES.COM

[Detour ❸ Freixo ● ● ● ● *5.3 km (+5.1 on to Castrelos). To take this option follow the green arrows around monte Coruxo onto quiet country lanes into the peaceful hamlet of Freixo.* ●*Alb.***O Freixo** *Asoc.[6÷1] €5 © 679 652 431 (see photo>). Limited facilities but bar adjacent. Continue to Vigo along waymarked country lanes into Parque de Castrelos].*

To continue on the main waymarked route carry s/o into Roteas *alto* down to the main road at Coruxo with ☕ & *Iglesia San Salvador*. Turn down right along the PO-552 to a second option point:

2.3 km **Opción** ***Río Lagares*** Focus is needed as this option is not obvious.

[Detour ❷ Paseo Río do Lagares ● ● ● ● *4.0 km to Castrelos. This pleasant and shorter alternative is marked with green arrows and continues s/o down the PO-552 past the Citroen showrooms (left) to roundabout then left under road bridge to paseo Río Lagares into Castrelos].*

To continue on the main route turn right down narrow Camino Pitasia (FCC factory right) under the motorway ☕ 🍴 *Os Albois* onto short track and up into **Matamá** with several cafes.

3.1 km **Matamá** turn down left onto Camino Real by ☕ *Príton* & *Iglesia de San Pedro de Matamá (S.Mauro)*. We next skirt the sprawling Citroen / Peugeot factory (left) onto Av. Alcalde Portanet opp. football stadium Estadio Balaídos and turn right into Av. & Parque Castrelos ☕ *Medalla de Oro*. Routes ❷ & ❹ (via paseo do Lagares) join main route ❶ at this point and head through pleasant Park ahead to join route ❸ (from Freixo). *Parque de Castrelos:*

2.9 km **Parque *de Castrelos* Pazo Quiñónes de León** *(Museo Municipal)* © 986 295 070. ***Igrexa S.M. de Castrelos*** *románico XIII.* ***[Vigo Balaídos.*** Here all routes (except the senda litoral) head up steeply into Rúa Emilia Pardo Bazán turn right> into Rúa do Loureiro to junction of Av. Madrid (N-120) *[the 'de facto' albergue hostel* ***Kaps*** *left 700m along N-120 see p.246). Bus station down right 300m].* Keep s/o over N-120 up past **Parque San Roque** [**2.4** km] into the modern suburbs around **Vigo *Alta*.** Somewhat disappointing arrival point with no defined 'centre'. Continue up Rua S. Roque & Couto S. Honorato to busy **Av. Alcalde Gregorio Espino** [!] Turn left by chemist (opp. ☕ *Melody*) and imm. right at next junction (50m *Olive tree in centre of road*) by Banco Santander into the pedestrian street **Rúa Urzaiz** [**1.0** km].

3.4 km **Vigo Alta** The area offers a wide selection of modern hotels and hostals (see city map p.247). ***Note:*** *If you opt to stay in the historic 'downtown' by the lively port area* ***Vigo Baja*** *it is 2.1 km down rua Urzaiz at this point to the* taxi rank by *Hotel Compostela* and the Cathedral & tourist office. *Fiesta Reconquista* marks the victory over Napoleon's army on March 28th when Vigo pulses to street music.

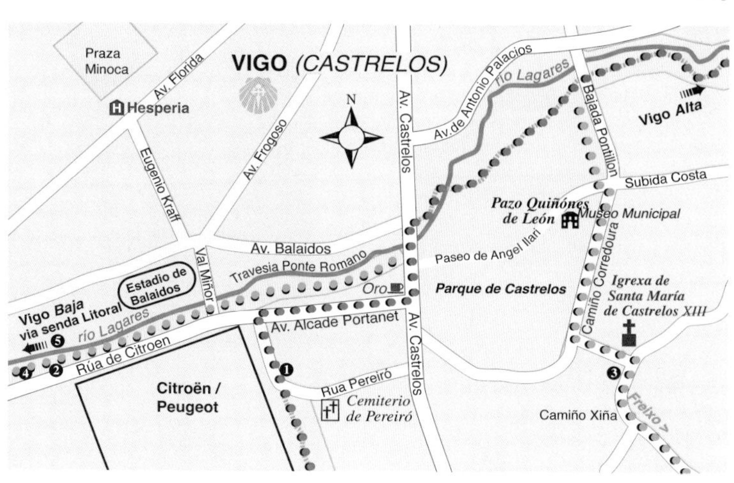

Personal Reflections:

Senda Litoral with the mythical Bali Ha'i & mystical Ilas de Cies *in the distance!*

20a *A Ramallosa – Vigo 20.7 km*

Practical Path: This delightful seaside route follows the coast via boardwalks, sandy paths and pavements. It is also popular with tourists so cafes, restaurants and lodging are plentiful. We pass by the Maritime Museum (pilgrims €1) *[now displaying the Irish currach used in the heroic Camino Voyage www.anupictures.com/project/camino. The museum occupies the site of an 8th c BC! Bronze age Castro]* and thence into the heart of Vigo Baja via the harbour area. The old quarter of Vigo has a very different atmosphere to upper town with its modern shops and hotels.

0.0 km **Ponte Ramallosa** The senda Litoral splits off from the Camino da Costa at this point and heads due North past the taxi rank and kids play park along a wide pedestrian path alongside the estuary. Turn <left into **Rua de Foz [1.0** km] and take the road right> back to coastal paths and pavements in **Av. Praia America** [**0.3** km] •*H*** **Miramar** *x48* €50+ ✆ 986 350 227 www.miramarhoteles.es .Continue along the pavements (opportunity to take grass path through the trees by parking area). Cross over the **Rio Muiños** [**1.1** km] along the paseo Maritímo to beach at **Panxón** [**1.4** km].

3.8 km **Panxón** ***port*** ☕ 🍴 restaurants and cafes around the central crossroads *[Opportunity to visit the Arco Xermánico ruins of a Visigothic arch with the imposing Iglesia San Juan behind 200m. Directions: At Crosroads keep s/o for 100m and Turn right by Taperia A Madorra. Arch is 100m]*. At the crossroads continue into Rúa Tomás Mirambell 🍴 *Taperia A Madorra* (right) and veer right after 300m (do not take the enticing coast road s/o along the beach – it goes in the wrong direction!). We continue up steeply passing •*P** **La Chica** *x8* €12pp ✆ 699 966 260 (opp. Escuela de Surf) and down to rejoin the seashore at **Praia Patos** [**1.2** km]. •*P* **Patos Beach Bar** *x10* €60 ✆ 691 571 818 www.patosbeach.com .Continue past Praia Areosa ☕*Areosa Beach Bar*. *[Note: From here to Praia Portiño there are several stretches of welcome dirt roads but some lead to cul-de-sacs so stay focussed for the infrequent waymarks]*. We make our way onto the Camiño do Portiño with a final stretch with magnificent views of the coast to **Praia Portiño** [**2.3** km]. 🍴 *Portiño* (evenings only). We make our way across the delightful small beach (good place to swim) and up the steep steps on the far side. We now enter a maze of narrow roads that lead up to the cycle path *ciclovia* alongside the PO-325 at **Saiáns** [**1.1** km].

4.6 km **Saiáns** ***Rotunda*** [**1.1** km] major roundabout 🍴 •*P** **Curbeira** ✆ 986 491 260. *[+800m up* Baixada á Praia ●*Alb.***San Xurxo** *Asoc.[8÷1]* €8 ✆ *986 491 918 r/Eira Vella, 4]*. We now have a long slog along the *ciclovia* to turn off <left into camino da Pirucha to **Campo de fútbol da Pirucha** [**0.6** km]. Continue down passing 🍴 *Churrasqueira Cabo Estay* and turn right> into Rúa do Arquitecto Antonio Cominges *[Praia Da Monduiña straight ahead. If you are feeling adventurous you can play hide-and-seek with the various beaches that run parallel all the way to Puerto Candido]*. Continue along pavements down to ☕ *Puerto* in **Candido** [**1.6** km].

2.2 km **Candido** ***Praia*** Continue along seafront to pass the Centro

Arqueolóxico da **Vila Romana de Toralla** [**0.5** km] in a weird juxtaposition with the modern eyesore tower block on Isla de Toralla. We now have a pleasant stretch of boardwalks by Play del Vao. Do not try to cross the rio Lagares by beach but stick to the main road and over road bridge to **option in Samil** [**1.8** km].

2.3 km **Samil *Option*** *[There is an option here to take the riverside walk to join the 'official' route into Parque de Castrelos to proceed up into Vigo Alta – see map].* Continue around sport complex *Complexo Deportivo de Samil* opp. •*H*** **Playa De Vigo** €40 ✆ 986 202 020 Av de Samil 95. Turn <left back on to beach promenade with tourist vibe past bars and restaurants. •*H** **Verdemar** Av Samil, 75 €40 ✆ 986 248 592. We next enter delightful woodland paths around rocky promontory. *[If you are agile and the tide is low you can continue by beach and scramble over various rock outcrops]* or continue along the busy Av Samil to the **Museu do Mar** [**2.8** km]. This excellent museum has a hall dedicated solely to the camino de Santiago *(see photo>). [Note the Celtic Castro underneath the currach that was rowed from Ireland and carried up to the cathedral in Santiago].* If you are not visiting you can proceed around the side of the building past the Celtic Castro that forms part of the museum grounds. •*H*** **Playa Santa Baia** €30+ ✆ 986 241 548 *www.hotelpsb.com* where Paz Lorenzo welcomes pilgrims on Av. da Atlántida, 121 (+250m from Museo do Mar). Several intimate beaches leads us to Priaia de Santa Baia and we continue via the woodland of Parque Carril. We continue **under VG-20** [**1.2** km] (access road to commerial port) along promenade to **Bouzas** [**0.6** km] with church of San Miguel de Bouzas and roundabout.

4.6 km **Bouzas *rotunda*** From the taxi rank by roundabout we have no other option but to slog along the busy two lane Av. de Beiramar with the port buildings on our left to veer right into Rúa da Ribeira do Berbés and arrive at the beautiful new **Vigo pilgrim hostal** [2.7 km] ●*Alb.* **Vigo** *Xunta.[**96**÷7]* €8 Praza do Berbés, 5. This was the original harbour front before it was extended out into the bay. We finally make our way up the Royal Road *Rua Real* to the the heart of old city of Vigo **Concatedral - Basílica de Santa María** [**0.4** km].

3.1 km **Concatedral** Several intimate plazas surround the cathedral with variety of hostals and eateries. The main port area with shopping centre and boat trips to the sky islands *Islas de Cies* from **Estación Marítima** is only 300m via the overhead pedestrian walkway back down towards the harbour. Here also is the homage to the emigrant *Homenaxe á Emigración*. See following pages for city map and accommodation.

▌**Vigo** ***Alta Lodging:*** •*Hs* **Kaps** *[24÷4]* €17+*14* €30 ✆ 986 110 010 www.hostelvigo.com Emilia Pardo Bazán 12. •*H*** **Tryp Los Galeones** *x50* €55+ ✆ 902 144 440 Av de Madrid 21. •**Pepe** ✆ 648 538 956 c/Badajoz 13. •*Hs* **Los Tres Luces** *x15* €40 ✆ 986 420 477 Venezuela 61. •*Hs* **Pio V** *x6* €25 ✆ 986 410 060 c/ Alcalde Vázquez Varela 46. ***Calle México*** *@N°22* •*H*** **Celta** *x40* €29-33 ✆ 986 414 699 &*@N°7* •*H*** **Casablanca** *x9* €35 ✆ 986 482 712. •*Hs*** **Lar Atlántica** *x18* €35 ✆ 616 706 948 Rúa Urzaiz, 83/1°A. ▌***Hotels:*** *€35-75:* •*H**** **Oca Ipanema** ✆ 986 471 344 Vázquez Varela 31. ***Rúa Lepanto*** *@N°4* •*Hs Int.* **Lapplandia** ✆ 605 457 792. *@N°16* •*Hs*** **Casais** ✆ 886 112 956. *@N°18* •*H*** **Panton** *x40* €29-34 ✆ 986 224 270. *@N°26* •*H*** **Lino** ✆ 986 447 004. •*H**** **Occidental** *México* €75+ ✆ 986 431 666 Vía Norte **N°10** & @ **N°9** •*H** **Solpor** *x8* €27-33 ✆ 986 416 036. **Iglesia de los Picos** *Inmaculada Concepción* ✆ 986 274 622 barrio del Calvario.

▌**Vigo** ***Baja:*** **Casco antiguo:** ●*Alb.* **Vigo** *Xunta.[96÷7]* €8 Praza do Berbés, 5. ●*Hs.* **R4** *Priv.[22÷1]* €20 ✆ 986 699 727 r/Real, 4. *Hs.* **Real** *x9* €20-25 ✆ 699 621 449 r/Real, 22. •*H*** **Compostela** €35+ ✆ 986 228 227 r/García Olloqui 5 *(Praza da Compostela).* •*Hs*** **La Colegiata** €25-40 ✆ 986 220 129 Plaza Iglesia 3. •*H*** **Puerta del Sol** *x25* €39-45 ✆ 986 222 364 Porta do Sol, 14. •*Hs* **Continental** €25-45 ✆ 986 220 764 Bajada la Fuente 3. •*H** **Aguila** €20+ ✆ 986 431 398 c/ Victoria 6. •*H** **Nautico** €25 ✆ 986 122 440 c/ Luis Taboada 28. •*H*** **Del Mar** *x32* €35-45 ✆ 986 436 811 r/ Luis Taboada, 34. •*H*** **Atlantico** €40 ✆ 986 220 530 r/ García Barbón, 35 (opp. Igrexa Santiago). *[Note missionary brothers **Hermanos Misioneros** Av. de Galicia no longer accept pilgrims].*

▌**Vigo BAJA** ❶**Turismo Vigo** ✆ 986 224 757 Estación Marítima C/ Cánovas del Castillo 3. **Turismo Xunta** *(Galicia)* ✆ 986 430 577 C/ Cánovas del Castillo 22. *Marítima*: Ferry Islas Cíes / Ons €22 July-Sept. ○ ***El barrio histórico de Vigo:*** ❶ **Concatedral** ***Colexiata de Santa María de Vigo*** neoclásico *XIX (*104.4 km to Santiago).* ❷ **Casa de Arines** *Ceta XV* (Instituto Camões) calle Real. ❸ **Ayuntamiento** *antiguo* Praza da Constitución. ***Marítima:*** ❹ Monumento a Xulio Verne *(20.000 leguas de viaje submarino; que menciana la Ría de Vigo).* ❺ **O Castro** *XVII (y Parque Monte del Castro).* ❻ Neo Gothic **Igrexa de Santiago** *XIX* Rúa García Barbón *(***103.2** km to Santiago Cathedral entitling the bona fide pilgrim to apply for a Compostela).*

The islands in the sky *Ilas de Cies (voted 'most beautiful beach in the world')* rise from the deep Ría Vigo which inspired Jules Verne to write *20,000 Leagues Under the Sea* which gives us the image of the giant Octopus (see photo below). *Pulpo* is a popular local dish! The islands can be visited by regular passenger ferry from the port.

Monumento a Xulio Verne

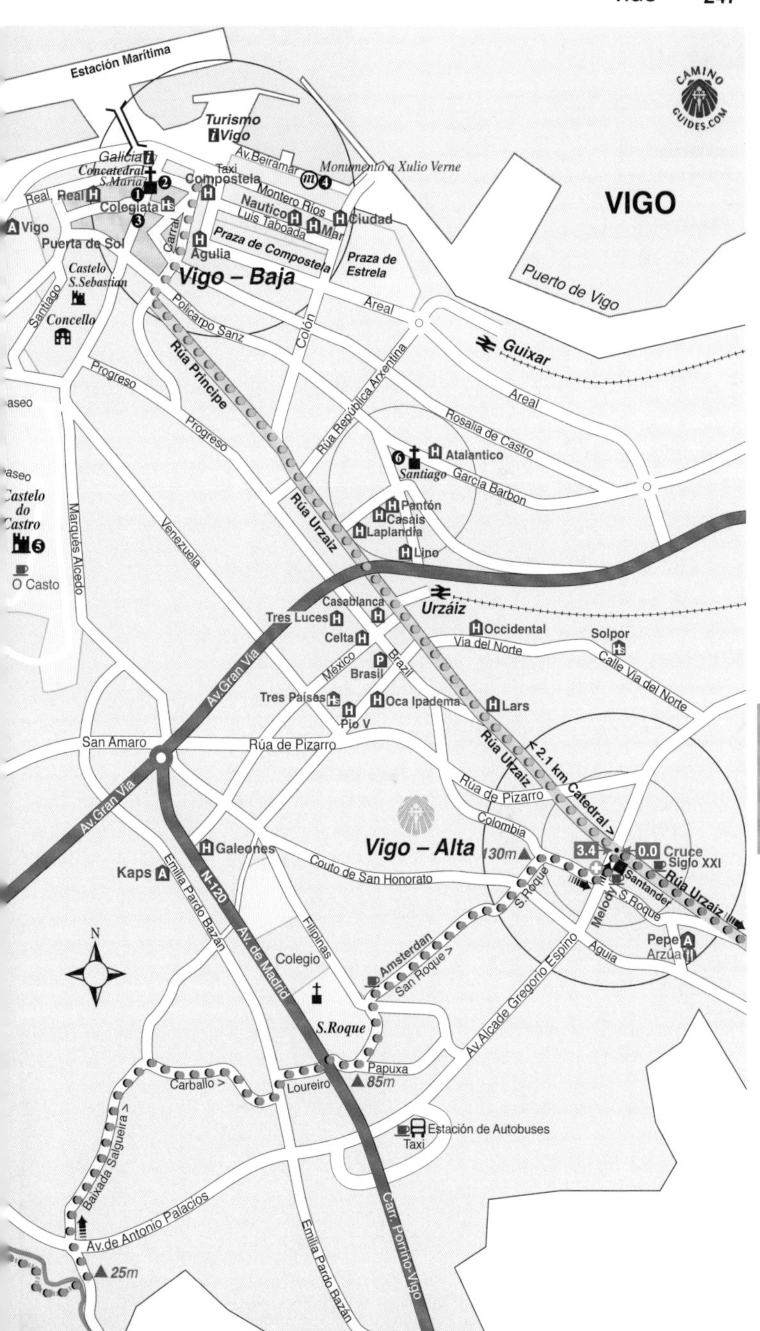

Estación Marítima
Turismo Vigo
Galicia
Concatedral S.María
Real
Colegiata
Compostela
Taxi
Av.Beiramar
Monumento a Xulio Verne
Montero Ríos
Nautico
Luis Taboada
Mar
Ciudad
VIGO
Vigo
Puerta de Sol
Carral
Agulia
Praza de Compostela
Praza de Estrela
Castelo S.Sebastian
Vigo – Baja
Puerto de Vigo
Santiago
Concello
Policarpo Sanz
Areal
Colón
Guixar
Rúa Principe
Rúa República Arxentina
Progreso
Areal
Rosalia de Castro
Atalantico
Santiago
García Barbon
Castelo do Castro
Marqués Alcedo
Venezuela
Rúa Urzaiz
Pantón
Casais
Laplandia
Lino
O Casto
Casablanca
Urzáiz
Tres Luces
Occidental
Solpor
Celta
Via del Norte
Calle Via del Norte
México
Brasil
Brazil
Av.Gran Via
Tres Países
Oca Ipadema
Lars
Pio V
San Amaro
Rúa de Pizarro
Rúa Urzaiz
< 2.1 km Catedral >
Rúa de Pizarro
Colombia
Av.Gran Via
Vigo – Alta
130m
3.4
0.0 Cruce
Siglo XXI
Galeones
Couto de San Honorato
S.Roque
Santander
Rúa Urzaiz
Kaps
Melody
S.Roque
N-120
Emilia Pardo Bazán
Pepe
Arzúa
Aguia
Av. de Madrid
Filipinas
Amsterdan
San Roque >
Colegio
N
Av.Alcade Gregorio Espino
S.Roque
Papuxa
85m
Carballo >
Loureiro
Baixada Salgueira >
Estación de Autobuses
Taxi
Av.de Antonio Palacios
Carr. Porriño-Vigo
25m
Emilia Pardo Bazán

21a VIGO – REDONDELA

(dotted)	--- ---	6.2	--- ---	*43%*
(grey)	--- ---	8.2	--- ---	*55%*
(dark)	--- ---	0.3	--- ---	*02%*
Total km		**14.7** km *(9.1 ml)*		

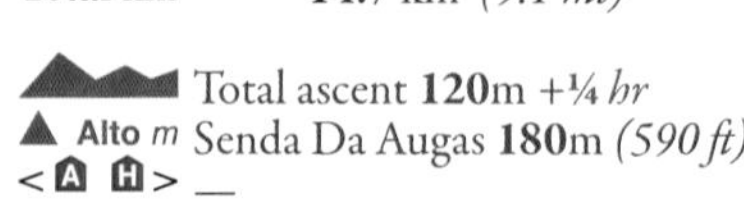

Total ascent **120**m +¼ *hr*

▲ Alto *m* Senda Da Augas **180**m *(590 ft)*

< Ⓐ Ⓗ > __

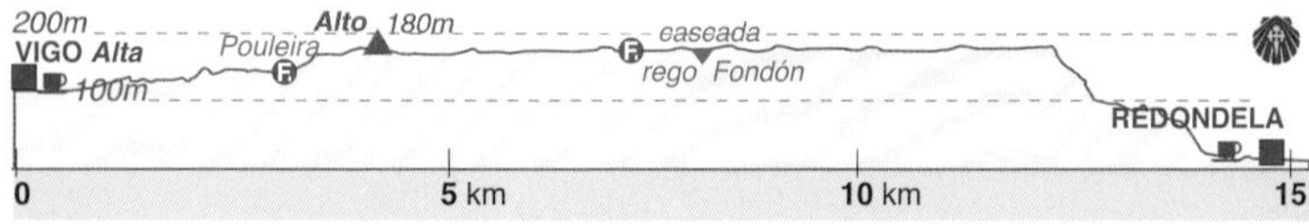

The two most important days in your life are the day you are born... And the day you find out why. *Mark Twain*

Mystical Path *The Inner Camino:* Many traditions celebrate the day we were borne, others mourn the day we separated from our Divine Origin and chose to take a detour into fear. Many religions disguise this decision by proclaiming we were banished from heaven; others claim we became so enamoured with our delusional drama that we forgot our heavenly Source. We need remember why we came before we can choose to go Home. The Garuda is a mythical bird; born fully grown symbolising the perfection of our essential nature, it is ready to fly Home as soon as our shell cracks open. The Heavenly Iles Iles *Islas de Cies* lies over the horizon but they not found by death... but by choice.

Practical Path •*Camino da Costa:* ● ● ● ● The well waymarked route continues through the upper suburbs of Vigo opening to wonderful views west over the *Ilas de Cies* and along 6 km of tranquil woodland paths all the way to the outskirts of Redondela. It is generally level following the lower contours around the Pico de San Vicente. While this is a short stage there are no facilities once we leave the Vigo Alta suburbs and enter the woodlands – bring water.

•***Senda Litoral:*** ● ● ● ● In the past there have been many ways to connect back with the main path as fading yellow arrows around the harbour area attest but they all require the steep climb up to Vigo Alta. The most straight forward way (recommended) is to connect via ruas Principe & Urzaiz to join waymarks at the *pedestrian* section of Rua Urzaiz (Banco Santander on corner).

0.0 km **Vigo *Alta Cruce*** the waymarked route continues along the pedestrian sections of Rúa Urzáiz (Banco Santander) into Rúa Toledo and s/o over dual carriageway *Rua Jenaro de la Fuente* up past *Parroquia Inmaculada Concepción* ***Iglesia de los Picos*** (distinctive pyramid shaped roof) into Rúa Toledo past ☕ *París* and over busy Av. Aeroporto into Rúa Cantabria to ☕ ***O Chato*** **Option [1.5 km]**. Ⓐ keep s/o along Rúa Cantabria into San Xoan Poulo with sports ground and kids play park (right) past ☕ *A Nosa Rua* and up into camiño Pouleira to wide **junction *Pouleira* [1.0** km] [⛲] *Fonte das Mozas Pouleira* where alt. route joins.

For alternative route Ⓑ by ☕ ***O Chato** Option* turn up right into Rúa Vista do Mar

VIGO – REDONDELA – 14.7 km

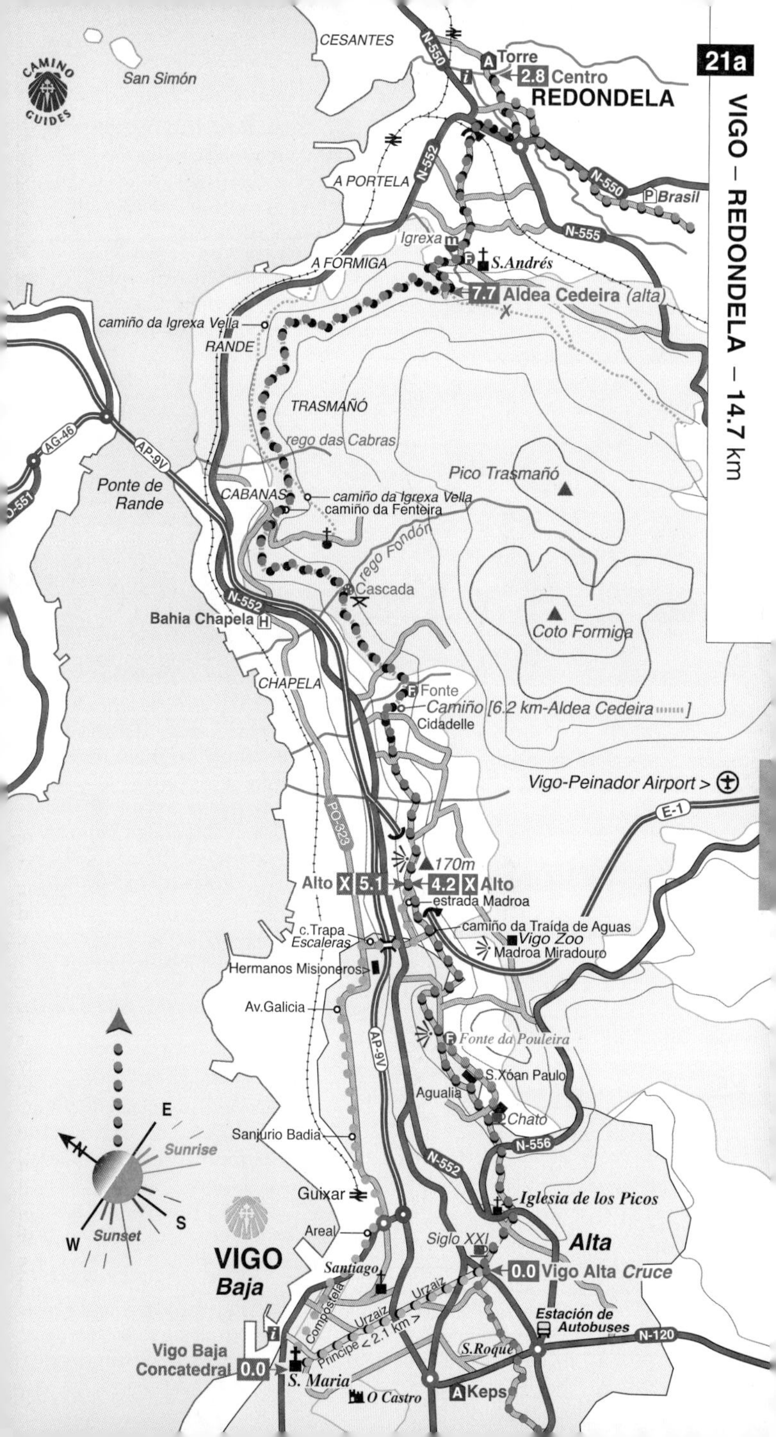

and follow it around the back of the sports ground with wonderful sea views as we drop again to join the original route at *Fonte das Mozas* ***Pouleira*** (same distance as route Ⓐ). We now veer left into camiño Poulo and Camiño da Traída das Augas to cross over **estrada á Madroa** [**1.7** km]

4.2 km **Junction** *[autostrada do Atlántico now in a tunnel below us. At this point an alt. connecting route from the Senda Litoral joins via Rua Trapas* *Taperia a Nosa Ria +200m down left].* All routes proceed past the 5.5t sign with splendid view over the Ria with Vigo's iconic suspension bridge *Puente de Rande* visible in the middle distance and the Islas Cíes on the western horizon (see photo below). **Alto** *180m Senda das Aguas.*

We now enter a wonderful woodland section 'where many paths and errands meet' including alternative local walks so stay focussed! The main route is marked with yellow arrows and essentially maintains the same contour throughout the next 6 km of forest paths so avoid any paths that have a pronounced ascent or descent. We cross **road** [**4.8** km] *[sign A Traida & +* ***500****m up right to popular* *O Eida Vella. Also* ***+1.5*** *km down left Chapela Av. Redondela •Hs* ***Bahía de Chapela*** *x12* €30 *near Puente de Rande – free pickup / transporte gratuito)* © *986 452 780].* We finally emerge from the forest paths to begin our descent in **Cedeira** [**3.6** km]:

9.4 km **Aldea Cedeira** ***Alta*** take steep asphalt road down into Cedeira *Iglesia San Andrés* [ ] & *Vilarosa* s/o along Estrada Subida Cedeira turning right into **Camiño das Cardosas** [**1.2** km] *[an alt. route via the N-550 continues s/o at this point]* keep on Camiño das Cardosas under railway and cross N-552 down to roundabout and into the centre of Redondela [**1.6** km]

2.8 km **Redondela** ***Centro*** See page 171 for list of albergues and information on this delightful town. As this is a short stage you may have lingered in Vigo but if you arrive early in Redondela you can ❶ meander around the old town and hang out in the lively squares. ❷ head down to the seafront Ría *Barrio de Portela* under rail and road bridges where boardwalks start and curve around the estuary all the way to *A Taberna De Paulina* where you can feast on inexpensive seafood 1.2 km (2.4 return). ❸ Redondela is where the coastal routes join with the main camino central. While this creates a lively pilgrim atmosphere it puts pressure on bed spaces. ❹ An alternative is to continue along the 'unofficial' coastal route and head out to the lovely beach around Cesantes and stay at the *•Hotel Antolín* or *•Casa A Vella* and continue on by the quiet coastal roads to albergue ●*O Recuncho do Peregrino* on Estrada de Soutoxuste and continue by woodland path to rejoin main route in Arcade (see next page).

REDONDELA: ***See p.171 for detailed town plan and description. See p.172 for main central route to Pontevdra and Santiago.***

This delightful town is where the coastal routes join the main Camino Central. From this point on the route becomes progressively busier. The albergues are located around the centre close to numerous cafés bars and restaurants. The town has a lively atmosphere and the *paseo* passes by the river and town park. The emblematic 15th century ***Iglesia de Santiago*** is located up cobbled rua do Adro.

❹ In past years the coastal way continued to Arcade via Cesantes but this route has been largely abandoned and waymarks are now faded. However, Hotel Antolín has placed signs at key junctions. ***Detour*** ● ● ● ● leaves main waymarked camino at **Option** [**2.1** km] junction of ***Rua Torre de Calle*** with ***Camiño do Picho*** *[140m before it crosses over railway]* continue up into **Cesantes** turn right by *Barros* left along railway to **road bridge** [**0.4** km] *[right 100m over bridge Furancho A Tasca]* (left 50m camiño da Vella, 4 •*CR* **Casa A Vella** €25 ✆ 658 535 935 Jesús, also runs taxi). Keep s/o (railway on right) and watch carefully for Antolín sign **down left** [**0.5** km] *Cño. da Fradesa* onto track by beach to **hotel** [**0.6** km] *[total 1.5 km from option point]*. •*H* **Antolín** €40 ✆ 986 459 409 Paseo da Praia. Picturesque seaside resort with fine sandy beaches *(busy and expensive during summer school holidays in July & August)*.

Continue along beachfront *O Mesón* & •*P.* **O Regato** €20+ ✆ 653 794 740. Take steps up to laneway and turn left (local railway right) past *Mariscos Inés* and take the slip road up to join **N-550** [**2.1** km] at •*H* **Santo Apóstolo** €30-50 ✆ 986 495 136. We now have a short stretch of **main road** [**0.7** km] to ●*Alb.* **O Recuncho do Peregrino** *Priv. [12÷1]+* €10 ✆ 617 292 598 where Miguel has created a welcoming hostel from a former roadside bar. *[The main camino central is now only 300m further along the N-550]*. To avoid dangerous bend on the N-550 drop down sharply at the side of the albergue to high-speed rail AVE (local line left along coast) and take a path around the perimeter fence to join forest track. Turn right at **junction** [**0.7** km] & next **right** [**0.3** km] and left onto asphalt road [**0.1** km] & up next right [**0.1** km] and down to join main waymarked route at the top of **Arcade** [**0.3** km] with ❶ *Alb.* **A Xesteira** (right). *[total 4.3 from Hotel Antolín]*.

● At this stage the majority of pilgrims who have been on the costal route will now join the main central way to Santiago via Pontevedra (see page 172). The next pages detail the Variante Espiritual from Pontevedra to Vilanova de Arousa.

Beach front at Hotel Antolín – Rande bridge in the distance.

22a PONTEVEDRA – ARMENTEIRA

Santiago – 108.3 km *(67.3 ml)*

▮▮▮▮▮▮▮▮	--- ---	8.9	--- --- *42%*
▬▬▬▬	--- ---	11.8	--- --- *55%*
▬▬▬▬	--- ---	0.7	--- --- *03%*
Total km		**21.4** km	*(13.3 ml)*

Total ascent **1,280**m +2¼ *hr*

▲ Alto *m* Outeiro Do Cribo **455**m *(1,490 ft)*

< A H > ➲Campaño **5.9** km. ➲Poio **8.2** km. ➲Combarro **11.3** km.

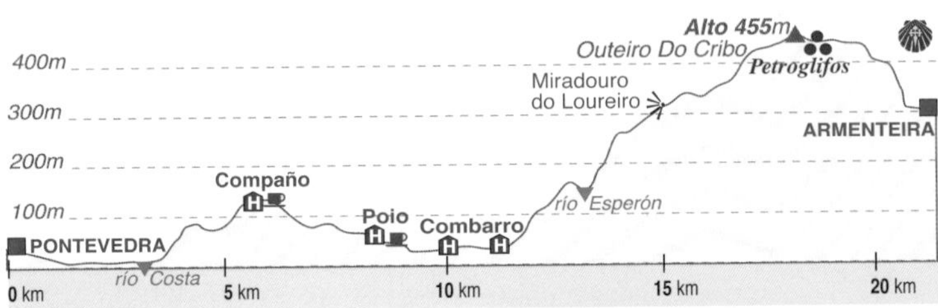

There are two ways of spreading light: to be the candle or the mirror that reflects it. *Edith Wharton*

Mystical Path *The Inner Camino:* Every religion has its guiding light. Christ was a candle of pure brilliance and his disciple James chose the Iberian peninsular to reflect that light into the darkness that covered the landscape. The ignorance remains and the need to embody the light is ever more urgent. Darkness cannot be reflected but we can choose to remove the veil drawn across the light. The Bible tells us that in the beginning, *A great sleep fell across Adam* and nowhere does it mention that he awoke. We are each a Sleeping Beauty and it is time to accept the kiss of peace that passes all human understanding and let the light in. All paths can become variations of a spiritual reality. The road ahead is steep but high places reflect the light.

The Practical Path: *Variante Espiritual* ● ● ● ● a wonderfully varied route and while all paths are overtly 'spiritual' the Landscape Temple is very evident along the coastal paths and woodland tracks. This first stage follows the coast around the Ria de Pontevedra before heading up steeply around the flank of Monte Redondo. *[**Note 1:** The final stage [3] is mostly on asphalt alongside busy main roads all the way to Padrón. An alternative is to take the spectacular boat trip along the only maritime Way of the Cross* Via Crucis marítimo *along the Ria de Arousa.* ***Note 2:*** *The boat is dependent on tides so the schedule changes daily and is dependent on at least ± 8 passengers. Tickets can be obtained from the albergue in Vilanova de Arousa* *(see p.258).*

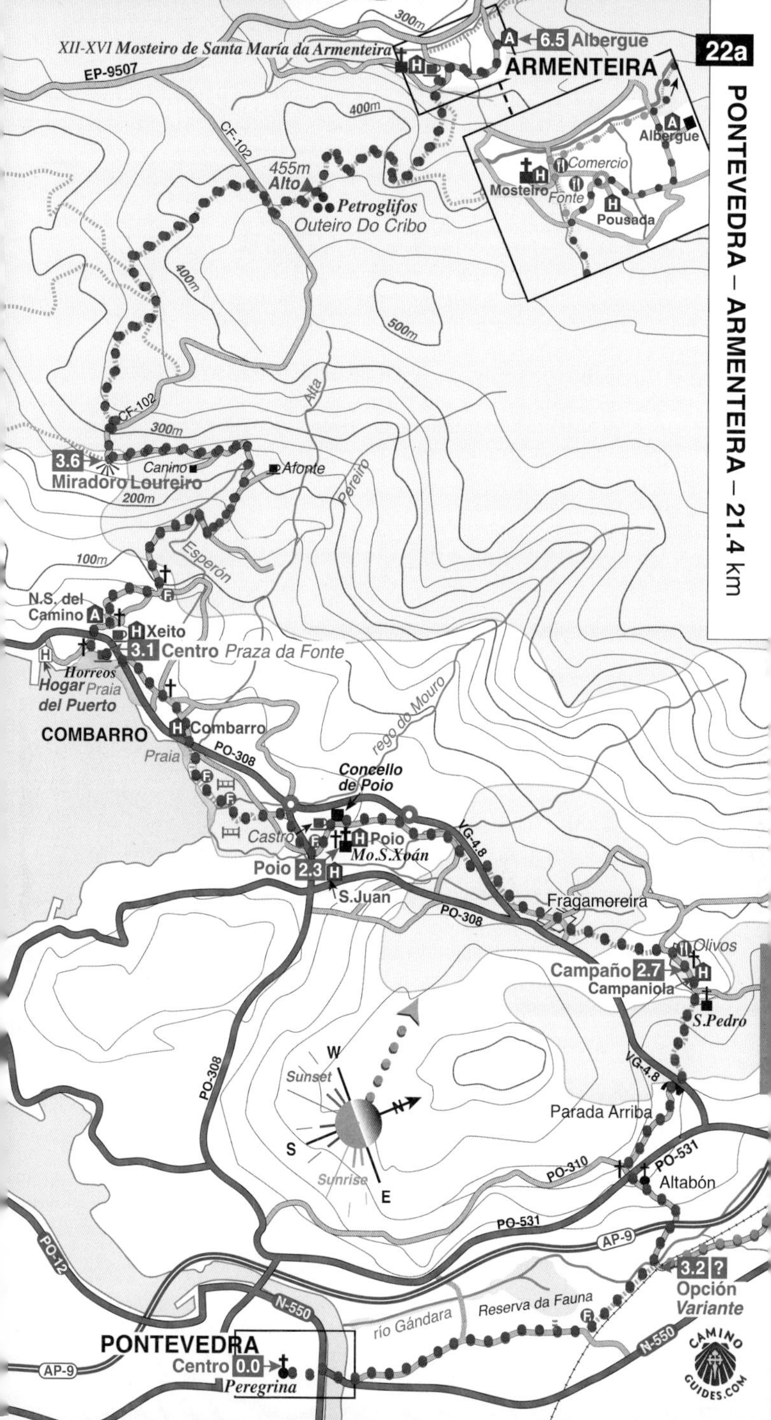

22a
PONTEVEDRA – ARMENTEIRA – 21.4 km
XII-XVI Mosteiro de Santa María da Armenteira
6.5 Albergue
ARMENTEIRA
EP-9507
300m
400m
CF-102
455m
Alto
Petroglifos
Outeiro Do Cribo
Albergue
Comercio
Mosteiro
Fonte
Pousada
500m
400m
CF-102
300m
3.6
Miradoro Loureiro
Canino
Afonte
200m
Alta
Pereiro
Esperón
100m
N.S. del Camino
Xeito
3.1 Centro Praza da Fonte
Horreos
Hogar Praia del Puerto
COMBARRO
Combarro
Praia
PO-308
rego do Mouro
Concello de Poio
Castro
Poio
Mo.S.Xoán
Poio 2.3
S.Juan
VG-4.8
Fragamoreira
PO-308
Olivos
Campaño 2.7
Campaniola
S.Pedro
W
Sunset
N
S
Sunrise
E
PO-308
VG-4.8
Parada Arriba
PO-310
PO-531
Altabón
PO-531
AP-9
PO-12
3.2 ?
Opción Variante
Reserva da Fauna
N-550
río Gándara
N-550
PONTEVEDRA
Centro 0.0
Peregrina
AP-9
CAMINO GUIDES.COM

0.0 km **Pontevedra Centro** ***Praza Peregrina*** head down Rua Real over Ponte do Burgo into Rua Da Santiña through the city suburbs into open countryside passing nature reserve and wetland [ ] onto track Rua Gándara to option point: *(see p.180 for detailed description and alternative routes to option point below).*

3.2 km **Opción** *Variante [At this point the main route to Caldas de Reis turns right under the railway bridge].* The Variant turns <left over the Rio Gándara over main road by chapel (right) and up through Parada de Arriba under **tunnel** [**1.7** km] onto woodland track to turn up sharp right> onto **path** [**0.5** km] to ***Iglesia S.Pedro*** *XVIII* with exterior pulpit into **Campañó** [**0.3** km].

2.7 km **Campañó** village square •*H* **Campaniola** *x30* €36 © 986 872 711 www.campaniola.es + café. *La Viuda* and *Los Olivos*. S/o into woodland past *cruceiro* in Fragamoreira [**1.0** km]. Continue down to track alongside main road (left) and over bridge to main road **roundabout** [**1.1** km] and turn <left to **Monasterio de Poio** [**0.2** km].

2.3 km **Poio** •*H* **Monasterio Poio** €35 © 986 770 000 r/Convento. S/o past Concello de Poio past *Castro* [**0.3** km] to main road PO-308. [ ]. •*H* **San Juan** *x28* €25-40 © 986 770 020 *+200m (left).* Turn right> along main road to roundabout and take narrow lane (left). Continue s/o down woodland track to seafront. Continue along the paseo maritimo and beach and over main road [**1.7** km] by •*H* **Combarro** *x30* €49 © 986 772 131 www.hotelcombarro.es (Apr-Sept) PO-308. Continue back over main road onto the beach at Combarro *Praia O Padron* past the historic horreos to the fountain square in the old quarter [**1.1** km].

3.1 km **Combarro** ***Praza da Fonte.*** Don't miss exploring the old town with its meandering streets and restaurants. *Pedramar* is the first you come to and good value with lower deck on the estuary. Along the harbour front is •*H* **Hogar del Puerto** €35-50 © 986 770 116 www.hogardelpuerto.com.es *Taperia O'Piorno* & •*H* **Stella Maris** €40+ © 986 770 366. Continue up to the main road which we cross for the last time by *&* •*H* **Xeito** €39 © 986 770 039. Last chance to buy food before the ***long and arduous climb ahead*** +100m ●*Alb.* **N.S. del Camino** *Priv. [12÷2]* €18 +5 €45+ © 649 053 236 www.nsdelcaminohostel.com Trv. Casalvito, 16. Continue up steeply past several *cruceiros* and [ ](right) [**1.0** km] past sign for Hotel Canino! (dog kennels) [**1.9** km] to viewpoint [**0.7** km].

3.6 km **Miradouro do Loureiro**. Fine views back over Ria de Pontevedra. Continue uphill and turn off left [**0.3** km] where we finally level out along lovely woodland paths all the way to Armenteira. There are many tracks but the way is well signposted and keeps to a level contour around the flank of Monte Redondo. Cross road [**2.6** km] back onto woodland track past ancient site with rock carvings ✤ ***Petroglifos Outeiro Do Cribo*** *alto* (right) [**0.8** km]. The path starts its descent to mountain brook to emerge on the outskirts of **Armenteira** [**2.0** km]. ***Option:*** To head directly to the monastery, restaurants and river route to the albergue continue s/o ***(left)*** down narrow path alongside the stream to the village centre.

To go direct to the albergue by asphalt road continue s/o *(right)* past ultra-modern •**Pousada Armenteira** *x30* €85+ ✆ 986 716 372 *www.pousadadearmenteira.com*. Turn right> at road junction down to the new albergue visible ahead adj. school [**0.8** km].

6.5 km **Armenteira** ***Meis*** ●**Albergue de Peregrinos** *Muni [34÷2]* €6 purpose built (2017) All mod cons and warm welcome from ✆ Carmen 670 757 777. Hot drink machine. •*Hs* **Mosteiro de Santa María da Armenteira.** The monastery serves as a retreat house and generally requires a min. 2 night stay. However, the welcoming nuns may accept pilgrims with credencial by prior arrangement. €35-50 (dinner €10) ✆ 627 097 696 *www.monasteriodearmenteira.org* Adj. the monastery are popular *O Comercio* ✆ 986 710 186 & *A Fonte* ✆ 986 710 003.

Personal Reflections:

Path into Combarro. *(Note: image on previous page 'Inner Camino' reflects the light over the tomb of Santiago taken from above the Cathedral roof lantern).*

23a ARMENTEIRA – V.N. de AROUSA

--- ---	17.2 --- ---	*70%*
--- ---	7.4 --- ---	*30%*
--- ---	0.0 --- ---	0%
Total km	**24.6** km *(15.3 ml)*	

Total ascent **1,190**m +**2.0** *hr*

▲ Alto *m* Armenteira 275m *(900 ft)*

< A H > ➲Barrantes **6.4**. ➲Av.Cambados **19.7** km (+200m) ➲Terrón **22.3** km.

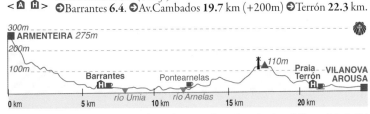

300m
ARMENTEIRA *275m*
200m
100m
Barrantes
Pontearnelas
110m
Praia Terrón
VILANOVA AROUSA
río Umia
río Arnelas
0 km 5 km 10 km 15 km 20 km

The Practical Path: This stage along the *Ruta da Pedra e da Agua* follows delightful bubbling mountain brooks to the sea. A magical 70% is on pathways including the first 12 km, one of the longest stretches of continuous pathway on any camino. The last stretch into Vilanova de Arousa is alongside golden sandy beaches. There are several café stops and good shade from sun or shelter from wind and rain. Enjoy!

0.0 km **Armenteira** ***Albergue*** from the municipal albergue head down to the river and take the woodland path alongside the river. *[Note the alternative path from the monastery joins at this point]*. We pass *muiño do Trinta* the first of many abandoned stone mills and over the first of several bridges where local walks meet. Pass picnic spot and cascade of mills at *muiño do Avispa* to:

3.9 km **Aldea Labrega** ***Meis*** major picnic area ☕ 🍴 *Taberna Aldea* (summer only) and public toilets. Cross over busy road at roundabout and under the autopista back onto the riverside path which we cross on stepping stones to arrive at *muiño do Con* and directly on the path are rock carvings from the 5th century *petroglifo* to roundabout on busy main road:

2.5 km **Rotunda** ***Barrantes*** Overlooking the river is the pleasant ☕ 🍴 *&* •*Hs* **Os Castaños** €25-35 ✆ 986 710 236 *www.oscastaños.es* rúa Torre, Ribadumia. Cross over by Turismo kiosk (summer) back onto path between road and river which leads into a nature reserve Espazo Natural and another delightful river walk alongside the imposing río Umia which flows through Caldas de Reis on the main central route and cross road bridge.

3.2 km **Ponte** Nautical park and nature recreational area Area de recreo refuxo de Cabanelas ☕ *Náutico*. Continue along other bank of the river to cross back via pedestrian bridge *pasarela* where the waymarked route takes a circuitous route back to a second bridge over the río Arnelas at:

3.3 km **Pontearnelas** small village *capela de Santa Marta* [✝] pass chemist to roundabout with service station and 100m off route (right) ☕ *Arnelas*. Continue to second roundabout and up (right) past Colegio San Bartolomeu and football ground opposite shop and ☕ *Chica* and just beyond welcoming 🍴 *Falcors.* We turn

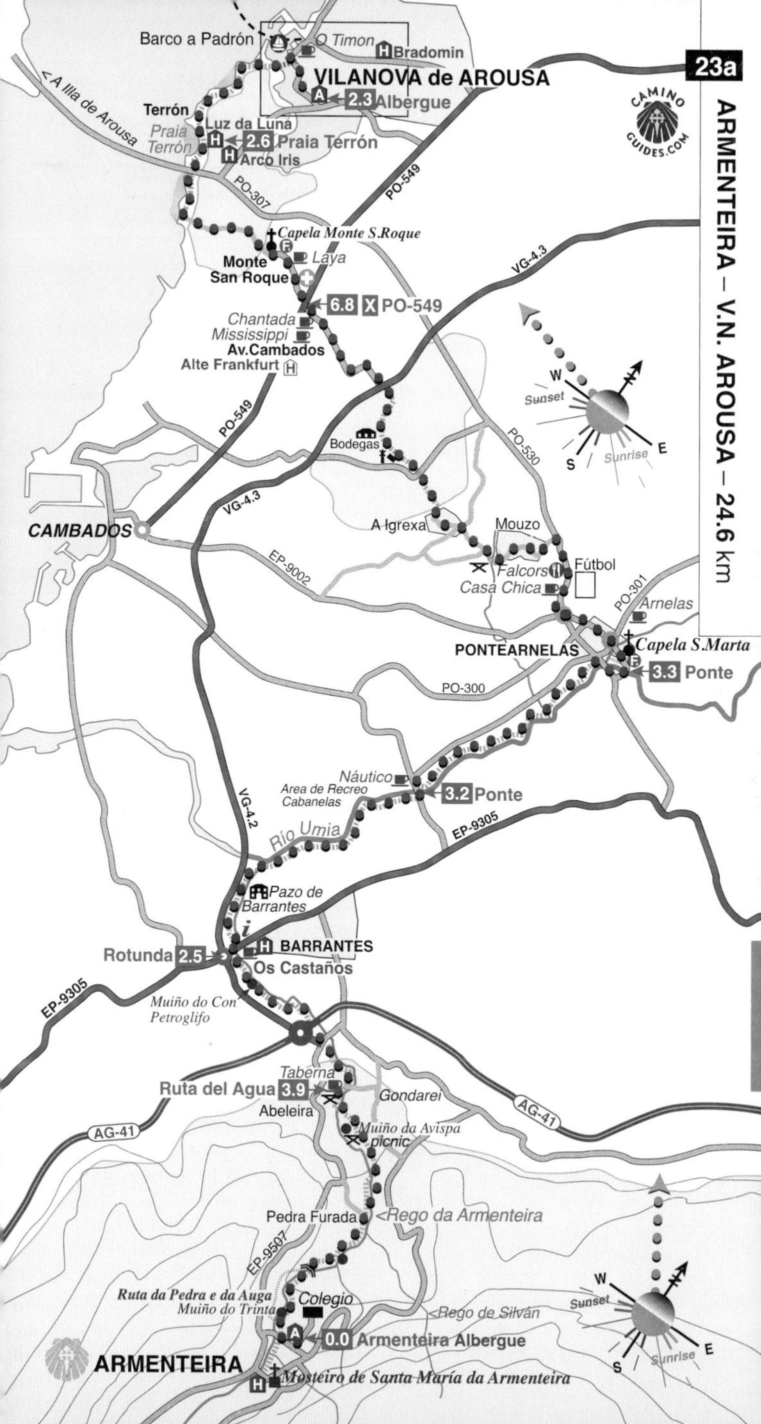

23a
ARMENTEIRA – V.N. AROUSA – 24.6 km
CAMINO GUIDES.COM
Barco a Padrón
O Timon
Bradomin
VILANOVA de AROUSA
2.3 Albergue
<A Illa de Arousa
Terrón
Praia Terrón
Luz da Luna
2.6 Praia Terrón
Arco Iris
PO-307
PO-549
Capela Monte S.Roque
Monte San Roque
Laya
6.8 PO-549
Chantada
Mississippi
Av.Cambados
Alte Frankfurt
VG-4.3
Bodegas
CAMBADOS
A Igrexa
Mouzo
Falcors
Fútbol
Casa Chica
EP-9002
PO-530
PO-301
Arnelas
PONTEARNELAS
Capela S.Marta
3.3 Ponte
PO-300
W
Sunset
S
Sunrise
E
Náutico
Area de Recreo Cabanelas
3.2 Ponte
VG-4.2
Río Umia
EP-9305
Pazo de Barrantes
Rotunda 2.5
BARRANTES
Os Castaños
Muiño do Con Petroglifo
Taberna
Ruta del Agua 3.9
Gondarei
Abeleira
AG-41
Muiño da Avispa
picnic
Pedra Furada
<Rego da Armenteira
EP-9507
Ruta da Pedra e da Auga
Colegio
Muiño do Trinta
<Rego de Silván
0.0 Armenteira Albergue
ARMENTEIRA
Mosteiro de Santa María da Armenteira

left off main road into **Mouzo** [**0.8** km] chapel [] and onto short stretch of path by stream picnic area into the old hamlet of **A Igrexa** [**1.3** km] veering <left by stone *cruceiro* and up right> into woodland. We head up to our high point of this stage by radio mast [**1.1** km] (110m) and one of several bodegas serving the vineyards in the area incl. Bodegas y Viñedos Don Olegario. The track continues down to cross bridge [**1.0** km] over the VG-4.3 with first views of the sea onto asphalt road to major crossroads [**2.6** km]:

6.8 km **Cruce** (PO-549) *Chantada* & *Mississippi* also •*H* **Alte Frankfurt** €25-45 ✆ 986 554 165 www.altefrankfurt.es (+200m Av. de Cambados). Cross over *[!]* by chemist into Monte San Roque *Laya* and capela Monte S. Roque []. Continue on quiet laneway through woodland straight onto the coast by sandy beach and path under the bridge to the Illa de Arousa to Praia Terrón:

2.6 km **Praia Terrón** *[Note V.N. Arousa and albergues + 2 km]*. If you want to stay beach-side a good option is welcoming •*Hs* **Luz de Luna** special pilgrim price *x8* €15-35 Elena ✆ 986 555 054 on the beach. To the rear •*H* **Arco Iris** + *Camping x40* €35-€55 ✆ 986 555 444 www.arcoirisweb.net •*H* **Dinajan** €40 ✆ 986 561 534 c/ Terrón. Continue along the sandy coastal path passing several restaurants, campsites & •*H* **Torres** *x24* €35 ✆ 986 561 010. Continue over the pedestrian bridge into the centre of Vilanova de Arousa and harbour area. To access the albergue turn right along the quayside (see town plan).

2.3 km **Vilanova de Arousa** *Alb.*❶ **Vilanova de Arousa** *Mun. [20÷1]* €6 ✆ Emilio 633 906 490 / 616 701 798 in town sports centre. Lovely seaside town with good facilities and a range of cafes and restaurants. The only hotel in town is the modern •*H* **Bradomin** *x51* €25+ ✆ 986 561 038 www.hotelbradomin.com Av. Juan Carlos I, 29 centrally located and good value. Also *Alb.*❷ **A Salazón** *[11÷2]* €18 *+2* €45 Fran ✆ 606 365 561 Callejón do Boliche, 7. *Alb.*❸ **A Corticela** *[10÷2]* €18 Angeles ✆ 655 884 136 Rua A Basella www.acorticela.com can arrange boat to Padron. Variety of cafes and restaurants including Meson *O Timon* on Av. Galicia facing the harbour front and quayside. Popular meeting place for pilgrims who plan to take the sea route to Padrón.

Boat trip to Padrón: The sea route is spectacular but note that the estuary is shallow and the schedule is dependent on tides so departure times vary each day. Time is of the essence as the boats have a limited time to get upriver (and return) before sections dry out – boats have been known to go aground! A reliable and regular daily passage has been established by ***Bahia-Sub*** ✆ 607 911 523. The price of €20 is dependant on 8 travelling (max 24) but a higher fare can be negotiated for fewer passengers. Book in advance (the albergue issues tickets) and arrive early. Santiago is the delightful skipper, is very knowledgeable and provides an interesting commentary of the estuary life in Spanish with a basic English translation. This is one of the most important fish farming areas in Galicia and the trip takes a look at some of the cages before heading upstream to pass the only maritime Way of the Cross *Via Crucis Marítimo-fluvial* where the ancient stone *cruceiros* rise majestically from the seabed. Journey time around 1 hour.

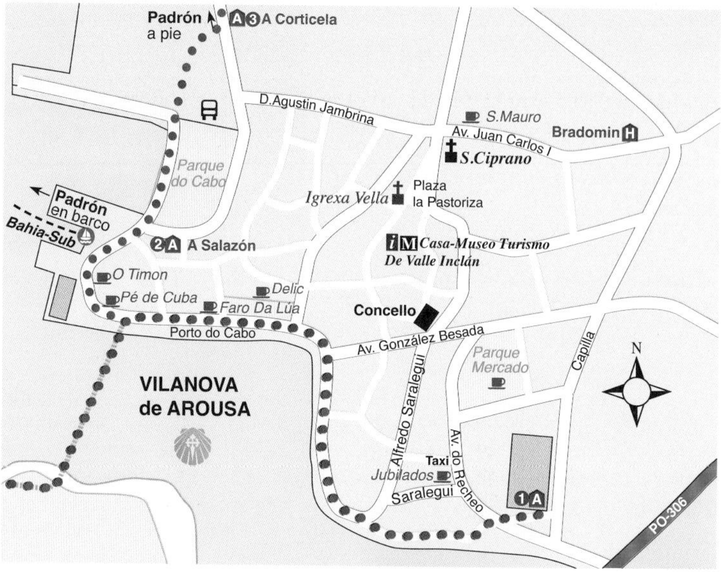

Padrón a pie
A 3 A Corticela
D.Agustin Jambrina
S.Mauro
Av. Juan Carlos I
Bradomin H
S.Ciprano
Parque do Cabo
Padrón en barco
Bahia-Sub
Igrexa Vella
Plaza la Pastoriza
2 A A Salazón
i M Casa-Museo Turismo De Valle Inclán
O Timon
Pé de Cuba
Delic
Faro Da Lúa
Concello
Porto do Cabo
Av. González Besada
Parque Mercado
Capilla
N
VILANOVA de AROUSA
Alfredo Saralegui
Av. do Recheo
Taxi
Jubilados
Saralegui
1 A
PO-306

Tourist office ***Turismo*** part of ***Casa-Museo De Valle Inclán*** (10-14 + 16.30-19.30) ✆ 986 555 493 on c/ Luces de Bohemia. Centrally located but tucked away behind a maze of lanes close to the Old Church *Igrexa Vella Da Pastoriza* off Plaza la Pastoriza adj. parish church of San Cipriano and *café S.Mauro*. Excellent small museum and well worth a visit. This is the house where Ramón María del Valle-Inclán y de la Peña was born in 1866. One of Spain's most noteworthy and radical dramatist. He died in 1936 in Santiago de Compostela.

Praia Terrón

24a VILANOVA de AROUSA – PADRON

Santiago – 62.3 km *(38.7 ml)*

--- ---	8.5 --- ---	*23%*
--- ---	22.9 --- ---	*63%*
--- ---	5.3 --- ---	*14%*
Total km	**36.7** km *(22.8 ml)*	

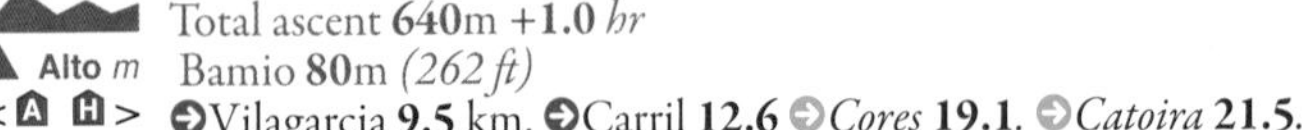

Total ascent **640**m **+1.0** *hr*

▲ Alto *m* Bamio **80**m *(262 ft)*

< A H > ➲Vilagarcia **9.5** km. ➲Carril **12.6** ➲*Cores* **19.1**. ➲*Catoira* **21.5**.

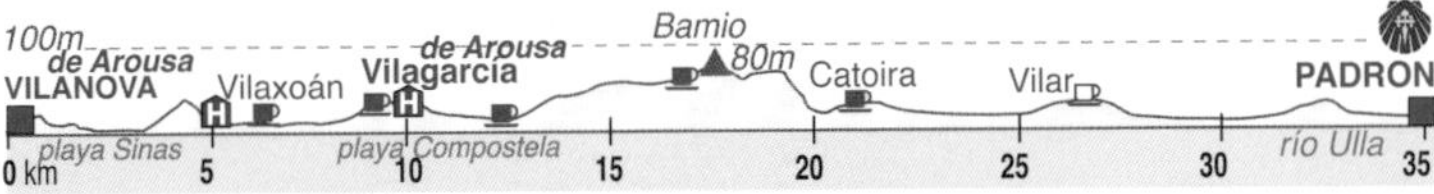

The Practical Path: This stage along the río Ulla appears from the map as a riverside walk but appearances can be deceptive! In reality it is a long and mostly gruelling hike with few river stretches. There is a monotonous uphill climb all on asphalt around Bamio. But pilgrims take all things in their stride and their are some wonderful exceptions – the first 12 km to Carril and 4 km of boardwalks and woodland paths along the river from the 'Towers of the West' to Vilar. Waymarking throughout is haphazard and most of the limited the accommodation is seasonal; busy in season and closed outside it! Public or private transport will preclude an honest application for a compostela but there are several rail stations en route direct to Padron. The river option by boat is popular with pilgrims and passes all the maritime crosses with a dramatic view of the historic *Torre de Oeste.*

0.0 km **Centro** ***Estación Marítimo*** from Vilanova de Arousa harbour head north along the coast to **Playa As Sinas** [**1.6** km]. •*H** **Leal La Sirena** €21-33 ✆ 986 554 112. ●*Alb.* **Juvenil** *Xunta* ✆ 986 554 081. •*H** **Playa Las Sínas** €35 ✆ 986 555 173 San Pedro, 31. Passing As Sinas pier to roundabout at Rial [**3.1** km]. •*H**** **Pazo O Rial** €46+ ✆ 986 507 011. Av. de Vilanova. ☕ *Carboa.*

4.7 km **Rial** ***Rotonda*** leave the main road for a short but delightful path around Dolphin Bay *Enseada do Rial* with its active harvesting of clams and cockles *almejas y berberecho* into **Vilaxoan** [**1.4** km] port area with park *Café Centro Socio.* S/o along busy coast road past seafood market *Lonxa de Vilaxoan* into rúa Valle Inclán to petrol station **Repsol** [**2.2** km] *[!]* and ***Parque Botánico Enrique Valdés*** opposite (easily missed). Archeological excavations have obscured the waymarks but you essentially head up north to the top of the park and down to pass *Convento de Vista Alegre (founded in 1648 by the archbishop of Santiago Don Fernando de Andrade y Sotomayor).* Over riverlet *rego do con* into pedestrian street Rua Castelao ☕ *Nata* to the central Praza de Galicia [**1.2** km].

4.8 km **Centro** ***Praza Galicia*** **Vilagarcia de Arousa.** •*H**** **Castelao** €50 ✆ 986 512 426 Rúa Arzobispo Lago, 5. •*Hs* **Nogal** *Cafetería* €30 ✆ 986 505 600 Rúa Alcalde Rey Daviña, 20. Veer left into Parque Miguel Hernandez and pick up the beach path at roundabout *Playa de la Concha* passing •*H*** **Playa Compostela**

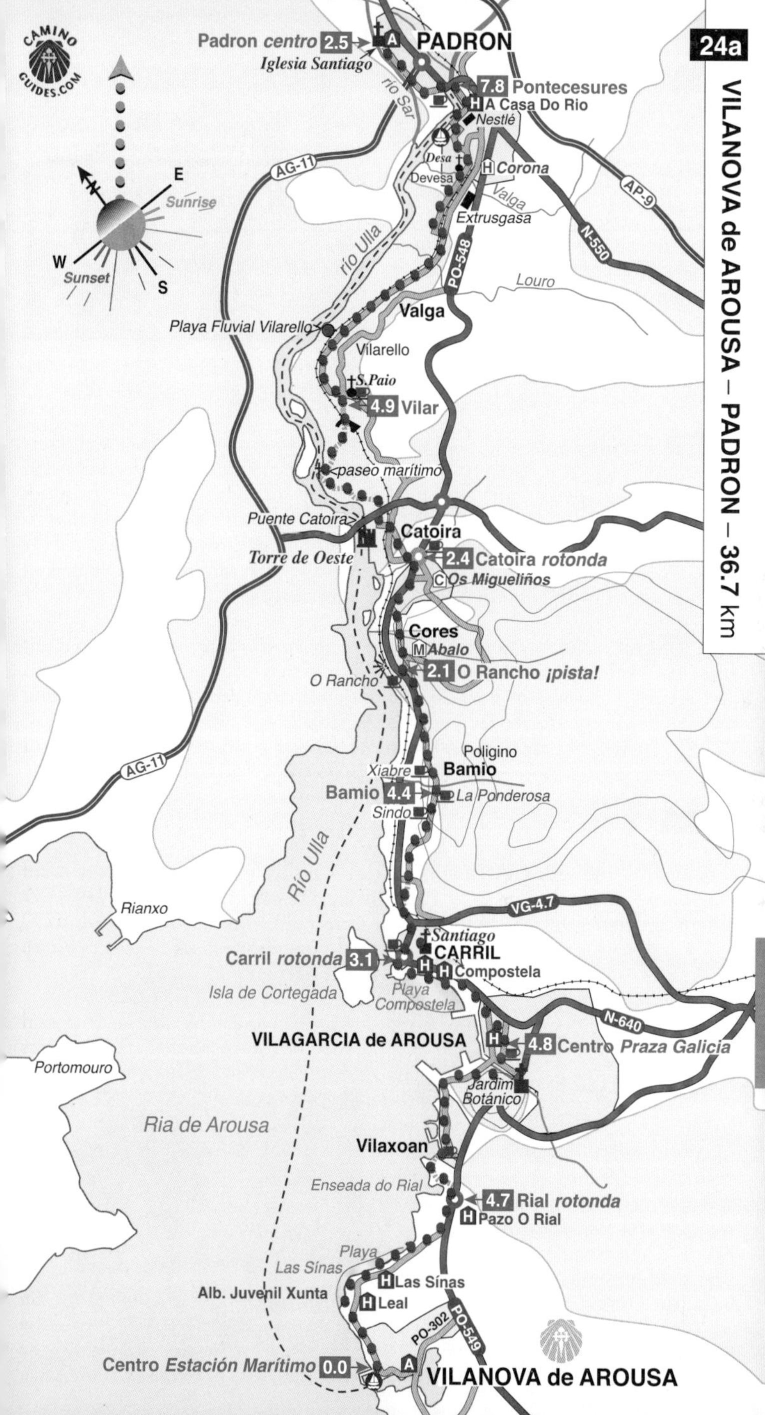

CAMINO GUIDES.COM
24a
VILANOVA de AROUSA – PADRON – 36.7 km
Padron centro 2.5
Iglesia Santiago
PADRON
7.8 Pontecesures
A Casa Do Rio
Nestlé
río Sar
Desa
Devesa
Corona
Valga
Extrusgasa
AG-11
AP-9
N-550
PO-548
E
Sunrise
W
Sunset
S
río Ulla
Louro
Valga
Playa Fluvial Vilarello
Vilarello
S.Paio
4.9 Vilar
paseo marítimo
Puente Catoira
Catoira
Torre de Oeste
2.4 Catoira rotonda
Os Migueliños
Cores
Abalo
2.1 O Rancho ¡pista!
O Rancho
Poligino
Xiabre
Bamio
Bamio 4.4
La Ponderosa
Sindo
AG-11
Río Ulla
Rianxo
VG-4.7
Santiago
CARRIL
Carril rotonda 3.1
Compostela
Isla de Cortegada
Playa Compostela
N-640
VILAGARCIA de AROUSA
4.8 Centro Praza Galicia
Portomouro
Jardim Botánico
Ria de Arousa
Vilaxoan
Enseada do Rial
4.7 Rial rotonda
Pazo O Rial
Playa Las Sínas
Las Sínas
Alb. Juvenil Xunta
Leal
PO-302
PO-549
Centro Estación Marítimo 0.0
VILANOVA de AROUSA

€35 © 986 504 010 Av. Rosalía de Castro, 138 and •H''' Carril €56 © 86 511 507 r/ Lucena, 18. Continue to the roundabout at Carril.

3.1 km **Carril *rotonda*** several cafes. Head up past emblematic *Iglesia de Santiago* (see photo>) on corner of rúa Extramuros and veer left and then imm. right along rua Santiago onto path through woods with picnic benches and [ ]. Head up past chapel and down past cruceiros at Os Anxos over rail line. We now follow the monotonous climb up the PO-192 through Bamio ***Alto** 80m*:

4.4 km **Bamio** *Casa Sindo* and up past *La Ponderosa* in Pedrosa with short detour over rego da Amproa (picnic area on busy main road – sign for Industrial estate *Polígono Bamio* right) ***Alto*** High point at 80m with distant views across the ria de Arousa *(see photo opp. page. Note the calvary centre, part of the Via Crucis Maritimo). [!]* WContinue along the busy PO-548 or cross over *[!]* for a short detour (camino naturales with red and white blaise) that runs parralel to the main road and emerges by *O Rancho* and viewpoint *mirador.*

2.1 km **O Rancho *restaurante mirador.*** *[!]* waymarks here are ***not*** obvious but veer right> off the main road via short path onto side road (signposted *Tanatoria de Catoira*). Continue to new roundabout and parking for the funeral parlour *Pompas Funebres / Tanatoria. [Off route +250m up right motel •Motel'' **Abalo** x5 €70 © 986 546 900 Aldea Cores, Catoira]*. continue down to join the **main road** [**1.6** km] to roundabout (right) passing *Taberna Vikinga* to next roundabout.

2.4 km **Catoira *rotonda*** . *[Off route right +200m •CR **Os Migueliños** x5 €55+ © 986 546 132 c/Barral, 12].* Turn <left over the bridge (do ***not*** take the enticing riverside walk at this point) but turn <left again and follow signs to ***paseo marítimo / Torre do Este*** as we finally make our way back to the río Ulla over railway and under the road bridge ***Puente Catoira*** [**1.6** km].to join the boardwalk and paseo *paseo marítimo* through woodland along the riverside to pass ***Cruceiro As Telleiras*** and join road out under rail bridge into **Vilar** [**3.3** km].

4.9 km **Vilar** (right). S/o past capela San Paio and turn <left at crossroad and s/o down to railway line [**0.4** km] the road now runs parallel taking a short detour around the road bridge to *Playa Fluvial Vilarello (left)* back to rail which we cross [**2.8** km] passing factory (right) *Extrugasa* in Valga under new road bridge (replacing level crossing) to underpass [**1.9** km] *[+½ km off route – multi-storey building visible on horizon •H'' **Corona De Galicia** x30* €40 © 986 557 575 *Rúa da Devesa, 28 Valga].* The road now veers away from the rail line into **Devesa** passing wayside cross adj. the diminutive chapel of the two disciples *capela da dos desa* with fine image of *Santiago Peregrino* in the niche.

At this point waymarks disappear and we are faced with a myriad of small laneways but they all lead back to the río Ulla at the Nestlé factory on Av. Eugenio Escuredo [**1.8** km] where a delightful new *paseo fluvial* has been built along the river bank past •*H*'' **A Casa Do Rio** €40 ✆ 986 557 575 Rúa Víctor García 1 to bring us to Ponte Cesures [**0.9** km] where we join the main flow of pilgrims on the camino central.

7.8 km **Pontecesures** Turn <left over the bridge (río Ulla) ☕ *Casa Farrucan* (left) and continue s/o (don't stay on the main road which is narrow and dangerous). We now make our way along a quiet country lane turning right> along the banks of the **río Sar** under C-550 ring road to the first of Padron's many albergues [**1.6** km] *Alb.*❶ **Camiño do Sar** *Priv. [20÷1]* €13-15 ✆ 618 734 373. Next +100m *Alb.*❷ **O Pedrón** *Priv. [43÷3]* €13 ✆ 881 121 266 & ☕ *La Hacienda*. Next +200m *Alb.* ❸ **Flavia** *Priv.[22÷5]* €12 +7 €25-38 ✆ 981 810 455 *(Isabel)* Campo da Feira + 🍴 *Flavia (50m right)*. Continue along the river Sar (replica Padron on the far bank) by shaded *paseo* lined with plane trees to the heart of Padrón with the statue of her most famous daughter and illustrious poetess *Rosalía de Castro* and the church of St. James [**0.9** km].

2.5 km **Padrón** ***Centro Igrexa de Santiago*** and *Alb.* **Rossol** ❹ *Priv.[18÷1]* €14 ✆ 981 810 011 m: 678 023 918 and popular ☕ *Rossol* that spills out onto the central plaza in front of the church *Plaza Rodriguez Cobián.* ***See p. 189 for full list of accommodation and p.191 for town map.***

Personal Reflections:

Ria de Arousa *Via Crucis Marítimo*

Stay in Touch: The evolution of human consciousness is gathering apace. One manifestation of this is the increasing interest in taking time out to go on pilgrimage and nowhere is this more apparent than along the camino where facilities struggle to keep up with demand. Information garnered in one month may be out of date the next as old hostels close and new ones open up. Paths are realigned to make way for new motorways and budget airlines suddenly announce new routes. Whilst great care has been taken in gathering the information for this guide we also welcome feedback from pilgrims who have recently walked the route to enable it to stay fresh and relevant to those who will follow on after us. Your comments and suggestions are always gratefully received so if you would like to offer something, ask something or simply stay in touch please e-mail us at: *info@caminoguides.com* or use the contact form on our website: *www.caminoguides.com*

NEXT STEPS?...

The official literature for a previous compostela jubilee year *año jubilar compostelana* stated boldly on the front cover, 'A Road with an END' *Camino que tiene META*. That may be so – but it is not the end of the road. Before you leave this corner of the earth why not visit the end of it *Finis Terra*.

"... Finisterre is one of the great hidden treasures amongst the many Caminos de Santiago. Only a small proportion of pilgrims arriving at Santiago continue *by foot* to the end of the road. The way to Finisterre truly follows *the road less travelled* and *that* may make all the difference. We need to search out the waymarks to the source of our own inner knowing. The light, while obscured, lies hidden in our memory – it is no coincidence that the path to Finisterre ends at the altar to the sun *Ara Solis* and a lighthouse." From *A Pilgrim's Guide to the Camino Finisterre.*

PILGRIM ASSOCIATIONS *(in English)*:

UK: ***The Confraternity of St. James*** +44 [0]2079 289 988 e-mail: *office@csj.org.uk* website: *www.csj.org.uk* the pre-eminent site in English with online bookshop.
IRELAND: ***The Camino Society Ireland***. Dublin: *www.caminosociety.ie*
U.S.A. ***American Pilgrims on the Camino***. *www.americanpilgrims.org*
CANADA: ***Canadian Company of Pilgrims Canada***. *www.santiago.ca*
SOUTH AFRICA: ***Confraternity of St. James of SA*** *www.csjofsa.za.org*
AUSTRALIA: ***Australian Friends of the Camino*** *www.afotc.org*

SANTIAGO:

Pilgrim Office *oficinadelperegrino.com/en*
Tourism: *www.santiagoturismo.com*
Luggage storage & camino forum *www.casaivar.com*
Backpack storage & local tours *www.pilgrim.es* Rúa Nova, 7 (adj. cathedral).

PILGRIM WEBSITES: *(in English) loosely connected with the Way of St. James or with the theme of spirituality and pilgrimage that may be helpful:*

Camino News: Largest English camino forum *www.caminodesantiago.me*
Alternatives of St. James (UK): *www.alternatives.org.uk*
British Pilgrimage Trust: *http://britishpilgrimage.org*
Gatekeeper Trust pilgrimage as personal/planetary healing *www.gatekeeper.org.uk*
The Beloved CommUnity (USA): *www.belovedcommunity.org*
Findhorn Foundation personal and planetary transformation *www.findhorn.org*
Lucis Trust spiritual education, meditation & World Goodwill *www.lucistrust.org*
Paulo Coelho reflections from author of The Pilgrimage *paulocoelhoblog.com*
The Quest A Guide to the Spiritual Journey *www.thequest.org.uk*
Peace Pilgrim Her life and work *www.peacepilgrim.com*

ALBERGUE, HOSTAL AND HOTEL BOOKING SITES:

List of albergues open in Winter: *www.aprinca.com/alberguesinvierno/*
Christian Hospitality Network: *http://en.ephatta.com*
Youth Hostels: *https://pousadasjuventude.pt/en*
Albergues: *www.onlypilgrims.com/en*
Hostals: *www.hostelworld.com*
B&Bs: *www.airbnb*
Hotels: *www.booking.com*
https://www.tripadvisor.co.uk/
Paradores: *www.paradore.es*

PILGRIM AND BACKPACK TRANSFERS / STORES:

Spanish Postal Service: *http://www.elcaminoconcorreos.com/en/*
General Listing: *www.amawalker.blogspot.co.uk*
Transfers: *www.pilbeo.com* + *www.tuitrans.com* + *https://caminofacil.net/en* + *(from Lisbon) www.pilgrim.es/en*

BIBLIOGRAPHY: Some reading with waymarks to the inner path include:

A Course In Miracles (A.C.I.M.) *Text, Workbook for Students and Manual for Teachers*. Foundation for Inner Peace.

The Art of Pilgrimage *The Seeker's Guide to Making Travel Sacred*, Phil Cousineau. Element Books

Anam Cara *Spiritual wisdom from the Celtic world,* John O'Donohue. Bantam.

A New Earth *Awakening to Your Life's Purpose*, Eckhart Tolle. Penguin Books

A Brief History of Everything *Integrating the partial visions of specialists into a new understanding of the meaning and significance of life*, Ken Wilber.

Care of the Soul *How to add depth and meaning to your everyday life,* Thomas Moore. Piatkus

Conversations with God Neale Donald Walsch. Hodder & Stoughton

From the Holy Mountain *A Journey in the Shadow of Byzantium*, William Dalrymple. Flamingo

Going Home *Jesus and the Buddha as brothers*, Thich Nhat Hanh. Rider Books

Loving What Is *Four Questions That Can Change Your Life*, Byron Katie. Rider

Handbook for the Soul *A collection of wisdom from over 30 celebrated spiritual writers*. Piatkus

The Hero with a Thousand Faces *An examination, through ancient myths, of man's eternal struggle for identity,* Joseph Campbell. Fontana Press

How to Know God *The Soul's Journey into the Mystery of Mysteries*, Deepak Chopra. Rider

Jesus and the Lost Goddess *The Secret Teachings of the Original Christians*, Timothy Freke & Peter Gandy. Three Rivers Press

The Journey Home *The Obstacles to Peace*, Kenneth Wapnick. Foundation for A Course In Miracles

The Mysteries *Rudolf Steiner's writings on Spiritual Initiation*, Andrew Welburn. Floris Books

Mysticism *The Nature and Development of Spiritual Consciousness,* Evelyn Underhill. Oneworld

Nine Faces of Christ *Quest of the True Initiate*, Eugene Whitworth. DeVorss

No Destination *Autobiography (of a pilgrimage), Satish Kumar*. Green Books

Pilgrimage *Adventures of the Spirit*, Various Authors. Travellers' Tales

Paths of the Christian Mysteries *From Compostela to the New World*, Virginia Sease and Manfred Schmidt-Brabant. Temple Lodge

The Pilgrimage *A Contemporary Quest for Ancient Wisdom*. Paulo Coelho

Peace Pilgrim *Her Life and Work* Friends of Peace Pilgrim. Ocean Tree Books

Pilgrim in Aquarius David Spangler. Findhorn Press

Pilgrim Stories *On and Off the Road to Santiago.* Nancy Louise Frey. University of California Press.

Pilgrim in Time *Mindful Journeys to Encounter the Sacred*. Rosanne Keller.

The Power of Now *A Guide to Spiritual Enlightenment*, Eckhart Tolle. New World

Peace is Every Step *The path of mindfulness in everyday life*, Thich Nhat Hanh.

Phases *The Spiritual Rhythms in Adult Life*, Bernard Lievegoed. Sophia Books

Sacred Contracts *Awakening Your Divine Potential*, Caroline Myss. Bantam

Sacred Roads *Adventures from the Pilgrimage Trail*, Nicholas Shrady. Viking

Secrets of God *Writings of Hildegard of Bingen*. Shambhala

Science and Spiritual Practises *Rupert Sheldrake.* Hodder & Stoughton.

Silence of the Heart *Dialogues with Robert Adams*. Acropolis Books

The Gift of Change *Spiritual Guidance for a Radically New Life,* Marianne Williamson. Element Books

The Inner Camino *Path of Awakening,* S. Hollwey & J.Brierley. Findhorn Press.

The Prophet. Kahlil Gibran. Mandarin

The Reappearance of the Christ. Alice Bailey. Lucis Press.

The Road Less Travelled *A new Psychology of Love,* M. Scott Peck. Arrow

The Soul's Code *In Search of Character and Calling,* James Hillman. Bantam

The Untethered Soul: *The Journey Beyond self,* Michael A. Singer New Harbinger

Wandering Joy *Meister Eckhart's Mystical Philosophy*. Lindisfarne Press

Wanderlust *A history of Walking*. Rebecca Solnit. Verso

Whispers of the Beloved *The mystical poems of Rumi*. HarperCollins

RETURNING HOME: *Reflections...*

Before a new chapter is begun, the old one has to be finished.
Stop being who you were, and change into who you are.
Paulo Coelho

When, after a prolonged absence, friends and family remark, *'you haven't changed at all'* I am hopeful they are either blind or following some meaningless social convention. I have spent the last 20 years of my life with the primary intention to do just that – to change myself. One of the more potent aspects of pilgrimage is the extended time it requires away from the familiar. This allows an opportunity for the inner alchemy of spirit to start its work of transformation. It's not just the physical body that may need to sweat off excess baggage – the mind needs purifying too. Our world is in a mess and we are not going to fix it with more of the same. We need a fresh approach and a different mind-set to the one that created the chaos in the first place. Hopefully, this re-ordering of the way we see the world will quicken apace as we open to lessons presented to us along the camino and begin to understand that... life itself is a classroom.

A purpose of pilgrimage is to allow time for old belief systems and outworn 'truths' to fall away so that new and higher perspectives can arise. We may also need to recognise that colleagues and partners at home or at work may feel threatened by our new outlook on life. Breaking tribal patterns, challenging the status quo or querying consensus reality is generally considered inappropriate at best or heretical at worst. The extent to which we hold onto any new understanding is measured by how far we are prepared to *walk our talk* and live our 'new' truth in the face of opposition, often from those who profess to love us. Christ was crucified for living The Truth.

These guidebooks are dedicated to awakening beyond human consciousness. They arose out of a personal existential crisis and the urgent need for some space and time to reflect on the purpose of life and its direction. Collectively we live in a spiritual vacuum of our own making where the mystical and sacred have been relegated to the delusional or escapist. Accordingly, we live in a three dimensional world and refuse to open the door to higher dimensions of reality. We have impoverished ourselves in the process, severely limiting our potential. Terrorised by the chaotic world we have manifested around us, we have become ensnared in its dark forms. We have become so preoccupied with these fearful images we fail to notice that we hold the key to the door of our self-made prison. We can walk out any time we choose.

Whatever our individual experiences, it is likely that you will be in a heightened state of sensitivity after walking the camino. I strongly recommend that you do not squeeze your itinerary so you feel pressurised to rush back into your work and general lifestyle immediately on your return. This is a crucial moment. I have often witnessed profound change, in myself and others, only to allow a sceptical audience to induce fear and doubt in us so that we fall back to the starting point – the default position of the status quo. Be careful with whom you share your experiences and stay in contact with fellow pilgrims who can support new realisations and orientation. Source new friends and activities that enhance and encourage the on-going journey of Self-discovery.

I have developed great empathy and respect for my fellow pilgrims who have placed themselves on the path of enquiry. We are embarking together on a journey of rediscovery of our essential nature and opening up to knowledge of Higher Worlds. We have, collectively, been asleep a long time and while change can happen in the twinkling of an eye it is often experienced as a slow and painful process. It is never easy to let go of the familiar and to step into the new. How far we are prepared to go and how resolute in holding onto our newfound reality is a matter of our own choosing. There is little point in garnering peace along the camino if we leave it behind in Santiago. We need to bring it back into our everyday life. After the camino comes the laundry!

Whichever choice you make will doubtless be right for you at this time. I wish you well in your search for the truth and your journey Home and extend my humble blessings to a fellow pilgrim on the path. The journey is not over and continues, as you will have it be, dedicated to the sacred or the mundane, to waking or sleeping. To help remind us of our true identity, I leave you with the following words of Marianne Williamson, distilled from A Course In Miracles and immortalised in Nelson Mandela's *freedom speech*.

Our deepest fear is not that we are inadequate.
Our deepest fear is that we are powerful beyond measure.
It is our Light, not our darkness, that most frightens us.

We ask ourselves, who am I to be brilliant, gorgeous, talented and fabulous?
Actually, who are you not to be? You are a child of God.
Your playing small doesn't serve the world.
There's nothing enlightened about shrinking,
So that other people won't feel insecure around you.

We were born to make manifest the Glory of God that is within us.
It's not just in some of us; it's in everyone.
And as we let our Light shine,
We unconsciously give other people permission to do the same.
As we are liberated from our own fear,
Our presence automatically liberates others.

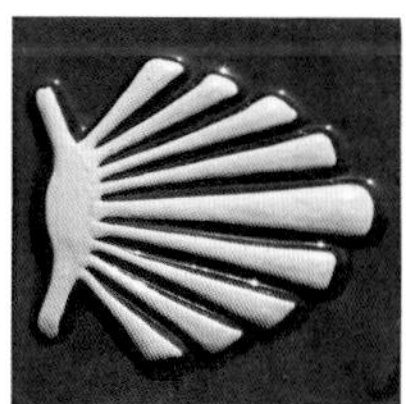

A tithe of royalties from the sale of this guidebook will be distributed to those who seek to preserve the physical and spiritual integrity of this route

The breeze at dawn has something to tell you. Don't go back to sleep.

Rumi

Personal Reflections:

12 Caminos de Santiago

❶ **Camino Francés*** **778** km
St. Jean – Santiago
Camino Invierno*
Ponferrada – Santiago **275** km

❷ **Chemin** de **Paris 1000** km
Paris – St. Jean via Tours

❸ **Chemin** de **Vézelay 900** km
Vezélay – St. Jean via Bazas

❹ **Chemin** du **Puy 740** km
Le Puy-en-Velay – St. Jean
Ext. to Geneva, Budapest

❺ **Chemin** d'**Arles 750** km
Arles – Somport Pass
Camino Aragonés **160** km
Somport Pass – Óbanos
Camí San Jaume **600** km
Port de Selva – Jaca
Camino** del **Piamonte **515** km
Narbonne - Lourdes - St. Jean

❻ **Camino de Madrid 320** km
Madrid – Sahagún
Camino de **Levante 900** km
Valencia – Zamora
Alt. via Cuenca – Burgos

❼ **Camino Mozárabe 390** km
Granada – Mérida
(Málaga alt. via Baena)

❽ **Via** de la **Plata 1,000** km
Seville – Santiago
Camino Sanabrés Ourense **110** km

❾ **Camino Portugués** ***Central**** **640** km
Lisboa – Porto 389 km
Porto – Santiago 251 km
Camino Portugués *Costa** **320** km
Porto – Santiago
via Caminha & **Variante Espiritual***

❿ **Camino Finisterre* 86** km
Santiago – Finisterre
via – Muxía – Santiago **114** km

⓫ **Camino Inglés* 120** km
Ferrol & Coruna – Santiago

⓬ **Camino** del **Norte 830** km
Irún – Santiago via Gijón
Camino Primitivo 320 km
Oviedo – Lugo – Melide